The RECONQUEST of MONTREAL

Language Policy and Social Change in a Bilingual City

Conflicts in Urban and Regional Development

a series edited by John R. Logan and Todd Swanstrom

The
RECONQUEST
of
MONTREAL

Language Policy and Social Change in a Bilingual City

MARC V. LEVINE

Temple University Press

PHILADELPHIA

Temple University Press, Philadelphia 19122
Copyright © 1990 by Temple University. All rights reserved
Published 1990
Printed in the United States of America

⊗   The paper used in this publication meets the minimum requirements of American National Standard for Information Sciences—Permanence of Paper for Printed Library Materials, ANSI Z39.48-1984

Library of Congress Cataloging-in-Publication Data
Levine, Marc V., 1951–
The reconquest of Montreal : language policy and social change in a bilingual city / Marc V. Levine.
    p.   cm.—(Conflicts in urban and regional development)
    ISBN 0-87722-703-9 (alk. paper)
    1. Language policy—Québec (Province)—Montréal.   2. Bilingualism—Québec (Province)—Montréal.   3. English language—Québec (Province)—Montréal.   4. French language—Québec (Province)—Montréal.   5. Montréal (Québec)—Social conditions.   I. Title.   II. Series.
P119.32.C3L48   1990
306.4′49714—dc20   89-20378
                                                               CIP

For Marta and Katie

Contents

A Note on Vocabulary

The vocabulary used to denote Montreal's language groups can be bewildering to those not familiar with the city and its linguistic divisions. The English-speaking community is variously described as "English-speakers," "Anglophones," and "English Canadians." Similarly, the French-speaking community is referred to as "French-speakers," "Francophones," and "French Canadians" or "French Québécois." I have primarily used "Anglophone" and "Francophone" in this book, but occasionally vary the usage for stylistic reasons.

Montreal's "third force"—the non-Francophone, non-Anglophone minorities—has been labeled in different ways throughout the twentieth century. They have been called Neo-Canadians, Neo-Québécois, Allophones, and, more recently, "Cultural Communities" and "Ethnic Minorities." For the most part, I have used the label "Allophone," but have also occasionally referred to these groups by some of the categorizations used historically.

Acknowledgments

Writing a book requires long hours of solitary work; yet without the help of others, most books would never be written. I have been fortunate to receive ample assistance in this project. Lee Benson, my mentor at the University of Pennsylvania, has taught me more about social conflict and social change than I can ever acknowledge. His indefatigable efforts to transcend disciplinary boundaries to develop a genuine science of society have been an inspiration to me, and his influence pervades my work.

I am particularly grateful to Todd Swanstrom, co-editor of the series in which this book appears. His detailed reading of the entire manuscript helped sharpen my arguments and mold the book in ways that, I hope, make it informative and accessible to both Canadian and American audiences. Several scholars helped by reading portions of the manuscript at various stages and generously offering valuable criticisms and much-appreciated encouragement: my thanks especially to Kenneth McRoberts, Andrew Sancton, Robert Whelan, and Louis Balthazar. I presented portions of my research on the Montreal language situation at the meetings of the Association for Canadian Studies in the United States (Montreal, 1987); the Urban Affairs Association (St. Louis, 1988); and the American Council for Quebec Studies (Quebec City, 1988), and this book benefited considerably from the constructive criticism I received at those meetings. Special thanks also to Michael Ames, editor-in-chief at Temple University Press, for his encouragement and his patience.

The financial assistance of several organizations facilitated the research for this book. I am grateful for research support granted by the Graduate School of the University of Wisconsin–Milwaukee, the Canadian

Embassy Faculty Research Grant Program, and the Quebec Government Research Grant Program. Norman London of the Canadian Embassy, Pierre Lavigne of the Gouvernement du Québec, Ministère des Affaires internationales, and Andrée Vary-Kinney of the Délégation du Québec à Chicago deserve special mention for their unflagging support of research by U.S. scholars on Canada and Quebec, and their help has been crucial to my own work.

Numerous individuals at various libraries and research institutions provided indispensable aid. I thank in particular the staffs of the interlibrary loan office of the Golda Meir Library at the University of Wisconsin–Milwaukee, the Bibliothèque nationale du Québec, the MacLennan Library at McGill University, and the social sciences library at l'Université de Montréal. Leo Gagné and Hermine Beauregard of the Service des communications, Conseil de la langue française responded warmly and promptly to the pleas of a U.S.-based researcher for CLF documents that were vital to my research, as did CLF demographer Michel Paillé whose own work on "demo-linguistic" trends in Montreal has been of inestimable value. I am also grateful to the staff at Alliance Quebec's offices in Montreal for permitting my free use of their library and their extensive clipping file. Paule Giguère of Statistics Canada and Albert Côté of the Conseil scolaire de l'île de Montréal expeditiously provided some of the important data for this study; and Jac-André Boulet of the Conseil économique du Canada graciously shared with me some of his unpublished data on language and earnings in Montreal. Bill McMahon, a graduate student at the Urban Research Center at the University of Wisconsin–Milwaukee, used his computer wizardry to produce the graphs and figures in the book, and I greatly appreciate his help.

The Departments of History and Urban Affairs at the University of Wisconsin–Milwaukee have been the most congenial and collegial settings imaginable to work on a book, and I am grateful to my departmental colleagues for their ideas and encouragement. The generosities of several dear friends were indispensable to my efforts. John Kushma and Ira Harkavy have been my friends and intellectual companions since graduate school, and much of what I understand about politics and social change comes from their insights. During some of my most difficult times, Andie King supported me in ways that I cannot fully express but will never forget. Dan Todes offered encouragement, jokes, and perspective as we simultaneously worked on our books, and John Zipp, a fellow refugee from the Big Five, provided numerous assists and rebounds. My parents, Edith and William Levine, brought me up in a household in which issues of politics, policy, and history were always under discussion and where I learned that ideas matter; for that, and a thousand other reasons, I will always be grateful to them.

In ways both large and small, Marta Levine has been my greatest source of support during the writing of this book. Her love and confidence kept me going throughout the process, and her disciplined pursuit of her own work inspired me. Our daughter Katherine Anne was born as I was writing the book. Although she offered almost no assistance on the project, she helped me understand that there are more important things than writing books.

List of Abbreviations

BCE	Bell Canada Enterprises
BNA Act	British North America Act
BNC	Banque nationale du Canada
CECM	Commission des écoles catholiques de Montréal
CEGEP	Collèges d'enseignement général et professionel
CEQ	Corporation (Centrale) des enseignants du Québec
CLF	Conseil de la langue française
CNR	Canadian National Railway
COEQ	Conseil d'orientation économique du Québec
COFI	Centres d'orientation et de formation des immigrants
CPR	Canadian Pacific Railway
CSIM	Conseil scolaire de l'île de Montréal
CSN	Confédération des syndicats nationaux
CSS	Centre de service social
CUM	Communauté urbaine de Montréal
FLQ	Front de libération du Québec
FQF	Front de Québec français
FTQ	Fédération des travailleurs du Québec
LIS	Ligue pour l'intégration scolaire
MEQ	Ministère de l'éducation du Québec
MIS	Mouvement pour l'intégration scolaire
MNA	Member of the National Assembly
MQF	Mouvement Québec français
MSA	Mouvement Souveraineté-Association
ME	Montreal Stock Exchange

OLF	Office de la langue française
OQCE	Office québécoise du commerce extérieur
PLQ	Parti libéral du Québec
PME	Petite et moyenne entreprise
PQ	Parti québécois
PSBGM	Protestant School Board of Greater Montreal
RCBB	Royal Commission on Bilingualism and Biculturalism
REA	Régime d'épargne-actions
RIN	Rassemblement pour l'indépendance nationale
SDI	Société de développement industriel
SGF	Société générale de financement
SSJB	Société Saint-Jean Baptiste
SSJBM	Société Saint-Jean Baptiste de Montréal
STCUM	Société de transport de la Communauté urbaine de Montréal
UN	Union nationale

Note to the Paperback Edition

The year since the original publication of *The Reconquest of Montreal* has been tumultuous for Canada and Quebec. The collapse of the Meech Lake Accord has plunged Canada into its gravest national unity crisis. Support in Quebec for independence has never been higher, and the machinery is in place for a 1992 referendum that could lead to Quebec's sovereignty. Whatever the outcome of Canada's latest constitutional crisis, language group relations in Montreal are certain to be affected. For example, Quebec's political climate has English-speaking Montrealers understandably anxious about the future, and many seem poised to renew the "Anglo flight" of the late 1970s.

Several matters of language policy covered in this book have evolved during the past year. The language of work in Montreal received renewed attention with the April 1991 publication of a study by the Conseil de la langue française which showed modest gains in the proportion of Montrealers working almost exclusively in French between 1979 and 1989 (from 51 to 56 percent). The continuing transformation of French-speaking Montreal into a multiethnic and multiracial community also engendered public controversy. Heated conflicts emerged over the use of English as a "language of the schoolyards" by immigrant children enrolled in French-language schools. As the Bourassa government introduces ambitious plans to increase immigration to Quebec and improve the "francisation" of immigrants, there is intense debate over Montreal's capacity to absorb large numbers of immigrants without endangering Francophone cultural and linguistic security.

For the immediate future, however, all linguistic issues will be overshadowed by the debate over Quebec's sovereignty. Whatever the outcome—and an independent Quebec is by no means a sure thing—Montrealers from all linguistic communities will have much at stake in the months ahead.

Milwaukee, May 1991

The RECONQUEST of MONTREAL

Language Policy and Social Change in a Bilingual City

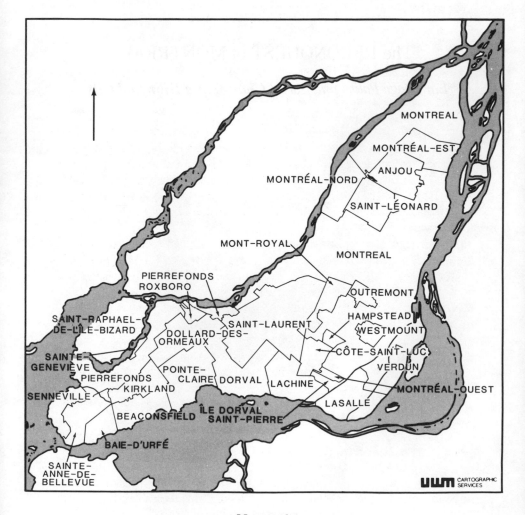

Montreal

Chapter 1

Introduction

Montreal has been a bilingual city, composed of French- and English-speakers, ever since French Canada was conquered by the British in 1760. For a brief period between 1830 and 1850, a flood of immigrants from the British Isles temporarily created an English-speaking majority in Montreal. In every census since 1871, however, French-speakers have accounted for more than 60 percent of the population in this island city on the St. Lawrence River.

Although Montreal has been demographically dominated by French-speakers for well over a century and a quarter, the city nevertheless appeared through the 1960s, in the words of Jane Jacobs, "to be what it had been for almost two centuries: an English city containing many French-speaking workers and inhabitants."[1] Until quite recently, Anglophone Montrealers could live and work using only the English language almost as easily as English-speakers in any city in the United States or English Canada. Montreal Anglophones had access to linguistically autonomous networks of educational, health, and social service institutions, all largely unregulated by the Francophone-controlled provincial and municipal governments. In sections of downtown and west Montreal, from the use of English in everyday social transactions and economic activities to English street names or public signs only in English, there was little to suggest that Montreal was the metropole of an overwhelmingly (80 percent) French-speaking province.

The prime factor giving Montreal this English "feel" before 1960 was unchallenged Anglophone domination of the city's economy. English was the language of industry and commerce—indeed, from their Montreal headquarters, Anglophone Montrealers controlled key sectors of the national Canadian economy. Montreal's labor market was characterized by a "linguistic

1

division of labor" in which Anglophones garnered a disproportionate number of the city's well-paying managerial jobs, and a substantial income gap separated English- and French-speakers. Cozy, back-channel political accommodation between Anglophone economic elites and Francophone politicians protected the autonomy of English-language institutions in Montreal and assured that vital English-speaking community interests were respected in Quebec politics.

All this would change as a rising generation of urbanized, French-speaking nationalists mobilized for a "reconquest" of Montreal. By the late 1960s the issue of Montreal's linguistic character dominated provincial politics. *La question linguistique,* as it was called, helped stoke the fires of the Quebec independence movement that burned so brightly in the 1960s and 1970s. The independence effort fell short, but by the mid-1980s, in the wake of three language laws and two decades of agitation over the places of French and English in the city, Montreal's linguistic dynamics had been radically transformed; the "English city" had been reconquered by the French-speaking majority. Schools, public administration, the economy, even the language of public signs in the city—all were reshaped by the surge in Francophone nationalism that began in the 1960s during what became known as Quebec's "Quiet Revolution."

The nature of this stunning transformation and, in particular, the role of public policy in promoting it are the central topics of this book. The reconquest of Montreal makes for interesting history: it includes episodes of intense conflict and even some violence, and it is the fascinating story of how an economically disadvantaged and culturally threatened linguistic community mobilized politically and used the state to redistribute group power in a major city. In addition, the history of Montreal's language question offers analysts of urban politics and public policy an excellent case study of some of the central issues facing cities containing more than one major linguistic community. Under what conditions do linguistic divisions become politically salient, and how can we explain patterns of conflict and accommodation? What is the role of the state, as a site for such conflicts or as a manager of them? How do class interests affect the politicization of linguistic divisions in the city? How can public policy alter linguistic hierarchies or affect patterns of language maintenance and language shift? What is the trade-off between collective and individual rights in bilingual cities? The Montreal experience has some answers to these important theoretical questions.

As Robert Dahl has noted, "Conflicts involving subcultures are likely to be especially intense, and therefore particularly difficult to manage because they cannot be confined to single, discrete issues; to the person sharing the perspective of a subculture, conflict over a 'single' issue threatens his 'way of life,' the whole future of the subculture."[2] Conflict over language in Montreal fits this description perfectly. The linguistic nationalism that erupted in Francophone Montreal in the 1960s was not simply "economic self-interest in fancy dress," as one scholar felicitously put it.[3] To be sure, economic issues figured prominently in the Francophone mobilization. On average, Montreal Anglophones earned 51 percent more than Francophones in 1961,[4] and the city's labor market fit the classic description of a cultural division of labor in which "ethnic groups within it are differentially stratified" and there is "an unequal distribution of resources between core and peripheral groups."[5] Particularly when the highly nationalistic and independence-minded Parti québécois held power in Quebec (1976–1985), provincial government policies in economic development and language planning attempted to eradicate this linguistic division of labor, create economic opportunities for Francophones, and redistribute economic power in Montreal from the Anglophone minority to the Francophone majority.

But, above all, the language question in Montreal after 1960 dealt with linguistic survival and cultural affirmation. French had survived in Quebec for over two centuries following the Conquest, but it had done so mainly in a world of isolated, rural parishes that were homogeneously French-Catholic and where contacts with English and the threat of Anglicization were limited. Outside metropolitan Montreal, Quebec's population has always been overwhelmingly French-speaking, except for once-substantial Anglophone communities in the Eastern Townships, Ottawa Valley, and on the Gaspé Peninsula that have declined dramatically in size throughout the twentieth century. In rural areas and in the provinces' smaller cities, such as Quebec City (97 percent Francophone in 1981), Trois Rivières (97 percent Francophone), or Chicoutimi (99 percent Francophone), the cultural and linguistic security of the Francophone community has never been in question.[6]

However, as Montreal developed into Canada's preeminent industrial metropolis in the late nineteenth century, thousands of Francophones migrated from the poverty of Quebec's rural hinterland in search of factory employment in the big city. By 1961 almost 40 percent of Quebec's Francophones lived in Montreal (up from 8.9 percent in 1871). This rapid urbanization, however, meant that the ability of French to survive in English North America would be put to a new and unprecedented test. In Montreal English was the language of upward mobility. Visible and powerful English-language institutions confronted Francophones every day, and Montreal was well integrated culturally and economically into the continental English-speaking world. Could French *flourish* in this modern, urban environment containing pervasive English influences or was it destined merely to *survive* in rural enclaves in a manner akin to the Amish or other "folkloric" linguistic communities? *That* was the crucial question facing Francophone elites as the 1960s began.

The cultural survival issue that brought Francophones to the streets and pushed the Quebec government to action in the 1960s and 1970s was the language of instruction in the Montreal public schools. This was no accident: more than any other public institution, schools are the central battleground for conflicts between urban ethnic and linguistic groups. Schools, of course, are institutions crucial to the vitality of linguistic communities. It is there that languages are taught, cultural values are transmitted from one generation to another, newcomers are integrated into a linguistic community, and numerous group members find employment as teachers and administrators. Language policy in education is integrally connected to patterns of language maintenance, language shift, and ultimately to group survival, especially in cities where speakers of "weaker" languages are more readily exposed to a dominant language and where the pressures to adopt the stronger tongue are greater than in more isolated, monolingual rural settings.[7] This is why, in bilingual cities such as Brussels or in debates over bilingualism throughout U.S. urban history, the language of schooling has been the focal point of group conflict.[8]

In Montreal, separate networks of English- and French-language schools had existed since the 1840s without unduly upsetting the city's linguistic equilibrium. But after 1945, a major wave of immigrants settled in Montreal and began sending their children to English-language schools. By the 1960s the Anglicization of the city's school clientele seemed to portend a Montreal in which the children of immigrants would become Anglophones and French-speakers would ultimately become a demographic minority. Thus, for important segments of the Francophone community, the individual right of parents to choose their children's language of schooling, historically respected in Quebec, now clashed with the "collective right" of Francophones to survive and prosper *as Francophones*. In the eyes of Montreal's rising Francophone elite, the new middle class of teachers, journalists, and policy professionals who had displaced traditional church elites as the leading force in French-Canadian society, Francophone *minorisation* in Montreal would spell ultimate doom for a living French language and culture throughout Quebec.

To block even the remote threat of an English-speaking majority in Montreal, this new class of Francophone nationalist elites rallied mass opinion behind legislation that would limit access to Montreal's English-language schools. Francophone pressures for restrictive language policies, and the vigorous response by Anglophones and immigrants in the city to this attack on their "rights," resulted in the most intense social conflicts in Montreal's history. Ultimately, however, the schools question was one on which Francophone nationalists would not compromise, for it was central to their vision of a reconquered Montreal in which the city's character would be unquestionably French. Montreal might always be a bilingual city in linguistic composition, but nationalists were determined to make French as dominant a language and culture in the city as English was in Toronto or Vancouver. Many issues regarding language and the Montreal economy were compromised in the 1970s, as nationalists scaled back radical plans to establish French as the city's language of work. But on a core cultural issue such as schooling, affecting the linguistic identity of Montreal and the viability of Francophone society, there would be no concessions.

Montreal's linguistic upheaval was a cardinal development in Canadian political history, inextricably linked to the country's national unity crises of the 1960s and 1970s. As Arnopoulos and Clift wrote in 1980: "The linguistic and cultural compromises that will be realized over the next few years in the Montreal area . . . will ultimately determine the manner in which the French majority considers its relations with the rest of Canada."[9] The issues were explosive: Which group would define Montreal's linguistic character? Did the survival of French in Montreal require an independent, French-speaking state of Quebec? In a Canada whose dominant language was English, what were the language rights of Montreal's English-speaking community in predominantly Francophone Quebec? In short, the Montreal language question was intimately related to the nettlesome problem of defining the boundaries of political authority and allegiance in Canada.

Such national conflicts between linguistic groups are often best resolved by the "principle of territoriality": the partition of plurilingual societies into distinct regions in which only one language is official.[10] This has been the policy adopted in multilingual countries such as Switzerland, where there are officially French- and German-speaking regions, and in Belgium, where the country is divided into officially unilingual French- and Flemish-speaking territories. But bilingual cities, located in nearly monolingual regions, cannot be easily incorporated into a national strategy of territorial partition: this is graphically illustrated in Belgium, where the chief ongoing battle between that country's language groups remains the linguistic status of the bilingual Brussels agglomeration.

Similarly, the existence of a substantial Anglophone community in Montreal represented a major stumbling block to any purely territorial solution to Canada's national language disputes. Quebec law declared the province officially French in the 1970s, and Francophone nationalists promoted a vision of Montreal as a fundamentally "French city." But the Anglophone concept of Montreal was of a city of "two majorities": English Canadians and French Québécois, each with inviolable, historically established rights. These clashing perspectives, combined with the strength of English-language institutions in a Montreal that was also the urban center of Francophone Quebec, made language in Montreal a continuing source of political friction in Canadian political life. The policy disputes in Montreal over language entailed more than just a big city sorting out its ethnic and linguistic hierarchies; whether Francophones felt culturally secure and "in control" in Montreal would go far in determining whether they felt at home in Canada. Those were perhaps the ultimate stakes in *la question linguistique*.

This, then, is a book about how political action and public policy produced major social and economic changes in a bilingual city. The book has two main parts. In the first section (Chapters 3–6), I examine the politicization of the language question in the 1960s and 1970s. In particular, I focus on the Francophone nationalist push for state intervention to alter Montreal's linguistic balance of power. In response to Montreal's deteriorating linguistic climate, the Quebec provincial government enacted three language laws between 1969 and 1977, and much of my analysis centers on the political conflicts and controversies surrounding these policies.

The second part of the book (Chapters 6–9) examines the changes in Montreal's linguistic landscape that occurred between 1960 and 1989, chiefly as a result of nationalist language policies. My main focus is on the impact of the province's far-reaching language law, the Charter of the French Language enacted by the Parti québécois in 1977, on such basic areas of Montreal life as schools, public administration, the economy, and the *visage* of the city. I also explore the effects of provincial government economic development policies since 1960 on patterns of linguistic control and language use in the Montreal economy. Finally, the book concludes with an examination of recent trends in language-group relations in Montreal, the changing cultural fabric of the city, and the outlook for both French and English in the new Montreal.

Before turning our detailed attention to Montreal's great transformation, we first need to understand the historical context from which *la question linguistique* emerged. Our initial task, then, is to analyze the political economy of language in Montreal before 1960, an era when Montreal was the economic center of Canada and the city's linguistic balance of power decidedly tilted in favor of English. That is the subject of the next chapter.

Chapter 2

An English City
Montreal before the Quiet Revolution

The uneasy coexistence of French- and English-speakers has been a fundamental part of Montreal history since the Conquest. In almost every sphere
of urban life, linguistic divisions have profoundly shaped Montreal's development. Before 1960, although Montreal's linguistic composition was predominantly French, its linguistic *character* was undeniably English. Montreal was
the urban center of English Canada where corporate boardrooms functioned
in English, the best neighborhoods were inhabited by English-speakers,
downtown was festooned with billboards and commercial signs in English,
and where the language of the city's minority—English—exerted a greater
assimilationist pull than the language of the majority.

These linguistic dynamics were rarely contested before 1960 by Montreal's Francophone community. Deference to the English character of the
city was part of Quebec's unwritten linguistic *modus vivendi;* as a result,
language had rarely surfaced as a divisive political issue in Montreal for any
sustained period before 1960. For Francophones, the price of this kind of
linguistic peace was heavy: limited economic opportunities for someone unable or unwilling to work in English, and a kind of cultural alienation in a city
that, by 1960, also had become the demographic and cultural center of
French-Canadian society. In this chapter, we examine the places of English
and French in Montreal before the 1960s: before the Quiet Revolution when
the city's Francophone majority decided that Montreal's linguistic dynamics
had to be contested.

Urban Growth and Linguistic Diversity, 1760–1960

When Montreal was conquered by the British in 1760, it was a fur-trading settlement of about 8,800 French colonials. British merchants accompanied the victorious army and immediately established a small, but powerful, English presence in the city. By the 1780s the British controlled the lucrative Montreal-centered fur trade, and historian Fernand Ouellet estimates that by 1820 almost two-thirds of all Montreal merchants were British.[1]

These British merchants, primarily of English and Scottish stock, represent some of the most venerable names in the history of English-speaking Montreal: Dunlop, McTavish, McGill, Molson, and Redpath. Their names still adorn street signs and important institutions in Montreal. Beyond this small merchant elite, however, the English-speaking population of Montreal grew slowly through the early 1800s; indeed, the most significant Anglophone presence in early-nineteenth-century Quebec was the 15,000 Americans, refugees from the Revolutionary War, who settled mainly in the farmlands of the Eastern Townships. By 1820, however, Montreal had developed into an important commercial center of 20,000 people, and the powerful Anglophone elite imparted a distinct English "character" to the city. Nevertheless, Francophones still constituted a solid majority of the city's population; demographically, Montreal was still *une ville française*.[2]

That changed dramatically between 1820 and 1850. Like cities on the Eastern seaboard of the United States during this period, Montreal received a steady stream of immigrants from the British Isles—approximately 60 percent of whom came from Ireland. Between 1829 and 1853, nearly 750,000 immigrants landed at Quebec City, the port of entry for British North America. While only a small minority remained in either Quebec City or Montreal—the rest settling elsewhere in North America—sufficient numbers settled in Montreal to alter radically the social and demographic character of the city. As early as 1831 Montreal had a British majority, and the census of 1851 revealed that 55 percent of the city's nearly 60,000 residents were of British ethnic origin.[3]

This period of British majority consolidated the hegemony of English and Scottish Protestants in Montreal. Moreover, migration of "Britain's dispossessed"[4] also meant that Anglophone Montreal was no longer what historian Paul-André Linteau has called "a handful of rich merchants and administrators."[5] English-speaking Montreal now had a substantial and diverse population, differentiated along ethnic and class lines. Anglophones of English, Scottish, and American stock continued to be vastly overrepresented among Montreal's "merchant class." As was the case in cities such as Boston, New York, and Philadelphia, however, a growing number of Irish-Catholic immigrants formed the ranks of the city's working strata, and by the 1840s, 20 percent of Montreal's population was Irish.[6]

In the 1860s, the linguistic composition of Montreal shifted decisively and, at least in demographic terms, Montreal became a French-speaking city. The continuing economic crisis of rural Quebec combined with the dynamic growth of Montreal's industrial economy drew thousands of rural and small-town Francophones to the city. Swelled by this rural exodus, the population of the city of Montreal grew from 90,000 to 800,000 between 1861 and 1931, with the population on the Island itself—including some of the newly established suburban communities incorporated outside the city limits—reaching one million by 1931.[7]

After 1871, as Table 2.1 shows, the French-origin population of the Island of Montreal remained above 60 percent through the early 1960s.[8] Increasingly, as Table 2.2 shows, Montreal became the demographic center of French-speaking Quebec.

While Montreal's Francophone population was growing rapidly after 1860, the city also increasingly became the central location for Quebec's English-speaking community. Anglophones began deserting other areas of Quebec in droves by the end of the nineteenth century. The Eastern Townships, a stronghold of mid-nineteenth-century British Quebec, became overwhelmingly French-speaking by the early twentieth century, a consequence of the late-nineteenth-century French-Canadian colonization movement and a precipitous outflow of British-origin population.[9] Similarly, by 1900 the Anglophone exodus from nineteenth-century, English-speaking areas such as Quebec City was well under way, and by 1930 the English-speaking population on the Gaspé Peninsula began declining.

Thus, while only 22.6 percent of Quebec's Anglophone population lived in Montreal in 1871, that figure rose to 61.4 percent in 1931 and 74.3 percent by 1961 (see Table 2.2). In short, by the 1960s Montreal was the demographic center of both Quebec's Anglophone and Francophone populations, a phenomenon that by itself multiplied the prospects for linguistic conflict.

After 1900 Montreal's ethnic and linguistic balance was also affected by new sources of international migration. As late as 1901 Montreal's population was still composed almost exclusively of British and French ethnics: the city's "charter" groups. Only 4.5 percent of the population was *not* of French or British ethnic stock. (By contrast, over two-thirds of the population in U.S. cities such as New York, Chicago, and Cleveland was of foreign ancestry.)

In two waves of immigration—between 1901 and 1931, and 1945 and 1961—Montreal became a multi-ethnic city. By 1931, with the immigration of Jews and Italians primarily, 13.5 percent of Montreal's population (135,000) was not of French or British ethnic stock. By 1961, as post–World War II immigration surged from southern and eastern Europe, the non-French, non-British component of Montreal's population reached 350,000 or almost

Table 2.1
Ethnic Composition of Montreal Island, in Percentages, 1871–1961

Year	French	British	Others
1871	60.3	38.1	1.6
1901	63.9	31.6	4.5
1921	60.7	27.3	12.0
1941	62.6	24.5	12.9
1951	63.8	22.2	14.0
1961	62.0	18.1	19.9

Sources: Norbert Lacoste, *Les caractéristiques sociale de la population de Grand Montréal* (Montréal: Les Presses de l'Université de Montréal, 1958), p. 77, and Statistics Canada, *Census of Canada: 1971* (Catalogue 92–726).

Table 2.2
Urbanization and Linguistic Concentration

The Percentage of Quebec's Population Living in Montreal by Language Group, 1871–1961

Year	% of Quebec Anglophones living in Montreal	% of Quebec Francophones living in Montreal
1871	22.6	8.9
1901	39.3	17.4
1931	61.4	26.6
1961	74.3	39.3

Sources: See Table 2.1.

Note on boundary definitions: For 1871, 1901, and 1931, Montreal Island is used, because the sparsely settled area off the Island was not then truly part of the Montreal metropolitan region. For 1961, with off-Island communities clearly linked to a metropolitan region, the Census Metropolitan Area is used for these calculations.

20 percent of the Island's population. "Ethnics" now outnumbered British Montrealers on the Island of Montreal.[10]

By the late 1940s this new ethnic mix began to influence Montreal's linguistic dynamics.[11] Through 1941 Anglophone Montreal was still almost entirely a British ethnic community. However, as non-Anglophone, non-Francophone immigrants came to Montreal and chose English as their "new world" language, Anglophone Montreal turned from a British community into a multicultural one. By 1971, as Jews, Italians, Greeks, and Portuguese joined the English-speaking community, British Montrealers constituted only 61 percent of the Island's Anglophone population, and only 37 percent of Montreal's entire non-Francophone population.

This "multiculturalization" of English-speaking Montreal had two important consequences. First, as immigrants became English-speakers, they obviously bolstered the demographic strength of the English language in Montreal. In the 1960s, as Francophone nationalists worried about the relative sizes of the English- and French-speaking populations in Montreal, the tendency of immigrants to become Anglophones surfaced as a major source of conflict in the city.

Second, the ethnic diversification of English-speaking Montreal transformed "Anglophone" into a statistical category instead of a communal social grouping. By 1960 English-speaking Montreal was a collection of subcommunities: a British community, with long historical roots in Quebec (itself divided into English, Scottish, and Irish ethnic groups); English-speakers from elsewhere in North America, who found themselves in Montreal for business or career reasons; older immigrant communities such as the Jews and Italians; and newer immigrants from southern and eastern Europe. These differences meant that Anglophones often fought among themselves, as, for example, British Protestants discriminated against Jews. It would take the politicization of the language question in the 1960s and 1970s to generate a common linguistic community out of these diverse ethnic groups. [12]

Linguistic Geography and the Two Solitudes

The basic contours of Montreal's remarkably persistent linguistic geography took shape by the mid-nineteenth century. By 1860 the greatest concentrations of British-origin Montrealers were in the western and central wards of the city, where they constituted 68 percent and 49 percent of the population, respectively; French-origin residents constituted 69 percent of the population in the city's eastern districts. [13] While the notion of "linguistic territory" in Montreal has often been exaggerated, this mid-nineteenth-century spatial distribution of Montreal's English and French-speaking communities became an enduring aspect of the city's social, economic, and political landscape. [14] Downtown and the western portion of Montreal Island would remain predominantly Anglophone through the 1960s, while the population on the eastern side of the Island became even more overwhelmingly French-speaking.

Montreal's rapid growth in the twentieth century followed these general lines of linguistic demarcation. By 1961 Montreal had become a genuine metropolis with a population of more than two million. The city continued its growth into the 1960s, but the chief characteristic of metropolitan development in twentieth-century Montreal was the proliferation of suburban communities across the Island and eventually to the North and South Shore regions "off-Island." Between 1941 and 1971, the city of Montreal's share of the metropolitan area's total population dropped from 79.2 percent to 44.2

percent. Linguistic divisions were apparent in this metropolitan sprawl: as in the city's earlier settlement pattern, western areas were predominantly Anglophone, while communities on the East Island and off-Island were over-whelmingly Francophone.[15]

Two socially and linguistically distinct types of suburbs emerged during Montreal's first phase of metropolitan growth. First, between 1870 and 1920, East Island working-class suburbs such as Hochelaga and Maison-neuve developed around industrial sites, transportation links, or the speculative ventures of real estate entrepreneurs.[16] Overwhelmingly Franco-phone, twenty-three of these suburbs were annexed by the city of Montreal between 1883 and 1918. These annexations, along with the continuing movement of rural Francophones to Montreal, helped bolster the emerging Francophone majority in the city.[17]

Second, in the early 1900s the city's British community began a "re-treat" to the suburbs.[18] In the late-nineteenth-century United States, elite suburbs developed around large cities as wealthy WASPs sought to escape the noxious urban industrial environment and the growing power of immi-grant-controlled political machines. Similarly, upper-income British Montre-alers reacted to industrialization and an expanding French presence by mov-ing to suburban communities west of the city. The advent of electric streetcars and telephones in the 1890s made elite, residential suburbs on the Island of Montreal feasible, and between 1890 and 1910 Westmount developed as Montreal's first upper-class, overwhelmingly British suburb. A small village of 3,000 in 1891 known as Côte-St-Antoine, Westmount grew to 14,600 by 1911 and more than 26,000 by 1941.[19] Incorporated as an autonomous muni-cipality in 1908, Westmount became "one of the wealthiest communities in Canada" and staunchly resisted any hint of political annexation to the in-creasingly French-speaking city of Montreal next door.[20] In its upper-class autonomy from the "French fact" in Montreal, Westmount would become a potent 1960s symbol of Montreal's Anglophone "establishment," perceived by increasingly nationalistic Francophones as "the last bastion of the British Empire" in Montreal.[21]

As the farmland of the West Island was subdivided into residential tracts after 1900, smaller communities such as Baie d'Urfé, Beaconsfield, Hampstead, Pointe-Claire, and Mont-Royal were incorporated; they also be-came English-speaking enclaves. In short, as Andrew Sancton points out, by 1921 "the patterns of municipal boundaries and linguistic segregation that exist today on the Island of Montreal were clearly established. . . . The im-age of wealthy English suburbs spreading west from a French dominated city of Montreal had become the central feature of Montreal's metropolitan development."[22]

Anglophone suburbanization began as an elite phenomenon, but by the middle of the twentieth century broad segments of the English-speaking

Table 2.3

Growth in Selected West Island Suburbs, 1941–1971

Population

Municipality	1941	1951	1961	1971
Beaconsfield	706	1,888	10,064	19,389
Côte-Saint-Luc	776	1,083	13,266	24,375
Dollard-des-Ormeaux	—	—	1,248	25,217
Dorval	2,048	5,293	18,592	20,469
Mont-Royal	4,888	11,352	21,182	21,561
Pierrefonds	—	1,436	12,171	33,010
Pointe-Claire	4,536	8,753	22,709	27,303

Source: Paul-André Linteau et al., *Le Québec Depuis 1930* (Montréal: Les Éditions du Boréal Express, 1986), pp. 260, 498.

middle class were moving to Montreal's suburbs. The percentage of the Island's Anglophone community living outside the city of Montreal increased from 13.8 percent in 1881 to 32.4 percent in 1931. After World War II, as was the case throughout North America, the pace of suburbanization accelerated in Montreal; as Table 2.3 shows, population growth in the heavily Anglophone West Island exploded after 1950. British-origin Montrealers were particularly prone to move to the West Island; in 1961, six West Island municipalities had British ethnic *majorities,* and the British were the principal ethnic group in several others.[23] In any event, by the end of the 1960s, almost 70 percent of metropolitan Montreal's English-speaking population lived outside the city of Montreal, the vast majority on the West Island.

Through 1931 only 12 percent of Montreal Island's Francophones lived outside the city limits, but by the 1950s the large-scale suburbanization of the French-speaking population had also begun. East Island suburbs such as Anjou, Montréal-Nord, and Saint-Léonard grew dramatically in the 1960s, as did predominantly Francophone suburbs off the Island such as Laval and Longueil on the North and South Shores.[24] Nevertheless, Francophones remained more concentrated in the city of Montreal than did Anglophones: 45 percent of the metropolitan area's Francophones lived in the city of Montreal in 1971, compared to only 30 percent of the region's Anglophones.

The relative linguistic segregation that shaped patterns of community development in Montreal from the nineteenth century through the suburbanization of the twentieth century was a source of both conflict and conflict management in the city. Even if the imagery of "two solitudes" uneasily coexisting in Montreal has been exaggerated, there apparently was sufficient territorial separation on the Island through the 1960s to help keep potentially conflict-producing linguistic contacts to a minimum—the consociational model of "good social fences" making "good social neighbors."[25] As

Douglas Fullerton, who grew up in central and western Montreal neighborhoods in the 1920s and 1930s recalls:

> We saw little of the French Canadians, never mixed with them socially;
> such contact as there was occurred mostly in the streets, tramways,
> in stores, with the milkman or the breadman. And I'm not just speak-
> ing of the wealthy Montrealers, the Westmount dwellers, but of the
> rest of us at every level of society. I did meet several French-Canadi-
> ans in school—they had been sent to learn English—but to the best of
> my memory, I was never a guest in a French-Canadian home, or a
> French-Canadian friend in mine, until my mid-twenties, in Ottawa. . . .
> We English Montrealers lived in different parts of town from the
> French-Canadians, went to different schools, attended different
> churches, socialized among our own.[26]

In one sense, then, the Anglophone retreat to the West Island (where
it became an easy matter to maintain an exclusively English-speaking existence) might have averted conflicts stemming from the transition to Francophone political control in the city of Montreal in the early twentieth century.

But, conversely, the existence of prosperous Anglophone enclaves
also engendered Francophone resentment. Through the 1960s Montreal's
British elite displayed both an opulence and imperial *hauteur* consistent with
its historical position as conqueror and colonizer. In the early twentieth century, before Westmount had emerged as the home of Montreal's Anglo establishment, 25,000 of the city's English-speaking elite lived in an area of
west-central Montreal called the "Golden Square Mile." The residents of
this neighborhood—where fur magnates such as James McGill and Simon
McTavish once had magnificent estates—were estimated to have controlled
70 percent of all Canadian wealth around 1900 and, even in the words of the
anglophile chronicler Stephen Leacock, "enjoyed a prestige in that era that
not even the rich deserved."[27] As an observer from that period put it:

> In perhaps no section of the Colonies, have Englishmen and Scotch-
> men made more of their opportunities than in Montreal. There is an air
> of prosperity about all their surroundings which at once impresses the
> visitor. Taken all in all, there is perhaps no wealthier city area in the
> world than that comprised between Beaver Hall Hill and the foot of
> Mount Royal, and between the parallel lines of Dorchester and Sher-
> brooke Streets in the West End.[28]

Through 1970, nearly 80 percent of predominantly Anglophone census
tracts on Montreal Island—all located on the western part of the Island—
had an annual family income higher than the metropolitan area median.[29]

Only one predominantly French-speaking municipality on the Island—Outremont—ranked among the top ten communities in real estate valuation in 1968; the assessed value of single-family houses in Westmount that year was double the Islandwide average.[30]

The existence of such "gilded ghettoes" helped sustain images of Anglophone "Rhodesians"—living luxuriously in places such as the Golden Square Mile or Westmount, and controlling the Montreal economy from offices on St. James Street—that would become commonplace in Francophone nationalist circles in the 1960s. Of course, all Anglophones did not live in the Square Mile or Westmount; a substantial English-speaking working class endured a harsh existence in "Griffintown" and the industrial districts of Verdun and Point-Saint-Charles along the Lachine Canal in southwest Montreal.[31] No matter. The obviously privileged position of Montreal's British elite in their prosperous, autonomous enclaves, coupled with that elite's arrogant disregard for the city's Francophone majority, helped fuel the mobilization of the Québécois independence movement in the 1960s along with agitation for pro–French language legislation.

In short, the existence of two solitudes may have helped preserve linguistic peace in Montreal through the 1960s. Ultimately, however, the image of privileged British conquerors controlling Montreal from Westmount and the West Island—even as English-speaking Montreal became less and less British—would help unleash the fierce linguistic conflicts of the 1960s.

Language Use and Language Choice through 1960

French has been the mother tongue of a solid majority of Montreal's population since the 1860s. Moreover, in the twentieth century, increasing proportions of Montreal's Francophone population spoke *only* French. Between 1931 and 1961, as thousands of unilingual Francophones migrated to Montreal from rural Quebec, the proportion of the Island's population classified as "unilingual French-speaking" grew by almost 33 percent.[32] The rate of bilingualism in the French-origin community declined by 20 percent during this period. With a critical mass of unilingual Francophones as an audience and market, the stage was set for a flowering of an urban, French-speaking culture. Since the 1930s, despite the exhortations of conservative Catholic church leaders that the essence of French-Canadian identity remained tied to rural and agrarian values, Montreal has become the cultural and social center of French-speaking Quebec.

Despite these changes, much of Montreal retained an aggressively English character through mid-twentieth century. André Siegfried, the European observer who visited Canada in 1898 and 1904 and wrote a "Tocquevillian" study of the country's linguistic character, was shocked by the English face of Montreal. He found:

Visitors may pass whole weeks there, frequenting hotels, banks, railway stations without ever imagining for a moment that the town is French by a great majority of its inhabitants. English society affects unconsciousness of this fact, and bears itself exactly as though it had no French neighbors. They seem to regard Montreal as their property.[33]

Siegfried's observations were echoed in 1942 when l'Université de Montréal rector Monseigneur Olivier Maurault commented: "If a stranger were content merely to circle the district of hotels, large stores, theatres, and offices, everything would lead him to believe that he was in an English city."[34]

Things were different—but only slightly—by the late 1950s. Downtown and western Montreal abounded with numerous signs in English only, imparting an English *visage* to major sections of the city. Anecdotal evidence is plentiful regarding unpleasant Francophone encounters with unilingual English-speaking clerks in downtown retail stores, a remnant of the days when stores such as Eaton's, Simpson's, Birk's, and Morgan's catered almost exclusively to an English-speaking clientele. By the 1950s, even as Anglophone-run stores took notice of a burgeoning French-speaking consumer market and the "language of the customer" was more frequently spoken, several downtown Montreal stores had "departments which cater to a clientele that might be largely English or at least bilingual enough to be served in English,"[35] and "the great bulk of the French . . . use English in the current intercourse of shops and streets."[36] In short, as one English-speaking observer has written: "Few French Canadians I have met did not have at least one story to tell me, or emotional bruises to display, resulting from their experience with the dominant and domineering English of Montreal."[37]

Data on patterns of language use reveal how easy it was for Montreal Anglophones to ignore the French-speaking majority and enjoy an English-only existence in Montreal through the early 1960s. Only 27.0 percent of British-origin Montrealers reported an ability to speak both English and French in 1961, compared to the 23.3 percent of 1931. (The rate of bilingualism among French-origin Montrealers was 24.8 percent in 1961, down from 30.6 percent in 1931.)[38] In west-center Montreal and the West Island suburbs, unilingual Anglophones vastly outnumbered all other linguistic categories.[39] Through 1960, as we explore shortly, the majority of Montreal Anglophones could work exclusively in English, live in generally homogeneous English-speaking neighborhoods, send their children to English-language schools, and enjoy a full range of English-language social service and health care facilities. Small wonder that so few bothered to learn the language of Montreal's majority: There was little need or incentive to do so. Leacock's 1948 observations nicely summarize the condescending Anglophone attitude on language use in the Montreal of that era: "Almost all

Table 2.4
Linguistic Transfers in Montreal, 1941–1961

Year	To English	To French	Percentage To English	Percentage To French
1941	21,319	7,339	74.4	25.6
1951	60,922	4,769	92.7	7.3
1961	103,163	11,722	89.8	10.2

Source: Hubert Charbonneau and Robert Maheu, *Les aspects démographiques de la question linguistique* (Québec: Éditeur officiel, 1973), pp. 71–73.

Note: Linguistic transfers are measured as follows: To English: English mother-tongue population minus British-origin population. To French: French mother-tongue population minus French-origin population.

the French people understand English and speak it well enough for the business of the day in shops or factories. . . . Most English people in Montreal cannot follow a French movie or a French speech or buy and sell in French. They don't need to. The French, conversely, have to [speak English]."[40]

A final measure of the strength of English in Montreal through 1960 was the degree to which "linguistic transfers" significantly favored English over French, as Table 2.4 demonstrates. Simply put, between 1941 and 1961, more non-British Montrealers adopted English as their language than non-French Montrealers adopted French. Thus, significant numbers of new immigrants as well as some (perhaps 10,000) Montrealers of French-ethnic origin became Anglophones, while almost no British Montrealers and very few new immigrants became Francophones.

Between 1941 and 1961, Montreal's French-speaking community remained essentially composed of the French-ethnic group, which constituted 99.7 percent of French-speakers in 1961. The size of Montreal's Francophone population during these years grew through natural increase and the migration of rural Francophones, not the "conversion" of new immigrants. On the other hand, as I have already noted, Montreal's English-speaking community expanded markedly beyond its British ethnic base during this period. In 1931, non-British ethnics constituted only 5 percent of the Island's English-speaking community; by 1961, that figure had risen to 27 percent. In sum, despite the fact that Montreal in 1960 was a solidly French-speaking city, the pattern of "linguistic transfers" was running strongly in favor of English.[41]

Language and the Economy: Historical Patterns

One central factor underpinned Montreal's English ambiance through 1960: Anglophone domination of the economy and the concomitant status of En-

glish as the language of work and upward mobility. From the 1780s—when
the Scottish merchants of the North West Company took control of the fur
trade—through the 1960s, English-speaking Montrealers ran the city's
economy, generally held the best jobs, and enjoyed substantially higher
earnings than Montreal Francophones.

On the eve of the Quiet Revolution, almost all of Montreal's major economic institutions—banks, heavy industry, and large commercial enterprises—were controlled by Anglophones. English was the language of work
above the middle-management level virtually throughout the private sector,
a situation that put Francophones at considerable disadvantage in competing for such employment. As a consequence, Montreal's labor market was
characterized by a linguistic division of labor in which Anglophones controlled capital and occupied command positions well out of proportion to
their numbers in the Montreal population, while Francophones were relegated to subordinate or peripheral economic activities.

Anglophone domination of the Montreal economy began shortly after
the Conquest. French merchants, who had relied during the colonial era on
military and government contracts as well as access to credit and markets in
France, quickly found themselves at a severe disadvantage to the British
"camp followers." [42] Some French–English partnerships developed, particularly in the lucrative fur trade where French-Canadians served as "middle-
men and couriers between Montreal and the interior posts." [43] With the establishment of the North West Company and other Anglophone-controlled
economic institutions, however, the Francophone role in the Montreal economy diminished. The profits from the fur trade were enormous, as were
returns from the incipient export trade in agricultural commodities and tim-
ber, and many of Montreal's oldest private fortunes were founded during
this period, so that by 1800 Anglophone economic control of Montreal was
firmly entrenched.

Traditional historical explanations of Anglophone economic dominance
focused on an alleged lack of "appropriate" commercial "values" in the
French-speaking community: in particular, the ideological aversion of the
dominant French-Catholic elite to capitalist values and, later, industrial society. Moreover, it was suggested that French-Canadian businessmen were
more risk-averse than their Anglophone counterparts, prefering the "security" of smaller, family-type enterprises to the risks of the more dynamic
sectors of the economy. [44]

As recent scholarship has made clear, however, the historical mar-
ginality of Francophones in the command positions of Montreal's economy
was at root "the product of the shift in access to the capital, suppliers, and
markets which followed upon the Conquest." [45] After the British took control, the Francophone businessman had to fend for himself in an English-
speaking business world where his chances of obtaining capital or securing

markets were lesser than those of Anglophone competitors. Anglophone-run banks, for example, rarely issued loans to Francophone entrepreneurs.[46] This structural disadvantage in post-Conquest Quebec may have been reinforced by a Francophone ideology that reacted to the "collective trauma" of the Conquest by disparaging the "British" world of commerce and industry and asserting the superiority of the values of traditional French-Canadian nationalism, agrarianism and Catholicism.[47] But, more than any antibusiness *mentalité* of Francophones, it was the pattern of Anglophone structural advantage established after the Conquest—superior access to capital and connections to Britain and the wider English-speaking North American economic markets and suppliers—that enabled English-speaking Montrealers to maintain economic control through the 1960s.

By mid-nineteenth century, the emergence of Montreal as Canada's major urban economic center consolidated the place of English in the city's economy. Montreal's English-speaking businessmen were "continental" economic actors, aggressively promoting Montreal as a central transportation link in Canada's expanding agricultural commodity export markets. By contrast, Francophone merchants were mainly small businessmen, conducting their activities in a regional market. Occasionally, there would be attempts by French-speaking entrepreneurs to penetrate some of the more continental-oriented sectors of the economy; but, as Fernand Ouellet argues, "At every turn the English-speaking were there too, and more and more seemed to be blocking the advance of the French-Canadians."[48]

For example, Montreal's banking industry developed along such linguistically differentiated lines. Throughout the nineteenth century, Anglophone-controlled institutions such as the Bank of Montreal catered mainly to English-speaking customers in Montreal, eschewed lending in the small towns of French-speaking Quebec, and operated in a national capital market. By contrast, Francophone-owned banks such as Banque Provinciale and Banque Canadienne Nationale, lacking access to English-speaking markets, developed by serving Francophone communities in Montreal and small-town Quebec.[49] As a result, Francophone banks were unable to reach the scale necessary to penetrate significantly the "continental" sector of Montreal finance. In 1896 Quebec's four Francophone banks held $15.2 million in assets; by contrast, the Bank of Montreal *alone* had assets of $59.3 million.[50]

These larger trends in urban economic development produced a discernible linguistic division of labor in Montreal by the early-nineteenth century. By 1840, for example, the vast majority (more than 70 percent) of Montreal's merchants were English-speaking, while French-speakers were overrepresented in "working class" occupations.[51] A century later, even as Montreal had grown into a metropolis containing more than a million residents, this pattern of linguistic hierarchy would linger. In 1934, 5.3 percent of all "English" employees were managers, compared to only 0.8 percent of

French-ethnic labor force participants. Conversely, while 28.6 percent of all English employees were "semiskilled and unskilled" workers, fully 51.7 percent of all French employees fell into that category.[52]

Confederation in 1867 created a national Canadian political economy, and over the next seventy years brought English-speaking Montrealers to the peak of their economic power. Montreal Anglophone business leaders such as Hugh Allan and John Rose had been among the staunchest advocates of Confederation, arguing that a strong central government was necessary to transcend provincial boundaries and build a transcontinental rail system in which Montreal would be the hub. Similarly, interests connected to the Bank of Montreal eagerly anticipated a centralized Canadian banking system in which their influence might be extended. Finally, English-speaking business leaders in Montreal believed that their interests would be better served in a new, national political system controlled by an English-speaking majority. In short, as Ronald Rudin points out, the British North America (BNA) Act that created the Canadian Confederation "was written, in certain regards, by and for the city's English-speaking business elite."[53]

Post-Confederation developments quickly turned out just as these elites had hoped. In the 1870s, an Anglophone-run Montreal syndicate won the contract to build the Canadian Pacific Railway (CPR), with extensive federal government support. The completion of the CPR in 1885 enabled Montreal's businessmen to assert "metropolitan" influence over a trans-Canadian market for Montreal-produced goods and services; thus, English-speaking Montreal industrialists controlling such companies as Canada Cement, Stelco, Dominion Textile, Ogilvie Flour, and Canada Power achieved national economic power in the late-nineteenth and early-twentieth centuries. In the financial world, the Anglophone-run Bank of Montreal became the repository for the accounts of the Canadian government and the banker for the new Quebec provincial government. By 1870 two-thirds of central Canada's banking assets were headquartered in Montreal, mostly at the Bank of Montreal.[54] The Bank of Montreal/CPR tandem emerged as Canada's dominant corporate power, and over the next fifty years Montreal Anglophone elites such as Donald Smith, R. B. Angus, George Stephen, and William C. Van Horne used their control of these corporate giants to become the lions of Canadian capitalism. St. James Street in old Montreal became Canada's Wall Street.

Several other factors in the late-nineteenth and early-twentieth centuries enhanced the economic power of Montreal's English-speaking business community. Close ties with British and American investors assured them a ready source of capital and credit. Furthermore, as was the case in the United States, corporate power became increasingly concentrated in Canada in the late-nineteenth and early-twentieth centuries; thus, Anglophone-controlled Montreal enterprises, already large to begin with, were excellently positioned to swallow up their competition and assert hegemony over local and national markets. The concentration of utility companies enabled Herbert Holt to build a spectacularly profitable empire out of the Montreal Light, Heat, and Power Company; other Montreal-based giants included Max Aitken's Canada Cement, the Sun Life Assurance Company, and Dominion Textile. The Canadian Pacific expanded its railroad and real estate empire in the early twentieth century, and Montreal-headquartered institutions such as the Bank of Montreal and Royal Bank consolidated their control over Canadian finance. The Bank of Montreal, for example, absorbed three major banks between 1913 and 1929—including Molson's Bank—to solidify its position.

In short, by the turn of the century Montreal was the industrial, financial, and commercial center of Canada, and its Anglophone elite "clearly dominated the economic activity of Canada as a whole."[55] In this heady atmosphere, the French-speaking majority of Montreal could easily be viewed as a historical accident of little relevance by Montreal's controlling English-speaking elite whose frame of reference was national and continental. The sense of destiny of these businessmen was boundless. As a business yearbook for 1915 put it:

> Montreal's future is not hard to prophesy. Each year its development becomes more rapid, its importance in the great world of commerce increases steadily and swiftly. Each year sees scores of new and great industries springing up, bringing to the city many thousands of new citizens and adding to the swelling millions of the city's wealth. If the rush of prosperity and progress which has marked Montreal's growth within the past half-century continues—and there is every reason to suppose it will—Montreal will some day rival New York as the centre of the continent's commerce. Even now, there are indications of nervousness on the part of the residents of Manhattan Isle. . . .[56]

In this context, as Siegfried observed in 1906, Montreal was like "London or New York—a preeminently Anglo-Saxon centre, in which the presence of more than a hundred thousand Frenchmen is a factor of secondary importance."[57] As a British-origin resident of the Golden Square Mile put it: "We were not a mere minority in the midst of a sparsely populated colony. We were proud citizens, builders of the largest and best empire the world had ever known."[58] For the city's Anglophone elites, early-twentieth-century Montreal was an economic and cultural extension of the British empire.

Even as the national power of Montreal Anglophones began eroding by the 1930s with the rise of Toronto as major financial center, the degree to which Anglophones continued to dominate economic life in Montreal through the 1960s was staggering. In 1921, for example, only 4 percent of the stockholders of the Bank of Montreal were Francophone, a situation that prevailed at other Anglophone-controlled banks in the city.[59] By 1929, Royal Bank and the Bank of Montreal controlled almost 90 percent of the total assets held by Quebec banks. One study of Montreal business in the 1930s found that 86 percent of the "estimated pecuniary strength" of major firms in the city was in Anglophone hands; and over half of that was held by the city's two hundred largest Anglophone-controlled corporations (a sign of how concentrated Anglophone economic power had become).[60] Moreover, the English-speaking business establishment began expanding beyond its British-Canadian ethnic base; by the 1930s, such non-British Anglophones as Samuel Bronfman (Seagram's and real estate) and Sam Steinberg (food and department stores) had emerged as powerful forces in the Montreal economy.

Montreal's main local business association, the Montreal Board of Trade, consisted chiefly of Anglophones from the city's largest firms, whose business activities spanned Canada; its focus tended to be on national business issues. The predominantly French business organization, the Chambre de Commerce du district de Montréal, was composed mainly of small businessmen functioning, for the most part, in the regional Quebec market. However, while English-speaking firms tended to national business, profitable local and regional markets were, by no means, left exclusively to Francophones. All of Montreal's leading department stores in the 1940s were owned by Anglophones, and the highly profitable energy sector was controlled by the Montreal Light, Heat, and Power Company which held a monopoly on the provision of gas and electricity in the metropolis.

French Canadians were not entirely absent from Montreal and Quebec corporate life by mid-twentieth century. Five major "family" groups— Simard, Bienvenu, Raymond, Brillant, and Lévesque—controlled several interconnected enterprises, primarily in finance, food-processing, leather, wood, paper, and printing and publishing.[61] Federal contracts during World War II enabled firms such as Bombardier and Simard to grow by selling military vehicles and ships to the Canadian Armed Forces.[62] The growth of a substantial urban, French-speaking consumer market in Montreal stimulated the growth of Francophone-controlled firms in banking (Banque Canadienne Nationale, Banque Provinciale), insurance (La Prévoyance, La Sauvegarde), real estate, cultural industries (radio, television, print media), and other service and commercial activity (Dupuis Frères department stores). However, the bulk of Francophone capitalist development before 1960 occurred *outside* Montreal; apparently, the concentrated weight of Anglophone power in the city left little room for the growth of large-scale Francophone industries.[63]

In short, by the end of the 1950s there was an emergent Montreal

Francophone business class. Nevertheless, Francophone capitalism remained confined chiefly to peripheral sectors of the economy, composed mainly of small businesses with low productivity, low salaries, and few export markets. The key sectors of the Montreal and Quebec economies, such as manufacturing, transportation, and finance, were controlled either by English-Canadians or foreign investors (largely Americans). A study by André Raynauld for the Royal Commission on Bilingualism and Biculturalism (RCBB), based on 1961 data, showed just how entrenched Anglophone economic power was and how marginal Francophone firms were. Only 21.8 percent of the Quebec manufacturing labor force in 1961 worked in establishments owned by Francophones; only 13 percent of Montreal's manufacturing establishments were owned by French Canadians.[64] The value-added in a Francophone establishment, on average, was less than 25 percent that of an Anglophone establishment and less than 15 percent that of a foreign-owned establishment.[65] Francophone firms were still oriented mostly toward local markets: They sold only 22 percent of their output outside Quebec, compared to 49 percent outside Quebec by Anglophone-owned establishments, and 60 percent by foreign-owned establishments.[66]

Anglophone control of Montreal's economy helped maintain linguistic segmentation in the city's labor market. A simple "ethnic class" model does not fit: All Anglophones were not capitalists, and all Francophones were not "workers." Through 1961, however, according to data gathered by RCBB, the ethnic-linguistic disparities in Montreal's occupational structure remained pronounced. Almost 39 percent of British-Protestant Montrealers in the labor force held professional, technical, or managerial positions; for French-origin Montrealers, the figure was 16.6 percent. On the other hand, while 25.4 percent of British-Protestant workers held jobs as craftsmen, production workers, or laborers, 42.7 percent of the French-origin workforce held such positions.[67]

These occupational differences translated into significant wage differentials between Francophones and Anglophones. Although Francophones accounted for 60 percent of Montreal's male labor force in 1964, they represented only 37 percent of the salaried personnel making more than $5,000 a year.[68] As Figure 2.1 shows, at the highest salary levels, Francophone representation shrank to 17 percent. On the other hand, although Anglophones constituted only 24 percent of Montreal's labor force in 1961, they totaled 56 percent of the metropolitan area's "best paid" wage earners.[69] Many of these jobs were in the Montreal head offices of Anglophone-controlled firms catering to markets across Canada. Such positions were generally reserved for people who could function in English, thus giving considerable advantages to Anglophones.

Overall, this concentration of Anglophones in the city's best jobs helped produce a 51 percent wage gap between English- and French-speak-

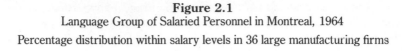

Figure 2.1
Language Group of Salaried Personnel in Montreal, 1964
Percentage distribution within salary levels in 36 large manufacturing firms

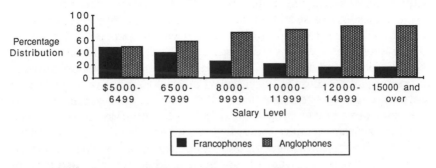

Source: Royal Commission on Bilingualism and Biculturalism, *The Work World* (Ottawa: Queen's Printer, 1969), p. 457.

ing Montrealers in 1961.[70] While research for the RCBB found that the inferior educational and occupational backgrounds of Francophones explained some of this income gap, almost 40 percent of the linguistic earnings gap could not be so explained and was attributable simply to a preference by Anglophone-controlled corporations to hire English-speaking employees.[71]

Through 1960 English was the working language of the upper echelons of Montreal business, and the burden of workplace bilingualism fell disproportionately on the city's Francophone majority. Indeed, the slot typically occupied by Francophone managers in Montreal firms was as a "bilingual buffer" between Anglophone senior management and Francophone workers, or in public relations as the "French face" of companies catering to the Quebec market. The RCBB found that while only 14 percent of Anglophones earning more than $5,000 a year in Montreal in 1961 were required to speak French in their jobs, fully 78 percent of the Francophones in this salary group were required to speak English.[72] This fact alone helps explain the persistence of Montreal's linguistic division of labor through the 1960s. English was entrenched as the language of management in corporate Montreal; thus, even highly bilingual Francophones faced a severe linguistic handicap competing for managerial employment against native English-speakers.

The upshot of all of these trends was that, in one of the best publicized conclusions of the RCBB, "Those of British origin fare far better in Montreal than anywhere else in the country."[73] In fact, in a striking finding that spoke volumes about the relative places of French and English in the city's economy, 1961 census data revealed that *unilingual* Anglophones had higher incomes than bilingual and unilingual Francophones, and virtually the same income as *bilingual* Anglophones.[74]

Linguistic discrimination—the preference of Anglophones for hiring other Anglophones—explained part of this disparity. In addition, the need for French-language abilities in Montreal was concentrated in lower-paying sectors, oriented toward the local and regional market. In higher-paying, higher-value firms, oriented toward the English-speaking continental market, there was little need for French and hence these positions were frequently held by unilingual Anglophones. Thus, as Stanley Lieberson points out, unlike French-origin Montrealers whose rate of bilingualism in 1961 increased sharply with education (reaching 94 percent for those with university experience), there was "virtually no association between educational achievement and bilingualism among those of British origin."[75] In the Montreal economy of 1960, educated Anglophones had little incentive to learn the language of the city's majority: a high standard of living was easily achieved without the ability to speak French. Thus, on the eve of the Quiet Revolution, unilingual Anglophones, living in exclusive neighborhoods and working in corporations catering to English-speaking markets, stood atop Montreal's social structure.

The Politics of Language through 1960

There were surprisingly few sustained or explosive political conflicts in Montreal over the places of French and English in the city through the 1960s. There were several historical moments—the Rebellions of 1837–1838, the Tory riots of 1849, and the Conscription controversies of 1917 and 1942 come to mind—when French–English conflicts in the city became raw and open. However, particularly after Confederation, linguistic peace was maintained through a combination of consociational-style elite accommodation, the existence of linguistically segmented social institutions, and, most important, a French-Canadian approach to Montreal's political economy that accepted linguistic hierarchies and eschewed state regulation of language.

Before Confederation, the main political issue regarding language in Montreal—indeed, throughout Quebec—was whether the French would be able to resist various British efforts at assimilation. The first British policy after the Conquest, the Proclamation of 1763, was aggressively assimilationist: Catholicism, the religion of French Canadians, was outlawed; the Church of England was declared Quebec's established Church; and Catholics—which meant, literally, French Canadians—were not permitted to hold colonial office. As Michel Brunet points out:

The evolution of this new British colony, it was felt, would be similar
to that of New York, first settled by Dutch colonists, and of New
Jersey, which had been founded by Swedes. In less than a century,
these two distinctive foreign collectivities had melted away. The British conquerors of the St. Lawrence Valley sincerely believed that a
similar fate awaited the Canadiens. [76]

The Anglophone merchant class in Montreal pushed particularly hard
for assimilationist policies, viewing the French as "backward" and French
civil law and the seigneurial system as an obstacle to the development of
commercial capitalism. James Murray, the first British governor of Quebec,
called these merchants "the most cruel, ignorant, rapacious fanatics that
ever existed," [77] and the conqueror's mentality of these merchants and their
successors was to structure linguistic politics in Montreal for the next
century.

Murray and his successor, however, did not vigorously pursue a policy
of assimilation, preferring to work out accommodations with the French
seigneurial and clerical elite. In 1774 British concern that French Canada
might become a fourteenth rebellious American colony led to a more culturally tolerant policy. The Quebec Act permitted the practice of Catholicism,
allowed French-Catholics to hold public office, and restored French civil law.
As part of the accommodationist approach of the first British governors,
French was used as a language of public administration. [78]

In the years following the American Revolution, thousands of English-
speaking "Loyalists," Americans, and British immigrants settled in the fer-
tile agricultural lands of the Upper St. Lawrence, an area that is now part of
Ontario. These settlers had little interest in even the mild cultural pluralism
of the Quebec Act, and clamored for an entirely English-speaking sociopolitical environment. The British authorities responded, in 1791, by dividing Canada into two provinces: Upper Canada (homogeneously British
and Protestant) and Lower Canada (predominantly French and Catholic).
Montreal merchants such as John Richardson argued vehemently in favor
of designating English as the official language of the new Lower Canada
Assembly; again, however, British authorities were more interested in
social peace with their French-speaking subjects than in immediately responding to the Montreal merchants, and official status was accorded both
English and French. [79]

While the Act of 1791 created a border that presumably "would sepa-
rate the two societies and prevent ethnic conflict," [80] the division of the
Canadas left a sizable and growing Anglo-Protestant minority in Lower
Canada, particularly in the developing commercial centers of Montreal and
Quebec City. Although, as we have seen, Anglophones became a majority in
Montreal by the early 1830s, their minority status throughout the province

(never constituting more than 25 percent of the population) made it difficult to control the Lower Canada legislature. While the British governor had broad decision-making authority—truly popular government had not yet come to the Canadas—linguistic conflict did occasionally ensue as Montreal merchants chafed when the Francophone-controlled legislature obstructed their economic development schemes. There was even some talk, in the 1820s, of "annexing" Montreal to English-speaking Upper Canada, and a bill to unite the two Canadas and create one English-controlled legislature was defeated in 1822.[81]

Wary of being part of a political entity numerically dominated by French Canadians, Montreal's merchant elite led the effort to establish English-Protestant cultural hegemony in Lower Canada. Education was seen as one powerful means of accomplishing that goal. In 1801 Anglophone merchants and the Anglican Bishop of Quebec, Jacob Mountain, persuaded the provincial legislature to enact "An Act for the Establishment of Free Schools and the Advancement of Learning in this Province."[82] Previously, the limited schooling efforts in Lower Canada received no government support and operated under religious auspices: the Catholic church for the French, the Anglican church for the English. The 1801 Act established a corporation called the Royal Institute for the Advancement of Learning, which was authorized to establish a single, English-language public school system of free primary and secondary schools.

The goal of the Royal Institute was plainly assimilationist. Bishop Mountain claimed that with such a system "in a few years a new race of men . . . will be found in the country . . . and the surest and most peaceful means will have been found to stimulate industry, to confirm the loyalty of the people by the gradual introduction of English ideas, customs, and sentiments."[83]

Naturally, Francophones vigorously resisted the public school plan, viewing it, in the words of historian Mason Wade, as "the first step in a campaign of anglicisation which endangered the basic elements of French-Canadian survival."[84] Francophone opposition to the plan was so intense that French-speaking legislators were able to attach disabling amendments to the final version of the bill so that effectively the "royal schools" were only put into operation in the English-speaking districts of Lower Canada (that is, mainly portions of Montreal, Quebec City, and the Eastern Townships). Ultimately, to avoid a head-on clash with the French-Catholic clergy that was rapidly emerging as the guardian of French-Canadian cultural survival, the provincial legislature passed school bills in 1824 and 1829 that permitted local French-Catholic parish control of publicly subsidized schooling. In a small way, this began the pattern of religiously and linguistically segmented schooling in Montreal and Quebec that persists through today.[85] By the 1840s, when "common" schools were emerging in U.S. cities, schooling in

Montreal was firmly divided into English-Protestant and French-Catholic networks.

Relations between Lower Canada's linguistic communities remained periodically tense through the 1830s, as British merchants, an emerging Francophone professional class, and French-Catholic clerical elites battled for political power. These tensions exploded in the Rebellions of 1837 and 1838. The rebellions had diverse and complex origins, many relating to class divisions *within* the French-speaking community.[86] However, as Fernand Ouellet persuasively argues, the conflicts fundamentally represented a breakdown in Montreal's linguistic equilibrium: the British had failed to assimilate the French; yet, in the context of Anglophone economic power and British immigration, French Canadians hardly felt secure about their prospects for cultural survival.

> Lack of class consciousness among the masses and manipulation on the part of a political elite opposed to social change served to focus hostility on the English-speaking merchants, "bureaucrats," and immigrants as the principal source of the perils hanging over French-Canadians and their culture. . . . The polarization of ethnic sentiment [was greatest] in the Montreal district. . . . Montreal was the city where the English presence was most keenly felt and where the continued existence of French-Canadians was most precarious.[87]

In this context of linguistic turmoil, the British sent Lord Durham to the Canadas to assess the situation and propose solutions. His famous assessment was that there were "two nations warring within the bosom of a single state," and he proposed resolving the situation through an aggressive policy to assimilate French Canadians. They were, he argued, a backward and uneducated people "with no history and no literature," and the best British policy would be to begin "the process of assimilation to English habits."[88]

Following the recommendations of the Durham report, the British proclaimed the Act of Union in 1840, the last systematic effort by the British to assimilate the French.[89] The legislatures of Upper and Lower Canada were abolished, and a single, English-dominated government of the United Canadas was created. English was the sole official language of record in the legislature, and the use of French was proscribed.[90]

English-speaking Montreal merchants, including Peter McGill, George Moffatt, and John Molson, supported the Union enthusiastically. With the frustrations of dealing with the French majority in the Lower Canada assembly behind them, and with interprovincial barriers to a St. Lawrence commercial system removed, Montreal's Anglophone elite looked forward to "glowing prospects of new commercial success" in the English-controlled

United Canadas (whose capital, incidentally, was located in Montreal between 1844 and 1849).[91]

Remarkably, however, Francophone political elites were able to thwart the assimilationist intent of the Act of Union. Splits within the English-speaking community over issues such as home rule for Canada left a political opening for French Canadians to act as a "swing" bloc in the legislature. French-Canadian leaders like Louis-Hippolyte LaFontaine were able to forge political alliances with English-Canadian reformers and gain political power. By the late 1840s, instead of the English-dominated, unitary government envisioned by the British, politics in Canada had evolved into a consociational pattern, in which leaders of each of the major linguistic groups had veto power over policy issues affecting community interests.[92] Improbably, linguistic dualism with genuine French power had developed a few years after the Act of Union. As early as 1842 French had been used by LaFontaine in parliamentary debate, and in 1849 the parliament sitting in Montreal lifted all official restrictions on the use of French. Symbolically, Lord Elgin, the British governor, delivered his annual parliamentary address in both French and English.[93]

The startling achievement of French power during the Union period engendered not only disappointment among Anglophone Montrealers, but also fear and hostility. The 1849 passage of the "Rebellion Losses Bill" by a parliament perceived as French-controlled, unleashed the linguistic tensions that had been building in Montreal in the 1840s as Anglophone leaders saw their assimilationist vision overturned. The bill proposed compensation to French Canadians whose property had been damaged by British soldiers in the Rebellions of 1837–1838. For LaFontaine and other Francophone leaders, the bill was an emotional symbol to demonstrate that "the union had truly been recast to bring them equality and power." For English-Tory Montrealers, the bill was an equally important symbol of dispossession, of "a world turned upside down." As Careless puts it: "As an enclave in a Lower Canada now thoroughly under French control, their past political authority lost, their economic future in jeopardy, they viewed the bill as a fearful demonstration of what newly triumphant French power might do to dictate to the British minority."[94]

Thus, the reaction of English-speaking Montreal to the bill was passionate and violent. There were angry confrontations in the legislature as Francophone leaders and their Reformer allies steered the bill to passage. The Montreal English-language press stirred up mass anti-French sentiment, the *Gazette* virtually issuing a call to arms.[95] On April 25, 1849, when British Governor-General Elgin accepted the bill, a Tory mass rally was called in the city, and "all the fever and fuming in Montreal exploded."[96] A mob of British Montrealers marched on the parliament building—the site of "French power"—and burned it down. Rioting in Montreal lasted a week, and Canada's capital was moved from the city permanently.[97] Tensions remained high throughout the year, and in October, despondent over a slumping economy and the emergence of "French power," numerous members of Montreal's Anglophone business elite signed a manifesto calling for annexation to the United States.

The annexation movement fizzled as economic prosperity in the 1850s lifted Anglophone Montreal out of its cultural doldrums. Moreover, in the wake of the obvious failure of assimilationist policies, Anglophone economic elites and Francophone political leaders began a pattern of elite accommodation that ultimately would manage linguistic relations in Montreal through the 1960s. With the exception of certain provisions of the BNA Act, there was no formal framework governing this elite "nonaggression pact";[98] however, its operation for the next century took place within a set of well-understood "rules of the game":

1. Francophones would run the provincial political system, with the ability to protect French-Canadian religious, educational, and legal institutions. In addition, there was an understanding, codified to some extent in 1867 in the BNA Act, that the status of the English language in public life and the autonomy of Anglophone institutions were untouchable.
2. Anglophones would continue to dominate the economy of Montreal and the province. Francophone leaders would not deploy the powers of the Quebec state to challenge these linguistic hierarchies and would support "probusiness" policies favored by the English-speaking economic elite of Montreal.
3. Any conflicts arising between the linguistic communities would be resolved through "back-channel" accommodations between Anglophone economic elites and Francophone political leaders. As a minority lacking mass electoral clout, Anglophones tended to abstain from participation in provincial politics and employed "their economic power to compensate for their lack of a more direct form of political influence."[99]

Several historical examples illustrate how this elite-managed "linguistic entente" operated. George-Étienne Cartier, one of mid-nineteenth-century French Canada's most important leaders, worked closely with Montreal's Anglophone business community on economic development initiatives such as the Grand Trunk Railway. During the Confederation debates in the 1860s, when Montreal's Anglo-Protestants expressed concerns about their minority status in predominantly French-speaking Quebec, Cartier was instrumental in ensuring an official status for English in the Quebec legislature and autonomy for English-Protestant educational institutions. Cartier's political career was financially supported by English-speaking Montrealers such as Hugh Allan, and Cartier himself was financially involved with the Grand Trunk as well as numerous other Anglophone-controlled enterprises. As

Brian Young points out, Cartier was "aware of the anglophone minority's political power in Montreal" and "distinguished himself by his tireless promotion of any communications scheme that might serve the Montreal business community." Cartier's efforts were appreciated by the Anglophone business elite: in the words of the Montreal *Gazette,* he was a "tried friend of the British population." [100]

In the twentieth century, sharing support for capitalist expansion and an interest in linguistic "nonaggression," Quebec's provincial premiers and Montreal's Anglophone businessmen solidified this pattern of elite accommodation. Premiers such as Louis-Alexandre Taschereau (1920–1936) avoided significant state intervention in the Anglophone-dominated private sector, even for the purpose of advancing the economic position of Francophones. [101] The power of the Anglophone economic elite ensured that the position of provincial treasurer was almost always held by English-speakers through 1944 (often appointed in consultation with the president of the Bank of Montreal) and "a citizen who wished to correspond with the department of the provincial treasurer could do so only in English." [102] Quebec premiers, including Taschereau and Lomer Gouin, openly sat on the board of directors of Anglophone-controlled corporations, notably the Bank of Montreal and the Sun Life Assurance Company.

This symbiotic relationship between Montreal Anglophone businessmen and Francophone politicians reached its apogee during the premierships of Maurice Duplessis (1936–1939; 1944–1959). Duplessis was a staunch conservative: a champion of free enterprise, believer in limited government, and vigorous foe of labor unions. All of these positions impressed Montreal's equally conservative English-speaking business elite. Duplessis enjoyed particularly close relationships with J. W. McConnell, owner of the Montreal *Star* and an especially influential voice of the Montreal business establishment, as well as John Bassett, owner of the Montreal *Gazette.* Although Duplessis would "wave the bloody shirt" of French-Canadian nationalism in his electoral campaigns, Anglophone institutions, the hospitals and schools, were generously treated by his Union nationale (UN) governments, and McConnell and other Anglophone elites contributed generously to the UN's coffers. [103] As Dale Thomson notes, for Montreal's Anglophone business community, "the rake off on profits taken by the Union nationale was not considered too heavy a price to pay for social peace and a good investment climate." [104] In short, as Kenneth McRoberts observes, Anglophone–Francophone elite accommodation under Duplessis was based on

> an acknowledged specialization of responsibilities. Duplessis was to enjoy full authority over the management of the province's political affairs (and all matters of mutual interest which lay within the French-Canadian community). In return, Anglophone business leaders were to enjoy full freedom from government intrusion in the management of

their enterprises, and from intrusion by overly aggressive union leaders for that matter. Cementing this alliance between the Union nationale and Anglophone business was strong mutual respect for the ability of the other to control affairs firmly within its particular sphere of influence.[105]

Language Policy before 1960

The few regulations governing language use in Montreal before 1960 were contained in the BNA Act. As we have seen, Montreal's English-speaking elite strongly supported Confederation; nevertheless, its members were concerned about their minority status in the new province of Quebec created by the BNA Act.[106] After vigorous debates in which Anglo-Protestant political interests were most vociferously articulated by Sherbrooke's A. T. Galt, two key clauses were inserted in the BNA Act. Article 133 stipulated that both English and French would be the official languages of Quebec's provincial legislature and courts. Article 93 sanctioned what had already existed in Montreal and Quebec since the mid-1840s, that is, separate Protestant and Catholic school systems. Because Montreal's religious and linguistic cleavages of the nineteenth century more or less overlapped, this provision functioned as a de facto guarantee of English-language rights in education in the city. Religious authorities—meaning essentially French Catholics and English Protestants—effectively managed public schooling in Montreal. Between 1875 and 1964, in fact, neither the province of Quebec nor the city of Montreal had had a public department of education.[107]

In Montreal separate Catholic and Protestant school boards developed across the Island. Anglo-Protestant boards federated in 1925 to become the Montreal Protestant Central School Board, which, in turn, became the Protestant School Board of Greater Montreal (PSBGM) in 1945. This board became the heart of Anglophone Montreal's educational establishment, and through the twentieth century the PSBGM evolved into a nondenominational, English-language school system educating Jews and other non-Protestants as well.

The chief Catholic school board in Montreal was the Commission des écoles catholiques de Montréal (CECM), a predominantly Francophone system with a small English-language network. In 1928 a quasi-autonomous committee was set up within the CECM to supervise English-language instruction, and by the 1940s, the English-language schools of the CECM—in curriculum, textbooks, and pedagogy—closely resembled those of the PSBGM.[108] The Anglo-Catholic schools were initially set up for Montreal's Irish Catholics, and through 1931 almost 60 percent of the students in these schools were of British ethnic origin. By 1960, however, with an influx of primarily Italian Catholics, the clientele of the Anglo-Catholic schools was only one-third British,[109] a trend that would soon emerge as Montreal's most explosive linguistic issue.

The Quebec provincial government provided meager funds for public education in Montreal before the 1960s. Protestant schools received a disproportionate share of these funds, a consequence of Anglo-Protestant economic and political power, a pro–public education attitude of Anglophone leadership, and a general indifference on the part of Francophone elites toward generating funds for an adequate public school system. Moreover, with a more substantial property tax base, the Protestant community was better able than the French-Catholic to raise revenues for schooling.[110] The result was: a markedly superior Anglo-Protestant school system in Montreal, better organized and administered than the CECM, with lower Anglophone dropout rates and higher proportions of Anglophone students moving on to secondary and postsecondary schools. In this fashion, the political economy of schooling in Montreal helped perpetuate the city's linguistic division of labor and provided compelling reasons for immigrants to send their children to Anglo-Protestant schools.[111]

Schooling typified the climate of linguistic laissez-faire that prevailed before 1960. Despite periodic concern among Francophone elites about the pro-English linguistic dynamics of Montreal, there was little inclination to use the power of the provincial government to alter the places of English and French in the city.[112] Major figures in French-Canadian society, among them Jules-Paul Tardival, Étienne Blanchard, and Athanase David, exhorted Francophones at various junctures to defend the quality of their mother tongue; yet there was a certain deference toward English and an acceptance of Montreal as a bilingual city in which French was a subordinate language. For example, after warning that English was corroding the quality of French in Quebec, Abbé Étienne Blanchard wrote in 1902: "This is not to say that one should neglect English. Far from it. The French Canadian should know both languages, above all if he is destined for commerce or the liberal professions. With the usage of both languages, we will attain summits that, in this country, the unilingual English will never reach."[113]

These attitudes stemmed from several sources. First, the ideology of traditional French-Canadian nationalism, *la survivance,* was a Church-based "defensive" strategy of cultural survival based on avoiding contamination by urban, English Montreal and maintaining French-Catholic purity in the homogeneous environments of rural and small-town Quebec. *La survivance* was not a strategy of linguistic promotion or confrontation with the English.[114] As long as it remained the dominant cultural strategy of French-speaking Quebec, Abbé Étienne Blanchard wrote in 1902: "This is not to say that one should neglect English. Far from it. The French Canadian should know both ment of an urban-based strategy of Francophone cultural development.

In addition, *anti-étatisme*—a distrust of strong government—dominated French-Canadian ideology through the 1950s. Francophone leaders opposed the development of a positive state in Quebec for a number of reasons: economic conservatism, a belief that politics was essentially corrupt, and a desire to leave education and social services, and other key services, in the hands of the church.[115] The Anglophone community was also uninterested in activist government in Quebec. Conservative Anglophone businessmen opposed state meddling in the English-dominated private sector. Moreover, since an aggressive Francophone-run state might promote the interests of the majority at the expense of the minority, Anglophones encouraged the Francophone "inclination to surrender the functions of government to semi-autonomous bodies controlled by interest groups. . . ."[116]

In short, an aversion to positive government in Quebec meant that little support existed before 1960 for aggressive state intervention to alter Montreal's linguistic dynamics. Provincial political party platforms through 1960 contained few references to language-use issues, and no proposals for government action.[117] When pressed to improve the economic opportunities of Francophones, Taschereau, Duplessis, and other leaders opposed any direct state role, arguing that the best way to provide jobs for Francophones was to encourage private sector growth and American multinational investment.[118]

Only twice before 1960 did the Quebec government enact a language law, and both instances reveal the timidity of the state in confronting Montreal's linguistic situation. In 1910 the provincial legislature passed the "Lavergne Law," which regulated the language practices of public utilities. Heretofore, railway, telephone, and electric power companies, particularly in Montreal, had often operated solely in English. The Lavergne Law required the use of both English and French in communicating with the public, specifying that items such as bills, signs posted in offices or railway stations, travel tickets, and contracts should be printed in both languages.[119] Despite the rather modest aims of the law, Lavergne's bill was passed only after overcoming the reticence of Francophone leaders of the Quebec Liberal party who feared antagonizing the Anglophone business community. Similarly, in 1937 the Quebec legislature passed a law giving primacy to the French-language texts in interpretations of laws and regulations in the province. This time, however, heavy pressure from the Anglophone business establishment persuaded Premier Duplessis to repeal the law one year later.[120]

Urban Governance and Linguistic Accommodation

Before 1960 Montreal's city politics also took place within this framework of elite accommodation and Francophone quiescence. Through the 1870s Montreal's Anglophone community controlled city government.[121] By the

1880s, however, with a Francophone majority firmly in command of Montreal's electoral politics, Anglophones increasingly relied on the power of their economic elites to influence municipal policy and protect community interests. In addition, certain consociational devices assured Anglophone influence in local government. By tradition, the office of mayor alternated between English- and French-speakers. This practice lasted through 1914 when Médéric Martin, the first of Montreal's Francophone "populist" mayors, broke the pattern in one of the few city elections in which the linguistic cleavage was openly politicized. The Province of Ontario had passed its infamous "Regulation 17," in 1912, proscribing French as a language of instruction in public schools; in this linguistically charged context, Montreal Francophones were prepared to depart from the tradition of alternating the office of mayor.[122] The thoroughly corrupt Martin remained in office largely by trading on ethnic–linguistic loyalties: his campaign slogan in 1926 was, "No more English mayors."[123]

Nevertheless, Anglophone influence in Montreal city political institutions was maintained by the creation of a complex system of city council representation. Between 1940 and 1962, when the system was abolished, one-third of the seats on the city council—Class "C" councillors—was allocated to representatives of designated public institutions such as McGill University, the Montreal Board of Trade, the Chambre de Commerce de Montréal, and so forth. Between 1940 and 1960, 40 percent of Montreal's Class C councillors were English-speaking. An additional one-third of the council was elected by property holders, another category in which Anglophones were overrepresented. Thus, combined with the tradition of an Anglophone vice-chairman of the council's powerful executive committee, this system of representation helped maintain Anglophone political influence in the city of Montreal, even as increasing numbers of Anglophones were moving to the West Island suburbs.[124]

In this institutional framework, and with the economic power of Anglophones an omnipresent concern, the Francophone-controlled Montreal city government rarely used municipal powers (for example, land-use regulations or the possibility of municipal ownership) to alter the places of English and French in the city. Anglophone-controlled public utilities, particularly the Montreal Light, Heat, and Power Company, generated much anger with their monopolistic pricing and high profits, and the specter of Anglophone enterprises exploiting Francophones was occasionally raised. However, the city government generally did not interfere with the power company's operations, and with the exception of the 1910 Lavergne Law, the provincial government did not intervene in company operations until 1944, when the monopoly was finally "nationalized."[125]

The proliferation of autonomously governed municipalities on Montreal Island also helped limit linguistic tensions through the 1960s. As already indicated, throughout the twentieth century, Montreal's English-speaking population moved in increasing numbers to suburban municipalities on the West Island where they could escape the Francophone control of the city. Although there were occasional calls for consolidated governance on the Island—in the early 1960s, Montreal Mayor Jean Drapeau moved for the creation of "One Island, One City"—the autonomy of these municipalities was virtually untouched through the 1960s. In the absence of any overarching provincial government policy regulating language use, Montreal's Anglophones were able to live a completely English-speaking existence in these West Island enclaves. The language of public administration in West Island communities was English, and schools, hospitals, and social services were operated in English without any interference from Montreal's Francophone majority.[126]

The Winds of Change: Language and Politics in the 1950s

By the 1950s, despite the continued privileged position of English in the city, Montreal began to experience harbingers of the linguistic conflicts that would explode by the late 1960s. In 1956 the provincial government's Tremblay Commission issued its landmark assessment of the status of French-Canadian culture. Although the commission called the Quebec government the "guardian of French-Canadian civilization," it never addressed the subject of language policy and failed to appreciate fully the need for an urban strategy for Francophone survival. Nevertheless, the Tremblay report did call to public attention the possibility that French-Canadian language and culture faced a dangerous future.[127]

In addition, several Francophone groups mobilized on linguistic issues in the 1950s. As William Coleman points out, the preoccupation of these groups—the Société Saint-Jean Baptiste de Montréal, the Société de bon parler français, the Comité permanent de la survivance française, and the Conseil de la vie française—was mainly on the English "external face" of Montreal rather than the "internal dynamics" of Anglophone control.[128] Typically, these groups promoted pride in the use of French and conducted campaigns to have businesses produce bilingual labels for their products and write their advertisements and signs in French and English. They pressured government to impart a more fully French character to Montreal through highway signs, street names, and public symbols such as wider display of the *fleurdelysé* provincial flag.[129] As Jean-Marc Léger, head of the nationalist Société Saint-Jean Baptiste (SSJB) wrote in 1959: "It would be elementary to prohibit English unilingualism on everything that reaches the public: signs, . . . billboards, menus, instructions, etc."[130] Note even here, however, the limited nature of these demands: nationalists before 1960 merely hoped to ensure that French had a place beside English in Montreal's public face.

Issues involving the linguistic consequences of modernization and new technologies also began to attract public attention. In 1952, when television broadcasts first began in Montreal, Francophone groups protested the bilingual programming on the city's one network; however, CBFT did not become all French until 1954 when an English-language station began broadcasting.[131]

The most heated linguistic controversy in the 1950s, typifying Francophone concern over Montreal's external face, concerned the naming of the new Canadian National Railway's complex of offices, shops, and a hotel to be built downtown. The CNR proposed to name the complex "The Queen Elizabeth." Opposition to the name developed among various segments of the Francophone community, who argued that the issue had profound cultural significance:

> We want a French name because we form the majority of the population in Montreal and in the province of Quebec.
> Toronto would not accept a French name for one of its great public buildings. Neither would Vancouver. Nor any important city outside of Quebec. We have shown a much greater broad-mindedness—or much greater stupidity—since our cities are plastered with English names. But we are not going to permit this misplaced generosity to continue, to apply to the largest hotel in Canada. We are the majority, and we want this to count, above all in a government service. We have the numbers; we want the name.[132]

The CNR's status as Canada's national rail line gave the matter additional cultural sting: the imposition of an English name was seen not only as a symbol of Anglophone power in Montreal but as yet another example of the insensitivity of the federal government to Francophone concerns. Francophone groups rallied around an alternative name: Le Château Maisonneuve, in honor of the founder of Montreal. An extensive media campaign was organized around the issue, and the Ligue d'Action nationale collected 200,000 signatures—including those of Mayor Jean Drapeau and several city council members—supporting the French name.[133] In the political climate of 1950s Montreal, however, in which there had not yet been a mass Francophone *prise de conscience* on the language issue, CNR President Donald Gordon was able to ignore the nationalists' concerns. The English name prevailed, a small but vivid symbol of the 1950s reality that English-speaking Montreal still very much controlled the city's linguistic dynamics.[134]

Thus, as the 1950s ended, the English character of Montreal remained intact. A Montreal-based Francophone culture was emerging, but visible institutions such as McGill University and the Bank of Montreal, flourishing Anglophone *milieux* including the West Island, St. James Street, and the

new predominantly English-speaking commercial and financial districts along
Dorchester Boulevard and rue Sainte-Catherine all reaffirmed the place of
English in city life. The Union Jack, a symbol of British imperialism, still flew
symbolically on the Red Enseign above federal buildings in Montreal,[135] and
Anglophones continued to exert political and economic influence well out of
proportion to their numbers.

Wedded to a conservative, rural, and church-centered nationalism, the
Francophone community had yet to develop a systematic strategy for confronting the internal dynamics of Anglophone influence that many were beginning to view as a threat to the French language and culture. Throughout
the twentieth century, Francophones had been leaving their homogeneous
villages for the bilingual–bicultural environment of Montreal. *La survivance*
was hopelessly inadequate as a strategy to protect the French language and
culture in Quebec when more and more Francophones were living in Montreal: a city firmly integrated into English-speaking North America, and economically dominated by English Canadians.

By the 1950s rumblings of discontent were heard in the Francophone
community over Montreal's language situation. Some Francophone groups
organized efforts to *francise* the external face of Montreal; moreover, by the
late 1950s, fringe groups such as the Alliance laurentienne were formed,
calling for an independent Quebec in which French would be the only official
language. These developments were too episodic and involved too few
people to challenge the basic dynamics favoring English in the city, but in a
few short years, these Francophone rumblings would be replaced by full-
scale political mobilization as the Montreal language question moved to the
center of Quebec political life.

Chapter 3

The Quiet Revolution and the Politicization of Language

After two centuries in which Montreal remained surprisingly free of overt linguistic conflict, in the 1960s the city's linguistic climate changed rapidly. As was the case around the world, the sixties were turbulent years in Montreal: it was a decade of street demonstrations (*"Québécois dans les rues"*), political agitation, riots, and terrorism. But, while racial divisions underlay the turmoil in American cities and class tensions surfaced in European cities, it was the linguistic cleavage that dominated Montreal life in those years. Before 1960 there was no serious, sustained political debate in Montreal over French or English rights in the city; by the end of the decade, the Montreal language question had become *the* provincial political issue.

Beyond this policy debate, the linguistic texture of daily life in Montreal was transformed in the sixties. The deferential attitude of Francophones to English vanished, as did the serene sense on the part of Anglophones that living in Montreal was no different from living in Toronto or Boston. In the 1960s, English-speaking Montrealers had to face up to the city's French fact in a hurry, confronted by a barrage of anti-English public rhetoric, threats of linguistic violence, and daily concerns that "addressing a stranger on the street or in a public place" might trigger "a minor linguistic confrontation."[1]

Montreal's linguistic upheaval began in the sixties with what has become known as Quebec's "Quiet Revolution": a Montreal-centered challenge by an emergent Francophone "new middle class" to the conservative, agrarian nationalism of *la survivance*. No longer willing to forego North American standards of living as part of a cultural survival strategy, new urban Francophone elites increasingly looked toward an energized Quebec state to bring French Quebec into the modern world while maintaining Francophone cultural security. Inevitably, the central theme of the Quiet Revolution—to make Francophones "*maîtres chez nous*" (masters in our own house)—politicized issues of language in Montreal. Francophones could never be "*maîtres chez nous*" if Montreal, the urban center of French-speaking Quebec, remained as it was: a city in which Anglophones—and the English language—were a dominant force. Thus, the logic of the Quiet Revolution inexorably led to a movement to dislodge the Anglophone elite and "reconquer" Montreal as the metropole of French-speaking Quebec.

Therefore, in the wake of the Quiet Revolution, the consociational *entente* that had structured Montreal's political economy since Confederation began to unravel. Montreal's brand of linguistic accommodation held through 1960 because Francophone elites accepted the legitimacy of Anglophone power and the privileged position of English in Montreal life. The Quiet Revolution, however, marked the displacement of the traditional Francophone elite by a French-speaking "new middle class" that rejected these historical arrangements. This Francophone changing of the guard, when combined with the mass politics of the 1960s, meant that back-door French–English "elite accommodation"—one of the hallmarks of consociational politics—became increasingly untenable. What is more, the themes of the Quiet Revolution—assertive Francophone nationalism, expansive notions of public action, and a clear mandate to promote the cultural and economic interests of Francophones—broke with the passivity of French Canada's historical strategy of cultural survival, and directly challenged the status of English in Montreal.

Montreal's linguistic consociationalism also was undermined in the early 1960s by the emergence of a number of groups in French-speaking Montreal advocating Quebec independence. The Rassemblement pour l'indépendance nationale (RIN) became Montreal's first mass-based, separatist political party. Composed chiefly of disaffected Francophone intelligentsia and radical students concerned "about questions of language and culture,"[2] the RIN fielded candidates in the 1966 provincial elections (garnering an estimated 10 percent of the Francophone vote in Montreal) and was a leading force in Montreal's linguistically charged "street politics" of the 1960s. The RIN led the nationalist demonstrations against CNR president Donald Gordon in 1962, when he questioned the business qualifications of Francophones, and the threat of RIN violence prompted Quebec officials to reroute the 1964 visit of Queen Elizabeth from "too turbulent" Montreal to Quebec City.[3] In 1965 the RIN brought some of the tactics of the U.S. civil rights movement to Montreal, demanding service in French and an end to unilingual English commercial signs in a series of well-publicized "sit-ins" at West Island commercial establishments.[4]

Even more radical than the RIN was the Front de libération du Québec (FLQ), a "revolutionary separatist underground" of self-styled Francophone "urban guerrillas" battling against the "economic colonialism" of Montreal's Anglophone establishment.[5] The FLQ came to public attention in the spring of 1963, when the group planted a bomb that exploded in the Canadian Army Recruitment Center on rue Sherbrooke (killing a night-watchman). Shortly thereafter, the FLQ began a campaign of mailbox bombings in such identifiable English-speaking neighborhoods as Westmount. Although small and always on the fringe of Montreal life, the FLQ's activities increased linguistic tensions on the Island and added an extremist edge to public rhetoric on matters of language. For example, an FLQ pamphlet asked:

> Have you ever seen an English library burning?
>
> Have you ever seen the president of a Yankee corporation under fire?
>
> Have you ever seen a can explode on the shelf of a supermarket in the British neighborhood?
>
> Have you ever seen a Protestant church burn?
>
> Have you ever seen Westmount without telephones or electricity and with its water supply poisoned?
>
> Have you ever seen sharp-shooters on roofs, shooting down traitors?
>
> Be sure you soon will!!![6]

This was not exactly the kind of rhetoric heard in Montreal before 1960. In October 1970, of course, the FLQ would bring Montreal to its greatest moment of linguistic crisis by kidnapping British Trade Commissioner James Cross, murdering provincial minister Pierre Laporte, and provoking the "occupation" of Montreal by federal troops.

In short, the speed with which Montreal's linguistic climate changed was breathtaking. In the 1950s, English-speaking elites could disdainfully ignore the Francophone community in naming the Queen Elizabeth Hotel; by the end of the 1960s, substantial segments of Montreal's Francophone community advocated unilingualist language policies and curbs on English-speaking institutions including Anglophone schools. Public demonstrations over language policy became commonplace, and, for the next two decades, the language issue would dominate Montreal's social and political life.

The Roots of the Quiet Revolution

Three important developments in Montreal set the stage for Quebec's "Quiet Revolution" and the momentous changes of the 1960s. First, between 1930 and 1960, Toronto replaced Montreal as Canada's national economic center.

As the United States eclipsed Great Britain as Canada's chief economic partner, Toronto benefited from the tendency of American corporations to locate their branch plants in Ontario and headquarter their Canadian operations in Toronto. In addition, the opening of the St. Lawrence Seaway in 1959 permitted ocean-going vessels to bypass the port of Montreal, reducing the city's status as Canada's transportation hub. Finally, the economic development of the western provinces and America's midwestern industrial belt enhanced Toronto's linkages to a growing periphery and to emerging regional economic centers such as Vancouver, Calgary, Edmonton, Chicago, Detroit, Cleveland, and Milwaukee.[7]

By the 1940s, these trends had helped Toronto assume Montreal's historical position as Canada's leading financial and commercial center. The volume of checks cashed in Toronto surged ahead of the volume in Montreal by 1940; moreover, the percentage of total Canadian stock transactions registered on Montreal's exchanges fell steadily from 86 percent in 1925 to 25 percent by the late 1960s.[8] Most tellingly, as Table 3.1 shows, by the early 1960s Toronto had emerged as the favored location for the head offices of Canada's largest corporations. Finally, despite the persistent availability of cheap French-Canadian labor in Montreal, in the same decade Toronto was also challenging Quebec's metropolis as Canada's leading industrial city, with manufacturing investment in Toronto actually outstripping Montreal's by 1962.[9] In short, on the eve of the Quiet Revolution, Montreal was no longer the economic center of English-speaking Canada.

These urban economic trends had important ramifications for French–English relations in Montreal. As Jane Jacobs argues, "had Montreal remained Canada's preeminent metropolis and national center . . . it would have remained an English-Canadian metropolis."[10] However, the decline of Montreal as a national economic center removed an important structural support to Anglophone power in the city and would give impetus to Fran-

Table 3.1
The Location of Corporate Head Offices in Canada, 1931–1988

Year	Toronto	Montreal	Vancouver	Calgary	Others
1931	25	49	1	1	21
1961	32	32	7	3	26
1971	39	29	7	3	22
1977	40	25	11	6	18
1988	48	20	8	13	11

Sources: James Lemon, *Toronto since 1918: An Illustrated History* (Toronto: James Lorimer, 1985), p. 198; and "The Canadian Business 500," *Canadian Business,* June 1989, pp. 127–160.

Note: Includes the top 100 Canadian corporations by assets. Those more than 50 percent foreign-owned are not included.

cophone efforts to establish the primacy of the French language and culture in the increasingly regional city. As Clift and Arnopoulos point out:

> The decline of Montreal would fundamentally alter the relationship between English and French. . . . As long as the English of Montreal remained in control of the Canadian economy, their position was secure and unassailable. However, as Montreal's English-speaking financial elites became the executors of decisions originating outside the province, their situation changed dramatically. . . . It was inevitable in this context that [French opinion leaders] would begin questioning the role of the English community in the management of the provincial economy.[11]

The Quiet Revolution also stemmed from cultural and demographic changes within the French-speaking community. Throughout the twentieth century, French Canadians had been leaving the farms and towns of rural Quebec for Montreal. The number of Francophones living in metropolitan Montreal doubled between 1931 and 1961, reaching 40 percent of Quebec's French-speaking population. Urban growth in Montreal provided the setting in which large numbers of French-speaking artists were brought into contact with one another and with a mass audience of unilingual Francophones. The result was an *ébullition culturelle,* a surge in cultural activity marked by the launching of new French-language publishing houses and theaters, and a proliferation of French-language literature, theater, music, journalism, and critical analysis that turned Montreal into a city of Francophone intellectual excitement and creativity.[12] These cultural activities drew more on the urban experiences of Francophones and began to redefine Francophone identity in an urban rather than rural context; the post-1945 novels of Gérard Bessette, Gabrielle Roy, Anne Hébert and others exemplified the growing importance of the city in portraying French-Canadian life.[13]

By the mid-1960s, the Francophone cultural renaissance had given Montreal much more of a French "feel" than had existed a decade earlier. But, more importantly, this "Montrealization" of French Quebec had made the traditional French-Canadian ideology, in which cultural survival was predicated on the rural isolation of French Catholics and in which Montreal's English character remained unchallenged, an anachronism. Montreal, not rural Quebec, was now the center of French-Canadian culture and the place where the future of French in North America would be determined. In this urban setting, English-language influences were infinitely stronger than in the homogeneously Francophone parishes of rural Quebec; thus, the continued survival and *épanouissement* of the French language and culture would seem to require confronting the status of English in Montreal.

Finally, the Quiet Revolution and the linguistic confrontations of the

1960s also were rooted in the changing social structure of the Francophone community. As Kenneth McRoberts has brilliantly shown, by the late 1950s a "new middle class" of Francophone technocrats, bureaucrats, and social scientists had emerged from three main quarters: the social and physical sciences departments of Université Laval and l'Université de Montréal, the burgeoning cultural industries of Montreal, and the growing bureaucracy of the Catholic church in the city.[14] Church institutions in health, education, and welfare were particularly important in the growth of the new Francophone middle class. As Francophones streamed to Montreal throughout the twentieth century, these institutions expanded to provide necessary services; and as these institutions grew larger and more complex, they increasingly required lay bureaucrats with the appropriate professional training to run them. Thus, in its efforts to cope with Quebec's new urban realities, the church inadvertently stimulated the development of a new Francophone class, "distinct from liberal professional and clerical elites, with a claim to power and status rooted in its monopoly of the specialized knowledge of the 'modern' social sciences."[15]

This new middle class found itself increasingly frustrated by conditions in Montreal during the 1950s. On one hand, "the middle class was increasingly intolerant of any clerical authority,"[16] which it viewed as an impediment to the efficient development of Francophone health, education, and welfare institutions. On the other hand, Anglophone domination of Montreal's economy meant that there were limited opportunities for members of this incipient Francophone technocracy to utilize their managerial and technical skills in the private sector. As we have seen, English was the language of administration in Montreal corporations through 1960, and managers worked in homogeneous, Anglophone milieux to which Francophone access was limited. Francophone entry into this world required not only perfect mastery of English, but the willingness to "renounce certain cultural traits"[17] and values, and to "think and act in English."[18] For the new class, assimilation was an unacceptable price to pay for economic mobility.

Thus, the emerging Francophone class had good reasons to promote social and political changes that would enhance their power vis-à-vis *both* traditional Francophone elites *and* Montreal's Anglophone establishment. The Quiet Revolution would do exactly that, as the new middle class dramatically expanded the role of the provincial government in Quebec. In a few short years, the Quebec state would replace the church as the locus of Francophone power and, under the political control of the new middle class, would begin to challenge the autonomy and power of Montreal's Anglophone institutions.

In addition to its support for a powerful, secular Quebec state, the new class was also attached to a neo-nationalism that would color the Quiet

Revolution and helped set off the language conflicts of the 1960s. This was not the defensive nationalism of *la survivance* that encouraged isolation and underdevelopment as the keys to French-Canadian cultural survival. For the technically competent, Francophone middle class, these ideas were anathema. To this new class, the survival and *épanouissement* of the Francophone community *depended* on effectively reconciling Francophone identity with the realities of modern, urban society. Otherwise, the French language and culture would survive in Quebec, as it did in Louisiana, merely as folklore, while English dominated the dynamic elements of Quebec life and inexorably threatened the cultural survival of the French-speaking community. Francophone Montreal could not flourish as a translated society—a French version of Anglo-American cultural and intellectual developments.

The new middle class emphatically rejected the traditional nationalist notion that French Canadians were *né pour un petit pain;* as Charles Taylor has argued, the self-esteem of this class was tied to the creation of a *modern,* French-speaking society.[19] Moreover, as educated, upward-striving individuals, members of the Francophone urban middle class often experienced episodes of cultural humiliation at the hands of Anglophone Montreal: discrimination in job searches, insulting commands to "speak white," or condescending public comments such as those of CNR president Donald Gordon explaining why French Canadians were unfit for the world of business. Thus, for the Francophone middle class, neo-nationalism—with its Francophone assertiveness and delegitimation of Anglophone power in Montreal—would represent an important declaration of collective self-worth in response to a history of cultural stigmatization.

Beyond these cultural considerations, the material interests of the new middle class were also served by neo-nationalism. This class was largely composed of what Marcel Fournier has called *travailleurs du langage:* teachers, administrators, journalists, and policy analysts, whose occupational skills involve the manipulation of knowledge and information.[20] Obviously, for Francophones, these skills are best used in French. Therefore, the persistent status of English in Montreal not only offended the cultural sensibilities of Francophone *travailleurs du langage,* but it also directly limited their employment prospects in the city. Albert Breton takes the point too far by arguing that neo-nationalism was merely "a tool used by the new middle class to accede to wealth and power."[21] Nevertheless, the state expansion advocated by members of the new middle class during the Quiet Revolution was a source of numerous well-paying jobs for the Francophone *travailleurs du langage.* And, as we shall see, even if the push for language policies promoting the status of French in Montreal had distinct cultural roots, the material interests of the new class would also clearly be served by policies promoting the use of French in all sectors of Montreal life.

Linguistic Tensions and the Quiet Revolution

By 1960 three key developments—the declining economic importance of Montreal in English Canada, the Francophone cultural awakening in the city, and the rise of the neo-nationalist Francophone new middle class—had set the stage for a "quiet revolution" in Montreal and across Quebec. In both popular and scholarly analyses, the Quiet Revolution of the early 1960s is viewed as a major turning point in Quebec history, a period of rapid change that

> spoke of a common liberation from the weight of the past, a sharing of an increasingly rich cultural life, and a collective exploration and assessment of all future possibilities to achieve the realization of those which best served the needs of the entire [Quebec] nation. In short, everything seemed possible.[22]

Two key aspects of the Quiet Revolution had a profound impact on linguistic relations in Montreal: neo-nationalism and the growth of the Quebec state. As we have seen, in the early 1960s, Quebec Francophones shed the outmoded ideology of *la survivance* and embraced an assertive neo-nationalism that called for Francophones to "catch up" with the twentieth-century world and "blossom" as a modern cultural community. Concomitantly, it was argued that Francophone underdevelopment required jettisoning Quebec's historical aversion to positive government and building a powerful state to promote the interests of the French-speaking community. René Lévesque, a provincial government cabinet member during the Quiet Revolution, called the state *un de nous, le meilleur d'entre nous* (one of us, the best among us), and argued: "Our elites scorned or disregarded the economic role of the state. In their eyes, the state had only one role: to act as a kind of insurance company and supplier of technical services to large corporations."[23]

During the administrations of Premier Jean Lesage (1960–1966), that situation changed dramatically: the provincial government became a powerful force affecting life in Montreal and across Quebec. Between 1959 and 1970, expenditures per capita by the provincial government rose, in real terms, over 200 percent.[24] The provincial bureaucracy expanded from 32,000 employees in 1959, to nearly 70,000 by 1970,[25] and, with the growth of new ministries, para-state boards, regulatory bodies, and so forth, the Quebec state rapidly replaced the Catholic church as the most visible presence in provincial life.

The role of the Quebec state was broadened in a number of policy areas. In 1964, after nearly a century of leaving educational administration solely in the hands of religious authorities, the Quebec government established a provincial ministry of education and embarked upon a crash program to improve public education in the province. During the 1960s, Quebec's investment in education tripled, and by the early 1970s state expenditures on education reached $1.3 billion—over 25 percent of the provincial government budget.[26] New elementary and secondary schools were built, standards were upgraded, a system of Collèges d'enseignement général et professionel (CEGEPs) was established to expand postsecondary educational opportunities, and in 1969 a nine-campus Université du Québec system was created, with a flagship campus in Montreal.

The *étatisme* of the Quiet Revolution was not limited to education. The provincial government took control of social and health care services from the church.[27] In addition, the Quebec state intervened more than had historically been the case in the provincial economy, setting up an investment fund (the Caisse de dépôt et placement), a holding company (Société générale de financement), and a state-run steel mill (SIDBEC); all these initiatives were designed to improve Francophone control over the Quebec economy. (See Chapter 7 for an analysis of these programs.)

Perhaps the most linguistically charged action of the provincial government during the Quiet Revolution was the Hydro-Québec "nationalization" of 1962–1963. The provincial government had purchased the Montreal Light, Heat, and Power Company in 1944, forming Hydro-Québec. Despite this purchase, Anglophones still controlled over 80 percent of the Quebec energy sector through the early 1960s. In 1962, confronting Montreal's English-speaking business community (and some Francophone businessmen as well), Natural Resources Minister René Lévesque proposed the provincial government buy out Quebec's remaining private electric power companies.

The Hydro-Québec "nationalization" battle was a watershed in French–English relations in Quebec, serving notice that the Francophone community's unqualified acceptance of Anglophone power was rapidly ending. The 1962 provincial elections were waged as a referendum on the Hydro-Québec plan, with the Liberals running on the slogan *Maîtres chez nous* to great success in Montreal. Lévesque candidly presented the Hydro-Québec plan as a step toward ending the subordinate status of Francophones in the Quebec economy,[28] and he was opposed not only by the Anglophone owners of the private electric companies, but also by the full weight of the Anglophone St. James Street establishment. English-speaking elites, represented in the Lesage cabinet by Montreal lawyer and businessman George Marler, tried to dissuade Lesage from supporting the nationalization scheme, and financial interests, the Bank of Montreal for one, tried to scuttle the plan by making it difficult for the Quebec government to sell the bonds necessary to pay for the purchase.[29] Nevertheless, the plan went through and, as we explore in Chapter 7, Hydro-Québec was to become a strategic lever in advancing Francophone control of the Montreal and Quebec economies.

The impact of Quiet Revolution neo-nationalism and *étatisme* on Montreal's linguistic cleavages was immediate and substantial. Most important was the changed Francophone attitude toward the status of English in the city. In the context of Quiet Revolution nationalism, Francophones began to think of themselves not as a French-Canadian minority, seeking merely to establish equal rights for French alongside English, but as a *Québécois* cultural "majority," with certain "normal" majority prerogatives.[30] In this changed ideological setting, increasing numbers of Francophones began to regard the lofty place of English in Montreal as inappropriate for a linguistic minority in the city, regardless of the continental context. Moreover, with *québécitude*[31] (an intense pride in French Quebec) at the core of Montreal's cultural effervescence, the persistent status of English in the city was increasingly viewed as an intolerable threat to the integrity and development of French language and culture. The architects of the Quiet Revolution argued that the Quebec state was the prime engine of Francophone advancement; thus, by legitimating this kind of "ethnic interest" state intervention, the Quiet Revolution would logically lead to Francophone demands that the provincial government more directly use its powers to alter Montreal's linguistic dynamics.

As for Montreal's Anglophones, the rise of neo-nationalism and *étatisme* were clear signals that historical patterns of language group relations in the city could no longer be taken for granted. Although many Anglophones supported the Lesage Liberals in 1960—apparently favoring the anticorruption and efficiency elements in the Liberal platform—they found the nationalist rhetoric and government expansion of those years were troublesome. As Michael Stein points out: "[State] interventionism on this scale was bound to encroach upon the hitherto autonomous operation of Anglo-Quebec local institutions. The Anglophones were no longer to be a self-governing community, but a minority group subject to the will and political aspirations of the governing Francophone majority."[32] After 1960, with the rise of a powerful Francophone-controlled provincial bureaucracy, venerable Montreal Anglophone institutions—McGill University, the Protestant School Board of Greater Montreal (PSBGM), and Royal Victoria Hospital—were "obliged to submit their policies and their budgets to civil servants in Quebec."[33]

Anglophone uneasiness over the reduced autonomy of English-speaking institutions in the early 1960s can be clearly seen in the area of educational reform. Before 1960 Montreal's Anglo-Protestants enjoyed nearly complete autonomy in education.[34] There was not yet even a provincial ministry of education, the PSBGM was virtually a self-governing body, and Section 93 of the BNA Act provided a constitutional guarantee for the existence of Protestant schools. The Anglo-Catholic network of schools in Montreal, its numbers beginning to swell with immigrant children, operated with relative independence within the CECM.[35]

Montreal's Anglophone community was obviously content with this privileged state of affairs. They possessed a high-quality, well-funded, autonomous school system that "reproduced" generations of English-speakers capable of manning the command posts of the Montreal economy.[36] Thus, Anglophone leaders reacted with undisguised chagrin to the massive expansion of the role of the Quebec government in education in the early 1960s. Even Bill 60—which simply established the provincial Ministry of Education in 1964, contained no regulations on the language of instruction in public schools, and left intact the governance structure of Montreal education— was viewed apprehensively by Anglophones. English-speaking educators expressed concerns that a coordinated provincial department, especially in the context of growing Francophone nationalism, might compromise the quasi-independent status their system had always enjoyed.[37]

Anglophone anxieties were heightened in 1966 with the release of the Parent Commission's recommendations for the reorganization of schooling in Montreal. The commission had been appointed by Premier Lesage to produce recommendations for a comprehensive modernization of Quebec education; one of its principal initial recommendations had been to create a provincial ministry of education.[38] The commission's report was *not* a fiery, nationalist document. In fact, it paid homage to Anglophone contributions to Quebec education, and stated that "in Quebec, the English-language schools have made secure for themselves a right to exist, which no one today, as far as we know, would think of contesting."[39]

However, to the consternation of the Anglophone community, the Parent Commission recommended sweeping changes in the governance of Quebec and Montreal education, calling for the elimination of separate confessional school boards and the creation of a unified administrative structure. The commission argued that the proliferation of independent school commissions in Montreal—there were forty-two operating by 1966—created serious administrative inefficiencies and perpetuated gross inequalities in the level of educational services offered throughout the metropolitan area. Wealthier districts, which generally were Anglo-Protestant, possessed a more substantial property tax base than poorer, primarily French-Catholic districts. This revenue inequality meant that Anglo-Protestant commissions were able to provide higher quality educational services than their French-Catholic counterparts. Programs such as continuing and special education were luxuries generally available only to these wealthier commissions, which were also able to spend more per capita than the *milieux défavorisés*.[40] Finally, there were serious inequities in school financing, as tax rates varied from commission to commission across the Island.

The Parent Commission's reorganization proposals sought to equalize school financing, streamline administration, and promote equality of educational opportunity in Montreal. The commission proposed consolidating the existing forty-two local school commissions into seven regional commissions that would administer all Montreal area schools, regardless of their linguistic or religious clientele. In addition, the report urged the creation of a Conseil de développement scolaire pour l'île de Montréal, a body that would coordinate the operations of the regional commissions and serve as a "central authority for all of the Island, charged with insuring as much equality as possible in school services and an equitable distribution of the school financing burden among taxpayers throughout the Island."[41]

In short, the Parent report envisioned a powerful, centralized school governance structure for Montreal possessing powers over financing, budgeting, service distribution, and resource allocation. Anglo-Protestants voiced immediate opposition to the plan, noting the loss of community autonomy and the absence of formal guarantees of Anglophone representation and mechanisms of community protection either within the unified regional commissions or on the sovereign Island Council. As one analysis put it: "Autonomy was seen as a guarantee that English-language education in Quebec would be responsive to the distinctive needs of the minority and would continue to reflect its distinctive aspirations. The Parent Commission . . . directly challenged this autonomy."[42]

Anglophones were able to delay consideration of the Parent report's recommendations, and further investigation of the plan was entrusted to a newly created body called the Conseil de restructuration scolaire de l'île de Montréal. Chaired by former Montreal school commissioner Joseph Pagé, the Conseil was carefully balanced along religious and linguistic lines, and would not issue its report until October 1968—by which time Montreal was already awash in much more heated linguistic conflicts. Nevertheless, the events surrounding educational reform and school reorganization in the early and mid-1960s alerted Montreal Anglophones to the erosion of the city's linguistic entente heralded by the growth of the Quebec state. The days of completely autonomous Anglophone institutions and "back-channel" accommodations between Anglophone and Francophone elites were ending; but it would take almost a decade before Montreal Anglophones truly recognized the city's changed linguistic environment and mobilized as a minority in defense of community interests.

Francophone Demands for a Government Language Policy, 1960–1966

In the climate of Quiet Revolution nationalism, Francophone groups in Montreal intensified the efforts of the 1950s to *francise* the external face of the city and province: to provide visible symbols of the French character of Montreal and Quebec. These efforts achieved some success. Although English commercial signs remained omnipresent in Montreal—even Francophone neighborhoods contained "Enjoy Pepsi-Cola" signs and the like—

by the end of the 1960s there was a noticeably enhanced French public face to Montreal and the province. The *fleurdelysé* flag was ubiquitously displayed in the province, the formerly bilingual provincial yearbook became the unilingual *Annuaire du Québec,* several ministries of the provincial government began releasing their annual reports in French only, and *Radio-Québec,* a French-language television network supported by the provincial government, began broadcasting.[43] Unlike a decade earlier, when Francophone protests were ignored in the naming of the CNR hotel, Montreal redevelopment projects in the early 1960s generally had French names: Place Ville-Marie, Place Bonaventure, and the Place du Canada complex developed by Canadian Pacific.[44]

Despite their French names, all of these projects were built in the new Anglophone business district of Montreal—centered around the western sector of Dorchester Boulevard—that had progressively supplanted the traditional core of Anglophone finance located on St. James Street in Old Montreal. This land-use pattern underscored the continuing status of English in Montreal's political economy, despite the nationalists' moderate success in *francising* the external face of Montreal in the early 1960s. By the mid-1960s, such pillars of the English-speaking establishment as Sun Life, Royal Bank, CNR, the Bank of Commerce, and Canadian Industries Limited all had major office buildings in this new city core.[45]

Nevertheless, by the mid-1960s, projects of the provincial, municipal, and federal governments began channeling redevelopment activity eastward to traditionally French-speaking areas of downtown Montreal. This was done not only to bolster the economy of these areas but to *francise* the external face of Montreal by moving the focus of daily activity in the city to more French-speaking *milieux.* The central station of the new Montreal Métro, Berri de-Montigny, was built in a distinctly Francophone quarter; provincial and municipal government buildings such as the Hydro-Québec offices and the Place des Arts were constructed on the eastern (Francophone) end of Dorchester Boulevard; and the federal government, presumably to emphasize its sensitivity to Francophone concerns in an era of neonationalist threats to Canadian unity, located the Radio-Canada building and the main federal offices in Montreal (Complexe Guy-Favreau) on the Francophone side of Dorchester as well.[46]

Notwithstanding these changes, Francophone pressure in the 1960s to deal more forcefully with the continuing English face of many sections of Montreal intensified. Between 1963 and 1965, the Société Saint-Jean Baptiste de Montréal (SSJBM) pursued an *Opération visage français* whose "final objective [was] to make Montreal, the national metropolis of French Canadians, a city of the French language and culture in the same way that Toronto, metropolis of Anglo-Canada, is an English-language city."[47]

Beyond these attempts to alter the external face of the city, the early

1960s witnessed a growing clamor among elements in the Montreal Francophone community for policies that would deal more directly with the forces underpinning English influence in the city. In 1962 the SSJBM presented a brief to the Parent Commission arguing that Francophone cultural security required intervention in the internal workings of historically autonomous Anglophone institutions such as English-language schools. The SSJBM proposed that: (1) all graduates of Quebec schools possess "knowledge" of French; (2) in Quebec's courts, the French text of laws be considered the sole authentic text—"the English version being considered as a translation"; (3) private enterprises in Quebec be required to have French names (that is, Eaton's should be Eaton, Smith's Hardware should be Quincaillerie Smith, and so forth); and (4) the language of instruction in all public schools in Quebec be French, with the exception of schools for children of English mother tongue, which should be "bilingual," in the manner in which schools for French Canadians in Ontario were bilingual.[48]

The SSJBM represented mainly the traditional Francophone *petite bourgeoisie* of Montreal (doctors, lawyers, shopkeepers, and clerics) that had always been concerned about the corrosive impact of English on the French character of the city. In the assertive nationalist climate of the Quiet Revolution, however, the interests of the SSJBM meshed with those of the new Francophone middle class, and the result was a move beyond preoccupation with external symbols to concerns with issues such as language policy in the public schools. By 1963 the provincewide SSJB supported a policy designating French as Quebec's "official" language of work, education, and public administration.

The first systematic calls for a provincial language policy of French unilingualism were made in the early 1960s, most loudly by the separatist Rassemblement pour l'indépendance nationale (RIN). A 1962 RIN pamphlet, *Le bilinguisme qui nous tue,* argued that bilingualism in Montreal was inherently unequal, and that the strength of English threatened the survival of the French language and culture. A year earlier, at its party convention, the RIN had resolved that: "Once independence is established, only the French language will be official in Quebec. In anticipation, the government of Quebec should proclaim itself *now* as unilingual French as the governments of the other provinces are unilingual English."[49] While French unilingualists in the 1960s and after would disagree over such issues as the place of English-language schools in an officially French Quebec, or how rapidly a French-only policy should be implemented, a

> common idea prevailed: the system of linguistic dualism, as it functioned in Quebec, logically promoted the degradation of the French language and risked leading, sooner or later, to its final collapse. The blossoming of the language of the majority, indeed, its simple survival,

demanded the abandonment of a bilingualism that was fundamentally unequal.[50]

A special concern of the RIN was language policy in education, labeled by party leader Pierre Bourgault as "the best means of assimilating" Anglophones as well as immigrants to Quebec.[51] By 1965, the RIN program proposed a system of public education in which French would be the exclusive language of instruction in state-supported schools.[52] The RIN's "street politics" were important in politicizing the issue of language in the schools. In September 1967, the RIN led demonstrations in the West Island suburb of Pierrefonds, calling for the creation of a French-language school in this predominantly Anglophone community. Riot police were required to break up clashes between Francophones and Anglophone counterdemonstrators, and the next day two bombs were set off in the local high school.[53]

Through the mid 1960s, the RIN and similar groups remained on the fringe of Montreal politics, and mainstream Francophone public opinion opposed French unilingualism. René Lévesque, although clearly the most nationalist member of the Lesage cabinet, opposed French unilinguism as unrealistic and "artificial." He favored a "priority" for French "by all legitimate means," but without imposing French unilingualism on the Anglophone minority.[54] Premier Lesage was steadfast in opposing any proposals he viewed as abrogating English-language rights in Quebec and, despite the nationalist tenor of his administration, was always anxious to maintain good relations with Montreal's Anglophone business community.[55]

Nevertheless, while language policy never became a major political issue during the Quiet Revolution, the Lesage administration did mark the first, tentative involvement of the Quebec provincial government in language policy and planning. In 1961, the government established a Ministry of Cultural Affairs, charged with the task of supporting the *épanouissement* of French language and culture in Quebec. The ministry was conceived as a French-speaking, provincial government counterpart to the federal government's Canada Council, which Francophone nationalist intellectuals viewed as an attempt to impose "Canadian" culture on Quebec Francophones. Headed by George-Émile Lapalme, Lesage's predecessor as leader of the provincial Liberal party, the ministry included divisions on the arts, historic places, urban design, and an Office de la langue française (OLF), designed to stimulate a *révalorisation* of the quality of French in Quebec.[56] Nationalist intellectuals had long expressed concern over the declining quality of French in Quebec as a serious threat to French-Canadian culture; thus, the Office was established to oversee "the correctness and enrichment of the spoken and written language." Jean-Marc Léger, a well-known nationalist intellectual, was named the OLF's first director.

The Ministry of Cultural Affairs was not a high priority of the Lesage government. Frustrated by the scant resources made available to the ministry, Lapalme resigned in 1964; Léger had left the OLF two years earlier having caused considerable difficulty with his overzealous nationalism (at one point he declared that the word "province" had been abolished, replaced by the term "State" of Quebec).[57] Lapalme was replaced by Pierre Laporte who, in an effort to revive the mission of the ministry, formed a working group to produce a White Paper on cultural policy. A draft of the document, written chiefly by the Deputy Minister Guy Frégualt, was presented to the Lesage cabinet in October 1965.

The White Paper contained the first call from within the provincial government for a coherent language policy. While much of the document focused on "corpus" language planning—policies to improve the quality of French in Quebec—the report also called for the Quebec government, as the "political incarnation of the French-Canadian nation," to make French "the priority language in Quebec." After sketching the "perilous state" of the French language in the province, the report argued that public policy should "take all necessary measures to imprint a new orientation in Quebec society that favors, in all domains of human activity, the normal development of the French language."[58]

The White Paper was vague on the meaning of French as a "priority language." Although the report called efforts such as the "*bon parler français*" campaign "absolutely insufficient to solve the grave linguistic problems facing French Canadians," no proposals were offered to alter the historical status of English in the economy or schools. The report did specify that English should be used by the state solely for the convenience of Anglophones, and that in public administration and certain private enterprises, "French will be the first language of working documents, of communication between management, and implementation." A strengthened OLF was recommended as an agency "to ensure the implantation of French as the common language in all sectors of human activity."[59]

Despite its urgent tone and call for dramatic government action, the White Paper received an unsympathetic reading from Lesage and was never released. According to Dale C. Thomson:

> Lesage reacted strongly against its cry of alarm about the pitiful state of the French language and culture, and its call for much more vigorous state intervention. It was not true, he noted in the margin of his copy, that the French language was continuing to lose ground to English; that trend had been reversed in the past few years, and to speak of the disintegration of the French language and culture was mere defeatism, reflecting an inferiority complex. He also rejected a proposal to make French the "priority language" in Quebec with English translations for the "convenience" of the English-language population.[60]

Despite Lesage's initial reaction, Laporte was confident that the cabinet would approve the White Paper after the 1966 provincial elections.[61] Indeed, the Liberal platform in 1966 included a section entitled *Le Québec français,* in which the party promised measures that would respect the "inalienable rights of the Anglophone minority," yet "guarantee the vitality of French . . . [and] assure a French face to the province," and establish the "priority position of French in public services and administration, public signs, industrial relations, commerce, and generally all sectors of human activity."[62] However, the Liberals suffered an upset defeat in the 1966 elections. The White Paper was never published, and its recommendations were never introduced as legislation.

Clearly, however, by the mid-1960s the issue of language policy was gaining attention in mainstream Francophone political circles. Although unilingualist groups were still at the margins of provincial political life, their agitation was forcing Quebec's established political parties into positions more responsive to growing nationalist sentiment.[63] Still, through the mid-1960s no major Francophone political figure dared advocate policies that would alter the legal status of English-language institutions in Montreal or across Quebec. After 1966, however, nationalist groups seized upon an issue that would turn language policy into the central concern of Quebec politics: the growing demographic presence of non-French, non-English-speaking ethnic minorities in Montreal and their tendency to enroll their children in English-language schools. Concerned about the impact of immigrant "Anglicization" on Montreal's linguistic balance and the security of French in the city, Francophone groups mobilized to limit access to English-language schooling. That mobilization ignited the worst sustained linguistic conflict in the city's history.

The Anglicization of Immigrants

As we examined in Chapter 2, the population composition of Montreal changed significantly after 1900. The non-French, non-British component of Montreal Island's population grew from 16,000 in 1900 to over 500,000 in 1970 (increasing from 4.5 percent to over 23 percent of the total). The immigrants' choice of whether to adopt English or French as their language would obviously affect Montreal's linguistic demography, and as Table 2.4 showed, linguistic transfers in Montreal through 1960 overwhelmingly favored the English-speaking community. These trends continued between 1960 and 1970 as Montreal received over 150,000 non-French, non-English immigrants. By 1971, 78,000 more Montrealers reported using English in their homes than claimed English as their mother tongue; the number using French in the home exceeded the French mother-tongue population by only

1,400.[64] Thus, while many immigrants continued to use their mother tongues at home, 98 percent of their "linguistic transfers" in Montreal in the 1960s involved adoption of English (in contrast to the rest of Quebec where 53 percent of net linguistic transfers went to French).[65] Francophones had remained a solid, 60 percent plus majority of Montreal's population through the 1960s, as a result of a high birthrate and large-scale Francophone migration from rural Quebec. Nevertheless, as the pace of European immigration to Montreal increased, by the 1950s some Francophone nationalists such as Jean-Marc Léger, André Allemagne, and Pierre Laporte began warning that immigrant Anglicization posed the most dire threat yet to the survival of the French language and culture in the city.[66]

The most politically explosive sign that immigrants were integrating into Montreal's English-speaking community was in the city's school enrollments. As late as 1935, over half of non-French, non-English-speaking children in the CECM (primarily Italians) were enrolled in the French-language sector (3,943 in the French sector and 3,899 in the English sector).[67] By the late 1960s, almost 40,000 of the 43,400 "Allophone" children (as non-English, non-French speaking immigrants are now called) in Montreal's public schools were enrolled in the PSBGM and the English-language network of the CECM.[68] English-language schooling in Montreal was fast becoming a multi-ethnic operation, with 61 percent of the students in Montreal's Anglo-Catholic schools and 19 percent of the students in the PSBGM schools reporting languages other than English or French spoken at home in 1970. Only 24 percent of the pupils in the Anglo-Catholic sector were of British origin, and just over 25 percent of the students attending English schools in the CECM reported English as their mother tongue.[69] English-language schools, particularly the Anglophone network of the CECM, were becoming the primary agency through which immigrants prepared their children for life in Montreal—in *English-speaking* Montreal.

Why did the immigrants decide, in such overwhelming numbers, to send their children to Montreal's English-language schools? The central reasons were economic. For most immigrants arriving in Montreal, the frame of reference was English-speaking North America, not necessarily French-speaking Quebec. Immigrants regarded command of English as essential, to exploit economic opportunities in North America fully and enjoy the consumer culture diffused through the English-language electronic and print media. For example, three-quarters of Montreal's Italians—the city's largest non-British, non-French community—surveyed in a 1970 study said they sent their children to English schools because "English facilitates moving in Canada" and "English makes it easier to get jobs."[70]

Even ignoring the North American context, continuing Anglophone domination over Montreal's economy meant that English was clearly the language of upward mobility in the city. Therefore, just like immigrants to cities in English Canada or the United States, newcomers to Montreal found it economically compelling to ensure that their children achieved a thorough command of English. Such mastery plainly could best be achieved in Montreal's English-language schools; hence the pattern of Allophone enrollments. As Paul Cappon noted, in the Montreal economy of the 1960s,

> There exists an economic bias that acts against the assimilation of immigrants to the francophone community, no matter what their ethnic origin. The tendency will be to assimilate to the group that economically dominates Quebec society. . . . The immigrant chooses the privileged anglophones because it is not *materially* and *economically* necessary that they have elaborate relationships with the francophone community. The immigrant can work and live in Montreal and never use the French language.[71]

Several features of the organization and administration of Montreal schooling also inhibited the enrollment of immigrant children in the city's French-language sector. First, the denominational structure of Montreal education precluded some immigrant parents from "freely" choosing between French and English language classes. The PSBGM was an exclusively English-speaking system through the early 1970s; thus, non-Catholic immigrants had no choice in their child's language of instruction unless they were willing to send their children to French-Catholic schools. However, the heavily religious content of the curriculum in Montreal's French-Catholic schools—in contrast to the essentially secular nature of the PSBGM curriculum—discouraged non-Catholic parents from sending their children to CECM schools simply to gain a French-language education (especially in view of the minimal need in Montreal for non-Francophones to be fluent in French before 1960). Moreover, in the unlikely event that non-Catholics wanted to enroll their children in CECM schools,

> Local Catholic authorities, directors, and even teachers refused to admit non-Catholic pupils, or those professing no religion, and the French-speaking sector thus lost a number of Orthodox Christian, French-speaking Jewish, and other non-Catholic immigrants, usually because of religious zeal or a desire to avoid complications. This isolationist trend did not favor close relations between ethnic groups and the French majority.[72]

Thus, a provincial government commission examining the problem of immigrant Anglicization in 1967 concluded that a crucial difficulty in Montreal was the absence of a *nondenominational* network of French-language schools. This Interministerial Commission, chaired by René Gauthier (who headed the immigration section of the Department of Cultural Affairs and formerly directed the CECM's Service des néo-Canadiens), recommended the development of such a network to facilitate the integration of immigrants in Francophone society—a proposal that never saw the light of day.[73]

Second, immigrants were wary of the quality of French-Catholic schools. As the Parent Commission concluded, the English-language school system was "adapted to the requirements of modern society"; conversely, the French-language schools provided "preferential treatment for a small group of students, who were expected to attend the university, and neglected the great majority of young people in the same age group who, after their public school studies, were confronted with a blind alley."[74] Expenditures per pupil were higher in English-language schools, the teachers were better trained, and the curriculum was better suited to modern, urban society—all crucial elements in the "Anglophone head start" in Montreal's linguistic division of labor. In addition, although immigrants were not opposed to having their children learn French, they were adamant about the need for their children to master English—and the quality of second-language instruction in the French-Catholic schools was abysmal. In some cases, Catholic immigrants even sacrificed their religious convictions and, to enable their children to receive the best-quality English-language instruction available, enrolled them in Montreal's historically superior Anglo-Protestant school system. Research for the CECM in 1941 estimated that 1,000 such "apostasies" by "néo-Canadiens" had occurred in Montreal in the 1930s, and the issue sufficiently troubled CECM officials to stimulate consideration of ways to keep Allophone children in the CECM.[75]

Finally, the administration of Montreal's Catholic school system also deterred immigrant integration into the French-language schools. Through the 1960s, CECM officials routinely channeled immigrant children into the English-language network.[76] In addition, the personnel of the French-language network of the CECM was remarkably homogeneous, a situation that did little to attract immigrants to the system. Through 1970, Allophones constituted only 2 percent of all elementary school teachers in the French sector, compared to 23 percent in the English schools.[77]

CECM officials were not completely oblivious to the immigrant Anglicization problem. In 1947, the Commission set up a Comité des Néo-Canadiens to develop strategies, first, to assure that the children of Catholic immigrants to Montreal attended CECM schools, and second, to facilitate the integration of immigrants into French-Canadian society.[78] Evening French classes were established for immigrants, and in 1948 the Comité proposed the creation of a semi-autonomous, "trilingual" sector within the CECM in which instruction in both French and English would be combined, during the first years of schooling, with instruction in the student's native language.[79] However, opposition from both Francophone and Anglophone elements in the CECM scuttled the plan. Immigrant Anglicization had not yet become an issue of communitywide concern for Francophones; hence, there was little support for reorganizing the structure of the CECM to accommodate immigrant needs. On the other hand, the infusion of Allophone children was an unmitigated boon to Montreal's Anglo-Catholic system; the number of schools and total enrollments in the network doubled between 1950 and 1960.[80] Thus, Anglophone commissioners on the CECM, led by Father Emmett Carter, were loathe to abandon the status quo.

A secret 1957 report prepared by a subcommittee of the Comité catholique du Conseil de l'instruction publique more directly addressed the issue of immigrant Anglicization. The report presented alarming statistics on the number of Allophones in the English-Catholic sector, and pointed out that without quality English-language instruction in the French sector, "néo-Canadien parents, determined that their children would learn English, had no choice but to send their children to the English sector."[81] The Comité proposed special bilingual "ethnic schools" in which Allophone children would be taught religion through grade three in their native language, and in grades four to seven would receive instruction in some subjects in French (history, French, geography, and so on) and other subjects in English (mathematics and English). Students in these ethnic schools would then move on to French-language high schools.[82]

In 1961, pressured by such advocates of bilingual schools as new Commissioner Ferdinand Biondi, the CECM implemented the new curriculum in twelve "ethnic schools," six attached to the French-language sector and six in Italian parish schools (the English-language sector refused to set up the six ethnic schools that were planned for that sector). By 1962, there were 1,217 Allophone students in thirty-eight ethnic classes. Nevertheless, debate continued to rage within the CECM over the proper policy regarding Allophones. In the neo-nationalist climate of the Quiet Revolution, Francophone nationalists in the CECM questioned the efficacy of the bilingual schools in integrating immigrants into French-speaking Montreal. As for English-Catholic educators, the new curriculum was viewed as a threat to their system and was denounced as pedagogically unsound and lacking qualified teachers to implement it. By 1963, the Comité des Néo-Canadiens "was left in a state of shambles"[83] and, although Italian leaders such as Biondi still advocated bilingual schools, there was little support for the program among French- or English-speaking Catholics.

Despite these efforts, the main policy of the CECM before the 1960s was *not* aimed at integrating the immigrants. This was hardly surprising: after all, the English-language sector of the CECM had been created in the first place by exponents of *la survivance* to ensure that non-Francophones did not "contaminate" French-Catholic schools as places in which French-Canadian values could be transmitted.[84] During the 1950s, as the Tremblay

Report reaffirmed, the Francophone self-concept of community was *not* a *pluraliste* one: the survival of the French language and culture, in this traditional view, hinged on maintaining the purity and homogeneity of the community. Little attention was paid to immigration as a factor shaping French-speaking society, especially since historically almost all of the immigration to Montreal had been Anglophone.[85]

Conversely, by the early 1960s leaders of many of Montreal's English-speaking institutions were sensitive to the growing place of ethnic minorities in the city. Anglo-Protestant Montreal had not always been so hospitable to newcomers. Well into the twentieth century, Montreal's Anglo-Protestant establishment was as ethnocentric as any in Canada or the United States. The novels of Mordecai Richler offer rich literary evidence of the Jewish–WASP tensions in Montreal, and for many years Anglophone bastions such as McGill, the Montreal Stock Exchange, and Board of Trade were off-limits to Jews or any other non-Protestant ethnic minorities.

As the century advanced, however, accommodations gradually developed between Jews—the city's largest non-Catholic immigrant group at the time—and Protestants. By the 1930s, with an agreement for enrolling Jewish students in the PSBGM's schools, Jewish immigrants quickly adopted English as their main language, and Anglophone Montreal was on its way toward becoming a multi-ethnic, rather than simply a British community.[86] In the wake of post-World War II immigration, it was clear to Anglophone leaders that the new ethnic minorities were a crucial "third force" in Montreal and that the vitality of Anglophone institutions increasingly depended on integrating immigrants into a pluralistic, English-speaking community. Consequently, in contrast to French-speaking institutions, which seemed closed to ethnic minorities, Anglo-Protestant Montreal "opened up" to immigrants in teaching positions, school administrations, and other community agencies. In certain ways, the ethnic accommodations *within* English-speaking Montreal began to resemble the processes of immigrant integration and acculturation that historically occurred in other United States and Canadian cities. On the other hand, under the influence of traditional nationalist ideology, the Francophone community remained insulated and homogeneous.

In summary, three factors—Anglophone domination of the Montreal economy, the structure of public education in the city, and differing attitudes toward immigrants in the Francophone and Anglophone communities—induced Montreal's burgeoning immigrant population after 1945 to send their children to English-language schools. Normally, in multicultural settings, immigrants integrate into the majority culture and attempt to learn the language of the majority. However, even as the Quiet Revolution was changing Quebec's social and political landscape, Montreal Anglophones remained in the mid-1960s a *minorité majoritaire,* a minority with the power, prestige, and privileges of a majority that assimilated immigrants in the city. Moreover, English *was* the language of *Canada's* majority; thus, in a culturally explosive sense, Montreal was a city with "two majorities," with immigrants free to choose between them. Under such circumstances, unless compelled by public policy or dramatic changes in the structure of Montreal's economy, immigrants would continue to enroll most of their children in the city's English-language schools.

The Political Ramifications of Immigrant Anglicization

By the end of the 1960s, these enrollment choices had clearly reshaped the linguistic composition of Montreal public education. Although only 22.6 percent of Montreal's population reported English as its mother tongue in 1970, nearly 38 percent of the Island's elementary school enrollments were in the English-language schools—a sign of how immigrant choices were bolstering Anglophone schools.[87] A reasonable projection was that immigrant Anglicization would place a majority of Montreal's first-graders in English-language schools by the early 1980s.[88]

By the early 1970s, plunging birthrates and the large-scale movement of Montreal families to suburbs on and off the Island had resulted in declining enrollments in both the CECM and the PSBGM. Replenished by a steady stream of Allophone enrollments, however, Montreal's English-language schools experienced much slower rates of "depopulation" than did those in the French-language sector. Between 1970 and 1974 (the years that school enrollments in the city began noticeably declining and before any government action was taken to limit access to English-language schools) enrollments fell 13.2 percent in the all-English PSBGM, but 23.2 in the French-language network of the CECM. In the English-language sector of the CECM, the destination of most Allophone pupils, enrollments declined only 4 percent between 1970 and 1974.[89]

These enrollment trends were fraught with explosive cultural and economic implications. In an era proclaiming Francophone *épanouissement* in Montreal, immigrant Anglicization represented a jolt to Francophone collective self-esteem. By sending their children to English-language schools, immigrants appeared to deem the language of the city's majority as less "worthy" than that of the minority and reject the message of the Quiet Revolution that Quebec was building a dynamic French-speaking society. This rejection was sure to ignite a strong Francophone response.

By 1967, many Francophones were expressing a more particular cultural concern over immigrant Anglicization: that if the linguistic composition of Montreal's population began to resemble the ratios in the public schools, then Francophones were well on their way toward becoming a minority in their cultural metropole. English-language schools, with their expanding Allophone enrollments, were seen as the primary institution promoting the Anglicization of Montreal—and, therefore represented the gravest threat to the French language and culture in the city. As the Gauthier Commission concluded in 1967, enrollment of 90 percent of the immigrant children in English schools "can only lead to a constant reduction of the importance of the French language in Quebec and result in a process of *minorisation* of the Francophone community." By sending their children to English schools, immigrants "reinforce the British element and increase the Anglophone character of Montreal."[90]

Highly publicized demographic projections in the late 1960s heightened Francophone fears of *minorisation* in Montreal. Even though immigration to Montreal had favored the English-speaking community since Britain's poor began arriving after 1815, Francophones had represented over 60 percent of Montreal's population since 1871 by virtue of an exceptionally high birthrate and steady flow of Francophone migrants from rural Quebec.

However, by the 1960s the Francophone birthrate had plunged precipitously, and migration from the hinterland had slowed. In an influential analysis published in 1969, demographer Jacques Henripin argued that, "If recent migration trends continue, and if immigrants continue to opt predominantly for the English language, the French-speaking community of Quebec is bound to see its majority seriously reduced, particularly in Montreal. This would mean losing their only real power: that of making laws and electing governments."[91] Henripin offered a series of possible scenarios for the future linguistic composition of Montreal. His most alarming projection, highlighted in the Montreal media, was that with a high rate of immigration of non-French speaking settlers, the Francophone proportion of metropolitan Montreal's population could shrink as low as 52.7 percent by the year 2000. In other words, an analysis by a respected demographer raised, as a realistic possibility, the virtual *minorisation* of Francophones in Montreal by the end of the century. Henripin himself regarded the threat to Francophone majority status seriously enough to recommend provincial government intervention to integrate immigrants into the French-speaking community.[92]

In retrospect, there were several variables that made Henripin's forecast unduly alarmist. First, at the same time immigrants were Anglicizing in Montreal, a substantial number of Anglophone Montrealers were leaving the metropolitan area. Drawn by the superior economic opportunities in Toronto, and repelled by growing nationalism and anti-English sentiment in Montreal, net Anglophone emigration from Montreal totaled 33,000 between 1966 and 1971.[93] Anglicizing immigrants were not augmenting a stable Anglophone population and Henripin's alarming forecast did not sufficiently account for increasing Anglophone emigration.

Second, Henripin may have underestimated the extent to which the migration of Francophones from rural Quebec might counterbalance Anglicizing immigrants in Montreal's linguistic equilibrium. Throughout the twentieth century, rural Francophones had migrated to Montreal in search of economic opportunity, creating a solid and growing core of unilingual Francophones in the city. Although this internal migration had slowed by the late 1960s, net Francophone migration to the Montreal region between 1961 and 1971 was still 156,500 (compared with 175,800 between 1951 and 1961).[94] Moreover, Henripin's forecast included no assumptions on the demographic consequences of various economic developments; yet the possibility existed that economic stagnation in the hinterland might renew Francophone migration to Montreal. Coupled with the increasing emigration of Montreal Anglophones, such a trend might have been a sufficient counterweight to immigrant Anglicization, thus preserving Montreal's clear French-speaking majority.

Taking these factors into consideration, other demographers produced population projections for Montreal that were considerably less distressing than Henripin's from the Francophone perspective. Charbonneau and Maheu, for example, offered estimates of a French-speaking majority in Montreal that ranged from 61.2 percent to 70.2 percent by 1991,[95] and Henripin himself revised his estimates after analyzing 1971 census data.

However, by the time these conflicting population projections became a matter of academic dispute, Montreal's linguistic cleavage had become openly politicized. Whatever the validity of predictions of *minorisation,* growing segments of Francophone community believed that the enrollment of Allophones in Montreal's English-language schools posed an imminent threat to the cultural security of French-speaking Montreal. In addition, although there was little public discussion of the issue, some nationalists raised the specter that *Francophones* were following the example of immigrants and enrolling more of their children in English-language schools, with devastating cultural and linguistic implications. By 1970, Francophones constituted 13 percent of the clientele in the English-language sector of the CECM, and almost 5 percent of the students in the PSBGM.[96] Projections of a possible Francophone *minorisation* in Montreal had assumed virtually no assimilation from the French- to English-speaking community. However, if significant numbers of Francophone parents began sending their children to English-language schools, the possibility of such assimilation would surely increase, and with it the prospect of an eventual non-Francophone majority in Montreal.

William Coleman goes too far in arguing that the *real* concern over language in the schools involved Francophone fears over losing *les nôtres:* clearly, the immigrant issue was a genuine worry by the late 1960s. Moreover, the number of French-origin students enrolled in Montreal's English-language schools was not particularly high (around 8,000 in 1970—only 3.1 percent of the Island's Francophone schoolchildren) nor growing at a rapid rate (the number of Francophone students in the English-Catholic sector increased from 4,518 in 1960 to 5,373 in 1970).[97] Nevertheless, there were some groups in the French-speaking community who did view *Francophone* Anglicization via Montreal's English-language schools as a significant threat, and the concern was sufficient for the Gauthier report in 1967 to recommend barring Francophones from enrolling their children in English-language schools.

Although the main concerns over Montreal school enrollments involved Francophone cultural security, there were also some vital economic issues at stake. Simply put, the declining enrollments in French-language schools threatened the jobs of Francophone teachers and school administrators. The rivalry for Montreal's new ethnic minorities was not only an issue of linguistic demography; it was also a battle over which linguistic community, in an era of shrinking school enrollments, would attract sufficient numbers of immigrant children to keep schools open and protect educators' jobs. It was no accident that Francophone teachers and their students formed the core of an expanding coalition calling for language policies restricting access to Montreal's English-language schools: their material well-being was at stake.

By the fall of 1967, the issue of immigrant Anglicization in the Montreal public schools began receiving considerable attention in the Francophone community. Letters and articles on the subject appeared with increasing frequency in *Le Devoir,* the newspaper catering to Montreal's Francophone intelligentsia. The 1966 electoral platform of the victorious Union nationale included vague wording on the need for "welcoming" policies to integrate immigrants into the Francophone majority.[98] Moderate Francophones endorsed "immigrant assistance" programs and improvements in English-language instruction in French schools as a means of encouraging Allophones to enroll their children in French-language schools.

More militant voices, however, began to be heard. Nationalist groups such as the SSJBM, the États Généraux du Canada Français, and RIN continued their calls for new school policies in Montreal that would compel immigrants (and, in some formulations, Anglophones) to send their children to French schools. The report of the Gauthier Commission, completed in January 1967 included the explosive proposal that "freedom of choice" in Montreal education be eliminated. As we have seen, the commission recommended that Francophone students be required to attend French-language schools; in addition, it called for Allophones (and eventually Anglophones) to be placed in a new, bilingual school system, with French as the predominant language. "[Linguistic] equilibrium can only be re-established," claimed the commission, "by the energetic intervention of public powers." To think that a "warmer reception" of immigrants by Francophones or that improvement in second-language instruction would encourage immigrants to send their children to French schools, stated the commission, "is to believe in Santa Claus." [99]

Despite the growing militance among Francophones, the unwritten consociationalism that had historically governed relations between Montreal's linguistic communities remained potent—even as it was showing signs of unraveling. Mainstream Francophone political figures were not ready for a frontal assault on the status of English in Montreal, and the UN government of Daniel Johnson, taken aback by the vigorous nature of the Gauthier Commission's recommendations, buried its report (it was not released until 1968).

Nevertheless, by 1967 a significant portion of Montreal's Francophone community had taken note of the problem of immigrant Anglicization. School enrollment patterns made it appear that Montreal was well on its way to becoming a multi-ethnic city, with *English* as the integrating language. In the context of Quiet Revolution neo-nationalism, this was clearly unacceptable. Although a Francophone consensus had not yet formed on the appropriate policy response, pressures were growing for government action.

By the late 1960s, Montreal had become both the center of French Quebec's new urban culture and the setting where immigrant Anglicization threatened that culture. It was now the center of French Québécois nationalism—and the locus of Anglophone power. In this setting, Francophone anxieties over cultural security and school system jobs made Montreal ripe for a major linguistic conflagration. All that was needed was a spark, some catalytic event, to make language and schooling in Montreal a major political issue. That spark flared in November 1967 when a local Catholic school board in the Montreal suburb of Saint Léonard declared French the sole language of instruction for Allophone children in the community. In 1968 and 1969, in Montreal's supercharged linguistic climate, this issue of local school policy quickly became a city- and provincewide concern. Once a preoccupation of Francophone linguistic purists, language policy was about to become a mass political issue.

Chapter 4

Linguistic Crises and Policy Responses, 1967–1969

Saint-Léonard is an independent municipality on Montreal Island, located about five miles north of downtown. Through the mid-1950s, like so many small towns on Montreal's East End, Saint-Léonard was a quiet, homogeneously French-speaking community with fewer than 1,000 residents. Change came swiftly, however, following the 1960 completion of Boulevard Métropolitain, Montreal's cross-island expressway. Commercial and residential development swept across the eastern portion of the Island, and by the end of the 1960s Saint-Léonard had become a bustling inner suburb of 52,000. Attracted by inexpensive bungalows and convenient location near both downtown and East End factories, thousands of lower-middle-class Francophones and large numbers of Montreal's growing Italian community moved to Saint-Léonard in the 1960s, turning the municipality into Montreal's quintessential multi-ethnic community. By the late 1960s, Francophones represented 60 percent of Saint-Léonard's population, Italians around 30 percent, and the remainder consisted of Anglophones and a smattering of other ethnic groups.[1]

Naturally, schooling in previously homogeneous Saint-Léonard had always been in French, but in 1963 the local Catholic school board took notice of the community's ethnic transformation by opening bilingual elementary schools in which classes would be taught in both French and English. This option, similar to the ill-fated program introduced by the Comité des Néo-Canadiens in the CECM, was designed to ensure that immigrant children mastered French while providing them with the quality English-language instruction desired by their parents. The board's expectation was that enrollment in the bilingual schools would be more the exception than the rule, but the program proved enormously popular with Saint-Léonard's Italians. By

1967, over 90 percent of Saint-Léonard's Allophone elementary school children were enrolled in the district's fifty-seven bilingual classes.[2]

However, much to the chagrin of the increasingly nationalistic and politicized Francophone community, by the mid-1960s it appeared that the bilingual schools were having the perverse impact of integrating Saint-Léonard's immigrant children into Montreal's English-speaking society. Through 1967, over 85 percent of the students finishing the bilingual classes went on to English-language secondary schools in the Jérôme Le Royer Regional School District (in which Saint-Léonard was located).[3] In short, Saint-Léonard presented in microcosm the dilemma facing French-speaking Montreal in the late 1960s: public schooling seemed to be functioning as an instrument for the progressive Anglicization of the city. What's more, a disturbing number of *Francophone* parents, presumably seeking a promising future for their children in Montreal's linguistic division of labor, were also sending their children to the bilingual schools; by 1967, 6 percent of Saint-Léonard's French-speaking elementary school pupils were enrolled in the bilingual classes.[4]

It was in this context that the Francophone-controlled Saint-Léonard Catholic school board decided, in a November 1967 decision that would change the politics of language in Montreal forever, to eliminate the district's bilingual schools. Students enrolled in the bilingual classes at the time of the board's decision would be permitted to complete the program, but all children entering Saint-Léonard's elementary schools in fall 1968 would be required to attend French-language schools. Because the bilingual program ran through grade seven, the board envisioned a gradual, six-year phase-out of the classes.

Allophone parents reacted quickly and negatively to the board's imposition of French unilingualism. They formed a group, the Saint-Léonard Parents Association, which advocated parental "freedom of choice" in the language of instruction and demanded restoration of the bilingual classes. The Association threatened to withhold school taxes, keep their children out of school, and take the school board to court in defense of their language rights in education. The school commissioners were taken aback by the intensity of the Allophone parents' reaction and, in the hopes of cooling growing linguistic tensions, decided in April 1968 to delay implementation of the new language policy for another year.[5]

However, the genie of linguistic conflict was now out of the bottle in Saint-Léonard, and the school board's waffling merely exacerbated community tensions. By April 1968, a Francophone organization, the Mouvement pour l'intégration scolaire (MIS), had been formed to fight for "French as the sole language of instruction in the public schools of Saint-Léonard."[6] Led by Saint-Léonard architect and Quebec separatist Raymond Lemieux, the intent of the MIS was not only to defend "French rights" in Saint-Léonard, but to politicize the language and education issue beyond the local community, across Montreal and the province. "From the very first meeting" of the MIS, stated Lemieux, "the parents were quite conscious of the broader aspects, that eventually Montreal would become more and more English."[7] The MIS quickly grew to over 3,000 members, and would later declare a goal of creating "10, 20, 50 Saint-Léonard crises" across Quebec.[8] With links to radical separatist organizations such as the RIN and the FLQ, the MIS's deployment of "shock-troop," street politics tactics in Saint-Léonard over the next two years played a major role in polarizing Montreal's linguistic communities and pressuring reluctant provincial politicians to wrestle with the explosive issue of language policy.[9]

By May 1968, in an effort to gain control over local language policy in the Saint-Léonard schools, both the MIS and the Parents Association announced plans to field slates of candidates in the June school board elections. It was a turbulent and bitter campaign, replete with charges of electoral fraud and subsequent court challenges, and the election was closely watched across Montreal. Fifty percent of eligible voters participated, in contrast to the normal 5–10 percent turnout in school elections. The MIS won a decisive victory, electing Jean Girard and Raymond Langlois to the board; when these two were added to holdover board member Jacques Déschenes, also a unilingualist, the MIS now controlled the Saint-Léonard board. Moreover, in an accompanying referendum, over 75 percent of Saint-Léonard's voters expressed support for schools in which French would be the only language of instruction.[10] With this apparent unilingualist mandate, the new majority on the school board acted quickly, declaring on June 27 "that in all of the first years of elementary school under the jurisdiction of the Saint-Léonard school commission, beginning in September 1968, the language of instruction will be French."[11]

In the summer and early fall, as the Parents Association and the MIS continued to mobilize, tensions mounted in Saint-Léonard and the issue of language rights in education rapidly became a Montreal-wide issue. Fresh from their triumph in the June school board elections, the MIS announced plans to spread their linguistic action to such Montreal Island communities as Pierrefonds, Laval, Anjou, and Saint-Laurent.[12] On the other hand, under the aggressive leadership of its new head, an Anglo-Catholic named Robert Beale, the Parents Association now sought the creation of a separate, English-language school network in Saint-Léonard, and enlisted support from Anglophone businessmen, educational leaders, and the Montreal English-language media for their demands. In addition, the Association initiated court challenges to the school board's decision, announced a boycott of Saint-Léonard's unilingual French classes, and established private, "basement" classes—one was called the "Citizens' School"[13]—in which Allophone first-graders could receive English-language education. In September, the Parents Association organized a demonstration of 5,000 in Ottawa to alert English Canada to the "violation of Anglophone human rights occurring in Saint-Léonard"[14] and to enlist the support of newly elected Canadian Prime Minister Pierre Elliot Trudeau.

Numerous groups from across Montreal came to the Allophones' defense. While the CECM discretely avoided any entanglement in *l'affaire Saint-Léonard,* perhaps fearful that Francophone teachers might set off a linguistic explosion by pressing the case for unilingualism in Montreal's largest school system, the PSBGM announced that Catholic children of Saint-Léonard could enroll in Protestant schools, contingent on available space and parental payment of a "special contribution."[15] The English-Catholic Teachers' Association, undoubtedly concerned about their employment prospects should other school commissions follow the Saint-Léonard example and force immigrants into French-language schools, voiced their support for the beleaguered Allophones.[16] Beale would later criticize Anglophone businessmen as "apathetic and indifferent": "When we needed them and I knocked on the doors of big business . . . to say we had to raise $50,000, they said, 'Hey, take it easy. We have to do business with the French.'"[17] Nevertheless, as we shall see, Anglophone business pressure, in the historical tradition of Montreal consociationalism, would be crucial in the last analysis, pushing the provincial government to enact legislation protecting parental freedom of choice in the language of instruction.

While Francophone groups such as the RIN, SSJB, and the Fédération des Enseignants de Montréal (Montreal Teachers Federation) expressed support for unilingualist action in Saint-Léonard, mainstream Francophone public opinion had not yet galvanized in favor of limiting the availability of English-language schooling. Editorialists in *Le Devoir,* the influential Montreal daily of the Francophone intelligentsia, warned that "majorities cannot trample the rights of minorities in a democracy," and defended parental freedom of choice by noting that "tradition and practice are sufficiently clear to speak of acquired rights."[18] Claude Ryan, the respected director of *Le Devoir* called Saint-Léonard a "test case" of the future of language rights in Quebec schools and wrote that, although "fanatics in the ranks of Saint-Léonard demonstrations may object . . . Montreal has been a bilingual city. It has remained one and it should remain one if it wants to retain its position as an economic and social metropole in North America."[19] Leaders of the Union nationale, the party in control of the provincial government, also called for moderation. Jean-Jacques Bertrand, Minister of Justice and soon-to-become premier stated: "Bilingualism is still official in Quebec, and it will remain so as long as the parliament does not decide otherwise. We do not play with acquired rights as toys."[20] Premier Daniel Johnson, in one of his final statements on the subject before his sudden death, acknowledged that the Saint-Léonard conflict underscored the need for a comprehensive provincial language policy, and asserted that "we cannot permit rights as basic as those of language to be manipulated by a local school board."[21]

The situation in Saint-Léonard deteriorated markedly with the beginning of the school year in the fall of 1968. The Francophone-controlled Jérôme Le Royer regional school commission had decided in August, for reasons of administrative efficiency, to change l'École Aimé-Rénaud, a French-language secondary school located in Saint-Léonard but drawing students from across the East Island region, into an English-language school. Aimé-Rénaud was located near the Italian neighborhoods of Saint-Léonard; thus, given the tendency of Allophones to send their children to English-language secondary schools in the district, the regional commission calculated that turning Aimé-Rénaud into an English school would save $150,000 in transportation costs and avoid the logistical difficulties of dispersing English-language students into other schools in the predominantly Francophone regional school district.[22]

The commission's decision was based strictly on considerations of rational resource allocation, and was unrelated substantively to the ongoing conflict in Saint-Léonard over the language of public instruction. Nevertheless, the Aimé-Rénaud question immediately assumed linguistic overtones in the superheated climate of Saint-Léonard. By expressing the need for additional school space for English-language classes in a community with few Anglophones, the regional commission highlighted the now-sensitive fact that immigrants were choosing to send their children to English instead of French schools in Montreal. Moreover, the symbolic significance could hardly be missed: because of immigrant language choices, a school was being "taken" from the Francophone community and given to English-speakers— what would such developments portend for the future of French in Montreal? The MIS announced that it would take "effective measures to protect French in the school," and in September organized student occupations of l'École Aimé-Rénaud. The "sit-in" was buttressed by crowds outside the school, including Pierre Bourgault (head of the RIN), Yvon Groulx of the SSJB, and members of the Fédération des Enseignants de Montréal. Stated Groulx: "Saint-Léonard has become the conscience of Quebec."[23] Bomb threats and concerns about street violence hung over negotiations to end the sit-in.

The Francophone community was far from united in support of the Aimé-Rénaud demonstrations. Vincent Prince, editorialist in *Le Devoir*, supported the commission's plan and noted that "Aimé-Rénaud should not become a symbol of Anglophone or Francophone supremacy. Aimé-Rénaud is a building that should be used in the best interests of the region's taxpayers."[24] René Lévesque, who by fall 1968 had declared himself an *indépendantiste* and was about to launch the Parti québécois, incurred the wrath of Lemieux and the MIS by refusing to support the demonstrations outside the school; later, in his memoirs, Lévesque would condemn the MIS for their "rhetoric of hatred" and manifestation of "an intolerance to which we ourselves [as French-speaking Québécois] had been exposed."[25] Finally, a week after it began, the student occupation ended with a compromise in which l'École Aimé-Rénaud would remain French. L'École George-Étienne Cartier, a modern, new school that had been slated to include both French- and English-language classes, would now become entirely Anglophone to accommodate the students displaced from Aimé-Rénaud.[26]

The conflict surrounding l'École Aimé-Rénaud, coupled with the ongoing boycott and pressure by the Parents Association for provincial government support, made clear just how much the Saint-Léonard situation was turning Montreal into a linguistic tinderbox over the issue of language in the schools. Other events in 1968 and early 1969 also contributed to a sense of linguistic crisis on the Island. On June 24, 1968, at Montreal's annual *Fête Saint-Jean Baptiste* parade, RINistes and other separatist militants participated in one of the city's bloodiest demonstrations. Dubbed the *lundi de la matraque* ("Monday of the truncheon"), demonstrators scuffled with police and threw stones at the car carrying Prime Minister Pierre Elliot Trudeau in the motorcade. One hundred thirty-five were injured and more than three hundred arrested.[27] Separatist bombings continued through 1968 and 1969, including such identifiable Anglophone targets as the Board of Trade, Eaton's Department Store, the headquarters of Domtar, the Gare Centrale of the CNR, and the Montreal Stock Exchange. In October 1968, stimulated by the "nationalist fever rising with events in Saint-Léonard,"[28] students, taxi drivers, and separatist militants participated in a coordinated "urban guerrilla" action to protest the monopoly on airport taxi services and private buses held by the Anglophone-controlled Murray Hill Company. Dorval Airport was cut off and traffic blocked for hours in several areas of Montreal; more important, the event seemed to symbolize the growing dissolution of the city's historical tradition of linguistic peace.

Increasing concern over the places of French and English in Montreal also fueled the growth of Quebec independence activity in the city. Most important, of course, was the formation in 1967 of the René Lévesque–led Mouvement Souveraineté-Association (MSA), which ultimately became, in October 1968, the Parti québécois (PQ). There was agreement in *indépendantiste* circles that "in a sovereign Quebec, French will be the sole official language" and that all immigrant children should attend French schools.[29] However, beyond this consensus, there were sharp divisions over policies regarding language and schooling. Separatists such as François Aquin and Pierre Bourgault endorsed policies that would abolish all English-language schools in Quebec, while René Lévesque insisted on guarantees for publicly supported English-language schooling for bona fide Anglophone children (that is, whose mother tongue was English). As Lévesque later recalled:

"The maintenance, not of the excessive privileges but of the fundamental schooling rights of Quebec Anglophones seemed to me a test of our maturity, of our aptitude to maintain comfortable relations with the rest of North America."[30] As for the Aquin–Bourgault position, Lévesque called it "injustice in response to injustice," and when the radical position initially carried at the MSA's founding convention, Lévesque resigned (only to return when the delegates reversed themselves and supported his position). It would be the first of numerous episodes between 1968 and 1980 when Lévesque would intercede personally to prevent *indépendantiste* radicals from adopting a hard-line unilingualist stance. Largely because of Lévesque's power in the movement, the early platforms of the PQ all recognized the right of English elementary and secondary schools "to be subsidized proportional to the English-speaking population."[31]

While *la question linguistique* was rapidly becoming the prime political preoccupation of Francophone Montreal, the Island's Anglophone community also began showing political concern over the city's deteriorating linguistic situation. In December 1968, provincial legislature by-elections in the predominantly Anglophone riding of Notre-Dame-de-Grâce, voters were urged by the Montreal *Star,* the city's leading English-language newspaper, to "remember St. Léonard" and vote for whichever provincial party promised to redress the situation and restore English-language schooling rights in the community. Both candidates—William Tetley of the PLQ and John Lynch-Staunton of the UN—denounced the abrogation of freedom of choice in Saint-Léonard and promised vigilance in defense of Anglophone rights.[32] Clearly, anxieties were rising in both of Montreal's linguistic communities, and the provincial government could no longer avoid the need to articulate a clear, comprehensive policy on the language of education in Montreal.

Policy Response I: Bill 85

As Montreal's linguistic situation worsened, Premier Bertrand announced in late November 1968 his intent to introduce legislation protecting minority language rights in education that would "regulate the problem of Saint-Léonard."[33] Accused of attempting to curry Anglophone favor in light of the upcoming Notre-Dame-de-Grâce by-election, Bertrand delayed introducing his legislation until early December. In the meantime, the MIS, SSJB, and other nationalist groups organized a mass protest in Quebec City to oppose the anticipated action of the Bertrand government to guarantee freedom of choice in the language of instruction. A group of three thousand, including many twelve- and thirteen-year-olds bused up from Montreal, demonstrated in front of the provincial legislature. Bertrand was joined by such varied

Francophone leaders as René Lévesque and Jean Lesage in condemning the MIS as fanatics and extremists and denouncing nationalist teachers who participated in this "brigading of students."[34]

In December 1968, the Bertrand government unveiled several measures to demonstrate its readiness to act on the language question. Earlier in the year, the provincial government had established Centres d'orientation et de formation des immigrants (COFI), immigrant training and orientation centers designed to "provide for immigrants' initial need to learn languages" and to "ensure contact with the French majority and promote integration into the French-speaking milieu."[35] In December, Education Minister Jean-Guy Cardinal announced the expansion of COFI, with adult language-education classes that would emphasize French instruction but also offer English-language courses. In addition, Premier Bertrand appointed a blue-ribbon commission to study the language problem and present recommendations for a comprehensive Quebec language policy; thus was born the Commission of Inquiry on the Position of the French Language and on Language Rights in Quebec, chaired by the noted linguist Jean-Denis Gendron.[36]

However, the centerpiece of Bertrand's response to the growing linguistic crisis in Montreal was Bill 85, an act specifying language rights in education. The bill, presented on December 9, sought a linguistic compromise that would emphasize French as Quebec's *priority* language while preserving individual linguistic freedom of choice in education. The heart of Bill 85 was its requirement that all school commissions provide instruction in either French or English, with *all* parents—regardless of their mother tongue—free to choose their child's language of education. A province-level "linguistic committee" was proposed, to be composed of ten Francophones and five non-Francophones and charged with the task of regulating controversies such as Saint-Léonard involving the language of education. Finally, Bill 85 required that all graduates of Quebec schools possess a *connaissance d'usage* (working knowledge) of French; presumably, Bertrand thought that such a requirement would satisfy nationalist concerns on the promotion of French.[37]

In short, Bill 85 attempted to regulate Montreal's schooling conflict by inscribing in provincial law the principle of linguistic freedom of choice in education. As would be the case throughout his sad tenure as Quebec's Premier, Bertrand badly underestimated the depth of growing Francophone concern over the language question in Montreal. Led by the MIS, SSJB, and an unprecedented number of witnesses who testified before the parliamentary committee reviewing the legislation, Bill 85 was vehemently attacked throughout the Francophone community. Raymond Lemieux denounced Bill 85 as "a proposal legalizing the theft of French in Quebec by the minorities."[38] Father Richard Arès, whose sociological analyses and demographic projections played an important role in raising public concern over language issues, concluded that "Bill 85 . . . if it is adopted without other guarantees for

French, can only aggravate an already alarming situation, one that is in the process of compromising forever the very future of the French-language community in the Montreal region."[39] René Lévesque, now sitting in the provincial legislature as the leader of the PQ, criticized Bill 85 as "maintaining the status quo that undermines French," and offered a PQ counterproposal that would require all non-Anglophone schoolchildren to attend French-language schools after January 1, 1969. Anglophones would continue to have access to fully subsidized English-language public schools, with an enrollment ceiling fixed by the number of students in 1968 enrolled in English-language schools. However, Lévesque and the PQ were vague on precisely how admission to the fixed number of English-language "slots" would be determined.[40]

The hearings on Bill 85 before the legislature's Education Committee permitted an almost daily airing of Francophone attacks on the proposal in January and February 1969, as "a sounding board for extremists" in Bertrand's view.[41] In addition, in late February the Conseil Supérieur de l'Éducation recommended to the education minister that Bill 85 be withdrawn, labeling it a "piecemeal approach to a much larger problem."[42] More ominously, the Conseil suggested that if the bill were enacted, a series of Saint-Léonard crises would ensue across the province. Thus, facing splits within his own Union nationale caucus over Bill 85 and unexpectedly fierce nationalist opposition, Bertrand withdrew the bill in March 1969, calling it "*un bébé dont personne ne veut*" (an unwanted baby).[43] While reiterating his support for open access to English-language schools, Bertrand indicated that he would await the recommendations of the Gendron Commission before proposing a new language policy.

Conflicts Become Crises: Linguistic Battles of 1969

Bill 85 was clearly not the solution to the linguistic tensions surrounding schooling in Montreal. Nevertheless, its demise left unresolved the contentious matter of language rights in education. The immediate consequence of governmental inaction was the continued festering of the Saint-Léonard situation through the spring and summer of 1969. Moreover, other "language rights" confrontations surfaced in Montreal during this period, further aggravating the city's already tense linguistic climate. The most passionate and symbolic of these conflicts involved Francophone efforts to convert McGill University into a French-language institution.

McGill University was founded in 1821 with a bequest of land and money in the will of James McGill, a prominent Montreal merchant of British origin. The university developed as an institution of some international renown in medicine and the sciences, but, most important for English-speaking Montrealers, it became the equivalent of an "Ivy League" training ground for the city's ruling class, the "place to go if one hoped to crash the gates of downtown business."[44] Well into the twentieth century, McGill typified British Montreal at its most imperial and exclusivist. Quotas limited Jewish enrollments at the university, and as late as 1965 the McGill Board of Governors was "almost totally WASP."[45] As Douglas Fullerton notes, the links between McGill and the Montreal Anglo-Protestant business establishment were "broad and deep. The ultimate accolade denoting arrival at the top of Montreal's business community was an invitation to join the Board of Governors of McGill—a much more exclusive club even than English Montreal's finest, the Mount Royal Club, a few blocks west along Sherbrooke Street."[46] Montreal Francophones also saw McGill as a crucial institutional bulwark of Anglophone control of the city, symbolically perched on the slope of Mount Royal, overlooking downtown Montreal and beside the mansions of the Golden Square Mile. For many Francophones, McGill was "the perfect symbol of [Anglophone] domination, the stronghold of a propertied minority that lived in a ghetto in the heart of overwhelmingly French-speaking Quebec."[47]

While this view undoubtedly fit McGill for much of the twentieth century, by the late 1960s it was a somewhat exaggerated, ethnocentric position; McGill's student body had become quite diversified. Nevertheless, for Montreal Francophones McGill was a "foreign" university, drawing large numbers of students from outside Quebec and having almost no discernible connection to French-speaking society. Even if the 1960s McGill was less British and imperial than it was through the early part of the century, the university was still the training ground for Montreal's English-speaking business class and intelligentsia, and it remained a potent symbol of the linguistic hierarchies that Montreal Francophones were now challenging.

In March 1969, a coalition of nationalist radicals—including members of the FLQ, the Ligue pour l'intégration scolaire (an expanded version of Saint-Léonard's MIS), and the Montreal branch of the Conseil central des syndicats nationaux—announced plans for *Opération McGill français,* a mass demonstration to protest the English character of the university. Francophone students had been particularly active in nationalist activity in Montreal since 1968, and the organizers of *Opération McGill français* sought to channel student sentiment for a second French-language university in Montreal into a symbolic assault on one of Anglophone Montreal's core institutions.[48] McGill officials defended the university as a central link between Montreal and English North America and, as such, vital to Montreal's growth and prosperity. Moreover, university officials claimed that McGill was becoming much more responsive to Montreal's French fact, offering more courses and public events in French, establishing a French-Canadian studies program, permitting students, since 1964, to take exams or write theses in French or English, and setting a target of 20 percent Francophone enrollment by 1974.[49] For the most part, however, these points fell on deaf ears in the Francophone nationalist community.

L'Opération McGill français took place on March 28. More than fifteen thousand marchers descended upon rue Sherbrooke in front of the university and despite fears of violence, a massive police presence limited incidents to a few broken windows in stores and restaurants along streets around the campus. University and city officials had feared that demonstrators would attempt to storm the campus and occupy buildings, in the manner of campus revolts in the United States at Columbia, Harvard, and Berkeley, but that did not occur and there was no physical damage to the university. All told, forty demonstrators were arrested, and twenty suffered minor injuries.[50] *Opération McGill français*, however, was a one-time event. Nationalists soon became preoccupied with other linguistic concerns in Montreal and, by the fall, pressure to *francise* McGill was lessened by the opening of l'Université du Québec à Montréal (UQAM). By 1974, UQAM had a student body of more than fourteen thousand (around 50 percent of the entire l'Université du Québec system enrollments), housed several important research centers such as INRS-Urbanisation, and was undeniably Montreal's second major French-language university.[51]

The open challenge to Anglophone institutions displayed in such events as *Opération McGill français* revealed how significantly Francophone acceptance of Montreal's hierarchical "dualism" had eroded by early 1969. Nevertheless, the most immediate threat to linguistic peace in the city remained the worsening school conflict in Saint-Léonard. In the aftermath of the demise of Bill 85, both the Parents Association and the MIS redoubled their pressure-group activities in Saint-Léonard. The Parents Association focused its energies on two main issues: trying to pressure Minister of Education Jean-Guy Cardinal into overruling the local school board and establishing English-language classes in Saint-Léonard; and, in lieu of government action, setting up alternative schooling for the Allophone children affected by the new unilingualism policy.

Cardinal soon became the Parents Association's chief villain by steadfastly insisting that he lacked authority to overturn the local board's policy; this led Robert Beale of the association to accuse Cardinal of using Saint-Léonard as a "pilot experiment" for the establishment of unilingualism throughout Quebec education.[52] Cardinal agreed that school boards should not make policy on as fundamental an issue as the language of instruction. However, he maintained that resolution of the problem would occur when the government introduced legislation in the fall that would abolish local boards such as the one in Saint-Léonard and reorganize school governance on Montreal Island along linguistic lines. As an interim "compromise," Cardinal suggested that Saint-Léonard's Allophones take advantage of the province's new law on private schools, Bill 56, which would permit parents to establish a private, English-language school in Saint-Léonard and receive a government subsidy of up to 80 percent of the average cost of instruction in the public schools. Beale and the Parents Association immediately rejected the "Cardinal solution," calling upon Quebec's Assemblée nationale to guarantee freedom of choice in the language of instruction and obligate local school boards to furnish education in English or French in appropriate public facilities.[53]

While keeping the pressure on Cardinal and the UN government, the Parents Association also organized an Allophone boycott of Saint-Léonard's first- and second-grade classes (those classes affected by the June 1968 unilingualism decision) and made arrangements for alternative schooling. Basement classes continued, although funding was a constant problem. In addition, with the opening of the fall 1969 schoolyear, the PSBGM enrolled around 60 percent of the boycotting schoolchildren (for a $25 a month fee that represented a significant financial burden for Allophone parents). Cardinal called the PSBGM action "an affront to Quebec society," and even moderates like Claude Ryan charged the PSBGM with "throwing oil on the fire" and undermining any possibility of compromise in Saint-Léonard to meet the legitimate concerns of the French-speaking community.[54]

Meanwhile, the Ligue pour l'intégration scolaire (LIS), the expanded version of the MIS, continued its agitation in Saint-Léonard. Boisterous public meetings, including some that ended in scuffles between Francophones and Allophone counterdemonstrators, were held to rally support for unilingualism policies. LIS rhetoric became increasingly shrill, with leader Robert Lemieux calling for the provincial government to "close the door to immigration until the language problem in Quebec is regulated." In early September, Saint-Léonard's mayor warned of an imminent "racial explosion."[55]

That explosion came on September 10 when the LIS staged a deliberately provocative march in support of unilingualism through the Italian neighborhoods of Saint-Léonard. Despite pleas from Robert Beale as well as public officials to ignore the marchers and remain in their homes, Italians lined the parade route and heckled the demonstrators. Confrontation spilled over into violence, and a riot broke out in which an estimated thousand marchers and residents were involved; one hundred were injured, and fifty arrests were made. For the first time since 1957, the Riot Act was read in Montreal, establishing curfews and other measures to restore order. One journalist characterized the event as "an explosion of English-French hostility unparalleled since the conscription crisis."[56]

The Saint-Léonard riot, culminating a year of growing linguistic unrest in Montreal, was perhaps the clearest sign yet that language-group relations in the city could no longer be governed, as they had been historically, by linguistic separation, elite accommodation, and Francophone docility. In a brilliant editorial written in the aftermath of the riot, Claude Ryan noted that "Montreal is today torn apart by the Saint-Léonard affair. We will eventually extinguish this fire. But nothing guarantees that others are not already in the making."[57] Linguistic peace, Ryan continued, had been maintained histori- cally by the acceptance of "two cities," one Anglophone, the other Fran- cophone, separate and unequal. Those days, however, were gone and An- glophones now needed to participate in a refashioning of the "Montreal spirit." While protecting the legitimate rights of the English-speaking com- munity, said Ryan, public policy must also now respond to the concerns of the Francophone community over economic inequality and immigrant An- glicization. Ryan still advocated policies of "moderation" and "gradualism," and condemned the "fanaticism" of the LIS and its supporters in Saint- Léonard. Nevertheless, the message from this influential Francophone mod- erate was clear: Montreal's French-speaking community had legitimate grievances that, if unresolved, could only lead to more conflict and violence.

Policy Response II: Bill 63

Wary of reigniting the kind of passionate linguistic debate that accompanied the Bill 85 misadventure, Premier Bertrand had vowed not to introduce lan- guage legislation until the Gendron Commission issued its recommenda- tions. However, the breakdown of civil order in Saint-Léonard suggested that tensions in Montreal had moved to a new, dangerous level. Despite sharp divisions in his cabinet over language policy, Bertrand decided to at- tempt once again to legislate on language rights in education. On October 23, 1969 the Bertrand government presented Bill 63, "An Act to promote the French language in Quebec."[58] Bill 63 was basically a reworked version of Bill 85, but the government presented it as "the first step toward making French the priority language in Quebec."[59] Several features of the bill aimed to bolster the status of French: all graduates of Quebec schools were re- quired to possess a "working knowledge" of French, COFI programs were expanded to encourage immigrants to learn French, and a new Office de la langue française was proposed to monitor the position of French in Quebec and advise the government on any future measures necessary to protect the French language.

But the key provision of Bill 63 dealt with the language of instruction. Pressured by the Montreal Anglophone business establishment, the Ber- trand government proposed to guarantee explicitly that schooling "shall be given in the English language to any child for whom his parents or the per- sons acting in their stead so request at his enrollment."[60] Immigrants would not be compelled to attend French-language schools; moreover, freedom of choice would exist for anyone, Francophones included, to send their children to English-language schools. In short, the bill represented a ringing affirmation of Montreal's historical dualism, a stinging rebuke to the growing French unilingualist coalition, and, insofar as the Saint-Léonard crisis was concerned, intervention by the provincial government on the side of the Allophone parents.

While the Anglophone community generally applauded Bill 63, the legislation set off an unprecedentedly intense mass reaction among Montreal and Quebec Francophones. Unimpressed with the "French promotion" features of the bill, the Montreal French-language media, cultural associations, labor unions, student and teacher organizations, and nationalist groups all denounced Bill 63. A survey conducted by researchers at l'Université de Montréal found that, while British-origin Montrealers and "Neo-Canadians" favored Bill 63 by a margin of 56 percent to 13 percent (the remainder undecided or having no opinion), "French Canadians" on the Island of Montreal opposed the bill by 46 percent to 26 percent. The rate of opposition was particularly high among young Francophones: 55 percent of those between the ages of eighteen and twenty-four reported opposing Bill 63 while only 21 percent approved.[61]

Inside l'Assemblée nationale, opposition to Bill 63 was led by René Lévesque of the newly-formed PQ, Union nationale renegades Antonio Flamand and Jérôme Proulx, and nominal PLQ member Yves Michaud. Dubbed the "Circumstantial Opposition," the group waged a tenacious filibuster using, as Lévesque would later recall, "all possible and imaginable" motions to paralyze the legislature.[62] Declaring that freedom of choice in the language of instruction would result in Francophone *minorisation,* Lévesque argued once again that English-language schooling should exist only for Anglophones in proportion to their percentage in the population; Allophones should be compelled to send their children to French-language schools.[63] Flamand argued that Bill 63 would achieve what Lord Durham could not in 1840—the eradication of the French fact in Quebec—[64]while Proulx maintained that Bill 63 mistakenly enshrined individual choice over "the well-being of the collectivity and the higher interest of the nation."[65]

Bertrand was determined not to repeat what he saw as the key tactical error of the Bill 85 fiasco: permitting the legislation to linger in committee where it would be subjected to prolonged, daily attacks. Bill 63 was placed immediately before l'Assemblée nationale; thus, the delaying tactics by the "Circumstantial Opposition" were crucial in giving Francophone pressure groups an opportunity to mobilize against the bill. While Lévesque and his parliamentary allies proposed numerous amendments and tied up the legislature with procedural motions, a formidable extra-parliamentary coalition emerged, embracing "hard-line" Francophone unilingualists as well as more moderate nationalists who acknowledged a place for English in Quebec but believed that Francophone cultural security required limiting access to English-language schools. In Montreal, a Front de Québec français (FQF) was formed, spearheaded by the SSJB de Montréal and including the LIS, Francophone teachers unions, and the Confédération des syndicats nationaux (CSN). The FQF broadened its operations across Quebec, organizing a multipronged campaign of propaganda, demonstrations, and petitions against Bill 63, and offering a concrete policy alternative—symbolically titled Le Projet de loi Québec numéro 1—that proposed French as the only official language of Quebec. In the FQF proposal, French would be the language of "factories, offices, and other places of work," all public administration would function in French, and English-language schooling would be gradually eliminated, not only for immigrants and Francophones but also "British descendants settled in Quebec."[66]

The FQF clearly offered the hard-line French unilingualist position, but it gained increasing support in the wake of public dissatisfaction with the Bertrand administration's seeming obliviousness to the threat to French in Montreal. François-Albert Angers, then president of the SSJB de Montréal and a leading force in the FQF, put the matter directly; Bill 63 posed a basic identity question: was Quebec fundamentally a French society or a bicultural one?[67] Bill 63 was clearly a policy flowing from the historical notion of Montreal as a "dual" city, a city in which the French and English languages possessed equal legal status. By late 1969, however, that image was unacceptable for vast numbers of Francophone Montrealers, from teachers to factory workers to middle-class professionals. As the provincial government continued to ignore the linguistic concerns of these Francophones, thousands in Montreal were radicalized on *la question linguistique* and increasingly embraced variants of the unilingualist position.

Perhaps the most effective tactic of the FQF was in mobilizing teachers and students in Montreal to participate in school disruptions and rallies opposing Bill 63. In the last week of October 1969, a wave of student and teacher "strikes" and "teach-ins" swept across Montreal. On October 28, an estimated ten thousand students marched in a giant Montreal teach-in and demonstration, ending with a giant rally at the Centre sportif of the Université de Montréal in which FQF speakers François-Albert Angers, Raymond Lemieux, Pierre Bourgault, and Michel Chartrand (of the Confédération des syndicats nationaux, a major Francophone union) blasted Bill 63 and promoted French unilingualism.[68] The next day, twenty-five thousand "calm, orderly" students and other opponents of Bill 63 marched in a huge Montreal rally; "the student world is completely paralyzed," read local headlines.[69] This week of activity culminated on October 31 in a demonstration, estimated at between fifteen and thirty-five thousand participants, in front of l'Assemblée nationale in Quebec to protest Bill 63. Bertrand and former Premier Lesage denounced the teachers for manipulating their students in

the Bill 63 battle, and Claude Ryan called "this use of adolescents for political show a shameful chapter in contemporary Quebec history."[70] Nevertheless, as Robert McDonald has pointed out, this politicization of Francophone
students was a crucial development in the Montreal language question:

> The disturbances . . . illustrated the extent to which the young in
> Quebec had been politicized, a fact which had serious implications for
> the political life of the Province. A clear link had been forged between
> French unilingualism and economic liberation. It was now a logical step
> to believe that a declaration establishing French as the only language of
> instruction in the schools would mean a French-only province. . . . In
> short, French unilingualism in schools was symbolic of economic and
> political and cultural liberation.[71]

In the wake of the Francophone uproar against Bill 63, thoughtful analysts such as Université Laval political scientist Léon Dion viewed the entire
episode as an "escalation towards anarchy." Dion and other moderates
urged Bertrand to withdraw the "hastily and ill-conceived" bill and to recon-
sider, in a calm, deliberate fashion, the entire question of language policy.[72]
Yet, despite the disastrous impact that Bill 63 was having on Montreal's linguistic cleavage, and despite the knowledge that he was committing political
suicide, Bertrand was determined to keep his promise to Anglophone leaders and pass the legislation.[73] Although there were a few defections from the
UN caucus, Bertrand had the support of his party as well as PLQ members
of l'Assemblée nationale, and by a vote of 89 to 5 Bill 63 became law on
November 27, 1969. The immediate crisis of Saint-Léonard was over; Italian parents once again were permitted to send their children to English-
language schools. But, as we shall see, Bill 63 hardly regulated Montreal's
linguistic conflicts. Between 1970 and 1974, nationalists would take advantage of the bill's overwhelming unpopularity among Montreal Francophones
to steadily build support not only to repeal Bill 63, but also to establish a
more radical language policy promoting the status of French in Montreal and
across Quebec.

Language and the Restructuring of School Governance

Bill 63 was one major piece of legislation dealing with language and schooling
in Montreal presented by the Bertrand government in the fall of 1969; the
other was Bill 62, an act to reorganize school governance on the Island of
Montreal. The two bills were twinned by Education Minister Cardinal into a
linguistic "package deal,"[74] in which, it was hoped, Bill 63 would meet Anglophone concerns over freedom of choice in the language of instruction while

Bill 62 would placate Francophone nationalists by replacing the existing forty-two Protestant and Catholic school boards on Montreal Island with eleven unified (that is, *not* linguistically or confessionally autonomous) boards. Following the recommendations of the Parent and Pagé commissions, Bill 62 also proposed a powerful, centralized "Island Council" to coordinate school policy and equalize school finance disparities across the Island. Given Montreal's linguistic demography and the proposed boundaries for the new school districts, the Island Council and at least seven of the unified boards would be controlled by the French-speaking majority on Montreal Island. Thus, although access for all to English-language schools would be guaranteed by Bill 63, the Bertrand government hoped that nationalists would be pacified by the increased Francophone control over Montreal education inherent in Bill 62.[75]

Francophone groups generally supported Bill 62,[76] although the Bertrand government's political calculus went awry when it became clear that Francophone approval of the school reorganization plan had done little to mute the mass outcry over Bill 63. On the other hand, Montreal's Anglo-Protestant establishment, with the curious exception of the Montreal *Star*, vehemently protested the restructuring plans.[77] Organizations such as the PSBGM, the Montreal Association of Protestant Teachers, the Provincial Association of Protestant Teachers, and the Quebec Federation of Home and School Associations, painted Bill 62 as a major linguistic threat.[78] Specifically, these groups bemoaned the loss of autonomy for English-language schooling contained in Bill 62, and criticized the bill's failure to guarantee Anglophone representation on the unified school boards or the powerful Island Council. Fresh from the experience of Saint-Léonard, Anglophones questioned whether the provisions in Bill 63 protecting linguistic freedom of choice would be respected by the Francophone-controlled, unified school boards. H. Rocke Robertson, the principal of McGill University, warned that under Bill 62, Francophones would control the unified boards, imposing their values in pedagogy and curriculum, and Anglophone schools "would not have voice concerning their own affairs . . . or formal contact with Anglophone schools in other municipalities."[79] Stanley Frost, McGill's vice-principal was even more alarmist: Bill 62, he said, "spells the end of the English language teaching profession in Quebec."[80] In place of Bill 62, Anglophone critics generally called for autonomous boards, based on language, and undergirded by *constitutionally* guaranteed freedom of choice in the language of instruction (these were the recommendations, more or less, of the Pagé Commission whose October 1968 report had called for replacing the existing boards with nine regional Francophone commissions and four regional Anglophone commissions—but with a stronger Island Council than Anglophones would have liked).[81]

The Anglo-Protestant educational establishment was strongly supported in its battle against Bill 62 by corporate Montreal, hardly an accident given the "substantial overlapping in the leadership positions of [Anglophone] educational and business institutions in Montreal."[82] During the parliamentary hearings on the bill, the PSBGM advanced what would become a staple Anglophone argument against all language policies promoting French in Montreal over the next decade. "The passage of Bill 62," claimed the PSBGM, "could be followed by a serious exodus of funds from the province."[83] Similarly, the Montreal Board of Trade stated that "to create a totally unified education system at this time would have a substantial retardant effect on the economic growth of Montreal."[84] In the Board of Trade's view, "the attitudes of anglophones are generally better adapted to purely economic goals than those of francophones into which considerations of another order tend to be introduced."[85] Since these differences flowed mainly from education, the clear implication from the Board of Trade was that Quebec's economic future hinged on avoiding the contamination of English-language schooling by Francophone values.

In short, in the same manner that corporations have historically used the threat of disinvestment to influence public policy in American cities, Montreal's English-speaking business elite threatened a "capital strike" if policies were enacted that altered the historical place of English or the autonomy of English-language institutions on the Island.[86] Bertrand decided not to press the matter, and in April 1970 permitted Bill 62 to die on the order paper. The confessional structure of Montreal schooling remained intact, underpinned now by a policy protecting freedom of choice in the language of instruction. The "package deal" crafted by Cardinal had yielded nothing for the burgeoning Francophone nationalist coalition.

Conclusion

As much as Montreal's linguistic climate had changed by the end of the 1960s, it is revealing that although mass Francophone protests had failed to dissuade Bertrand from forging ahead with Bill 63, the opposition of Anglophone capital to Bill 62 was sufficient to kill the school reorganization plan. In many ways, the battles over Bills 63 and 62 represented the last gasp of Montreal's old order: an urban linguistic regime in which elites from both major linguistic communities conceptualized Montreal as a dualistic, bilingual city (rather than a primarily French city with a large English-speaking minority), and in which Francophone politicians largely deferred when the English-speaking elite flexed its muscles on matters of Anglophone community interest. After withdrawing Bill 62, Bertrand called for an early provincial election in April 1970. Mass dissatisfaction with his handling of the language question was evident in the election results: Bertrand's Union nationale, the party of Duplessis that had ruled Quebec with one brief interruption between 1936–1960, was thoroughly trounced and, for all intents and purposes, eliminated as a viable force in provincial politics. The lesson of the Bertrand debacle was transparent: any Quebec government that ignored the groundswell of Francophone concern over the language question would now do so at its political peril.

The Saint-Léonard school crisis, and the subsequent mobilization of Francophone nationalism in opposition to Bills 85 and 63, were watershed events in reshaping language-group relations in Montreal. A powerful, mass-based Francophone coalition had come together as an unprecedented "common front," committed to using state policy as a weapon in the battle for linguistic supremacy on the Island. For the first time, Francophones openly challenged Montreal's longstanding assumptions on language rights, and the events of 1967–1969, accompanied by a heavy dose of intergroup invective, revealed that language disputes could no longer be contained by the old patterns of elite accommodation. Even though the political economy of language in Montreal remained such that the nationalists were thwarted in the language-policy battles of 1969, the outcry in the French-speaking community over Bills 85 and 63 plainly foreshadowed the shape of things to come. The language question was now an issue of mass politics, and the intensity of the Francophone response to Bills 85 and 63 made it clear that the question of language policy in Montreal was far from settled by the legislation of 1969.

The schools issue, touching as it did on Francophone concerns about the demographic strength and the ultimate cultural and linguistic security of French in Montreal, became the flashpoint for growing English–French tensions, especially as job-conscious and culturally sensitive Francophone teachers and their students took the lead in politicizing the question of language policy in education. Anglophones were not disposed to relinquish what they regarded as basic, community rights—nor the school system jobs that would vanish if Allophones were barred from enrolling in English-language schools—and Anglophone leaders defended the status quo with an admixture of philosophical appeals ("freedom of choice," "individual rights") and threats of capital flight and plant closings. In the aftermath of the crises of 1967–1969, however, growing segments of the Francophone community endorsed policies that would assert the primacy of Francophone "collective" rights—most basically, the "right" to cultural survival—in reshaping schooling and other linguistically vital areas of life in Montreal.

By the end of 1969, there was a near-consensus in the Francophone community that immigrant Anglicization via public schooling posed a fundamental threat to French in Montreal (and, eventually, to all of Quebec as Montreal progressively Anglicized). The main division among Francophones—and it was an important one—was over how to direct the Allophone children of Montreal into the French-speaking sector. Should immigrants be compelled to send their children to French-language schools, or should freedom of choice be respected while the government "encouraged" immigrants to attend French-language schools with "welcoming classes" and other adjustment mechanisms? These issues would be debated through the 1970s as surging Francophone nationalism would continue to pressure the provincial government to enact a comprehensive language policy establishing the primacy of French in Montreal education—as well as in other spheres of public and private life in the metropole.

Chapter 5

A Polarized City, 1970–1976

The 1960s ended in Montreal with a year of unprecedented linguistic unrest. By 1969, with the festering Saint-Léonard crisis and the conflict over Bill 63, Francophone discontent had spawned a veritable wave of street demonstrations, fiery speeches, terrorist violence, and riots. However, few Montrealers were prepared for the linguistic turbulence with which the city began the 1970s. Montreal did not become a Belfast or a Beirut in 1970—far from it. But events in that year, from divisive spring elections to the terrorist violence of the October crisis, confirmed the arrival of a new era in language relations in Montreal. The city's French- and English-speaking communities were now polarized in ways that seriously threatened social peace. For the remainder of the decade, life in Montreal would be dominated by linguistic discord, with the possibility of violence always lurking in the background. The government of Canada enacted policies it hoped would lessen linguistic tensions, and in 1974 a reluctant Quebec government was forced by surging Francophone nationalism to pass a language law that declared French as the province's (and thus Montreal's) only official language. But the Montreal language crisis remained unresolved.

Montreal 1970: A City in Turmoil

The 1970s began with perhaps the most linguistically divisive electoral campaign in Quebec history. The April elections marked the first test of voter support for the Parti québécois, and PQ opponents used every scare tactic imaginable to dissuade Francophones from voting for "separatists." Montreal's English-speaking establishment was particularly aggressive in attempting to discredit the PQ. An editorial in the Montreal *Star* noted the "proclivity of Quebec [Francophone] leaders toward authoritarianism and dictatorship," and likened PQ leader René Lévesque to Kerensky before the Bolshevik revolution: a benign revolutionary "then replaced by lawless fanatics."[1] In addition, the city's Anglophone economic elite heavy-handedly attempted to influence the April elections by orchestrating incidents that darkly hinted at impending economic chaos should the PQ win. On April 4, *La Presse* published a "leaked" letter from the Montreal investment firm of Lafferty, Harwood, and Company advising clients to transfer securities and liquid assets outside Quebec until after the April 29 elections. Another "confidential" Lafferty, Harwood letter, published April 11, warned that the provincial government's credit rating, and hence ability to finance capital projects in Quebec, would plummet with a strong PQ showing in the elections.[2]

More flagrant was the "Brinks Show" in which the Royal Trust Company ostentatiously assembled a convoy of nine Brinks trucks, allegedly carrying securities from its Montreal headquarters to Toronto. The entire event, occurring just three days before the election, was designed for public show as the press was "tipped off and present both at the Montreal point of departure and the Ontario border";[3] to say the least, banks did not ordinarily make the loading of valuables into armored trucks a public event. The desired front page articles appeared the following day in all four major Montreal daily newspapers.[4] The episode was pure political theater, underscoring the Anglophone establishment's staple argument against Francophone nationalism: Anglophones were the effective managers of the Quebec economy and, therefore, to avoid a massive flight of capital from Montreal and the province, Francophones should resist the false allure of nationalism and separatism.

Despite these antics—or, perhaps, because Francophones were so offended by them—the PQ did quite well in the elections. The PQ took 23 percent of the popular vote across the province, far above the vote for separatist parties in 1966, and finished a respectable second behind Robert Bourassa and the Quebec Liberal Party (PLQ).[5] The PQ gained substantial support among Francophone voters in Montreal, winning five seats in working-class districts on the East End where unions, such as the CSN and FTQ, had been particularly active on behalf of the party, and capturing 39.5 percent of the vote in predominantly Francophone ridings on the Island.[6] Discontent with Bill 63 apparently helped the PQ in Francophone Montreal, as a Université de Montréal voter survey showed a solid plurality of anti-Bill 63 Francophones supporting the party.[7]

The April vote reflected a linguistically polarized Montreal. The Island's electorate seemed divided into two hostile camps: a party of Anglophones, Allophones, and federalist Francophones (the PLQ) and a growing party of Francophone nationalists (the PQ). Moreover, the campaign and its

aftermath included some of the most explosive rhetoric dealing with language-group differences ever uttered in mainstream Quebec politics. The
Anglophone establishment continued the drumbeat that Francophone nationalism would wreck the Montreal economy. "Imagine Montreal with no
skyscrapers, no commuter trains, no Métro. Imagine it without its swarm of
taxis, its multiplicity of restaurants and hotels"—that was the threatening
tone of a Montreal *Star* article on the likelihood of Anglophone-controlled
head offices leaving Montreal if the PQ ever came to power.[8]

On the other hand, during and after the election, PQ leaders lashed
out in particularly bitter terms at Anglophone actions such as the "Brinks
Show" and the distortions that appeared in English-language newspapers.
Jacques Parizeau warned that "these people arc just waving a red flag in
front of a fuming bull . . . they are really asking for trouble."[9] René Lévesque declared his "disgust" at "the way information was manipulated in
the Anglo-Saxon establishment in Montreal with its propaganda media, its
disrespect for a population which is treated like 'natives.'"[10] He warned
against "those forces, from St. James Street to the Montreal *Star,* who
seem intent on poisoning the Quebec climate with all kinds of panics, in
order to create divisions between the French-speaking majority and its
many minorities."[11] Lévesque was particularly infuriated with the "chaos
and dictatorship" scare tactics of the April 21 *Star* editorial, labeling it a "collective insult" to French Canadians and fuming that "we've no lesson on that
score to take from the owners of the Montreal *Star*—from anyone that has
been dominating Quebec like a bunch of Rhodesians—the white group. If we
had colors here, you'd feel it."[12] Lévesque's rare anti-English remarks encouraged radicals within the PQ to propose resolutions at the 1971 party
congress that would eliminate English-language schooling rights in an independent Quebec—a resolution that the essentially moderate Lévesque
blocked. Nevertheless, the Anglophone approach to campaign '70, and
Lévesque's fiery response, clearly radicalized sentiment in the Francophone
community.

Montreal also experienced its worst year of linguistic violence in 1970.
Following the April elections, the "urban guerrillas" of the FLQ resumed
their Montreal area bombings, setting off explosions at the Montreal Board
of Trade offices in old Montreal and at residences in Westmount.[13] In October, the FLQ brought Montreal to its most intense moment of linguistic
crisis, kidnapping Great Britain's trade commissioner James Cross and, five
days later, abducting and eventually murdering Pierre Laporte, the provincial minister of immigration and labor.[14] The Bourassa government retreated
into heavily guarded quarters at the Queen Elizabeth Hotel, and for three
weeks no one in Montreal was quite certain how extensive the FLQ operation was or whether a genuine upheaval was underway. The FLQ forced the
broadcast of its "manifesto," a *mélange* of Marxism and Québécois national-

ism, that called upon Francophones to "use all our means, including arms and dynamite, to rid ourselves" of "the big shots who live in Westmount, the Town of Mont Royal, Hampstead, and Outremont, and the fortresses of high finance on St. James and Wall Streets."[15]

The FLQ manifesto seemed to strike a responsive chord among students at Montreal's French-language universities, sparking an *Opération Débrayage* (Operation Walkout) and a wave of "teach-ins." On October 15, the federal government declared that Montreal was in a state of "apprehended insurrection": troops were sent to maintain order in the metropolis and the "War Measures Act" was invoked, suspending civil liberties and permitting the round-up of five hundred suspected FLQ "sympathizers."[16] Montreal was an occupied city.

Several weeks after the tragic murder of Laporte, Cross was released and his kidnappers were permitted passage to Cuba. The FLQ, whose size had been drastically exaggerated during the October crisis, was demolished by the police. For a period, the crisis was effectively exploited by anti-separatists to discredit the PQ and Francophone nationalism. PQ membership, for example, declined from eighty thousand in April 1970 to thirty-five thousand by mid-1971, although the party was able rebound in time for the next provincial elections in 1973.[17] The October crisis was an isolated event: the FLQ was a fringe group, and the rise of the PQ in the 1970s would provide a nonviolent, democratic outlet for growing Francophone nationalist sentiment. Nevertheless, the October crisis provided a vivid illustration of what could happen if Montreal's linguistic passions surged out of control.

The Federal Government and Montreal's Language Question

Aside from the extraordinary brandishing of military force during the October crisis, the federal government also began in the late sixties and early seventies to implement policies designed to respond to the deepening Francophone discontent in Montreal. The rise of separatism in Quebec, fueled by Montreal's linguistic tensions, was increasingly viewed as a genuine threat to Canadian national unity, and the election of Pierre Elliot Trudeau as Canada's prime minister in 1968 was, in part, based on the perception that he could "manage" the Quebec problem. Trudeau was a vigorous opponent of Francophone nationalism, viewing ethnic "particularism" of any sort as reactionary and authoritarian.[18] The interests of Francophones would not be served by turning inward and creating a secure French-speaking ghetto in Quebec. Rather, Trudeau's vision was of a "coast-to-coast" bilingual Canada, in which minority language rights would be entrenched in a constitution and in which Francophones could maintain their language and culture while becoming full participants in Canadian life. "The answer to separatism," believed Trudeau "is making French-speaking Canadians at home . . . in Vancouver and Toronto as well as Montreal."[19]

Before the 1960s, there was little to make Francophones feel "at home" in Canada anywhere outside Quebec. Provincial governments in Western Canada and Ontario systematically refused to establish French-language educational systems.[20] The national capital, federal public administration, and Canadian armed forces functioned entirely in English, and there was little Francophone representation in the middle and upper level of the civil service.[21] Federal statutes were drafted in English, with generally inadequate French translations and, in the absence of simultaneous translations, a Francophone visiting Ottawa rarely heard the Parliament of Canada functioning in French.[22] The "face" of the federal government was resolutely English: for example, a 1960 survey of federal buildings by the Conseil de la vie française, a Quebec-based French-language pressure group, found that only 13.2 percent had bilingual signs, 36.8 percent "had a little French," and 50 percent were exclusively in English.[23] Government services in areas outside Quebec were seldom available in French.

This was the situation diagnosed by the Royal Commission on Bilingualism and Biculturalism, appointed in 1963 to "inquire into and report upon the existing state of bilingualism and biculturalism in Canada and to recommend what steps should be taken to develop the Canadian confederation as an equal partnership between the two founding races."[24] The RCBB prescribed a wide range of policies designed to ensure equal status for French and English throughout Canada, and these recommendations served as the basis for the Trudeau language policies. The central proposals of the RCBB were incorporated in the Official Languages Act of 1969, and many also made their way in Trudeau's crowning political achievement: the Canadian Charter of Rights and Freedoms that was inserted in the Constitutional Accord of 1981.[25] Specifically, federal language policy would be based on the following principles:

1. French and English would be explicitly identified as Canada's official languages;
2. Canadians should be able to communicate with and obtain services from federal institutions in either French or English, in the nation's capital and "wherever there is sufficient demand" for such bilingual services;
3. Bilingual districts would be designated in regions where Francophone or Anglophone minorities exceed 10 percent of the population; these districts were envisioned as places where a full range of federal, provincial, and local government services would be available in both official languages;

4. Canadians of both official language groups should have equal opportunities for employment and advancement in federal institutions, and to work in the official language of their choice;

5. Although education was under provincial government authority, the federal government would provide financial support for second-language education and encourage the provision of schooling in both official languages where numbers warranted (an "encouragement" that became part of the 1981 constitution).

The federal government allocated an estimated $5 billion between 1969 and 1982 to achieve these goals.[26] In the space of a decade, the English face of the federal government was transformed. Federal services were bilingualized and, although the use of French as a language of work in the federal bureaucracy was spotty, by the late 1970s the proportion of Francophones in the civil service had reached 27 percent—slightly higher than the French-speaking share of Canada's population.[27] A Commissioner of Official Languages served as a visible advocate of bilingualism, and the financial inducements of the federal government encouraged second-language teaching in public schools and some expansion in the availability of French-language classes outside Quebec.

Although many Montreal Francophones took advantage of the bilingualization of the federal government to pursue careers in Ottawa, federal policy had little impact on the language situation in the city itself. Francophone mobilization since the early 1960s focused on linguistic inequalities and threats to the French language and culture that existed in Montreal and throughout Quebec. Thus, federal guarantees of French-language services in Ontario or support for French-language schools in Manitoba did little to deflect these basic, Montreal-centered nationalist concerns.

The one area that might have directly affected linguistic dynamics in Montreal, the policy of "bilingual districts," was strongly opposed in Quebec Francophone circles. In 1971, the Bilingual Districts Advisory Board[28] recommended that the entire province of Quebec, with its substantial Anglophone minority, be designated a federal bilingual district. Opposition from even the federalist Quebec provincial government of Robert Bourassa as well as Francophone nationalist groups scuttled the plan.[29] In 1975, a second advisory board considered designating Montreal-only as a bilingual district. The Quebec government, again, strenuously objected, arguing that "matters pertaining to language were policy issues for Quebec to settle within its jurisdiction." After a long and divisive debate, the board decided not to recommend Montreal as a bilingual district because such a designation "might well affect adversely the position of the French language in Montreal." "Treating Montreal differently from other urban centres in Canada," noted the board, especially in view of the "strong, compact, and forceful" position of the city's Anglophone minority, would "increase the disparity of French and English [and] run counter to the intent of the Official Languages Act, which seeks equality of status between the two languages."[30] Ultimately, resistance from virtually all provincial governments forced the federal government in 1977 to abandon the concept of bilingual districts, a tool that had once been considered the key element of federal language policy. Whatever language regime developed in Montreal, it would be forged in the arena of provincial politics.

Holding Action, 1970–1973

The shock of the October crisis and perhaps an ebbing of passion following the emotional events of 1969–1970 seemed to lower the intensity of the language question in Montreal during the early 1970s. Nevertheless, Francophone groups continued to mobilize on the issue. In March 1971, a Mouvement Québec français (MQF) was formed, joining Francophone unions, teachers, and nationalist groups in a common front to repeal Bill 63 and force legislation declaring French as Quebec's sole official language. Headquartered at the offices of the Société Saint-Jean Baptiste de Montréal (SSJBM), the MQF functioned as an important unilingualist pressure group, and by virtue of its petition campaigns, demonstrations, marches, and "popular assemblies," kept the language issue in the public eye. In 1974, when language policy again returned to Quebec's political center stage, the MQF would play a leading role in articulating the Francophone nationalist position.[31]

Quebec's new premier, thirty-seven-year-old Robert Bourassa, was in no hurry to venture into the turbulent waters of language policy during his first mandate (1970–1973). The existence of the Gendron Commission, appointed by Bourassa's predecessor to study the language question and recommend a provincial policy, provided a convenient pretext for delay: before acting on such explosive matters as the language of instruction, Bourassa averred that it was only proper that the Quebec government await the in-depth analysis of the commission. In the meantime, Bourassa hoped that economic growth—his main 1970 campaign theme was "100,000 jobs"—would defuse nationalism and ease concomitant linguistic tensions.[32] In any event, the cautious premier would not be rushed into precipitate action, and was not displeased that the Gendron Commission continually delayed submission of its final report.

Although Bourassa was able to postpone action on a comprehensive language policy through his first mandate, his first administration did venture into several policy matters that involved Montreal's language situation. In January 1971, the Ministry of Education promulgated Regulation 6, a directive specifying how Quebec public schools should ensure, as required by

Bill 63, that students in English-language schools possess "a working knowledge of the French language."[33] Regulation 6 mandated six years of elementary school instruction in French as a second language and five years of similar study in secondary school. Where "pedagogically feasible," English-language schools were encouraged to use French as a medium of instruction in as many courses as possible.[34] Graduation requirements from English-language high schools would now include passing oral and written examinations in French-language proficiency. By the mid-1970s, all Montreal school commissions had implemented Regulation 6, and the rapid development of "French immersion streams" in English-language schools—programs in which a majority of the curriculum was taught in French—demonstrated a growing willingness on the part of Anglophone parents to "bilingualize" in response to Montreal's changing linguistic climate.[35]

But the political impact of Regulation 6 on growing Francophone unrest over language and schooling in Montreal was nil. Improving the French-language skills of Anglophone schoolchildren was perhaps welcome, but unrelated to the central Francophone concerns over the Anglicization of immigrants in the Montreal public schools. Moreover, there was some thought among Francophone school officials that Regulation 6 might have the perverse effect of making English-language schools even more attractive to immigrants interested in ensuring mastery of English *and* French for their children.[36]

The Bourassa government also moved to reorganize the administration of schooling on Montreal Island. In July 1971, Education Minister Guy St. Pierre unveiled Bill 28, a plan that reintroduced the main elements of the Bertrand government's Bill 62. Bill 28 retained the plan to abolish Montreal's hodgepodge of denominational school boards and create eleven unified boards, but several provisions were included to meet Anglophone concerns with the original legislation. Each school board would be elected by universal suffrage, but linguistic minorities would be guaranteed representation. Moreover, each board would have a Catholic and Protestant committee to oversee denominational education in their jurisdiction. Finally, the central authority that Anglophones had feared being vested in a Francophone-controlled Island Council was significantly mitigated: minority representation on the council was guaranteed, and school property and the administration of buildings and equipment would remain under the control of the local boards.[37]

Despite St. Pierre's efforts to enlist broad support for Bill 28, the legislation fell victim to Montreal's increasing polarization over language. Although some Anglophone groups such as the Montreal Board of Trade publicly supported the bill, the PSBGM and Montreal Teacher's Associations both opposed Bill 28 as a threat to Anglophone interests and came out in favor of linguistically autonomous boards.[38] On the other hand, Francophone teachers' unions and other labor groups argued that the weakened powers of the Island Council jeopardized the goal of reducing linguistically based educational inequality in Montreal. Nationalists had envisioned a powerful Island Council redistributing resources from richer, predominantly Anglophone school commissions to disadvantaged, predominantly Francophone boards, but Bill 28 implied that poorer districts would be limited to "the same inferior buildings, equipment, and facilities they had previously." [39]

The Parti québécois and Francophone teachers also polarized matters by injecting the language of instruction issue into the debate over Bill 28. Although the PQ supported unified boards, it insisted that repeal of Bill 63 accompany any school reorganization plan; moreover, the PQ also outlined amendments to Bill 28 that would block non-Anglophones from attending English-language schools and would mandate French as the working language for all school boards. The Corporation des enseignants du Québec (CEQ), the Francophone teachers' union, condemned Bill 28's guarantees of Anglophone representation on the unified boards as making Montreal a "bilingual district" in schooling—an obvious reference to the unpopular federal policy—and asserted that "school structures in Montreal must serve the Francophone majority." [40] This Francophone opposition, and a PQ filibuster in l'Assemblée nationale, led the government to withdraw Bill 28 on December 23, 1971. By linking Bill 28 to the controversial issue of access to English-language schools, the PQ transformed school reorganization from an issue of administrative efficiency to one of language policy, and the Bourassa government simply was not yet willing to endure such a divisive and potentially volcanic debate. [41]

Finally, in December 1972, Bourassa's new Education Minister François Cloutier was able to navigate a school reorganization plan through l'Assemblée nationale. Bill 71 backed away from the controversial plan for unified school boards. Instead, the bill retained Montreal's confessional school structure and reduced the number of school boards on the Island to eight: six Catholic and two Protestant. Bill 71 also created an Island Council, composed of five representatives from the CECM, two from the PSBGM, one each from the six other commissions, and three appointed by the provincial government. However, the policymaking powers of the council would be as limited as in Bill 28. Finally, in an effort to dampen potential opposition to Bill 71, the law was explicitly labeled as temporary: the Island Council would be responsible for formulating a permanent reorganization plan by December 31, 1975. [42]

Although Bill 71 was crafted not to offend the main participants in Montreal's school politics, only Anglo-Protestants and the city's French-Catholic educational establishment strongly favored the bill. [43] Anglo-Catholics opposed Bill 71 because it left them under the jurisdiction of Francophone-controlled boards, a situation that since the Saint-Léonard crisis had become increasingly uncomfortable. A Committee for the Coordination of Anglophone Catholic Education called for Cloutier to set up two Anglo-Catholic commissions on the Island, "to ensure cultural survival," but Cloutier refused.[44]

Francophone nationalist groups also opposed Bill 71, denouncing it as "not changing anything significant in the existing situation. It does not correct the menaces weighing on the Francophone majority. In short, it has not gone far enough."[45] Claude Charron, the PQ spokesman on education, argued that confessional school boards undermined Francophone cultural security and perpetuated "privileges and injustices in Montreal public education, for the benefit of Anglo-Protestants."[46] Charron insinuated that the prominence of Anglophones in the Quebec Liberal party accounted for the Bourassa government's "pro-Anglophone" school reorganization bill.

In the last analysis, the limited and temporary nature of Bill 71, combined with the general lack of public emotion on the issue,[47] permitted the government to enact the legislation. When the Island Council, entrusted with the task of developing a permanent reorganization plan, finally made its recommendations in November 1976 (more than a year behind schedule), it voted by 8–7 to maintain confessional commissions and a weak Island Council: every other alternative was voted down.[48] There simply was no public consensus on the school reorganization issue and, as the PQ discovered in the early 1980s when it controlled the provincial government and made the next major attempt to restructure the administration of Montreal's schools, little public interest in developing one.

Bourassa Prepares to Act

On December 31, 1972, Robert Bourassa lost his main rationale for avoiding action on language policy. After extensive hearings, the preparation of over forty research reports, and the expenditure of $2.3 million, the Gendron Commission finally presented its eagerly awaited (and often delayed) final report. The commission offered an exhaustive analysis of the positions of French and English in schooling, public administration, and the economy in Montreal and across Quebec, and its findings generally mirrored those of the RCBB. In particular, the Gendron Commission emphasized the dominant position of English in the Montreal economy as the key threat to French in the city and across Quebec, and the main reason immigrants chose to send their children to English-language schools. Nonetheless, despite the attraction of English for Montreal's ethnic groups, the demographic studies conducted for the commission projected a solid Francophone majority in Montreal through the twentieth century. Even the demographers' "worst-case" scenarios, assuming migration and fertility trends highly unfavorable to the Francophone community, still projected little danger of *minorisation*.[49]

The commission's policy recommendations were decidedly moderate. As an overarching language policy, it suggested that French be designated the "official language" of Quebec but that English have special status as a "national language." This seemed to be a reworking of Pierre Laporte's 1965 concept of French as a priority language and it left unclear precisely what these designations would mean specifically for language use.[50] The commission argued that making French the language of work in Quebec was vital to the preservation and development of the French language and culture, but it did not delineate any program in which the government would force firms to use French in their operations or hire more Francophones. The Gendron report was particularly moderate in regard to Montreal's most explosive issue: the language of instruction. The commission recommended a buffer-period of three to five years, before considering repeal of Bill 63, to gauge the law's impact fully. Immigrants should be "induced" rather than "coerced" into the French-language schools, through *francisation* of the Montreal economy and special programs such as French-language nursery schools for immigrant preschoolers, summer camps in French for immigrant children, and expansion of the COFI language classes for adults.[51] "A repetition of the Saint-Léonard crisis must at all costs be avoided," stated the commission. "In some situations, the positive solution lies in refraining from action rather than the alternative of precipitate interference."[52]

Montreal's English-speaking community reacted positively to the temperate recommendations of the Gendron report, particularly those concerning Bill 63. The city's Anglophone business establishment, whose leading representatives had paraded before the commission's public hearings to warn that coercive language policy would drive capital and industry from Quebec, pronounced the report acceptable.[53]

On the other hand, the hope that Francophones would embrace the Gendron recommendations, and thus provide a moderate resolution to the language crisis, was dashed. Groups such as the MQF, Montreal's Francophone teachers and labor unions, and the PQ all denounced the Gendron recommendations as "cowardly" and "a Trojan Horse" insofar as Francophone cultural and linguistic security was concerned.[54] Even moderate observers such as Claude Ryan and Université Laval political scientist Léon Dion criticized the report for ambiguity and excessive timidity.[55] Eventually, Commission Chairman Jean-Denis Gendron himself acknowledged the negative Francophone reaction and began to back away from his own commission's recommendations on language and education. Although the demographic studies of the commission should have been reassuring to the French-speaking community, Gendron admitted that the commission "had not fully accounted for the psychological factor: the Francophone fear of *minorisation*," and said that, given the state of Francophone public opinion, "there was now no other option except to modify Bill 63 to obligate immigrants to send their children to French schools."[56]

Premier Bourassa took all of this in, and by the spring of 1973 began private meetings with Anglophone business leaders to discuss language policy. Bourassa told executives of Royal Bank, Royal Trust, the Bank of Montreal, Molson, and other venerable Anglophone-controlled corporations that he could no longer avoid legislating on language, or "he would be destroyed politically."[57] Bill 63 would have to be repealed, French would be symbolically declared Quebec's official language, and measures would be introduced to encourage companies to use more French. While the executives reportedly told Bourassa that they would "go along with a few crazy things in order to achieve the larger result"[58] of defusing the language question, Anglophone business people warned Bourassa that tampering with the language of the economy would drive head offices out of Montreal and discourage investment in the province.[59]

In the October 1973 provincial elections, Bourassa said little about language policy, vaguely mentioning the need to make French the language of work and running on a theme of "cultural sovereignty with a profitable federalism" in deference to growing Francophone nationalist sentiment in Montreal.[60] Bourassa's PLQ was returned to power by an overwhelming margin, garnering 102 of the 110 seats in l'Assemblée nationale. In view of this formidable parliamentary majority, the time seemed propitious for Bourassa to act on the language question, and two major political considerations would influence his approach. Despite the sizable PLQ victory in 1973, the PQ had continued to gain support, winning 44.5 percent of the vote in predominantly Francophone ridings on Montreal Island.[61] Clearly, the PQ was claiming a growing share of the Francophone electorate with its aggressive stand on the language question, and Bourassa believed it important to defuse the issue in a way that blunted the PQ's nationalist appeal and avoided "mortgaging his political future."[62] On the other hand, Montreal Anglophones represented, by some estimates, 25 to 30 percent of the PLQ's provincewide electoral base; thus, Bourassa also needed to avoid alienating these voters as he drafted a language law to quiet nationalist rumblings.[63] In his politically inspired effort to find a middle ground between Anglophones and Francophone nationalists, Bourassa would create a political and policy disaster.

Bill 22: A Policy Disaster

During the fall and winter of 1973–1974, Bourassa worked with Education Minister François Cloutier to draft a language bill. Apparently there was little consultation with other members of the cabinet on the matter, and Bourassa's discussions with Anglophones on language policy were limited mainly to business elites.[64] This insulated approach may account for the fiasco that followed, for, in the end, Bourassa's language legislation was opposed by Anglophones, Allophones, *and* Francophone nationalists; more-over, even as the outcry over his policy grew, the premier seemed oblivious to the true state of public opinion. Elements of the Bourassa plan were floated in the Montreal press in February 1974.[65] The reports hinted at efforts to encourage the use of French in the workplace, repeal of Bill 63, and access to English-language schools limited on the basis of some vague linguistic proficiency tests. The response to these trial balloons was not promising: criticisms emerged immediately from Francophone linguistic pressure groups, important voices in the Anglophone community, and both the French- and English- language media. The Montreal English-language press denounced the contemplated repeal of Bill 63 as an "intrusion by the state into individual choice and personal liberty";[66] on the other side, the Mouvement Québec français warned that failure by the Bourassa govern-ment to formulate a "sharp and clear" language policy would contribute to "a deterioration in the social climate and risk starting a brutal confrontation be-tween Anglophones and Francophones in Quebec."[67]

Despite these warning signals, Bourassa forged ahead. On May 22, 1974, he presented Bill 22, entitled "The Official Language Act," to l'As-semblée nationale. The bill marked an end to the officially equal status that French and English had held in Montreal and Quebec since Confederation. Bill 22 forthrightly declared that "French is the official language of Quebec" and declared the government's intention to promote French as "the ordinary language of communication" in all spheres of Quebec life. As the preamble stated:

> The French language is a national heritage which the body politic is duty bound to preserve, and it is incumbent upon the government of Quebec to employ every means in its power to ensure the pre-eminence of that language and promote its vigor and quality.[68]

Bill 22 required that all texts and documents in public administration be drawn up in French and that "the French language must be in use at every level of business activity, especially in corporate management and firm names, on public signs . . . and in consumer contracts."[69] However, Bill 22 was emphatically *not* a French unilingualist policy: although it mandated a form of French priority in most areas, English-language rights were explic-itly written into the bill, and Anglophones retained control over their com-munity institutions. For example, local governments and school boards in areas that were at least 10 percent English-speaking were required to draw up official documents in French and English. Moreover, both French and En-glish were permitted as the languages of internal communication for public institutions in these communities. Finally, while billboards and other public signs were now required to be in French—a stipulation meant to meet nationalist concerns over the insufficiently French face of Montreal—English was not proscribed. In short, despite the bold rhetoric of French promotion in the preamble of Bill 22, there was a healthy dose of bilingualism throughout the bill itself.[70]

The two central areas in the language issue were the economy and schools, and Bill 22 addressed both. French would be promoted as Quebec's language of work through a program of business *francisation* administered by a Régie de la langue française. Firms wishing to receive subsidies, contracts, or other benefits from the provincial government would be required to receive certificates of *francisation* from the Régie. Bill 22 listed several ways in which a company could manifest *francisation:* knowledge of French on the part of management and "personnel"; a "francophone presence in management"; and the general use of French as a language of written and oral communication in the firm.[71] Based on these criteria, the Régie would then conduct an analysis of the language practices of the firm and determine whether a certificate of *francisation* should be granted.

However, the ambiguity of these provisions, coupled with the lack of meaningful enforcement mechanisms, made it unclear how seriously Bill 22 would affect linguistic dynamics in the Montreal economy. For example, Bill 22 did not specify how the *francisation* criteria should be weighed or evaluated by the Régie. Concepts such as "the francophone presence in management" or "knowledge of French" by company personnel were ambiguous— for example, how many Francophones constituted a Francophone managerial presence? This ambiguity meant that the discretion of the Régie would be crucial in determining the rigorousness of the government's *francisation* program, and Francophone nationalists were wary of how the Régie would regulate corporate language practices in the absence of firm legislative guidelines.[72] The Régie was given further latitude by wording, inserted into Bill 22 at the behest of Minister of Trade and Commerce Guy St. Pierre, that evaluation of corporate *francisation* programs take into account "the situation and structure of each firm, of its head office, and of its subsidiaries and branches."[73] It did not require much imagination to envision many thoroughly English-speaking Montreal corporations, particularly those with operations outside Quebec, receiving certification under these guidelines from a Régie interested in maintaining a good investment climate.

In addition to these ambiguities, the efficacy of Bill 22 was inherently limited by its reliance on incentives as opposed to coercion to promote the position of French in the economy. An economist by training, Bourassa shared the neo-classical assumptions of most in his profession and was loathe to interfere in the internal workings of private enterprise. Moreover, the English-speaking business community, with whom Bourassa had closely consulted on Bill 22, had made it clear that coercive *francisation* was unacceptable. As the Montreal Board of Trade stated in its brief on the bill:

The Board is opposed to the institution of "francization" certificates as contemplated in the bill because of the strong possibility of discrimination and abuse. If certificates are to be introduced at all, they should only be used as a means of qualifying their recipients for subsidies [and] grants. . . . The Board reaffirms its belief that incentives rather than coercion have a far greater chance of accelerating the progress already made in obtaining greater participation of Francophones in all levels of business enterprises in Quebec.[74]

Thus, the only coercion in Bill 22 involved companies doing business with the government: if firms were willing to forego provincial government contracts or subsidies, they could avoid the costs of *francisation* altogether. Although some Anglophone businessmen fretted over the discretion given the Régie,[75] most understood that Bill 22 was not about to disrupt Anglophone control or the use of English in the Montreal economy.

The most controversial and, ultimately, most disastrous portion of Bill 22 dealt with access to English-language schools. Freedom of choice in the language of instruction, inscribed in provincial law by Bill 63, had resulted in a continuing Anglicization of Montreal public schooling. "Persuasion" programs such as COFI or the CECM's *classes d'accueil* had not altered the basic tendency of Montreal's Allophones to enroll their children in the Island's English-language schools: By 1973–1974, 88.6 percent of Montreal's Allophone schoolchildren received their instruction in English.[76] Although, contrary to nationalist rhetoric, there was no surge of *Francophone* enrollments in the Island's English-language schools,[77] approximately 3 percent of Montreal's French-speaking schoolchildren were being educated in the Island's English-language schools on the eve of Bill 22.[78]

As a result of these trends, the share of total Montreal school enrollments claimed by the English-language sector had risen from 36.8 percent in 1970 to 40.3 percent in 1974.[79] The end of the baby boom and slowing immigration had reduced Montreal Island's school enrollments starting in 1970. But under Bill 63, Francophone schools lost their clientele at roughly *three* times the rate of the Anglophone network (a decline of 18.4 percent in the French-language schools as opposed to only a 5.7 percent reduction in English-language enrollments). In some districts, such as the Jérôme Le Royer Catholic School Commission, which covered the East Island suburbs and included the "hot-spot" of Saint-Léonard, the trends were even more ominous from a Francophone perspective. Under freedom of choice, enrollments in the English-language schools of Jérôme Le Royer increased by 69.7 percent between 1970 and 1974, bolstered by Italian-origin pupils who constituted over 80 percent of the district's "Anglophone" school clientele.[80] By contrast, French-language enrollments in the district declined by 1.4 percent under Bill 63.

These trends reinforced the Francophone anxieties that had developed over the schools issue in the late sixties. The rhetoric of the MQF, PQ, and the CEQ had begun to mold mass opinion and, as Jean-Denis Gendron observed, by 1974 the perception seemed widespread among Francophones that the Anglicization of public schools presaged a Francophone *minorisation* in Montreal. Moreover, the rapid drop in French-language school enrollments, with attendant school closings and potential staff reductions, increased pressures from Montreal's Francophone educational bureaucracy for policies that would require all non-Anglophones to enroll their children in the Island's French-language schools. The highly vocal teachers' union, the CEQ, called for an immediate end to freedom of choice and a "repatriation" into the French-language schools of all Francophones enrolled in English-language schools since Bill 63 came into effect in 1969.[81] Similarly, by 1973–1974, the officials of the CECM were clearly on record in favor of requiring non-Anglophones to attend French-language schools. As Thérèse Lavoie-Roux, president of the CECM, stated: "The CECM, daily witness of the Anglicization of the majority of immigrants coming to Montreal as well as a percentage of the French-Canadian population, has taken vigorous positions on the necessity to integrate non-Anglophones into the French-language school and for priority status to be accorded French as a language of instruction."[82]

Sensing that the nationalist mobilization on this question had reached proportions that threatened Montreal with perpetual "social tensions,"[83] Bourassa decided to end parental freedom of choice in the language of instruction. Bill 22 declared French the language of instruction in the public schools, although "school boards . . . shall continue to provide instruction in English."[84] Access to English-language schools would be limited to pupils possessing "sufficient knowledge" of English; all others were required to receive their instruction in French. School boards were required to determine, on the basis of linguistic aptitude, the assignments of pupils; however, Bill 22 authorized the Minister of Education to "set tests to ascertain that pupils have sufficient knowledge of the language of instruction to receive their instruction in that language."[85] The Minister could, on the basis of these tests, overturn assignment decisions made by the school boards. Although Bill 22 did not require immigrants or Francophones to attend French-language schools, the obvious hope of the government was that the English proficiency tests would have that effect.

Bourassa was completely unprepared for the firestorm that followed the presentation of Bill 22. Anglophone groups, stunned by the abrogation of free access to English-language schools and the generally diminished status of English proclaimed in the bill, reacted furiously. The English-language press, in Montreal and across Canada, condemned Bill 22 as a discriminatory denial of Anglophone "rights." The ambiguities in the bill, coupled with the discretionary power left in the hands of the Minister of Education and local school boards in administering the Bill 22 tests, were denounced as opening the door for abuses by linguistic "extremists." Said the Montreal *Gazette:*

> With this legislation the English-speaking would lose the right established by custom and tradition to an education in English. Instead, education in English would become an exceptional privilege. This would be a law providing, not for the rule of law, but for the rule of men through regulation.[86]

Groups associated with English-language education also ferociously attacked Bill 22. Briefs were presented by the PSBGM, the Montreal and Provincial Associations of Protestant Teachers, the Federation of English-speaking Catholic Teachers, and the Quebec Association of School Administrators, each calling for Bourassa to withdraw the bill.[87] Common themes ran through the presentations of all these organizations. First, Bill 22 was deemed unacceptable by any philosophical standard, abrogating individual rights in the name of a distorted concept of Francophone collective rights. Second, by declaring French Quebec's sole official language, the legislation unjustly denied the historical place of English in Montreal and Quebec society. Third, the concerns over Francophone cultural security motivating Bill 22 were spurious: the primacy of French in Quebec was already assured, and Anglophones accepted this fact by sending increasing numbers of children into French immersion programs. Fourth, the bill was poorly crafted, leaving far too much discretionary authority to be abused by zealous bureaucrats. Finally, Anglophone educators predicted that Bill 22 would have disastrous consequences on their organizations by drastically reducing the potential clientele of English-language schools.

Montreal's Italian community was more circumspect in its opposition to Bill 22, wanting to avoid a recrudescence of the Saint-Léonard violence in which Francophone nationalists painted Italians, because of their schooling demands, as a threat to French-speaking society. The Fédération des associations italiennes du Québec, led by Pietro Rizzuto, endorsed the "broad goals" of Bill 22 to build a *Québec français*. But, the fédération denounced the educational provisions of the bill as discriminatory and arbitrary. Putting four- and five-year-old children through traumatic tests was criticized, as was the absence of "acquired rights" that would guarantee Italian children enrolled in English-language schools at the time Bill 22 was implemented the right to continue in them. Moreover, Italian parents were horrified at the prospect that some of their children might fail the Bill 22 tests and be unable to join older siblings in the English-language schools. Immigrant parents, counting on older siblings to help with schooling, now faced the frightening possibility of linguistic splits within their own families.[88]

Reaction from the Francophone nationalist community to Bill 22 was

equally negative. The linguistic proficiency tests were widely viewed by nationalists as a sham, especially in view of the discretionary powers granted
the Minister of Education. Various Francophone educational groups appeared before the parliamentary committee studying Bill 22, armed with
data outlining the precarious state of French-language education in Montreal
and cogently making the case for stronger government action.[89] The Bill 22
tests were criticized as likely to be ineffective, particularly if administered
by a lax Minister of Education. The MQF criticized the concessions to bilingualism contained throughout the bill, but especially denounced Bill 22 for
maintaining the status of English as an official language of instruction rather
than a privilege for genuine English-speakers.[90] Québécois were urged "to
rise as one to protest vigorously this hypocritical treason toward our most
sacred rights."[91] After Bill 22 was passed, the MQF intensified its opposition, organizing a march of fifteen thousand persons in Quebec City in October 1974 to demand a new, stronger language law.

    Bourassa serenely believed that opposition to Bill 22 was the work of
linguistic extremists, and that the "silent majority" from all communities
would see that he had put together a genuine compromise.[92] The premier
considered Bill 22 the middle ground on the language question between "Anglophone 'Orangemen' and the separatist Parti québécois," and viewed the
uproar as a "passing effervescence."[93] In fact, however, there was no middle ground; Bourassa had proposed legislation that fell "between two poles
of public opinion representing two conflicting principles."[94] What's more, in
Bourassa's attempt to avoid a clear statement on access to English-language
schools by leaving many decisions to the discretion of his Education Ministry, *both* linguistic communities feared that their educational interests would
not be served by Bill 22. This uncertainty about how the bill would operate
could only fuel anxiety and promote further conflict.

    Hearings were held on the bill in June, and only a handful of the sev-
enty-four groups presenting briefs expressed support for the legislation.
These tended to be business groups such as the Francophone Chambre de
Commerce du district de Montréal and Anglophone companies such as Bell
Canada.[95] In addition, Bourassa faced a mini-rebellion within his parliamentary caucus over Bill 22, from both Anglophone backbenchers and some
Francophones in the cabinet.[96] Thus, in July, the government amended the
bill slightly to meet some of the concerns of both linguistic communities.
English-language schooling had not been formally guaranteed in the first
version of Bill 22; the final version wrote such recognition into the legislation, although limits were placed on the expansion of English-language instruction (see the following). The business *francisation* program was slightly
strengthened. However, aside from these changes, Bill 22 went forward as
originally presented by Bourassa. The scene at l'Assemblée nationale was
rowdy: there was a PQ filibuster and, at one point, some protestors in

chains appeared in the gallery to disrupt debate. Nevertheless, Bourassa was determined to enact the bill by the end of July. With his massive parliamentary majority, the premier invoked cloture and on July 31, 1974, having passed by a vote of 92 to 10, Bill 22 became law.

Implementation of Bill 22 on the language of schooling produced all of the uncertainties, inequities, and conflicts that critics had predicted. Although the bill was enacted in July 1974, the articles regarding the language of instruction did not take effect until the 1975–76 school year; thus, there was a one-year delay in which controversy and anxiety over the Bill 22 tests intensified. An organization called the Consiglio Educativo Italo-Canadese, formed to represent the Italian community on the language issue, set up Saturday morning "clandestine classes" in church basements and private homes to tutor four- and five-year-old Italian children for the language-proficiency tests they would now have to pass to gain admission to English-language schools.[97] In the meantime, controversy grew as it became apparent that vast differences would exist among local school commissions over the criteria used to admit children to English-language schools. In the PSBGM, for example, the Bill 22 "test" consisted of a simple parental declaration of their child's linguistic competence. The CECM was slightly more demanding, assigning pupils to English-language schools on the basis of interviews that determined their knowledge of English, but liberally sprinkling the process with exemptions.[98] As a result, for the 1975–76 school year, the CECM accepted 76 percent of the applicants for admission to English-language schools; only 8 percent of the rejected applicants enrolled in French-language schools, with the remaining 16 percent not enrolling at all (and presumably attending either CECM English-language classes illegally or enrolling in the PSBGM).

In contrast to the PSBGM and CECM, admission to English-language schools in 1975 was much more difficult in the Jérôme Le Royer School Commission. Bill 22 had included the following provision, inserted in a last-minute amendment to placate nationalist dissatisfaction with the bill:

> An existing or future school board . . . cannot validly decide to commence, cease, increase, or reduce instruction in English unless it has received prior authorization from the Minister of Education, who shall not give it unless he considers that the number of pupils whose mother tongue is English and who are under the jurisdiction of such body warrants it.[99]

For districts such as the PSBGM or CECM, with declining enrollments in both linguistic sectors, this provision was innocuous. But, in districts such as Jérôme Le Royer, with swelling Italian-origin enrollments causing annual *increases* in the number of pupils receiving instruction in English, there were potential problems. Increases in English-language instruc-

tion could only be authorized by the Minister of Education, and these additional slots could only be for pupils whose mother tongue was English. In
other words, Italian children could pass the Bill 22 tests, and still be denied
admission to English-language schools by this "enrollment cap" amendment—which is precisely what happened to three hundred and fifty Italian
children in Jérôme Le Royer in August, 1975. Italian parents, through the
Consiglio, demanded that their children be admitted to the English-language
schools—after all, they had passed those odious language tests—but the
new Education Minister Jérôme Choquette insisted on enforcing the cap. In
late September, however, when Bourassa seemed to side with the Consiglio, the mercurial Choquette abruptly resigned.[100] The additional places to
accommodate Italian schoolchildren in Jérôme Le Royer were eventually authorized, proof to nationalists that the Bourassa government would not use
Bill 22 to make French the language of instruction in Montreal.

On the other hand, the Jérôme Le Royer affair heightened uncertainty
over precisely what criteria determined access to English-language schools,
serving only to reinforce the growing insecurity of Montreal's Anglophone
and Allophone communities regarding their language rights in schooling.
Anxiety among these groups was compounded in 1976 when the Ministry of
Education (MEQ) asserted its powers under Bill 22 to administer its own
language-proficiency tests and to require school boards to revise the assignment of pupils on the basis of the MEQ tests.[101] In May 1976, for example,
the MEQ accepted only 499 of the 2,413 applications for English-language
schools deemed admissable by the CECM; the other children were required
to take MEQ language tests. Approximately 50 percent of these children
passed the MEQ tests, leaving many others in the "gray area": having "sufficient knowledge" of English according to the local board, but not in the
eyes of the MEQ.[102] Ultimately, the minister left final placement decisions to
the local school boards. The entire process, however, involving varying admissions standards from board to board and with "double jeopardy" as children faced MEQ evaluations that could overturn local board decisions, was
harrowing for Allophone parents and left Montreal schooling in a state of
tension and disarray.

During its two years in force, Bill 22 had a mixed impact on enrollment
trends in the Montreal schools. By no means did the law channel most immigrants into the French-language schools, but by 1976–77, 22.3 percent of
the Island's Allophone pupils received their instruction in French, double the
ratio that prevailed before Bill 22 was adopted.[103] Concomitantly, Bill 22
slowed down the relative depopulation of Francophone schools that was occurring under Bill 63. French-language school enrollments declined by 11.5
percent while Bill 22 was in effect, compared with a 7.8 percent drop in the
English-language clientele; clearly, the gap in the rate of enrollment change
between the two networks was much closer under Bill 22 than Bill 63.[104]

However, although the gap may have closed, enrollments in the French-language schools continued to decline more rapidly than in the English-language sector. As a result, the Anglo-network share of total Montreal Island enrollments grew from 40.3 percent to 41.2 percent under Bill 22, and the Conseil scolaire de l'île de Montréal projected in 1976 that if Bill 22 remained in force, by 1985, 43.3 percent of Montreal's school clientele would be receiving their instruction in English.[105] By late 1976, with continuing agitation over Bill 22, it was clear that Bourassa had not solved, to anyone's satisfaction, the core problem animating language conflict in Montreal: regulating access to English-language schooling on the Island. Calls for repeal of the Bill 22 tests came from all quarters, and by early November, in the midst of a tough electoral campaign, Bourassa announced that he would attempt to "humanize" the Bill 22 school assignment process after the elections.[106] He never got the chance.

Conclusion

Rejected by Francophone nationalists as insufficiently vigorous in its promotion of French, Bill 22 nevertheless marked an important shift in Montreal's linguistic balance of power. For the first time since they rioted and burned down the Parliament in 1849, Montreal's Anglophone community clearly felt that it had lost control of the city's linguistic agenda. Bill 22 proclaimed a "French Quebec": Montreal was no longer officially bilingual, and although Bill 22 protected Anglophone privileges in a number of key areas, the "majority psychology" of Anglophones was shattered by the bill.[107] Anglophones were simultaneously enraged and bewildered at what was happening. English was the language of Canada's majority: how then could the Quebec government restrict the rights of Canadian citizens living in Quebec to send their children to English-language schools?[108] Even though Montreal's linguistic climate had obviously changed since the early 1960s, most Anglophones still regarded the threat of *any* restrictions on English in Montreal as an impossibility. Montreal in 1974 was still, in the perception of most Anglophones, a city in which English was the truly significant language, even if the Anglophone elite had begun making tactical concessions to concepts of dualism and bilingualism. Thus, the new linguistic regime delineated in Bill 22 put Anglophones in a state of collective shock.

English-speaking Montreal was politically ill prepared for the changes in linguistic practices entailed by Bill 22, particularly the erosion of the consociational structure through which Anglophone elites had historically ensured the autonomy of English-language institutions. Montreal's Anglophones had always relied on the economic power of its elites and the threat of capital flight to control the city's linguistic dynamics, and in drafting the economic sections of Bill 22, Bourassa conducted numerous, behind-the-scenes negotiations with Anglophone business leaders. This historical reliance on back-channel, elite accommodation, however, had left the Anglophone community with little sophistication in political mobilization and in-fighting. As a result, when elite accommodation failed to protect their position on language and schooling, Anglophones angrily flailed out, gathering for mass meetings at places like Loyola College to denounce Bourassa and the "repression" of Bill 22, and raising tensions in the city by mindlessly comparing 1970s Quebec to Nazi Germany.[109]

Robert Bourassa had made two calculations in introducing Bill 22 that backfired badly. First, he assumed that Francophone nationalists would be satisfied with the repeal of Bill 63 and his business *francisation* program and that he would break the momentum the PQ was building on the language issue. Not only did Bourassa utterly fail to mollify groups such as the MQF, CEQ, and other nationalist organizations in the vanguard of Montreal's *action linguistique,* but his perceived incompetence in drafting a clear, unambiguous policy alienated many moderate Francophones and actually helped the PQ gather support. As the implementation of Bill 22 exacerbated rather than mitigated tensions and uncertainty in Montreal, confidence in Bourassa's ability to manage the language question plummeted.

Second, Bourassa gambled, in attempting to meet the concerns of Francophone nationalists, that Anglophones and Allophones would generally accept his language policy because the only alternative—the Parti québécois—would obviously be even worse. Here again, the premier was dead wrong. He called a snap election in the fall of 1976, presumably hoping to gain another mandate and put the language question behind him. Anglophone and Allophone outrage at Bill 22 was obvious throughout the campaign and in the election results. A Montreal-based party, the Democratic Alliance, ran on a platform asserting that French "should be encouraged in all sectors of Quebec life, but not imposed," and advocated freedom of choice in the language of instruction. Its candidates received 10 percent of the vote in the heavily Anglophone riding of Notre-Dame-de-Grâce and 13 percent in equally English-speaking Westmount.[110]

But the main way in which Montreal's recalcitrant Anglophones vented their electoral anger at Bourassa and Bill 22 was by voting for the heretofore moribund Union nationale, which opportunistically advocated repeal of Bill 22's provisions on the language of instruction.[111] As Table 5.1 shows, UN support skyrocketed in 1976 in the five chief Anglophone ridings on Montreal Island. This was a protest vote; after 1976, the UN all but disappeared from Quebec politics, and Anglophones returned to a PLQ no longer headed by *ex*-Premier Robert Bourassa.

Nevertheless, in 1976 Anglophone voters punished Bourassa for Bill 22, demonstrating the depth of their disaffection with Montreal's changing

Table 5.1

The 1973 and 1976 Provincial Election Vote in Montreal's Predominantly
Anglophone Ridings, by Percentage Vote

Riding	PLQ 1973	PLQ 1976	UN 1973	UN 1976
D'Arcy-McGee	93.8	68.0	0.5	22.5
Pointe-Claire	87.8	35.1	0.9	45.0
Jacques-Cartier	69.2	35.4	2.5	31.1
Notre-Dame-de-Grâce	81.6	43.9	1.5	29.1
Robert Baldwin	81.0	35.9	0.8	26.2
Westmount	76.9	50.7	0.9	20.6

Sources: Rapports du président général des élections pour 1973 et 1976 (Québec: Gouvernement du Québec, 1973, 1976).

linguistic landscape. Any Anglophone comfort derived from defeating Bourassa was short-lived, however, for the stunning victor in the 1976 provincial elections was none other than the Parti québécois. The result would be a new, more radical language policy that not only wiped out the last vestiges of Montreal's consociational linguistic regime, but radically affected English-language institutions in ways that actually made some Anglophones look back with nostalgia at the policies of Bill 22.

Chapter 6

Bill 101 and the Politics of Language, 1977–1989

November 15, 1976, was a landmark date in Quebec political history. On that date, the Parti québécois scored a stunning triumph in the provincial elections, and by nightfall all of Montreal knew that a new and uncertain era in language group relations was about to begin. Pre-election polls had indicated a PQ victory was possible, but no one—not even party leader René Lévesque—had truly expected that the PQ would win an election as early as 1976. The PQ triumphed chiefly on the basis of popular discontent with the bumbling PLQ government, but there were clear signs in Montreal that the party's success also stemmed from the continuing politicization of Francophone nationalism in the city. The PQ swept all seventeen predominantly Francophone ridings on the east end of the Island, garnering over 52 percent of the vote there, and carried many of the Francophone suburbs on the North and South Shores.[1] Standing before an exultant throng of *péquistes* at Montreal's Paul Sauvé Arena, PQ leader and soon-to-be provincial Premier René Lévesque emotionally exclaimed: "I have never been so proud to be *Québécois*." Celebrations lasted through the night in Francophone Montreal, and even for non-*indépendantiste* Francophones there was a feeling of cultural exhilaration attached to the PQ triumph. Said one prominent federalist Francophone: "Many people had tears in their eyes and could not tell why."[2]

In English-speaking Montreal, the reaction was profoundly different. Shock, dismay, apprehension, and not a small amount of panic were manifested in the days and weeks following the "separatists'" triumph. "Make no mistake, those bastards are out to kill us," said Charles Bronfman, the powerful Anglophone capitalist whose holdings included Seagram's, CEMP (the family trust with major real estate holdings), and the Montreal Expos

111

baseball team.[3] In the weeks following the PQ victory, wrote Mordecai Richler, "there seemed to be more For Sale—*A Vendre* signs than impatiens on the lawns of the privileged suburb of Westmount . . . and rare was the West Island home that couldn't be had at a bargain price."[4] A crackpot organization called "the Preparatory Committee for an Eleventh Province" was formed, declaring that if Quebec separated from Canada, "Anglophone territory" in central and western Montreal would not leave with it.[5] All of these reactions were signs of how the tremors of November 15 had shaken English-speaking Montreal. The "unthinkable" had occurred and "separatists" were now in power, a development for which Montreal Anglophones were completely unprepared. Yet, now facing a hostile provincial government over which they had little influence, Anglophones could no longer pretend that Montreal was composed of "two majorities," nor expect that the power of English-speaking business elites would necessarily protect community interests as in the past. Montreal Anglophones were suddenly a vulnerable *minority* desperately in search of a coherent strategy to cope with the changes about to ensue from the PQ triumph.

November 15 promised that, one way or another, a new "linguistic regime" would finally emerge to take the place of Montreal's now defunct consociational framework. The PQ victory offered two main scenarios. First, there was now the real possibility that Quebec might soon become a sovereign, French-speaking state in which Anglophones would have little place and English would have a diminished official status—or none at all.[6] Not surprisingly, then, much energy in both Montreal linguistic communities during the first years of the PQ government was devoted to political mobilization on the "national unity question," cresting in May 1980 when a long-awaited referendum was held on whether the provincial government should begin sovereignty negotiations with Ottawa.[7]

In addition to the independence issue, however, lay *la question linguistique*. For the Montreal-based new middle-class *travailleurs du langage* in the PQ vanguard, the results of the November 15 election presented an opportunity to climax the struggles of the past decade by enacting a language policy that would "accompany, symbolize, and support a *reconquest* by the French-speaking majority."[8] The PQ had capitalized throughout the 1970s on nationalist dissatisfaction with the language situation in Montreal and had pledged during the 1976 campaign to replace Bill 22 with a more aggressive language policy. Now in power, the PQ was expected to deliver. The result, barely nine months after the November elections, would be Bill 101, a law that irrevocably transformed Montreal's linguistic landscape.

The PQ Enacts a Language Policy

The PQ was not a monolithic force, and divisions had always existed within the party over language policy. Ever since the party's founding in 1968, René Lévesque had battled with hard-line unilingualists, particularly those in the Montréal-Centre chapter of the party, over guarantees for the existence of English-language institutions in an independent Quebec.[9] Lévesque agreed that, in the absence of independence, the situation in Montreal required legislation to bolster the position of French; nonetheless, he regarded the whole process as "fundamentally humiliating" and thought that language laws were "instruments that only a colonized society would give itself."[10] Lévesque believed that in Quebec's sovereignty lay the solution to *la question linguistique;* an independent Quebec, with French as its official language, would be a "normal country" not needing "legislative crutches" such as restrictive language legislation.[11]

On the other hand, Camille Laurin found nothing at all "humiliating" about language policy.[12] Laurin, the PQ Minister of State for Cultural Development, immediately after assuming office was entrusted with the task of developing a language policy. Unlike Lévesque, Laurin viewed the enterprise not as "mere legislation," but as a *projet de société* that would codify the Francophone reassertion of collective self-esteem launched during the Quiet Revolution. Passing a language law would be a moment of national affirmation that would push Quebec closer to nationhood.[13] Dr. Laurin, a psychiatrist, "saw language legislation as a kind of shock therapy . . . which would give French-speaking Quebecers a sense of their identity, and bring the English-speaking community 'to its real proportions.'"[14] This hard line represented the majority view in the PQ caucus, and the language policy promulgated in 1977 was Laurin's handiwork.

In December 1976, Laurin assembled a working group to help him draft a White Paper delineating a PQ language policy. Composed of well-known nationalist sociologists Guy Rocher and Fernand Dumont, MQF veteran Henri Laberge, former Office de la langue française head Gaston Cholette, and party activist David Payne, the group toiled with uncommon zeal; they believed that theirs was a historic mission. Their intensity was also fueled by the social, psychological, and sociolinguistic assumptions they brought to the endeavor. Laurin viewed language policy as the "collective psychotherapy" necessary to undo the Francophone "experience of conquest and domination, frustration and insecurity,"[15] while Dumont and Rocher saw language in general (and thus the French language in Quebec) not simply as a means of communication but as the core of collective identity, social reasoning, and consciousness.[16] In short, the working-group members saw nothing less than the future of Francophone culture at stake in their enterprise; not surprisingly, the tone of the White Paper they produced reflected this "messianic" fervor.

The White Paper, entitled *Quebec's Policy on the French Language* and released at the end of March 1977, unveiled the PQ policy—"The Charter of the French Language"—and laid out its underpinning logic. Applying the perspective of Dumont and Rocher, the paper argued that if language were the core of collective culture, then French-Québécois culture could not survive in a bilingual framework. As the White Paper stated:

> Francophone demands have nothing to do with "English translations" that policies of bilingualism will guarantee. It is a matter of protecting and developing, in its fullness, an original culture: a mode of being, of thinking, of writing, of creating, of socializing, of establishing relations between groups and individuals and even the conduct of business. This necessity . . . cannot be reached simply because we are accorded a French terminology for realities that remain culturally foreign or hostile.[17]

Thus, whatever the past traditions of linguistic dualism in Quebec policy, the PQ proclaimed that "there will no longer be any question of a bilingual Quebec":[18]

> The Quebec we wish to build will be essentially French. The fact that the majority of its population is French will be clearly visible—at work, in communications, and in the countryside. It will also be a country in which the traditional balance of power will be altered, especially in regard to the economy; the use of French will not merely be universalized to hide the predominance of foreign powers from the French-speaking population.[19]

The White Paper restated the standard post-1960 Francophone concerns about cultural security thus: "If population trends in Quebec continue, there will be fewer and fewer French-speaking Québécois." Immigrant Anglicization was cited as a major threat to Francophone survival; thus, "there is no doubt that the situation of the French language in Quebec justifies vigilance and intervention by the government."[20]

The document then specified what this intervention would entail. A far-reaching *francisation* program for the economy was outlined (see Chapter 7 for a detailed analysis). Public and commercial signs would be in French only, chiefly to give Montreal a *visage français* appropriate to a French city (and to eliminate what the *péquistes* saw as physical reminders of historical Anglophone dominance). Over the initial objections of Premier

Lévesque, the White Paper proposed that Quebec ignore Section 133 of the BNA Act and declare French the sole official language of the provincial legislature and courts.[21] Moreover, the paper called for *all* municipalities, school boards, local health and social service institutions in Quebec, regardless of the linguistic composition of their workforce or clientele, to use French as their language of internal communications, draw up all official texts and documents in French, and communicate with the provincial government and other public agencies in French. Hiring and promotions could only occur if the employee had "appropriate" knowledge of French.[22]

Finally, the White Paper turned to the issue that had proven so explosive in Montreal since the late 1960s: the language of instruction in the public schools. The paper was blunt: while "there can be no question of abolishing English education," the English school "must cease being an assimilating force and must be reserved for those for whom it was intended." "The English minority" should have guaranteed access to English schools, but "it is legitimate to make sure that persons who settle in Quebec in the future send their children to French schools."[23]

The days of "freedom of choice," of course, had ended with Bill 22, but an incendiary question remained: how would it be determined who should have access to the English-speaking schools? The PQ's pre-election program called for "the maximum number of places" in English schools to be "fixed once and for all by the percentage of Anglophones in the total population,"[24] but the Laurin working group rejected this approach as impractical because of the difficulties in defining and verifying who constituted a proper "Anglophone."[25] Employing mother-tongue as an admissions criterion, with Brussels-style linguistic declarations and registration, also was rejected as "open to deceit and false declarations."[26] The Bill 22 approach, testing to verify a child's "native language," was viewed as too ambiguous, ineffective at limiting enrollments in English-language schools, and rather odious (in forcing five-year-old children to take an examination their parents believed would determine the child's future).[27]

Instead, the White Paper opted for clear regulations that would limit access to English-language schools to the following individuals:

1. Any child, one of whose parents received elementary school education in Quebec;
2. Any child already receiving instruction in English, as well as his younger brothers and sisters;
3. Any child, one of whose parents attended English elementary school outside Quebec, provided that the parent is domiciled in Quebec at the time the Charter is adopted.[28]

This "Quebec clause," while far from the radical unilingualist position that proposed abolishing all English-language schooling in Quebec, nevertheless marked a dramatic departure from historical traditions in Montreal and across Quebec. English-language schools would henceforth be limited, once the "grandfather" clauses of the Charter were exhausted, essentially to Anglophones with historical roots in Quebec. Not only would future Allophone immigrants be required to send their children to French schools, but so too would bona fide Anglophones coming to Quebec from the United States, Great Britain, or most controversially, elsewhere in Canada. Montreal Anglophone leadership rightfully saw the "Quebec clause" as a policy that would drastically limit enrollments in English-language schools and reduce the size and vitality of this crucial Anglophone institution. Moreover, by using the boundaries of Quebec to define access to English-language schools, the White Paper reflected "a determination that Quebec, not Canada, should be the preeminent community"[29] making the "Quebec clause," in the minds of many, a separatist gesture.

The PQ caucus itself was divided over the measure. All agreed that Allophones should be compelled to send their children to French-language schools. However, such notables as Lévesque, Intergovernmental Affairs Minister Claude Morin, and MNA Gérald Godin favored a "Canada clause" that would permit English-Canadian children from other provinces to have access to English-language schools in Quebec.[30] Lévesque attempted to compromise the issue by proposing "reciprocity accords" with other Canadian provinces under which any Anglophone child coming to Quebec from a province that guaranteed instruction in French for Francophone children would be permitted to enroll in Quebec's English-language schools. But, Lévesque's offer was spurned by the premiers of English-speaking provinces on the grounds that negotiating such bilateral accords with Quebec would legitimate the PQ's sovereignty aspirations.[31] Thus, Lévesque's compromise failed, and the "Quebec clause" remained part of the PQ language policy.

On April 27, after almost a month of intense public debate on the White Paper, the PQ deposited its language bill, symbolically numbered Bill 1, before l'Assemblée nationale. Bill 1, "The Charter of the French Language," was a faithful legislative translation of the White Paper, containing a Francophone "Bill of Rights" (enshrining the rights to work, consume, receive education, and have government and businesses communicate in French) and the key proposals on education, the economy, and public administration. In addition, the bill proposed the creation of a new "linguistic bureaucracy," designed to implement the Charter and monitor linguistic trends in Quebec.[32] The key new institutions were: the Office de la langue française, which would implement the business and public administration *francisation* programs and "standardize and publicize" French terms and expressions; the

Conseil de la langue française, which would be responsible for research on language questions and advisory reports to the minister in charge of the Charter; and the Commission de surveillance de la langue française, which would investigate alleged violations of the Charter, attempt to mediate disputes, and, as a last resort, report violators to the attorney general for prosecution. Fines ranging from $25 to $5,000 were mandated for violations of the Charter.

The debate over Bill 1 raised linguistic tensions in Montreal to their highest levels since the October crisis of 1970. The city's English-language media riveted almost daily attention on testimony before the parliamentary committee studying the bill.[33] A brief from the PSBGM protested that the bill treated Anglophones as if their very existence in Montreal were a "menace" to French language and culture. The Charter, claimed the PSBGM, threatened "the survival of English-language education,"[34] while others more polemically called the bill "cultural genocide" and compared the PQ to Nazis.[35] On the other hand, briefs from the SSJB de Montréal and the MQF, while generally supportive of Bill 1, insisted that the bill did not go *far enough* because it permitted Allophones and Francophones currently enrolled in English-language schools, as well as their brothers and sisters, to continue their education in English; clearly, these groups sought nothing less than the gradual elimination of Quebec's English-language schools.[36] Anglophone and Allophone[37] groups testified that Bill 1 violated basic human rights, particularly in its provisions on schooling and signs, while business groups warned that Bill 1 would promote capital flight and economic chaos.[38]

Camille Laurin belittled the Anglophone opposition. "English-speaking Quebecers," he warned, "had best learn to see themselves as a minority and not as the Quebec wing of the English-Canadian majority."[39] In language reminiscent of the "Westmount Rhodesian" caricatures of the late 1960s and early 1970s, Laurin scoffed at the Anglophone claim that they were battling for universal human rights:

> The privileges of the Anglo-Québécois minority are the fruit of historical and accidental forces, but they try to mask this incontestable fact and look for ways to perpetuate these privileges, all the while presenting their position as the expression of an absolute right that must be maintained in the interests of humanity. . . . However, it has become clear that the respect for individual rights . . . becomes a delusion and hypocrisy if one does not take into account the social inequalities that limit the use of them.[40]

Anglophones were not the only Montrealers disturbed by Bill 1 and Laurin. Claude Ryan, in a series of editorials in *Le Devoir*, criticized Laurin for his Manichean division of Quebec into "good" Quebecers (pro–Bill 1) and "bad" Quebecers (Anglophones and anti–Bill 1 Francophones).[41] As for Bill 1, Ryan wrote that "the Lévesque government will have succeeded in saddling Quebec with some of the most stifling restrictions ever seen in linguistic and administrative matters. At first glance, the shocking thing about this bill is the rigid, dogmatic, possessive, and authoritarian manner with which it attempts to decree the exclusive use of French."[42] Ryan's concerns, like those of the Anglophone community, were ridiculed by Laurin.

Hearings on Bill 1 continued through July, and the government began to worry that the PLQ might filibuster, thus preventing the bill from being passed in time for the beginning of school in September. To avoid that possibility, the government withdrew Bill 1 and reintroduced the Charter as Bill 101. The new bill, in the words of René Lévesque, "was purged of some excessively authoritarian vocabulary."[43] For example, Bill 1 was liberally sprinkled with phrases such as "the French language is the language of the Québécois people," with the clear subtext that non-French-origin residents of Quebec were not included as "true" citizens of the province. These references were replaced in Bill 101 by wording that left room for non-Francophones to be Quebecers as well.[44]

The new bill also modified the Charter on a number of key policy matters. The most notable revisions were in the private-sector *francisation* program that had been severely attacked by Anglophone *and* Francophone business groups (see Chapter 7). Bill 101 also loosened the original bill's public administration *francisation* program. Although municipal governments would still be required to use only French as their internal working language, Bill 101 permitted school boards and health and social services agencies to "communicate internally" in French and "another language," if the majority of their clientele were non-Francophone. The Office de la langue française would be responsible for designating such "Anglophone" institutions.[45] All local bodies would have until December 31, 1983 to *francise* in accordance with the new requirements of Bill 101. Other major changes from Bill 1 included softening the linguistic surveillance mechanisms of the Charter, exempting businesses employing fewer than five persons from the unilingual French sign requirements (a particular concern of Lévesque's), and permitting temporary residents freedom of choice on the language of instruction for their children.

Despite these revisions, Bill 101 left intact the core of Bill 1, most significantly the highly controversial regulations on the language of instruction.[46] The Anglophone community remained thoroughly opposed to Bill 101, viewing it as an equally odious, if slightly toned-down, version of Bill 1. Finally the PQ, with its sizable majority in l'Assemblée nationale, ended debate and called for the vote. On August 26, 1977, by a vote of 54 to 32, the Charter of the French Language became law. Laurin, in a triumphant speech, lauded Bill 101 as an "act that fundamentally reverses the course of our history of the last two centuries."[47] The legacy of the Conquest, declared Laurin, was now shed: "Quebec is hereafter and forever French."[48] François-Albert Angers, the nationalist leader of the FQF during the Bill 63 battle of 1969, called the passage of Bill 101 "the greatest moment in our history since the founding of Quebec in 1608."[49]

Despite this exuberance, as well as the doomsday scenarios being painted by some Anglophone leaders, Bill 101 was not the radical unilingualist policy envisioned by activists in the language battles of the 1960s and 1970s. In most areas, Bill 101 essentially extended the approach already begun in Bill 22.[50] In particular, while Bill 1 contained some radical regulations on language and the economy, pressure from mainly Montreal-based "employer groups"[51] forced revisions that left Bill 101's *francisation* program only incrementally stiffer than that of Bill 22. Bill 101 was more restrictive than Bill 22 on the language of instruction; yet, on issues such as permitting the siblings of children already enrolled in English-language schools to receive instruction in English, the PQ law was more liberal than Bill 22.

Nevertheless, Bill 101 was unmistakably the policy of an *indépendantiste* party, breaking new ground on matters such as the "Quebec clause," French-only public signs, and mandating French as a language of work in local public institutions regardless of their linguistic composition. Reflecting the particular cultural and economic preoccupations of Francophone *travailleurs du langage,* these aspects of Bill 101 were clearly policies of an "embryonic nation-state," that placed almost all social institutions under a French-language umbrella.[52] To be sure, crucial Anglophone institutions, such as English-language schooling, would continue not only to exist but to receive public support. Their autonomy, however, was clearly reduced and, under Bill 101, the number and size of English-language schools would unavoidably shrink. Most important, the bill's unequivocal affirmation of a *French* Quebec and a *French* Montreal irrevocably transformed the city's linguistic rules of the game. Bill 101 culminated the push, begun during the Quiet Revolution, to assert Francophone hegemony in Montreal, and the law quickly gained near-consensual support within the French-speaking community as the legal and symbolic cornerstone of the Francophone reconquest.[53]

On the other hand, opposition to Bill 101 would become the touchstone of Anglophone resistance to the new linguistic regime. Small wonder: Bill 101 limited Anglophone rights and privileges, threatened English-language schools with a demographic crisis, and reduced the status of the Anglophone community from one of Montreal's "Charter" groups—indeed, a historically "controlling" group—to the most important of many minority "cultural communities" in a French-speaking society. As we will see, Anglophone Montreal changed significantly in the years following Bill 101. But one factor has remained constant in survey after survey: overwhelming opposition to every aspect of Bill 101.[54] By the mid-1980s, Anglophone Montrealers, by and large, had learned to live with the new Montreal created by Bill 101. But very few Anglophones accepted the law as legitimate, and most viewed it as oppressive.

Anglophones and Bill 101

Once the immediate shock generated by the events of 1976–1977 subsided, Montreal's English-speaking community adjusted to Quebec's new linguistic regime in several ways. The initial response, for many Anglophones unable to accept the PQ victory and Bill 101, was simple: they left the province. Montreal Anglophones have always been highly mobile; a 1978 survey, for example, revealed that only 58.6 percent were born in Quebec.[55] Despite this tradition of mobility, Montreal's Anglophone population grew in the past because "out-migration" from the city historically was outweighed by three other migration streams: (1) Anglophones leaving the Eastern Townships and other areas of small town and rural Quebec for Montreal; (2) Allophones coming to Montreal and integrating into the English-speaking community; and (3) English-speaking immigrants, from Britain in the nineteenth century and then from elsewhere in Canada, drawn to Montreal as the urban center of the Canadian economy.

However, by the mid-1960s, as Montreal lost its national economic status and its linguistic climate deteriorated, migration patterns shifted noticeably. There was an increase in Anglophone departures for Ontario and Western Canada, while fewer English Canadians emigrated to the city to replace them. The result, between 1966 and 1976, was the net loss of 68,000 English-speaking Montrealers through interprovincial migration (although the absolute number of Anglophones[56] in Montreal increased through the early 1970s as a result of international migration and "linguistic transfers").[57] After 1976, however, this "negative interprovincial migration balance" of the 1970s became a full-fledged Anglophone flight from Montreal. Between 1976 and 1981, the number of Anglophones living in metropolitan Montreal fell by 83,000, a decline of 14 percent. Although the rate of out-migration slowed significantly between 1981 and 1986, the metropolis' Anglophone population nevertheless dropped by another 16,000.[58]

Thus, in the ten years following the 1976 PQ triumph, the Anglophone population in metropolitan Montreal declined by one-sixth (99,000). Table 6.1 shows how this Anglophone exodus transformed the linguistic composition of Montreal's West Island, the heartland of English-speaking Quebec. By 1986, the majority of West Island residents no longer were of English mother tongue (although the adoption of English as a "home language" by West Island Allophones and Francophones has enabled the area to retain a strongly English character). Municipalities such as Beaconsfield, Hampstead,

Table 6.1
The Changing Linguistic Composition of the West Island Suburbs: 1971–1986

Year	% by Mother Tongue			% by Language Spoken at Home		
	English	French	Other	English	French	Other
1971	62.7	27.2	10.4	68.9	25.7	5.3
1976	62.7	27.6	9.7	Not available		
1981	53.2	30.1	16.7	64.9	28.8	6.3
1986	48.9	33.2	17.9	61.8	31.8	6.4

Sources: Statistics Canada, *Census of Canada,* 1971, 1976, 1981, 1986 (catalogues 92–726, 92–822, 93–929, 95–130).

Côte-Saint-Luc, Kirkland, and Pointe-Claire, once almost homogeneously Anglophone, now boasted significant Francophone minorities.[59]

Why did so many Anglophones abandon Montreal after 1976? A detailed study by Uli Locher found that English-speaking out-migrants cited primarily economic factors in their decision to leave Montreal: job transfers, new employment offers, or simply the search for better economic opportunities. Thus, he concludes: "Nothing suggests that the 'Anglophone exodus' should be interpreted as a flight motivated principally by political and linguistic factors."[60]

However, strictly "economic" and "politicolinguistic" factors are not easily disentangled in post–Bill 101 Montreal. As we examine in Chapter 8, Bill 101 strongly influenced the "opportunity structure" in Montreal, increasing the value of French in the city's labor market and narrowing the range of options open to unilingual Anglophones. Thus, a self-described "economic" exit from Montreal may very well have been a response to conditions shaped by Bill 101. Moreover, Locher's own survey of expatriate Anglophones shows that over 73 percent attached at least "a certain importance" to language legislation as a reason for their departure, and 28.9 percent cited language laws and political conditions as the primary reason for leaving Montreal.[61] Certainly the timing of the exodus suggests the importance of political factors: while long-term economic trends exerted ineluctable pressures for Anglophones to leave Montreal and discouraged English Canadians from moving to the city, the sharp downturn in Montreal's Anglophone migration balance after 1976–1977 surely was a response to the new linguistic regime proclaimed by the PQ.

"Anglo flight" affected Montreal's linguistic dynamics in ways that still have not been fully sorted out. The existence of an English, North American "safety valve" may have helped preserve social peace in Montreal in the late 1970s as disaffected Anglophones exited for Toronto and points west. But, Anglophone out-migrants were disproportionately young and well educated;

Table 6.2

The Changing Class Structure of Anglophone Montreal, 1970–1985

Distribution of Anglophone Male Labor Force among Earnings Classes
Metropolitan Montreal, 1970–1985

% of total Anglophone male labor force in
each earnings class (in 1985 constant dollars)

Annual Earnings	1970	1980	1985
Under $15,000	25.1	28.1	31.4
$15,000–24,999	26.4	21.9	20.1
$25,000–39,999	29.2	28.1	25.6
$40,000–49,999	7.4	9.4	9.7
$50,000 and above	11.7	12.2	13.2

Source: Unpublished Special Tabulations, Statistics Canada.

thus, the exodus denuded English-speaking Montreal of some of its "best and brightest."[62] Moreover, the exodus had a profound affect on Montreal's Anglophone class structure. As Table 6.2 suggests, it was mainly middle-class Anglophones who departed after 1970, leaving behind a "two-tier" community increasingly composed of the wealthy and the poor. Such economic divisions may further fragment an already beleaguered community.

In addition, the Anglophone exodus raised fundamental questions about the "survivability" of English-speaking Montreal. Demographic shrinkage has a corrosive impact on community institutions, sapping their vitality and threatening their viability. Part of the impact is symbolic: the flight of large numbers of a community sends a negative signal to others about prospects in the city, discouraging in-migration and encouraging further out-migration.[63] More concretely, however, demographic decline forces schools and hospitals to close or change their cultural orientation and makes difficult the maintenance of such vital community institutions as newspapers and libraries.[64] All of these problems have surfaced in Anglophone Montreal in the wake of Bill 101 and the departure of thousands of English-speakers.

Although many Anglophones left Montreal after 1976, the vast majority stayed—and many chose to defy Bill 101. The central battleground was schooling, where the bill's provisions threatened a radical depopulation of Montreal's English-language schools. In September 1977, both the PSBGM and the Anglophone sector of the CECM vowed defiance of the newly enacted law. The PSBGM declared its doors open "to all students seeking an English-language education" and announced its intention to take the provincial government to court if subsidies to the PSBGM were cut because "ineligibles" were in the system.[65] Seeking to avoid ugly confrontations, PQ Education Minister Jacques-Yvan Morin announced that the government "had no intention of having police evict children illegally enrolled in English-language schools."[66] Nonetheless, Morin stated that provincial grants for the "illegals" would be withheld and warned that Anglophone disobedience of the law threatened social peace. The PSBGM actions were denounced throughout the Francophone community. As Michel Roy editorialized in *Le Devoir*:

> By all legitimate means at their disposal, the schooling sectors of the Montreal Anglophone community may denounce, combat, and challenge Bill 101, in particular the chapters on the language of instruction. But nothing justifies—morally or politically—the campaign of civil disobedience that has commenced in the educational institutions of the Anglophone community. *It will only contribute to the poisoning of relations between the Québécois of the two languages, who must live together whatever happens.*[67]

The Ministry of Education maintained that of the 47,234 students enrolled in the PSBGM for 1977–78, only 42,000 were eligible under Bill 101 to receive English-language instruction. Therefore, Morin threatened to withhold $9 million in provincial government subsidies for the 5,200 illegals. In July 1978, the Quebec Superior Court ruled that the PSBGM had "employed guerrilla tactics to obstruct the law," and that the Ministry of Education had the right to reduce funding of the PSBGM until it complied with Bill 101.[68]

At first, the PSBGM pledged to keep the illegals in English classes and called for private contributions to compensate for the loss of provincial subsidies.[69] However, few Anglophones were willing to foot the bill for such expensive defiance of the law. Therefore, the PSBGM capitulated. On August 1, 1978, school board members voted 9 to 3 to send the remaining illegals—now estimated at 1,600—into the PSBGM's French-language sector. In Montreal's English-language media, the PSBGM decision was bemoaned as one "that ends freedom of choice in the language of education."[70]

Anglo-Catholic schools also defied Bill 101, although resistance was on a school-by-school rather than a sectorwide basis.[71] Individual principals of Anglo-Catholic schools agreed to accept Bill 101 "ineligibles," meeting the extra burden by enlarging classes, expanding teaching loads, and hiring "volunteer" teachers. A Committee for the Coordination of Anglophone Catholic Education tried raising $300,000 to help defray these added costs, but Allophones soon lost interest in sending their children into "the margins" of the school system; nevertheless, through the 1980s, between 1,200 and 1,600 Allophone "illegals" remained enrolled in the English-language sector of the CECM.[72] In some Italian neighborhoods, where parents complied with

Bill 101 and sent their children to French-Catholic schools, resistance to the bill took the form of creating de facto "bilingual schools" where intensive instruction in English as a second language would begin early in elementary school. This was strictly against Ministry of Education policy, and Morin angrily denounced these *classes diversifiées* as an abuse of power by the CECM. Despite the energetic efforts of CECM Commissioner Angelo Montini, these classes never enrolled significant numbers of Montreal's Italian community.[73]

Civil disobedience was a short-lived strategy, and by the early 1980s there were increasing signs that Anglophones were adapting, both politically and institutionally, to the linguistic regime established by Bill 101. Despite aberrations such as the 11th province group, and a sizable vote in a 1978 provincial by-election for an eccentric, "freedom of choice" candidate, English-speaking Montrealers began organizing as a linguistic minority "operating within the rules of the democratic political game."[74] After deserting the PLQ in the 1976 elections, Anglophones returned to the party as their best hope of defending community political interests. A new generation of Anglophone Liberal leaders emerged, typified by MNAs Reed Scowen, Richard French, Herbert Marx, and Clifford Lincoln who battled within the political arena for the Anglophone "right to share . . . with the majority group the political, economic, and social space of Quebec."[75] Anglophone leadership gave up the futile effort to restore freedom of choice in schooling, acknowledged the need for Anglophones to accept French predominance in Quebec, and concentrated on such Bill 101 issues as loosening the Quebec clause, restoring bilingual signs, and guaranteeing government services in English.

The re-election of the PQ in 1981 ended any Anglophone nostalgia—nourished understandably by the shattering defeat of the PQ in the May 1980 referendum on sovereignty-association—that Montreal might somehow return to a pre-PQ linguistic regime. Anglophones would have to continue organizing to defend community interests, and the 1982 formation of Alliance-Quebec was an important development in that regard. Supported by $1 million a year in federal funds, Alliance-Quebec quickly emerged as the most visible and sophisticated Anglophone organization in Quebec. It lobbied the provincial government for changes in language policy and supported legal challenges to selected aspects of Bill 101.

Alliance-Quebec's tenacity in defending English-speaking rights sometimes obscured, at least in the eyes of some Francophones, how different it was from past traditions of Anglophone leadership. Unlike Montreal's unilingual British-origin old-guard, the fluently bilingual leaders of Alliance-Quebec, notably Eric Maldoff, Michael Goldbloom, Peter Blaikie, and Royal Orr, recognized that English-speaking Montrealers constituted a minority in a predominantly Francophone society—an admission that would have been "tantamount to cultural treason" in the 1970s.[76] Alliance-Quebec staunchly challenged those aspects of Bill 101 that were anathema to Anglophones and fought hard for the concept of Quebec as a fundamentally *bilingual* society—a position that irreconcilably clashed with the Francophone nationalist view. But, Alliance-Quebec pursued Anglophone interests not by advocating freedom of choice, or other code words of the "English city" era, nor by having English-speaking economic elites exert covert pressure on key policymakers. Rather, Alliance-Quebec sought to carve out a realistic strategy for Anglophone survival, based chiefly on clearly articulated *minority* language rights, in a Montreal (and Quebec) that, the Alliance realized, had been fundamentally reshaped by the Francophone mobilization of the 1960s and 1970s.

Beyond these political adjustments, Anglophones began restructuring key community institutions to cope with Montreal's new linguistic realities, most notably in the area of education. Blocked from enrolling immigrant children in English-language classes, PSBGM administrators looked for ways to maintain as large an Allophone clientele as the constraints of Bill 101 would permit. Historically an all-English network, the PSBGM announced its intention to become a "bilingual network that would permit all children to master the two languages of Quebec by secondary school."[77] The French-language sector of the PSBGM, with fewer than 1,000 students prior to Bill 101, was significantly expanded and by 1988 contained 9,200 students, or 30.4 percent of the total PSBGM enrollments. The *francisation* of the PSBGM was even more striking at the preschool and first grade levels, the best guide to the future linguistic composition of the system. By 1988, 42.6 percent of these pupils in the PSBGM were enrolled in the French-language network (compared with 3.7 percent in 1976–77).[78]

In addition to expanding its French-language sector, the PSBGM in 1978 greatly enlarged its *classes d'accueil* program. These were special classes, first started in 1969 by the CECM, to ease pupils of diverse ethnic backgrounds into French-language schools through a combination of special language training and cultural curriculum. The PSBGM, however, saw these classes as a way of holding immigrant enrollments while meeting the concerns of Anglophones seeking to give their children a head start in acquiring bilingual skills—all at provincial government expense. By the 1979–80 school year, over 22 percent of the children in Quebec's *classes d'accueil* were in the primarily Anglophone PSBGM and Lakeshore school systems.[79]

The purpose of these organizational adaptations was clear. As Bill 101 curtailed the pool of students eligible for English-language instruction, the heretofore all-English PSBGM hoped to maintain its institutional viability by attracting Allophones into their French-language network. System jobs would be saved, if not for Anglophone teachers then at least for administrators. The attractiveness of the "new" PSBGM for Allophones—and, perhaps for Francophones interested in a kind of bilingual education—was obvious. Allophones would fully comply with Bill 101 by placing their children in French-language classes; but these French-Protestant classes would be situated in the *Anglophone*-governed PSBGM, often in *linguistically mixed* schools where the teaching of English as a second language would be superior and where their children would come into daily contact with English-speakers. Because Montreal's 'school system was organized on a confessional rather than linguistic basis, the PSBGM could create situations of "linguistic cohabitation" in individual schools within the Protestant system, affording Allophone children "extensive knowledge of the English language and culture they could not acquire anywhere else."[80] Nor was the PSBGM the only Montreal school system creating "linguistic cohabitation"; according to a study prepared for the Conseil de la langue française (CLF), 20,423 schoolchildren on Montreal Island (11,117 in English-language classes and 9,306 in French-language classes) received their instruction in 1977–78 in settings of linguistic cohabitation, representing almost 7 percent of the Island's school population.[81]

Linguistic cohabitation, and conditions generally in the French sector of the PSBGM, came under fire from Francophones. Critics noted "the absurdity of the Anglophone community tending over the integration into French society of growing numbers of immigrant children" and chastised the PQ for permitting "covert bilingualism" in the French sector of the PSBGM.[82] This sector was labeled "a detour around Bill 101" for Allophones in which "the instruction is in French but the environment . . . and second-language instruction is English." The PQ was accused of "buying social peace in the Anglophone school system by actively consenting to the multiplication of bilingual schools."[83] The CLF strongly condemned linguistic cohabitation as "pedagogically unsound and a threat to the quality of French-language instruction."[84]

Responding to this barrage, as well as the constraints of the 1981–82 provincial budget crisis, the Ministry of Education sharply slashed spending for the *classes d'accueil* from $30 million annually to $13 million. Admission standards also were tightened—to ensure that immigrants rather than Anglophones attended the classes—and linguistic cohabitation was prohibited. All *classes d'accueil* were required to be located only in schools where all pedagogic and administrative activities were carried out in French.[85]

Despite these regulations, a combination of three factors—the declining school-age population in Montreal, the desire to avoid extensive busing of pupils, and the persistence of the Island's confessional structure of school governance—made linguistic cohabitation inevitable through the 1980s as administrators sought optimum use of school buildings, libraries, equipment, and so forth. Until the matter of school restructuring was resolved, Montreal's Anglophone school establishment would retain some organizational space in which to maneuver in defense of their interests.

A final way in which Anglophones adapted to Montreal in the 1980s was to accept the not-so-subtle message of Bill 101: "learn French or leave." Alliance-Quebec consistently clamored for improved French-language instruction in English-language schools.[86] Moreover, Anglophone parents across the Island enrolled their children in the burgeoning "French immersion" streams available within the technically English-language schools. "Immersion" began in Montreal in 1965, when Anglophone parents in the off-Island suburb of Saint-Lambert persuaded the local school board to set up a program in which Anglophone children would be taught all subjects during the early grades in French.[87] In French immersion, English is gradually introduced through elementary school, and then partial immersion is carried on through secondary school. The results of most studies reveal that immersion graduates become relatively fluent in their second language.[88]

Throughout the 1970s, as Montreal's linguistic climate changed, increasing numbers of Anglophone parents sent their children to French immersion programs: 18.4 percent of Montreal's Anglophone kindergarten enrollments in 1974 were in French immersion.[89] By 1987, however, immersion was practically the norm in many Anglophone schools. In the West Island's Baldwin-Cartier Catholic School District, 90 percent of the students in English-language elementary schools were in French immersion; the figure for elementary schools in the PSBGM was 41.6 percent.[90] What's more, an astonishing number of Anglophone parents went *beyond* immersion and, although their children were eligible to attend English-language schools, voluntarily chose to send them to the *regular* French-language network—a decision that would have been inconceivable a mere decade earlier. By 1985, 7.8 percent of Anglophone children in the Lakeshore School Commission, encompassing many West Island suburbs, were enrolled in the regular French-Protestant sector, while 4.9 percent of the Anglophone children in the PSBGM attended French-language classes.[91] "Today," wrote a Francophone reporter in 1987, "one can see in the West Island angry parents demanding more places for their children in French-language schools"—a development that spoke volumes about how Anglophones were adapting to the *francisation* of Montreal mandated by Bill 101.[92]

Conflicts and Compromises in Language Policy, 1979–1985

As Anglophones adjusted to life in Montreal after Bill 101, a combination of political pressures and court decisions resulted in important modifications of the language law. Between 1979 and 1988, Quebec courts and the Canadian Supreme Court handed down several judgments that abrogated sections of Bill 101.[93] In December 1979, the Supreme Court declared that Chapter III of the law, making French the sole official language of the provincial legislature and courts, was an unconstitutional violation of Section 133 of the BNA Act guaranteeing the use of English and French in these bodies in Quebec. In a mad rush, the Quebec government was forced to translate into English all laws passed since August 1977; technically, until an English version was published, these laws were not in force.

In 1981, over the heated objections of René Lévesque and the PQ government, Pierre Trudeau succeeded in his career-long goal of "repatriating" the Canadian Constitution.[94] However, Article 23 of the new Constitution included the guarantee of access to English-language schools in Quebec to children of parents who had received their primary school education anywhere in Canada, a stipulation that directly clashed with the provisions on the language of instruction in Bill 101.[95] In 1984, the Canadian Supreme Court upheld Quebec lower-court decisions that abrogated Article 73 of Bill 101—the celebrated "Quebec clause"—as incompatible with Article 23 of the Canadian Constitution. The core of Bill 101 on the language of education remained intact—non-Canadian immigrants to Quebec would still be compelled to send their children to French-language schools—and there was little suggestion that the Court's ruling would result in surging enrollments in English-language schools in Montreal or elsewhere in Quebec. Nevertheless, the 1984 verdict alarmed some in the Francophone community as it weakened Bill 101 by imposing the "Canada clause" that Laurin and the PQ hard-liners had rejected in 1977. As the CLF concluded, in reviewing this and other court rulings since 1979, "Even if the judgments have not affected the essential elements of the Charter of the French Language, they have begun to seriously modify its dynamism and social impact."[96]

Despite the disturbing trend in court decisions, it was evident by the early 1980s that Bill 101 had generated a sense of "relative linguistic security" in the French-speaking community.[97] Thus, in late 1982 Lévesque and the PQ, in an effort to reach out to the Anglophone community, began negotiations with Alliance-Quebec on "rounding the edges" of Bill 101.[98] The timing was right, as several incidents in 1982–1983 made Bill 101 seem petty and vindictive, and Lévesque had always been uncomfortable with the law's excesses. In 1982, despite Camille Laurin's assurance that no one would lose employment because of Bill 101, a nurse named Joanne Curran was forced to resign her job because she failed the written examination in French required of professionals in Quebec under the language law. Ms. Curran was sufficiently fluent in French to plead her case on French-language television and radio, thus making the government and its test look silly. In early 1983, the Commission de surveillance had opened an investigation of linguistic transgressions at St. Mary's Hospital in Montreal, on a complaint that a terminally ill patient did not have the comfort of "dying in French" because some of her nurses and doctors were unilingual Anglophones. As Alliance-Quebec put it, the Commission

> sent a wave of fear and outrage through our community when it condemned St. Mary's Hospital because it was not satisfied with the French language competence of 37 percent of the employees. . . . Subpoenas and summonses were served on doctors and nurses. Compulsory appearances by hospital staff dragged before the Commission de surveillance to account for their rendering of quality health care. All of the trappings of a criminal proceeding without the right of the "accused" to see the complaint or even know the identity of the "accuser." All of this when the hospital was able to provide service 100 percent of the time in French.[99]

Incidents such as these seemed to support Mordecai Richler's polemical description of Quebec's linguistic bureaucracy as "tongue troopers," and even PQ cabinet members urged the "hawks" at the Commission to adopt a more conciliatory approach.[100] Articles began appearing in Montreal's French-language newspapers urging changes in Bill 101 in the name of social peace and social justice.

As a first step toward modifying Bill 101, Lévesque had appointed Gérald Godin, considered a moderate on language issues, to replace Camille Laurin as the Minister in Charge of Bill 101. Clearly, Laurin's almost mystical identification with the law and his Mephistophelean image in the Anglophone community would have made negotiations impossible. In October 1983, Godin opened parliamentary hearings on revising Bill 101. His task was formidable: to find a middle ground between Francophone nationalists who viewed Bill 101 as an untouchable "sacred text" and Anglophone groups who wanted wholesale changes in the law. His opening statement, it is widely agreed, set the tone for a calm, rational discussion of the most divisive issue in Quebec political life. Godin outlined the constant battle against assimilation faced by Quebec *français* as a tiny island in the sea of North American English, especially in an era of high-technology, sophisticated communications, and a global economy, but then added, "Let us be clear. Anglo-Quebecers have very little to do with this assimilation, and it is not them that we should consider responsible, or their institutions."[101]

More than sixty briefs were presented during the hearings, including those of Montreal Mayor Jean Drapeau and Alliance-Quebec. Drapeau claimed that Bill 101 had damaged the Montreal economy and its international image, and said that the city should be given "special status" exempting it from parts of the law. In particular, he called for amendments that would permit bilingual signs and services in Montreal, a "Canada clause" in education, and the easing of French-language tests for professionals. Godin immediately rejected Drapeau's call for "special status," pointing out that the language situation in Montreal was "at the heart of the changes aimed at by Bill 101," and that "the city should find glory as a French, not a bilingual city."[102]

The longest and most important brief, presented by Alliance-Quebec, demanded nothing less than a thorough overhaul of Bill 101. The chief proposals were:

1. Formal status in Bill 101 of "English-language rights," and official recognition of linguistic dualism in Quebec;
2. Abolition of requirements that French be used as the language of internal communication in Anglophone institutions and of external communications between them;
3. Abolition of French-language testing for professionals;
4. Permitting all "English mother tongue" immigrants to Quebec to send their children to English-language schools;
5. Permitting bilingual public and commercial signs.[103]

There was, of course, no chance that a PQ government would accept the major items on this wish list, particularly the demands on access to English-language school and bilingual signs. Having thrown open the possibility of revising Bill 101, PQ leadership now was exasperated by the refusal of Alliance-Quebec to limit discussion to a few relatively minor amendments. Said Godin: "Alliance-Quebec's demands constitute virtually an invitation to demolish, piece by piece, the Charter of the French Language."[104] Although undercurrents of tension persisted throughout the hearings, there were none of the vituperative exchanges and visions of linguistic apocalypse that had prevailed during the language debates of 1974 and 1977, and the government moved resolutely to find a compromise.

After two months of hearings, the government presented and then passed Bill 57, modifying Bill 101 at the margins to meet some of the Anglophone community's concerns. The preamble of the French Language Charter was amended to include explicit recognition of the institutions of the English-speaking community as "precious to the development of Quebec."[105] Other substantive changes were in the language of public administration, where Bill 57 met Anglophone demands for "institutional" as opposed to "personal" bilingualism in English-language hospitals, schools, and social service agencies. Article 20 of Bill 101, required, for all intents and purposes, fluency in French for public employees no matter the clientele of their agency; it was amended to permit English-language institutions to designate which employees must be bilingual to ensure that "their services to the public are available in the official language [French]."[106] French proficiency tests for professionals who also were graduates of Quebec English-language high schools were abolished. Moreover, Anglophone municipal governments were no longer required to use French as a language of internal communication—an exemption granted school boards and health and social services agencies in Bill 101—and all Anglophone local institutions were now granted the right to use English when communicating with each other.[107] Although Alliance-Quebec criticized the limited nature of the changes, the Montreal *Gazette* hailed Bill 57 as a "major advance for Anglophone institutions. . . . It should enable English-speaking institutions to retain their English character and remain valuable sources of employment for Quebecers who are not fluent in French."[108] Montreal's French-language press also praised Bill 57 as a sign that Francophone society had reached a new "maturity" on linguistic matters.[109]

Bourassa Reignites the Language Question, 1985–1989

Bill 57 was the PQ's final language legislation. Beset by internal factionalism and directionless as its independence project stalled, a moribund PQ was thrashed in the November 1985 provincial elections by a politically rehabilitated Robert Bourassa and the PLQ. Bourassa's triumph inaugurated what Michel Plourde has aptly called an era of "equivocation" in Quebec language policy.[110] Massively supported by Montreal Anglophones, Bourassa had promised during the campaign to amend "useless irritants" in Bill 101, including the provisions on unilingual French signs.[111] Three Anglophones and an Allophone received prominent cabinet appointments in the Bourassa administration, and there was every expectation in the English-speaking community that major *assouplissements* to Bill 101 were at hand.

In 1986, the Bourassa government presented three language bills. In June, the government passed Bill 58, a law granting "amnesty" to the 1,013 "illegals" still enrolled in Montreal's English-language schools (all in the Anglophone network of the CECM). The PQ had attempted, in 1982, to coax what was then estimated as 1,200 to 1,600 of these Allophone children into the French-language schools with a $3.6 million program of special linguistic and pedagogic services.[112] Nevertheless, most remained in the English-language network and, with the problem nearly ten years old, PLQ Education Minister Claude Ryan declared that the time had come "to conclude this emotional phase of our linguistic history."[113] Bill 58 accorded the remaining illegals "official" status in Montreal's English-language schools; and since all of the children had received their primary school education in English, Article 23 of the Constitution guaranteed their brothers, sisters, and descendants access to English-language schools. The PQ attempted to rouse public sentiment against the bill, but with the party deeply factionalized and nationalist forces generally dispirited, there was little public reaction against Bill 58. Moreover, the bill entailed no changes in the application of Bill 101; it merely dealt with a fixed number of cases that would hardly affect the demographic balance in Montreal schools.

In November, Bourassa presented two more bills affecting language policy. Bill 140 proposed a radical streamlining of the linguistic bureaucracy created by Bill 101. Anchored in the Bourassa administration's overall strategy of reducing the size of the Quebec state, Bill 140 proposed merging the Office de la langue française (OLF) and the Commission de protection de la langue française, replacing the CLF with a less elaborate advisory group, and abolishing the autonomous appeal board that ruled on business *francisation* programs. Critics contended that the changes would significantly weaken Bill 101: there would be fewer employees and less money spent on language planning; daily operations of these agencies would be more directly under the control of the provincial government; it would be more difficult to register complaints about infractions of the law; and there would be no independent agency informing "the public on questions concerning the French language in Quebec." [114] The intent of Bill 140 was clear: to rein in the administrative arms of aggressive language policy. Ultimately, however, strong opposition—from inside and outside the bureaucracy—forced Bourassa to abandon the bill. [115]

Along with Bill 140, the government also proposed Bill 142, an act to guarantee Anglophones the right to receive social and health services in English. [116] Bill 101 had dealt rather nebulously with this issue, offering no explicit guarantees but authorizing the OLF to recognize as "Anglophone" those institutions serving a clientele with an English-speaking majority. Such Anglophone institutions presumably had the right to serve their clientele in their own language as long as they also made services available in French. On Montreal Island, social services had evolved since 1977 on a territorial-linguistic basis, with three social services centers—the predominantly Anglophone CSS Ville-Marie, the Francophone CSS Montréal Métropolitain, and the Jewish Family Services—expected to serve constituencies concentrated in distinct areas of the Island. It was anticipated that arrangements among social service centers would be made to serve linguistic minorities located outside the center's own boundaries (for example, CSS Montréal Métropolitain serving West Island Francophones). [117]

Unlike this territorial model, Bill 142 proposed inscribing in law the "personal" right to English-language health and social services to all individuals "who express themselves in English" (*toute personne d'expression anglaise*). The PQ and other nationalist groups protested that this ambiguous phrase would expand English-language health and social services from being a special right for Anglophones located in areas with a large English-speaking population, such as Montreal's West Island, into an option available from *all* health or social service agencies in Quebec to *any* non-Francophones speaking English. The notion that the government might require health and social services to be available in English outside Anglophone enclaves, combined with the specter of ethnic minorities "who express themselves in English" utilizing such services across Montreal, infuriated numerous Francophones. Radical nationalists viewed any enshrining of English-language rights as "a step on the return route to a bilingual Quebec," [118] while Francophone health and social service professionals saw the plan as a dangerous step back toward immigrant Anglicization. [119] In the end, nationalist mobilization and strong opposition in the French-language media forced Bourassa to retreat. Bill 142 was passed in December 1986, but in its final form it only applied to regions where the linguistic composition of the population warranted such services; ultimately, the bill strengthened only moderately a right implicit in Bill 101. [120]

At the same time that Bourassa was trying to shepherd these bills through l'Assemblée nationale, the issue of the language of commercial signs erupted, reigniting *la question linguistique*. As we have seen, Bourassa proposed amending the French-only signs policy during the 1985 campaign. This seemed an astute political maneuver at the time: Anglophones felt strongly about the issue ("We want to be visible," said the Alliance-Quebec's Eric Maldoff), while support among Montreal Francophones for unilingual signs had dropped in surveys from 66 percent in 1979 to 46 percent in 1985. [121] Bourassa calculated that the signs issue offered an opportunity to assuage his Anglophone constituency while not touching the essentials of Bill 101— the provisions on education and the language of work—that were sacrosanct in the French-speaking community.

The premier was deliberately vague as to what his signs policy would entail. The 1985 PLQ program called for a Bill 22–type policy: French priority in all signs, but no proscriptions on other languages. In 1986, Bourassa hinted that he might create "bilingual districts," such as the West Island, in which bilingual commercial signs would be permitted. One trial balloon after another was floated. [122]

Whatever Bourassa's eventual policy, his election seemed to signal a relaxation in enforcement of the signs provisions of Bill 101 in Montreal (see Chapter 8), and with a proliferation of illegal bilingual and even unilingual English signs came a Francophone reaction. Nationalists accused Bourassa of ignoring the "guerrilla warfare" being waged by Anglophones against Bill 101. Gaston Cholette, the outgoing president of the Commission de la protection de la langue française blasted the Ministry of Justice for failing to pursue cases turned over to it by the Commission. [123] The PQ attempted to bolster its sagging electoral fortunes by presenting itself as the defender of Montreal's "French face." "In Montreal, the situation is alarming," said

Claude Filion, PQ spokesperson on language policy. "The proliferation of bilingual and unilingual English commercial signs has reached a degree where one could count by thousands the cases of infractions. If Montreal falls, all other regions will follow."[124] "*Ne touchez pas à la loi 101*" (hands off Bill 101) became the PQ's rallying cry.

In December 1986, the Quebec Court of Appeal ruled that, while Bill 101 could legally require that signs include French, barring other languages violated the Canadian Constitution's guarantees on linguistic equality and the guarantees of freedom of expression in Quebec's own Charter of Rights. The court's decision, coupled with general Francophone uneasiness over the direction of Bourassa's language policy, led to a revival of mass linguistic action reminiscent of the battles of the 1960s and 1970s. A renewed Mouvement Québec français, along with the SSJB de Montréal, organized a demonstration of about five thousand persons at Centre Paul-Sauvé in Montreal following the Court of Appeal decision around the theme: *Québec, je t'aime en français.* Camille Laurin spoke, calling Bill 101 not "the law of the PQ" but a "law coming from the core of our collective history."[125] There were even modest reminders of the linguistic violence of the 1960s: after the court's ruling, disgruntled nationalists shattered the bilingually posted windows of Zellers' stores in Ville LaSalle, and there was periodic vandalism (spray painting, broken windows, and so on) in Anglophone areas of Montreal Island in 1988 by a group calling itself Action pour un Québec français. The sudden death of René Lévesque in November 1987 seemed to give a nostalgic impetus to nationalist efforts to remobilize around the language question, and in April 1988 linguistic "street politics" returned to Montreal when twenty-five thousand "defenders" of Bill 101 marched through downtown, shouting slogans and waving placards and Quebec flags.[126]

Startled by the public reaction and growing opposition to revising Bill 101 by Francophones in the PLQ legislative caucus, Bourassa attempted to buy time on the signs question by ruling out action until the Canadian Supreme Court had decided on the issue. Moreover, he began backing away from his 1985 commitment to the Anglophone community by noting that "social peace" came before "electoral promises."[127] Translation: the premier would not risk policies that would rekindle the street politics and linguistic disorders that plagued Montreal in the 1960s and 1970s.

In December 1988, the Canadian Supreme Court ruled, as expected, that Bill 101 illegally proscribed bilingual signs. Chastened by the growing nationalist mobilization on the question, Bourassa declared that his "first responsibility" as premier was the protection of the French language and culture, and he immediately invoked the "notwithstanding clause" of the Canadian Constitution that permitted provincial governments to override for a period of up to five years certain provisions in the Charter of Rights and Freedoms that might conflict with provincial law. After overruling the court decision, by way of compromise Bourassa offered Bill 178 that would maintain unilingual French signs on the outside of buildings, but permit bilingual signs (with French "predominance") on the inside.[128] With his crushing majority in l'Assemblée nationale, Bourassa was able to limit parliamentary debate on the matter and ram the bill through before the Christmas recess.

However, Bourassa's actions unleashed a firestorm of controversy in Montreal and the province. Fifteen thousand Francophone protestors crowded into Centre Paul-Sauvé to denounce Bourassa's plan, and PQ leader Jacques Parizeau criticized the government for diluting Bill 101 and reviving "façade French" in Montreal. Linguistic violence flared up on December 30 when a firebomb gutted the downtown Montreal offices of Alliance-Quebec. (Police investigation and a special inquiry on the crime failed to produce any arrests.)

Anglophones were equally furious over Bourassa's "compromise," accusing the premier of reneging on his 1985 campaign promises. Communications Minister Richard French, Environmental Minister Clifford Lincoln, and Minister of Justice Herbert Marx, all powerful English-speaking members of the Bourassa cabinet, resigned in protest. Moreover, English Canadians in other provinces reacted strongly to Bourassa's invoking of the "notwithstanding" clause to maintain unilingual French signs outside buildings. The English-Canadian backlash threatened to undermine ratification of the Meech Lake Accord, the constitutional amendment package negotiated in 1987 to entice Quebec to sign the 1982 Constitution. The Meech Lake Accord was the centerpiece of Canadian Prime Minister Brian Mulroney's and Premier Bourassa's approach to the "national unity" question. It included explicit "special status" for Quebec as a "distinct society" in Canada and was widely supported by Francophones in the province. Should the Accord run aground, a possibility that seemed a near certainty by the end of 1989, an opening might then exist for the PQ or some other group to question again Quebec's place in Canada, resurrecting the independence issue and all of the related implications for language politics in Montreal.

At least initially, Bourassa's actions on the signs issue looked eerily like his mishandling of the language of instruction question in Bill 22, finding a "middle ground" that satisfied no one. Although both major Montreal French-language dailies, *La Presse* and *Le Devoir* issued editorials supporting Bill 178 as "the best compromise under the circumstances,"[129] the *Gazette* denounced Bourassa, and surveys indicated widespread opposition in both linguistic communities to the Bourassa plan.[130] Bill 178 was sufficiently ambiguous and dependent on future regulations to enrage all parties. Questions abounded: What did "predominantly" French on inside signs mean? Would bilingual signs posted inside buildings but visible from the outside be permitted (display windows)? Bill 178 promised a Byzantine array of controversial regulations.

Throughout the winter of 1989, the Bourassa government floated numerous trial balloons on precisely how Bill 178 would be implemented, seemingly afraid to commit itself to clear and unambiguous regulations. At one point, it was hinted that bilingual signs would be permitted at ski centers and other tourist attractions, as well as on signs relating to matters of health and public safety. Another idea refined the notion of "interior bilingualism" so that only unilingual French signs would be permitted in common areas inside commercial malls, but establishments inside the malls could display bilingual signs, unless they were "franchises" with more than five employees, in which case unilingual French signs were required, and so on.[131] The more Bourassa delayed in specifying how Bill 178 would be implemented, the more convoluted his thinking seemed to become.

Bourassa expressed confidence that calm would prevail after the initial protest over his signs policy. "In between the total rejection of the Supreme Court judgment and complete bilingualism," he said, "we have opted for a measured solution that in the long run will be supported by the silent majority."[132] But the numerous ambiguities surrounding Bill 178 resulted in continuing agitation through early 1989 over the signs issue. In March, a massive demonstration organized by the MQF drew an estimated sixty thousand Québécois to the streets of Montreal to protest Bill 178 and the erosion of Bill 101.

As Francophone antagonism to the new law continued to grow, and with little sign that Anglophone leadership appreciated his effort at compromise, Bourassa retreated from the initial spirit of Bill 178. In March 1989, the premier appointed none other than Claude Ryan as minister in charge of Bill 101—the same Claude Ryan who had been so vehement, as editor of *Le Devoir,* in denouncing Bill 101 in 1977. By 1989, however, Ryan understood the special place of the law in the hearts of Quebec Francophones, and on March 15 he served notice that the Bourassa government's equivocation surrounding the language of commercial signs was over. Ryan announced that in shopping malls, in all establishments with more than fifty employees, on mass transit vehicles, in large department stores such as Eaton or in chains such as McDonald's, Dunkin' Donuts, or Radio Shack, "signs on the interior as well as exterior should continue uniquely in French."[133] Essentially, Bill 178 would apply to a select number of commercial establishments with fewer than fifty employees, and Ryan underscored that it was not "obligatory" for such establishments to post bilingual interior signs. Moreover, all interior signs were required to be marked by a "clear predominance" of the French language; May 1989 regulations defined "clear predominance" as French signs twice as large or twice as numerous as those in the other language.[134]

In short, cowed by the Francophone nationalist reaction to Bill 178 and determined not to be seen as "soft" on the language question, by mid-1989 the Bourassa government's policy on the language of commercial signs had evolved into something only slightly less rigorous than Bill 101. Critics accused the government of cynically engaging in political maneuvering, trying to quell nationalist sentiment before the September 1989 provincial elections, and nationalists in the PQ and MQF made clear that they were not appeased. The elections revealed, however, that Bourassa had generally succeeded in defusing immediate Francophone anxieties over the signs issue, as his party was handily returned to power with a solid majority of the Francophone vote. On the other hand, a dispirited Anglophone leadership, disillusioned by Bourassa's reneging on his 1985 campaign promises, groped toward a new strategy to defend community interests. The depth of Anglophone discontent was revealed in the September 1989 provincial elections when the "Equality Party," created as an "English rights" party and running on the single issue of opposition to Bill 178, captured four Assemblée nationale seats on Montreal's West Island. The Equality party represented a throwback to the pre-1976 era in English-speaking Montreal: two of its newly elected MNAs were unilingual Anglophones, and its leader, a twenty-eight-year-old Montreal architect named Robert Libman, was a political neophyte who seemed more gadfly than credible community leader. The strength of Equality in the September elections was an unmistakable sign of Anglophone alienation and disgust with Bourassa's handling of the language question.

The signs issue is symbolically explosive. Many Montreal Francophones see anything short of unilingual French signs as the continuing legacy of the "Conquest," while Anglophones view bilingual signs as a symbol that Montreal is a "social contract" between two linguistic communities. In short, the debate over Montreal's "French face" revolves around anithetical visions of the city: Montreal as a fundamentally French city versus Montreal as a dualistic city. In culturally divided societies, such polarized and symbolic issues are rarely amenable to compromise. Moreover, the philosophical issues raised in this *dossier*—individual versus collective rights— are equally difficult to resolve in multicultural settings. As Léon Dion puts it: "No compromise will satisfy both Alliance Quebec and the Société Saint-Jean Baptiste."[135]

Nevertheless, although the signs issue is loaded with emotion, it seems unlikely that it will carry the same, sustained political heat over the long haul that the language of instruction issue did in the 1970s. Indeed, polls by mid-March 1989 showed majorities in both the Anglophone and Francophone communities declaring themselves "tired" of debate on the language question.[136] The education issue cut to the core of Francophone survival, and by the late 1970s 70 percent of French-speaking Montrealers favored Bill 101's provisions blocking immigrants from enrolling in English-language schools.[137] By contrast, an extensive survey taken in the summer of 1988— admittedly, before the Supreme Court ruling and Bill 178—revealed that over 60 percent of Montrealers from both linguistic communities favored bilingual signs—in short, *opposing* the stipulations of Bill 101 on this issue. When asked what factors contributed the most to a "more Francophone Quebec," only 4 percent of Montreal Francophones cited French-only signs (the main factor cited was integrating immigrants into the French-language schools). [138]

The survey also revealed, however, that both communities contained substantial "radical cores" on the signs issue: 32 percent of Francophones favored "French-only signs," and 34 percent of Anglophones supported "free choice," including the right to display signs in English only. We should recall that *la question linguistique* began with a "radical core" in the vanguard, and then events such as the Saint-Léonard crisis and Bill 63 turned the issue into a mass preoccupation. Francophones overwhelmingly (90 percent) concur that it "is important that Montreal have a French face," and a majority (60 percent) believe that the "face of Montreal is inadequately French." [139] Thus, there was considerable space in Francophone public opinion for linguistic radicals to rekindle *la question linguistique* around the issue of French-only signs. At the very least, despite Bill 101 and its clear assertion of French as the "public language" of Montreal, the signs controversy illustrated graphically that there remained passionate disagreement over the places of English and French in the city at the end of the 1980s.

The Impact of Bill 101: Education

We have explored the *politics* of language policy in Montreal during and after the passage of Bill 101. We turn now to the impact of Bill 101 in transforming various social and economic trends in Montreal. The Charter of the French Language had two prime objectives: *francising* the economy, to improve the economic prospects of French-speaking Québécois, and reshaping public schooling to protect the demographic position of the Francophone community in Montreal. Chapter 8 examines the economic impact of Bill 101; here we analyze changes in the all-important educational sector.

As Tables 6.3 and 6.4 reveal, Bill 101 effectively curtailed access to Montreal's English-language schools and reduced the percentage of schoolchildren receiving instruction in English. During the eras of Bills 63 and 22, Montreal's English-language schools absorbed an ever-expanding share of the Island's school clientele. As Table 6.3 shows, however, Bill 101 reversed this trend and ended any possible threat of a Francophone *minorisation* in Montreal public schools. The English-language networks of Montreal's eight school commissions held 41.5 percent of the Island's schoolchildren in 1977–78, the first school year in which Bill 101 was in effect; by 1989–90, that share had fallen to 29.0 percent. [140]

Table 6.3

Enrollments in Montreal Island Public Schools, 1970–1990

By Language of Instruction (in percentages)

	Language of Instruction	
Year	French	English
1970–71	63.2	36.8
1974–75	59.7	40.3
1976–77	58.8	41.2
1977–78	58.5	41.5
1982–83	64.9	35.1
1987–88	69.7	30.3
1989–90	71.0	29.0
1991–92 [a]	72.0	28.0

Sources: Conseil scolaire de l'île de Montréal, "Série de données d'inscription depuis 1970 et prévision des populations scolaires du territoire du Conseil scolaire de l'île de Montréal" (Montréal: CSIM, 1986); Conseil scolaire de l'île de Montréal, "Les inscriptions officielles au 30 septembre 1987," 7 décembre 1987; and Conseil scolaire de l'île de Montréal, "Les inscriptions officielles au 30 septembre 1989," 6 décembre 1989.

[a] Projection

Table 6.4

Distribution of Allophone Pupils by Language of Instruction, Montreal Island, 1970–1988, in Percentages

	Language of Instruction	
Year	French	English
1970–71	7.9	92.1
1973–74	11.4	88.6
1976–77	22.3	77.7
1983–84	45.4	54.6
1984–85	51.3	48.7
1985–86	54.0	46.0
1986–87	60.0	40.0
1987–88	66.2	33.8

Sources: Gendron Commission, *Volume 3: The Ethnic Groups* (Québec: Éditeur officiel du Québec, 1972), pp. 218, 485; Conseil de la langue française, *Vivre la diversité en français: Le défi de l'école française à clientèle pluriethnique de l'île de Montréal* (Québec: CLF, 1987), p. 162; and Michel Paillé, *Nouvelles tendances démolinguistiques dans l'île de Montréal: 1981–1986* (Québec: CLF, 1989), p. 70.

Allophone enrollment patterns, the source of Montreal's fiercest language battles between 1967 and 1977, were redirected by Bill 101. As we have seen, Bill 22 had made some progress on the issue, doubling the percentage of Allophones enrolled in Montreal's French-language schools. However, on the eve of Bill 101, over three-fourths of the Island's Allophone student clientele remained enrolled in English-language schools. Bill 101 reversed this pattern, and by the mid-1980s, as Table 6.4 reveals, a clear majority of Montreal's Allophones were enrolled in French-language schools. The *francisation* of total Allophone enrollments has been gradual, because the "grandfather clauses" of Bill 101 permit students enrolled in English-language schools at the time the bill was passed, as well as their siblings, to receive instruction in English. For example, through 1987, 70 percent of the Italian-origin children in Montreal's public schools remained in English-language classes because so many fit the grandfather clauses of Bill 101.[141] Overall, however, by the mid-1980s over three-fourths of Allophones first entering the Montreal public schools were enrolling in the French-language network—precisely the opposite of the pre–Bill 101 pattern—and the Anglicization of immigrants via public schooling is no longer a Francophone concern.[142]

This *francisation* of Allophone enrollments transformed both English- and French-language schooling in Montreal. Before Bill 101, *both* networks were losing enrollments as birthrates plummeted and suburbanization drew potential pupils off the Island. However, as we examined in Chapters 3 and 5, English-language enrollments before 1975 were bolstered by Allophones, and the rate of enrollment decline was much steeper in Montreal's French-language schools.

Bill 101 inverted these trends. Between 1976 and 1987, the number of schoolchildren on Montreal Island receiving instruction in English-language schools fell by a staggering 53.0 percent (56 percent in the PSBGM, 63 percent in the CECM, and 35 percent in the suburban Baldwin-Cartier and Lakeshore School Commissions). French-language enrollments, now buttressed by an Allophone clientele, declined by a more modest 23.9 percent. Moreover, as we examined earlier, these figures understate the decline in students receiving their education in English, because by 1987 well over one-third of the pupils in the English-language network were enrolled in French immersion programs. Figure 6.1 shows how dramatically Bill 101 affected the linguistic patterns of enrollment decline in Montreal's public schools.

These enrollment trends represent nothing short of a survival crisis for English-language schooling in Montreal. The raw figures are graphic: enrollments dropped from 148,000 in 1970–71 to 61,000 in 1987–88 in Montreal's English-language schools.[143] In the PSBGM, over fifty English-language schools closed or were converted into French-language schools between

Figure 6.1

Linguistic Patterns of School Enrollment Decline in Montreal, 1971–1987

Annual percentage change in enrollments, by linguistic network for all school commissions, Island of Montreal

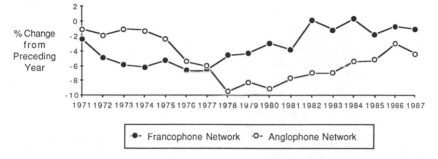

Source: Conseil scolaire de l'île de Montréal, "Série de données d'inscriptions depuis 1970 et prévision des populations scolaires du territoire du Conseil scolaire de l'île de Montréal" (Montreal: CSIM, 1986); and Conseil scolaire de l'île de Montréal, *Les inscriptions officielles au 30 septembre 1987* (Montreal: CSIM, 1987).

1977 and 1987, and employment for English-speaking teachers and support staff has declined an estimated 35 percent.[144] These results are hardly surprising: all immigrants to Montreal, except those covered by the Canada clause of the Constitution, must now send their children to French-language schools; substantial clientele for English-language schooling has been lost through Anglophone out-migration; and a significant number of Anglophone parents are electing to send children eligible to receive instruction in English into the French-language schools.

Bill 101 accomplished the Francophone nationalist goal of turning English-language education in Montreal into a "privilege" for a narrowly defined community of Anglophones, not a system that integrated immigrants and threatened the Anglicization of Montreal. The percentage of "non-English mother tongue" students in the Anglophone sector of the CECM has declined from 74 percent in 1972 to 64 percent in 1987, and it is inevitable that the clientele of Montreal's English-language schools will become progressively limited to Anglophones.[145] Thus, unless there is an unexpected increase in the Quebec Anglophone birthrate, or an equally unlikely surge of in-migration from English Canada, Bill 101 has effectively eliminated the sources of demographic replenishment for Montreal's English-language schools.

The impact of Bill 101 on French-language schooling in Montreal has been equally dramatic. First, as Figure 6.1 indicates, Bill 101 slowed the depopulation of Montreal's French-language schools and helped allay the job security and cultural concerns of Montreal's militant and heavily unionized Francophone teachers. Education jobs were at stake as Montreal's school systems competed for clientele, and in Bill 101 the PQ made policy that responded to the economic interests of one of its most important constituencies: Francophone teachers.[146]

Second, the Bill 101-induced growth of Montreal's French-Protestant schools introduced a new range of educational conflicts on the Island. Despite the rapid expansion of the French-Protestant sector, through 1988 the PSBGM remained an Anglophone-run board. There were no Francophones among the PSBGM commissioners, and some French-Protestant schools had principals transferred from the English-language sector.[147] Francophone parents complained about inferior services compared with the English-language sector: textbook shortages, fewer pedagogic aides, and overcrowded schools (at the same time that several Anglophone schools remained under-populated).[148] The PSBGM denied discrimination, blaming inter-sector inequalities on the system-straining surge in French-language enrollments caused by Bill 101, and refused French-Protestant demands for administrative autonomy along the same lines it was granted to Anglo-Catholics after 1940.[149] As long as Montreal schooling remained organized along confessional lines—housing two linguistic networks within the denominational school commissions—the uncomfortable coexistence of a declining (but still controlling) English-language sector with a growing French-language network promised to continue within the PSBGM.[150]

Finally, the most radical impact of Bill 101 on Montreal's French-language schools has been to introduce a function that urban schools throughout the United States and English Canada have performed since the mid-nineteenth century: integrating newcomers into the language and culture of the city's majority. As we have seen, through the mid-1970s, almost all of Montreal's ethnic minorities enrolled in English-language schools and the Island's French-language schools were composed almost exclusively of French Québécois. However, by 1987, as a result of Bill 101's impact on Allophone enrollments, the clientele in French-language schools was over 25 percent non-Francophone and over 35 percent were *not* of French-Québécois ethnic origin.[151] In addition to more established ethnic groups—Italian, Greek, and Portuguese—French-language schools were increasingly populated by children of Montreal's newer immigrant communities: Haitians, Vietnamese, Salvadorans, and Jamaicans. In the words of one analyst, with three races and over eighty ethnic groups represented in its clientele, the French sector of the CECM had become a "league of nations."[152]

The speed with which these historically homogenous institutions have become multicultural has been staggering. By 1986, Haitians constituted, after French Québécois, the largest ethnic group in the French-language sector of the CECM, with 6.3 percent of its total enrollment.[153] In 116 of the

CECM's 176 French-language schools, the clientele was more than 20 percent non-Francophone; in thirty-two of these schools, over half the students were not Francophone.[154] By 1986, only 38 percent of the students in the French-language sector of the PSBGM were French Québécois. In over one-third of the French-Protestant schools, more than half the student body was non-Francophone.[155]

Adjusting to ethnic diversity in the schools is now widely recognized as one of the central challenges facing Montreal's Francophone community. There are numerous, unprecedented pedagogic problems for Francophone educators:

1. Teaching in French to students with little mastery of the language;[156]
2. Introducing "multicultural" education to the heretofore "pure" French-Canadian Catholic curriculum and personnel. Representatives from various cultural communities complain that non-French-Québécois cultures are treated, at best, in a "folkloric" way in Montreal's French-language schools.[157] Concomitantly, the staff of these schools remains overwhelmingly composed of Francophones *de vieille souche* (of native-origin). For example, through 1986, only 3.2 percent of the CECM's French sector's principals and top administrators were from ethnic minorities (6 of 186), while only 10.7 percent of the system's teachers were not French-Québécois.[158] By contrast, Allophones constitute an estimated 25 percent of the staff in the PSBGM, prompting many immigrants to enroll their children in the more culturally congenial French-Protestant schools rather than the CECM. In times of budgetary compression, hiring the ethnic minority staff necessary to change the ratios in the French-Catholic schools will be difficult.
3. Dealing with the general problems associated with educating an influx of children from disadvantaged households (compounded by their deficiencies in French). An astounding 94.5 percent of Haitian students in Montreal secondary schools have been "left back" at least one year, and community leaders are concerned that school administrators avoid the special problems of Haitians by "dumping" them in "slow-learner tracks" in the public schools.[159]

Montreal's French-language schools have made a number of strides in all of these areas. Ethnic diversity among teachers and support staff is much greater than in the 1960s. In addition, special *classes de francisation* have been developed for immigrants needing extra attention in French instruction, and the *classes d'accueil* for cultural and linguistic adjustment have been continued.[160] In 1977 the CECM introduced the "P.E.L.O." program permitting Allophone students to be taught some subjects in their native tongue; by 1985, the program had enrolled over 4,300 students.[161] These developments, however, mark only a beginning, and Francophone educators are still groping toward solutions to the enormous pedagogic challenges facing them.

The multi-ethnic French-language schools also face numerous socio-linguistic problems. A detailed assessment by the CLF concluded that there are serious obstacles to the diffusion of French as the common language of communication in these schools. Fewer than half the multi-ethnic schools are located in neighborhoods with a Francophone majority; thus, the ambiance surrounding the schools often is not conducive to the use of French in extracurricular and non-classroom interaction.[162] Moreover, the allure of North America's English-language mass culture is powerful: Allophone children enrolled in the French-language network watch more English than French television and listen more to English radio stations than they do French.[163] Immigrants to Quebec remain highly conscious of the importance in North America of learning English. Finally, with ethnic and racial conflict in some French-language schools, and evidence of ethnic "cliques" in most, some question how effectively these schools are "integrating" immigrant children into the French-speaking community. As Beauchesne and Hensler note, immigrants will not learn French simply by absorbing "techniques"; Allophones must interact frequently with Francophones in "significant, numerous, and diversified situations" to integrate fully into the Francophone milieu.[164] However, school officials are still searching for ways to promote this full-scale "interaction."

As Francophone educators experiment with the appropriate strategies for multi-ethnic schooling, Francophone intellectuals have only begun to grapple with the potentially transforming consequences of Montreal's multi-ethnic French-language schools for the culture and politics of French Quebec.[165] The clauses in Bill 101 on schooling flowed from the nationalist argument that Francophone Québécois demographic and therefore cultural survival depended on integrating Montreal's immigrants into the French-speaking milieu. Yet, as Arnopoulos and Clift point out, "the possibility that French society might be profoundly influenced by immigrants it was forcibly integrating did not even cross the minds of the sociologists, civil servants, and politicians who drafted the legislation."[166] Arnopoulos and Clift perceptively speculated that Bill 101 might be a "Trojan horse": a bill that, in ensuring Francophone demographic survival, would also recast French-Québécois culture in ways that might disturb many nationalists.

Historically, the French-Catholic school system was the core institution transmitting the monolithic culture of French Quebec to succeeding generations of Francophones. However, Bill 101 turned Montreal's French-language schools into crucibles out of which a new, multi-ethnic Francophone Québécois identity will emerge. As the birthrate of "native-born" Francophones continues to plummet, and immigrants constitute an ever-growing proportion of the French-language school clientele, these ethnic minorities will put an increasingly powerful stamp on Montreal's Francophone culture.

There are already signs that this cultural transformation is producing several rifts within the Francophone community. On one hand, some nationalists are openly uneasy about the new role of French-language schools in promoting a multi-ethnic Francophone community. For example, Jean-Marc Léger, a long-time participant in Quebec's linguistic battles and an early advocate of greater Francophone openness to immigration, has questioned whether the high concentration of non-Francophones in some French-language schools may promote the "deracinating of young Franco-Québécois."[167] Léger proposes that the impact of immigration on Quebec culture be diluted by reducing the concentration of immigrants in Montreal and spreading them out across Quebec where their influence on "native" French-Québécois culture would presumably be lessened. Moreover, Léger called for a slowdown in immigration until Quebec comes up with an appropriate strategy for safeguarding its French culture.

On the other hand, a rising element in the Montreal Francophone community looks positively on the dawning of a new Quebec in which French will function as a *lingua franca*, connecting diverse ethnic communities as "partners in a new Quebec culture."[168] In this context, as Pierre Laplante has written, the French-language school is not viewed as a cultural threat but as the institution where the "distinctive character of the rising generation will emerge."[169] Laplante raises the possibility of a new cultural cleavage within Quebec's French-speaking community, pitting Montreal, where virtually all of the multi-ethnic French-language schools are located, against the rest of the province. In Montreal, he writes, "we are already far removed from *je me souviens* [the traditional nationalist motto adorning Quebec license plates] or the "purity of our origins."[170] The great French-Canadian nationalist symbols and cultural heros, transmitted in schools for generations, have little meaning for Haitian-Canadian Francophones living in the Montreal of the 1980s, while they continue as the "patrimony" of 3.2 million "native" Francophones living outside the metropolis (and most in Montreal as well). Moreover, the Montreal-based ethnic groups will increasingly expect the culture transmitted in French-language schools to reflect *their* symbols and *their* heritage.

Thus, the same kinds of native-born versus immigrant, and urban versus rural tensions that shaped the development of U.S. cities now loom in French-speaking Quebec, in the schools and in society at large. In the past, Quebec's Francophone hinterland saw Montreal as a cultural threat because of its English character; in the future, Montreal may be viewed warily because of its multi-ethnic Francophone culture.[171] If these rifts become politically salient, with Francophone Montreal internally divided along ethnic lines and Francophone Quebec fragmented on a Montreal versus "hinterland" axis, then the impact of Bill 101 may turn out to be more radical than anyone had imagined. Whatever the outcome of these cultural struggles, Montreal's French-language schools will be at the heart of them.

Conclusion

Despite this looming debate over the future of Francophone culture, there is overwhelming support in French-speaking Montreal for Bill 101. The law has become, as Camille Laurin had hoped, widely accepted as the corner-stone of Francophone linguistic security and a powerful symbol of the "Re-conquest." The backlash against Robert Bourassa as he attempted in 1988 to revise Bill 101 on the language of signs made clear the law's powerful meaning to Francophones.

Bill 101 codified the Francophone ascendancy in Montreal and changed the city's linguistic rules of the game. Immigrants were required to integrate their children into French-language schools, and the autonomy of Anglo-phone institutions was reduced. A new linguistic climate emerged in which French became Montreal's "public language": interactions in stores, restau-rants, or other public places seemed much more likely to at least begin in French, and "Francophones lost the habit of switching automatically to En-glish when an Anglophone joined the conversation."[172] While issues such as the language of commercial signs revealed continuing Francophone anx-ieties over how "French" Montreal really had become, there was no gain-saying the new sense of Francophone linguistic security spawned by Bill 101. Ironically, as René Lévesque and others speculated, the cultural secu-rity provided by Bill 101 may have taken some of the steam out of Fran-cophone dissatisfaction with the Canadian Confederation and unwittingly undermined the PQ's effort to secure a majority in support of Quebec independence.[173]

The core issue that had stimulated language conflicts in Montreal since the mid-1960s—the specter of an Anglicization of the Island via the public schools—was resolved by Bill 101. The law's provisions routing immigrants into the French-language schools are as close to inviolable as any matter can be in politics. No serious Anglophone or Allophone group publicly questions the policy of immigrant *francisation* any longer, an extraordinary shift from the turbulence on the issue that prevailed through the late 1970s. Alliance-Quebec's education demands center on broadening access to English-language schools to all genuinely English-speaking immigrants—ironically, a position close to the provisions of Bill 22 that some Anglophones found akin to "Nazism" in 1974. Allophone groups mainly seek better instruction in En-glish as a second language in the French schools and recognition of ethnic diversity in the curriculum. The provisions of Bill 101 on the language of instruction remain anathema to non-Francophones—surveys consistently show nearly 70 percent in opposition—but it is well understood that re-opening this *dossier* would menace social peace in Montreal and is a political impossibility.[174]

Bill 101 was more than an exercise in language planning: it was the most important political symbol of a new era in Montreal's linguistic history. Any dreams that Anglophones may have harbored that Francophone neo-nationalism would prove ephemeral, and the "mistake" of Bill 22 might be reversed, were dashed with the election and re-election of the PQ and the passage of Bill 101. Many Anglophones left Montreal and, as the editor of an Anglophone community newspaper put it in 1987, "we have become much weaker, our population is in decline, we have lost many of our schools, and above all we have lost our language which is not even any longer recognized in Quebec."[175] Despite these traumatic changes, Anglophones remain a rather privileged linguistic minority, with autonomous schools and social institutions and, as we shall examine in Chapter 8, a still prosperous position in the Montreal economy. Moreover, almost 60 percent of Montreal Anglophones surveyed in 1987 reported that, Bill 101 notwithstanding, it was still possible "to live completely in English in Montreal."[176] But the demographic future of the community is in doubt, with few possibilities for replenishment and with the economic lure of out-migration to English Canada an omnipresent reality. The new Anglophone leadership, far removed in temperament and circum-stance from the British-origin *minorité majoritaire* of Montreal's past, faces a daunting task in developing a community survival strategy.

For Francophone Montreal, the cultural ramifications of Bill 101 have already been substantial, and will continue to unfold. By directing Allo-phones to French-language schools, Bill 101 has assured a *Montréal fran-çais*. But, as immigrants are integrated into Francophone society, a collec-tivity whose cultural identity has historically been based on homogeneity and isolation will be transformed into a multi-ethnic community. A new French-Québécois culture will be forged out of this Montreal integration process and major accommodations will have to be worked out between Francophones *de vieille souche* and the emerging Francophone ethnic minorities. As we ex-amine in Chapter 9, predictable ethnic and racial conflicts have already ac-companied this great transformation, and the rise of Francophone multi-culturalism has potentially profound implications for Quebec nationalism and regional divisions within Quebec. Language will always be an issue in Mon-treal as Francophones struggle to safeguard their language and culture in a continent of English. Now, as a result of Bill 101, Francophone Montreal faces an internal "cultural question" that may prove as vexing and conflictual as *la question linguistique*.

Chapter 7

Public Policy, Language, and the Montreal Economy, 1960–1989

The Montreal economy was characterized by unmistakable linguistic hierarchies through the 1960s. The city's major corporations were largely under the control of English–Canadian and foreign capital, and Anglophones monopolized senior management positions.[1] The Gendron Commission put the matter succinctly in 1972: "[T]he French language is particularly characterized by inferior duties, small enterprises, low incomes, and low levels of education. The domain of the English language is the exact opposite, that of superior duties involving initiative and command, and large enterprises, and high levels of income and education."[2]

Eradicating this linguistic segmentation of economic activity was a matter of considerable material interest to Montreal's Francophone community. In addition, the issue of language and the economy was also a *cultural one* as Anglophone economic power seemed to threaten the French language and culture in the city. As we saw in Chapter 3, the greatest menace of the 1960s and 1970s—immigrant Anglicization—was closely linked to the economic strength of English in Montreal. Moreover, as long as English persisted as Montreal's language of management, Francophones faced an unenviable choice: maintain fidelity to their cultural and linguistic roots, at the cost of limited economic opportunity, or pursue material success by adopting English as their language and helping their children succeed by sending them to English-language schools.

A more insidious cultural consequence of Anglophone economic power, as Francophone nationalists from Jules-Paul Tardival in 1879 to Camille Laurin in 1977 argued, was the *devalorisation* of the French language and culture.[3] As Peter Leslie points out:

The language of economic elites is presumed to have a corrosive impact on other languages, even one spoken by a majority, and to invade it with foreign vocabulary, foreign turns of phrase, and foreign habits of thought (which can scarcely be dissociated from language). Eventually, it is argued, non-elite languages are relegated to the sphere of "folklore" and survive, if at all, in corrupted form.[4]

René Lévesque, as usual, put the matter succinctly: when you control economic life, he said, you control linguistic life.[5] To survive and *s'épanouir* (blossom) culturally, Francophone Montreal needed to represent something more than a French translation of the economically dominant English-speaking world. "That is why," as Leslie notes, "quite apart from the economic aspirations of a [Francophone] middle class, the language of high technology, senior management, and the boardroom is considered to have special significance."[6]

As Francophone nationalists mobilized over these and other language issues, every Quebec provincial government between 1960 and 1985 deployed various instruments of public policy—economic development programs, educational reform, and language policy—to reshape Montreal's economy in the interests of the French-speaking majority. Between the Quiet Revolution and the early 1980s, the Quebec state actively intervened in the economy to attack linguistic disparities in income, establish French as the normal language of work and consumer activities in Montreal, *francise* the "external face" of business in the city, and promote Francophone control over key economic institutions. The policies were undertaken at the provincial level, where Francophones solidly controlled the levers of power, but it was the Montreal situation that motivated policymakers in Quebec City.

By the 1980s, aided by certain market trends, state policy had helped transform Montreal's economy and promote an economic reconquest of sorts by French-speaking Montrealers. The power of Anglophone capital, and the use of English as a language of management, remained substantial. Nevertheless, by the 1980s, Montreal boasted a dynamic and innovative Francophone managerial elite, greater use of French in city workplaces, and pronounced reductions in income disparities based on language.

The nature of these economic changes, and an analysis of the forces promoting them, is the focus of the next two chapters. In this chapter, we examine the policies put into place between 1960 and 1985 that sought to improve the positions of Francophones and the French language in Montreal's economy. Chapter 8 then provides a detailed assessment of the economic impact of these policies.

The Quebec State and
Francophone Economic Development

The role of the provincial government in Quebec's economy expanded dramatically after 1960. Public expenditures represented 17 percent of Quebec's gross domestic product in 1961; by 1983, that figure had climbed close to 30 percent. The provincial bureaucracy grew from around thirty thousand employees in 1960 to nearly a hundred thousand by 1980, and thousands more were employed in local health, education, and social service "parapublic" institutions funded by the provincial government.[7]

The size of governments at all levels increased throughout Canada between 1960 and 1980 (although the Quebec state grew at a substantially faster rate than government in comparable jurisdictions such as Ontario).[8] State expansion in Quebec during this period was shaped by many of the same forces promoting public-sector growth in all advanced capitalist societies: a Keynesian consensus on the role of public spending in promoting economic growth, and public demands for social welfare programs. But, as we saw in Chapter 3, the rise of the Quebec state took place within a Francophone nationalist framework. In the ideology of the Quiet Revolution, the Quebec state was explicitly "conceived as an instrument in service of the interests of French Canadians."[9] In contrast to other areas in Canada or the United States, ethnic promotion became a *central* (though not exclusive) concern shaping public policy in Quebec. Thus, as the state assumed a more prominent position in Quebec society, its nationalist "mission" inexorably affected the places of English and French in the Montreal economy.

Quebec's rapidly growing state became a major source of quality employment for Montreal Francophones. Through the early 1970s, shockingly few Francophones held middle- and senior-level management positions in Montreal's Anglophone-controlled private sector. However, the growth of the provincial bureaucracy, combined with expanded employment in schools, social services, and health care institutions, produced a Francophone-controlled public alternative to the Anglophone-controlled private-sector labor market. Unlike the upper echelons of private industry, French was established as the main language of communication in the state sector. A 1982 survey by Sales and Bélanger found that 88.2 percent of senior and intermediate managers in Quebec's public administration worked "almost exclusively in French," compared to only 31.6 percent in such posts in private enterprise.[10]

By 1981, as a result of the twenty-year expansion of the state, 18.1 percent of metropolitan Montreal's labor force was directly employed in the public sector, either by the provincial government, the city of Montreal, or parapublic institutions. An additional 2.4 percent of metropolitan Montreal's labor force was employed by the Canadian government. All of these institutions employed Francophones to a much greater degree than did the private sector, and by 1981 an estimated 23.4 percent of metropolitan Montreal's Francophone labor force worked in the public sector.[11] Thus, in the face of limited economic opportunities in the upper echelons of Anglophone-controlled businesses, increases in public-sector employment in Montreal and across Quebec after 1960 provided jobs for an upwardly mobile new Francophone middle class of technocrats, teachers, social service workers, and policy entrepreneurs.

The "state sector" also emerged after 1960 as a Francophone-controlled locus of managerial jobs: over 98 percent of the senior and intermediate-level managers in Quebec's public administration in 1982 were Francophone. There were, of course, Francophone managers entering the private sector in the 1960s and 1970s. But, the numbers were small: in 1970, only 12.7 percent of the recent graduates of the Université de Montréal were working in the private sector.[12] Until private corporations in Montreal significantly *francised*, Quebec's public administration and state corporations would represent a crucial source of managerial jobs for Francophones. Moreover, the public sector would serve as an important training ground for Francophone managers who, as Montreal *francised* in the 1970s and 1980s, could then move into the private sector.

Beyond providing employment for Montreal's Francophone new middle class, the expanded Quebec state also sought to nurture the development of a Francophone capitalist class in Montreal and across the province. I argued in Chapter 3 that Montreal's emergent Francophone middle class was the driving force behind the state expansion that began in the early 1960s. However, as William Coleman, Dorval Brunelle, and others have documented, certain elements of a nascent Francophone "bourgeoisie" also envisioned "state capitalism" as a vital tool to advance their economic aims.[13] Michael Behiels notes that by 1960 "French-Canadian businessmen, suffering from the powerful competition of the larger and more dynamic Anglophone and American corporations, became increasingly supportive of the demands being made by this new professional middle class for an active, secular, Francophone-oriented Quebec state."[14]

In the early 1960s, some Francophone businessmen had ambitious plans for elaborate, corporatist state planning in Quebec. Representatives of the Montréal Chambre de Commerce, the Mouvement Desjardins, and several Francophone financial and industrial companies joined with the Lesage government in 1960 to establish the Conseil d'orientation économique (COEQ), a public–private industrial strategy council along the lines of corporatist entities emerging at the time in Europe. Although Brunelle maintains that COEQ functioned as a "strategic locus" whereby the interests of Francophone businessmen "could be directly articulated to the provincial political power,"[15] the evidence is that COEQ's impact was limited. As Dale Thomson points out, "meeting only once a month in Quebec City or Montreal, [COEQ] could not produce well-documented recommendations." COEQ members "were busy men who found it difficult to do much more than attend the meetings." Thus, under these circumstances, COEQ "found it easier to endorse recommendations put forward . . . by government departments." Ironically, according to Thomson, despite the ambitious plans of Francophone businessmen for COEQ, it was individuals identified with the Francophone new middle class, such as René Lévesque, Jacques Parizeau, and Claude Morin, who used COEQ to exert influence over the Lesage government's economic development agenda.[16]

Although Francophone businessmen did not control the agenda of Quiet Revolution *étatisme,* policymakers were nevertheless committed to using state power to expand the Francophone presence in the private sector. The architects of the Quiet Revolution were nationalists, not socialists, and the state was seen as a valuable tool in rectifying the historical weakness of Francophones in Quebec capitalism. During the Quiet Revolution and after, two main economic development strategies were pursued: public support for Francophone-controlled firms in the private sector and the development of Francophone-run public enterprise. By 1978, Quebec-based enterprises had access to more than 160 programs of economic assistance, including low-interest loans, loan guarantees, research and development assistance, and provincial government equity and debt financing; Francophone-controlled enterprises have been the conscious beneficiaries of these programs.[17] The most important of the Quebec government's direct business assistance programs has been the Société de développement industriel (SDI), created in 1971. The SDI provided "gap financing"—supplementing the funds private financial institutions might be willing to lend a firm—to stimulate economic development in sectors promising high productivity, export potential, and good wages.[18] Between 1971 and 1981, the SDI extended $602 million in financing to firms in the Montreal region (approximately 60 percent of total SDI allocations).[19]

In addition to business assistance programs, public enterprise was a central feature of Quebec state capitalism. Five state corporations were established or expanded during the Lesage administration, and nine more were created between 1967 and 1978.[20] As we explore below, the purpose of these state corporations was clear: to establish large-scale, Francophone-controlled enterprises in strategic sectors that could counteract Anglophone economic power while fostering the development of a Francophone entrepreneurial class.

The nationalist economic policies of the Quiet Revolution culminated during the late 1970s under the Parti québécois. The PQ came to power in 1976 with clear nationalist goals, but also with a social-democratic program and the perception of being antibusiness. The PQ had little support in the Francophone business community, and in party platforms the PQ often attacked corporate power and promised that social concerns would take precedence over purely economic (that is to say, business) ones. Economic policy statements early in the Lévesque administration extolled the virtues of "mixed economies," and called for government intervention "to compensate for weakness in the private sector, to ensure coherent development, and the presence of domestic influence in strategic sectors."[21] Nevertheless, by the end of the first Lévesque administration, and certainly during the PQ's second mandate (1981–1985), the fiscal imperatives of advanced capitalism and the triumph of pro-business technocrats in the party had resulted in economic policies that veered away from public planning and social democracy, toward the more corporatist model of public support for private enterprise. After 1980, according to Thomas Courchène, the PQ became "the most business-oriented or market-oriented government in Canada."[22] In 1978, PQ Finance Minister Jacques Parizeau castigated Quebec corporate executives for complaining about progressive taxation and the "social-democratic" direction of PQ policy; by 1983, Parizeau would proclaim that the promotion of a Francophone business class was the PQ's greatest achievement.[23]

The PQ created and expanded numerous programs to aid Francophone firms. The SDI was expanded, with an increased focus on small- and medium-sized firms—precisely the sector most likely to include Francophone-controlled enterprises. New PQ economic development initiatives included Opération solidarité économique (a coordinated program linking public works and business assistance), the Office québécoise du commerce extérieur (an export promotion agency), and PME-innovatrice (a special assistance program for small- and medium-sized firms).[24]

Three PQ programs in particular demonstrated the party's deepening commitment to Francophone businesses during its years in power. In 1977 the PQ instituted a *politique d'achat:* a "Buy Quebec" government purchasing policy that set aside more than $5 billion to support Quebec-based (primarily Francophone) enterprises. Such preferential purchasing ranged from buses ordered by municipal transport commissions, to household appliances purchased by the Société d'habitation du Québec (Quebec Housing Corporation), and computers procured by local school boards.[25] In 1979, the Régime d'épargne-actions, or REA (the Quebec Stock Savings Plan) was established, providing tax credits for stock purchases; the plan bestowed millions in tax breaks on wealthy Quebecers, and also raised over $5 billion in first-issue share purchases on the Montreal Stock Exchange, primarily in small-

and medium-sized Francophone corporations (see Chapter 8). Finally, in 1984 the PQ passed Bill 75, deregulating the insurance industry and permitting insurance companies to invest in finance companies, use public deposits to grant commercial loans, and to diversify into areas such as mutual insurance, property management and, through holding companies, into commercial and industrial investments.[26] All told, this was quite a record for a government labeled "antibusiness."

We should not exaggerate the extent to which promoting the interests of Francophone capitalists was a top priority of the PQ. "Ethnic" criteria never completely displaced conventional "economic" criteria in state economic policy—for two main reasons. First, English-Canadian and American capital occupied an integral place in the Montreal and provincial economies. Thus, any provincial government wishing to stimulate economic growth and create jobs was a hostage to the disinvestment power of non-Francophone capital. This was especially true for the Parti québécois in the late 1970s as it sought to boost a sagging economy amid public fears that the party's sovereignty option was a formula for economic disaster. It was no accident that one of René Lévesque's first actions upon becoming premier was an attempt to reassure New York financiers that fiscal restraint and economic stability were PQ priorities.

Second, contrary to the analyses of scholars such as Gilles Bourque, Anne Legaré, and Pierre Fournier, although the PQ was interested in helping Francophone capitalists, the promotion of a Francophone "national bourgeoisie" was not the *defining goal* of the party.[27] Many of the important PQ programs of its first years in power—language policy, public automobile insurance, campaign finance reform, anti-strikebreaker legislation, and, for that matter, the party's Quebec sovereignty option—generally incurred the wrath of the Francophone business community. The limits of nationalism in PQ economic development policy were displayed in 1977 when the provincial government awarded a $92 million contract for 1,200 buses to General Motors, rejecting a bid from Francophone-controlled Bombardier. In defending the government's decision, Premier Lévesque emphasized the economic need to attract investments from multinationals such as GM, and cautioned against adopting "a criterion of pure 'cultural' preference that would soon lead to the creation of a genuine economic ghetto."[28] In preparing for its referendum on sovereignty, the PQ did not want to alienate a major U.S. multinational corporation—even at the risk of offending a powerful Francophone corporate "success-story." Not unexpectedly, the PQ decision met with a stinging reaction from Bombardier President Laurent Beaudoin:

> I do not understand why a nationalist government cannot fully measure the disastrous consequences for Quebec companies of a decision

that enshrines, for generations to come [and] in a sector where the state has important influence, the absolute supremacy in Quebec and in Canada of the world's largest multinational, and destroys as a consequence, any hope of developing a Quebec company in that area.[29]

Beaudoin, of course, conveniently neglected to mention the numerous government contracts Bombardier had received throughout the 1970s and the substantial financial assistance it had been given by state corporations. In addition, both the Canadian and Quebec governments would provide important export assistance to Bombardier as it penetrated mass transit vehicle markets abroad in the late 1970s and 1980s. Nevertheless, the 1977 GM–Bombardier episode does reveal that the Quebec state was not the pure instrument of Francophone capitalists and that conventional macroeconomic concerns—stimulating growth and investment—often took precedence over the immediate interests of the Francophone business class.

State Corporations and Francophone Economic Development

Among the various economic development tools deployed by the Quebec government after 1960, none was more instrumental in helping create a Francophone capitalist class than state enterprise. Three important state corporations—the Société générale de financement (SGF), the Caisse de dépôt et placement, and Hydro-Québec—were created or expanded during the Lesage administration to attack the two main historical sources of Francophone weakness in Montreal's private sector: inadequate capital for large-scale development and lack of access to dynamic sectors of the economy. These public enterprises should not be misinterpreted as socialism *québécois:* the logic underpinning them was pure Francophone state capitalism. As Jacques Parizeau put it in 1970: "In Quebec, the state must intervene. It is inevitable. It is what gives people the impression that we are more to the left. If we had, in Quebec, 25 companies like Bombardier, and if we had important banks, the situation might be different. We have no large institutions, so we must create them."[30]

The SGF was created in 1962 as a public–private fund to invest in modern, Francophone-run enterprises, capable of competing with foreign and English-Canadian corporations. Premier Lesage had touted the importance of a provincial investment fund as tool to "reconquer the French-Canadian place in the economy," and Francophone business elites, led by René Paré of the Montréal Chambre de Commerce enthusiastically supported the idea.[31] Montreal's Anglophone business establishment viewed such an investment fund as a threat, and George Marler, who represented the views of "St. James Street" in the Lesage cabinet, voiced his opposition.

Despite Anglophone business resistance, the SGF was established, with an initial $25 million public–private subscription, and with Paré as the first chairman of the board. By all accounts, the SGF was a disappointment in the 1960s, functioning more as a bail-out mechanism for nearly bankrupt, family-owned French-Canadian businesses than as a supporter of new, dynamic Francophone enterprises.[32] Almost half of the SGF's holdings in 1965 was in Marine Industries, the Simard family's troubled construction company, and in 1971 the SGF lost $8 million on investments of $50 million.[33]

In the 1970s, however, the SGF was reorganized, established as an autonomous state corporation, and given an infusion of new capital. Under the leadership of aggressive Francophone managers emerging from the province's revitalized educational system, the SGF began having a real impact as a holding company that nurtured the development of large private corporations under Francophone control. For example, in 1975, a $6.8 million investment by the SGF helped Bombardier acquire and modernize the Montreal Locomotive Works complex. SGF assistance—along with other loans from public agencies, government contracts, and marketing assistance—enabled Bombardier to become one of Quebec's most successful corporations, with 1988 sales of $1.4 billion and international market niches in the production of mass transit vehicles and snowmobiles. In 1982, Bombardier outbid several leading U.S. companies to gain a $1 billion order for New York City subway cars and become the North American leader in mass transit equipment. By 1989, Bombardier had diversified into a wide range of transportation fields, including aircraft manufacturing, acquiring Canadair Inc. from the federal government in 1986 and gaining a foothold in 1989 in the European aircraft industry by buying Short Brothers of Belfast from the British government. At present, 80 percent of Bombardier's business is located outside Canada, and the company "represents one of the greatest successes of state-supported private enterprise" in Quebec.[34] The Bombardier story illustrates how the SGF had become a prominent contributor to the development of a Francophone capitalist class by the late 1970s. By 1986, the SGF itself held assets of $1.4 billion.[35]

A second state corporation that helped cultivate Francophone capitalism was the Caisse de dépôt et placement. The Caisse was established in 1965 after a bitter battle with the federal government and "the representatives of St. James Street."[36] In 1965, in one of the numerous Quebec–Ottawa squabbles of the 1960s over federal–provincial authority, the Quebec government set up the Quebec Pension Plan ("opting out" of the federal system, to the chagrin of Ottawa). The Caisse de dépôt et placement was created to manage the funds accumulated in the Quebec Pension Plan, investing in stock markets and purchasing bonds for provincial capital projects such as schools, hospitals, and highways. Ironically, in view of the major role the Caisse would play in bolstering Francophone enterprise, French-Canadian businessmen joined the Anglophone establishment in denouncing the plan to use pension funds for economic development as "galloping socialism."[37] Nevertheless, the nationalist-technocrats of the new Francophone middle class established the Caisse as an investment fund to modernize the Quebec economy and "challenge somewhat the economic and political dominance of the English minority in Quebec."[38]

Initially, the Caisse concentrated on gaining Francophone control over the government bond market, crucial for a provincial government embarking upon a massive exercise in nationalistic state-building. Regulating the ability of governments to borrow is a strategic mechanism through which economic elites maintain control over the content of public policy.[39] Through the 1960s, Montreal's Anglophone bankers and brokers functioned as "gatekeepers" to the bond markets from which the Quebec government sought to raise billions for the capital projects of the Quiet Revolution. One Montreal Anglophone syndicate, composed of the A. E. Ames Group and the Bank of Montreal, had been the exclusive underwriter of Quebec government bonds since 1929.[40] Jacques Parizeau recalls the influence of the Anglophone-controlled bond market on Quebec governments:

> It was amazing the power those guys had. The usual practice was to dump $50 million worth of Quebec bonds onto markets after a provincial election and frighten stiff new governments. They would be in a panic, in 1962, 1966, and 1970. In the first months of any new provincial government, the spread between Ontario and Quebec bonds would be usually 35 to 40 basis points [a difference in interest of 3.5 or 4.0%]. The record was 120 basis points with Bourassa in early 1970, even before the trouble [the October crisis]. I saw ministers of finance enter the boardrooms of these guys and come out mesmerized.[41]

In the early 1960s, there were several episodes in which Montreal's Anglophone financial establishment attempted to use its historical control over the bond market to "discipline" the nationalist *étatisme* of the Quebec provincial government. In 1962–1963, for example, the A. E. Ames/Bank of Montreal syndicate sought to discourage the Hydro-Québec nationalization program by suggesting that the funds required could not be raised on the bond markets.[42] Ultimately, the Lesage government assembled a new syndicate to underwrite the project, including two Francophone brokerage firms, Lévesque Beaubien and René T. Leclerc, as well as Royal Bank and Wood Gundy (Montreal's "financial oligarchy" remained sufficiently powerful for the Ames/Bank of Montreal group to receive some of the Hydro underwriting contracts).[43] It was in the aftermath of these kinds of linguistic financial power plays that the Caisse de dépôt et placement was created. The Caisse became an indispensable tool for breaking the grip of English-Canadian capital over Quebec public finance and saving the Quebec government "from falling flat on its financial face, because it couldn't sell its bonds through other channels."[44] Through 1988, over 55 percent of the Caisse's portfolio was in Quebec government bonds, and bonds issued by Quebec municipalities and school boards.[45]

As was the case with the SGF, the Caisse generally had little impact on Francophone economic development through the early 1970s. Paradoxically, aside from purchases of Quebec government bonds, the early investments of the Caisse were in safe, medium-yield, primarily English-Canadian economic institutions. Apparently, the early managers of the Caisse were more concerned about a satisfactory return on the pension funds than a social or ethnic investment calculus. In addition, some have argued that even by the mid-1960s, state planners were not yet fully committed to massive state intervention in the economy—even in the interests of promoting Francophone private enterprise—and thus were cautious in their early economic development efforts.[46]

However, the election of the PQ in 1976 introduced a more explicitly nationalist and venturesome lending program by the Caisse, helping augment Francophone economic control in Montreal. By 1988, the Caisse had become Montreal's most important Francophone financial institution, managing the investment portfolios of eleven Quebec public funds and possessing assets of more than $30 billion.[47] The Caisse now holds shares in a hundred major Canadian companies, including such Montreal-headquartered giants as Alcan, Canadian Pacific, Provigo, Steinberg, Domtar, Gaz Métropolitain, and the Banque nationale du Canada. In addition, the Caisse holds more than $14.7 billion in Quebec provincial and municipal government bonds, and has substantial real estate investments in Montreal (through the Société Immobilière Trans-Québec, in which the Caisse is the principal shareholder, and in partnership with such developers as Le Groupe Immobilier St.-Jacques, Prevel, Cadillac Fairview, Dévencore, and Le Groupe Ruel).[48]

One of the Caisse's most important contributions to Francophone business development has been in financing the growth of Francophone corporations, and then supporting them in corporate struggles. In the early 1970s, for example, the Caisse was instrumental in providing financing for three Francophone food retailers to merge and form Provigo, and the new company quickly emerged as Montreal's largest Francophone food retailer. In 1977, Provigo further expanded by acquiring Ontario's Loeb Stores, a takeover made possible by the Caisse transferring the 25.3 percent of Loeb's capital stock that it held to Provigo.[49] In the world of corporate "Pac Man," Provigo then became an inviting target for a takeover attempt by the Sobey Stores of Nova Scotia. The Sobey offensive was blocked because the Caisse held 24 percent of Provigo's stock and refused to sell—despite the economic attractiveness of Sobey's offer.[50]

By the early 1980s Provigo had surpassed the then Anglophone-controlled Steinberg's as the leading food retailer in Quebec. Provigo's annual sales have increased from $200 million to $7.4 billion over the past two decades, and the company has penetrated markets in English Canada and the United States (with several retail stores and warehouse outlets in California). The decade ended with Provigo in some disarray: overexpansion and overdiversification resulted in declining earnings in 1989 and apparently forced the resignation of boy-wonder company president Pierre Lortie.[51] Nevertheless, Provigo has been promoted as a model of the new Francophone "entrepreneurship" gripping Montreal and Quebec in the 1980s; one columnist even labeled this cult of entrepreneurialism *L'État-Provigo*.[52] Yet, this icon of Francophone free enterprise owes its existence to the Quebec state.

In addition to supporting Francophone corporations, in the early 1980s the Caisse was used as a "bridgehead" in a Quebec government effort to increase the Francophone presence in corporations under Anglo-Canadian control.[53] In 1981, in concert with Paul Desmarais' Power Corporation, the Caisse began maneuvering for a possible takeover of the Canadian Pacific, and demanded two seats on the CP's board of directors. CP executives reacted by requesting the aid of the federal government, and the anti-PQ administration of Pierre Trudeau was happy to oblige. The federal government proposed Bill S–31, prohibiting provincial state corporations from holding more than a 10 percent share in corporations engaged in interprovincial transportation—such as the CP. Although S–31 never became law, it "constituted a clear warning to the Caisse to limit its ambitions regarding pan-Canadian enterprises."[53] The Caisse had become so powerful that it not only altered the linguistic balance in Montreal's financial community, but also had the power to influence key segments of the Canadian national economy.

By the 1980s, the Caisse had actively deployed huge financial resources for the development of Francophone-controlled enterprises in Montreal and across Quebec. Indeed, by 1989 the Caisse had become so large and influential in Quebec capitalism that some critics protested its "distorting" effects on markets: "One agency . . . should not be picking the winners and losers in the Quebec economy."[54] The Caisse now ranks as North America's fifth-largest pool of capital, only slightly behind the first-place California teachers' pension fund.[55] The nationalist concerns of the Caisse made it a "heritage fund for Francophones,"[56] and, critics notwithstanding, the strength of Montreal's visible Francophone capitalist class in the 1980s owes much to the presence of the Caisse in Quebec financial markets.

Hydro-Québec is a final major state corporation that contributed, symbolically and substantively, to Francophone economic development in Montreal. As we saw in Chapter 4, this state corporation was created in two nationalizations: in 1944, when the provincial government took over the Montreal Light, Heat, and Power Company, and in 1963 when the Lesage government purchased the remainder of the Quebec energy sector.

These developments placed a profitable, high technology sector of the economy under Francophone control, and in the past twenty-five years Hydro-Québec has become a central force shaping the linguistic dimensions of economic development in Montreal and across the province. With assets of over $30 billion, Hydro has a steady stream of profits and is among Canada's largest public or private corporations. Its annual investments typically represent a huge component of total new capital spending in Quebec.

The magnitude of these investments strongly shapes Quebec industry, as does the sheer volume of Hydro-Québec's purchasing. From the outset, the corporation adopted a policy of preferential purchasing from Francophone enterprises, paying up to 10 percent more for locally produced items. [57] Since 1964, this policy has resulted in $10 billion in contracts to Montreal manufacturers and providers of advanced corporate services; the result has been the spin-off of new, Francophone corporations capable of competing in private markets. For example, two Francophone engineering firms based in Montreal—Lavalin and SNC—initially developed as a result of Hydro-Québec contracts. Today, they are multinational corporations, among the ten largest engineering firms in the world, with only a small fraction of their income now derived from Hydro-Québec contracts. [58] All told, Hydro-Québec's purchases have contributed to the creation of an estimated thirty-one Francophone-controlled companies. [59] In addition, Hydro has provided discounts on energy rates to local firms, attempting to lower their production costs and thereby improve their economic competitiveness.

Finally, Hydro-Québec has been important as an employer of Francophone managers and engineers and as an example of the successful introduction of French as a language of work in large-scale, technologically sophisticated industry. Prior to nationalization, the working language of private power companies was English, and top management was primarily composed of unilingual Anglophones. Even at the "first" Hydro-Québec (the former Montreal Light, Heat, and Power Company), although the number of Francophone managers and engineers grew in the 1950s through preferential hiring, "English maintained its privileged position . . . particularly at the higher levels, because of tradition, the unilingualism of some Anglophone managers, and the bilingualism of the Francophone employees." [60]

The nationalization of 1963, however, introduced radical changes in Hydro-Québec's language practices. By 1968, French had become the working language at Hydro-Québec, with all management personnel and 95 percent of the employees speaking French at work; French was used exclusively at business meetings and for internal correspondence.[61] By the end of the decade, over 80 percent of the top managerial and engineering positions at Hydro-Québec were held by Francophones, contrasted to less than 20 percent at the prenationalization electric companies.[62] Hydro-Québec's working-language practices set a standard for Quebec state corporations: By 1982, 82.9 percent of managers and senior executives in all of Quebec's state corporations reported working almost exclusively in French.[63] In short, Hydro-Québec represented a large-scale, high-tech enterprise, run by Francophones with French as its working language. Hydro-Québec was a striking symbol of the emerging technological and managerial competence of the new Francophone elite and a linchpin for Francophone economic development throughout the private sector.

The Linguistic Impact of Public Works

The public works projects of Hydro-Québec in northern Quebec in the 1960s and 1970s—the Manic 5 dam, the James Bay project—fueled the growth of Montreal Francophone enterprises in construction, consulting, architecture, and engineering. Montreal itself also was replete with public works projects in the expansionary 1960s and early 1970s and these, too, offered new opportunities to Francophone firms.[64] A short list of such Montreal projects would include the following:

- Infrastructure expenditures by the provincial and federal governments that included several highway and bridge projects, and a new airport (Mirabel);
- Schools, hospitals, and social service facilities to fulfill the education and social welfare commitments of the Quiet Revolution;
- Public offices for the expanding functions of the provincial and federal bureaucracies, such as the Place Victoria, Hydro-Québec headquarters, the Palais de Justice, Radio-Canada building, and Complexe Guy Favreau, and buildings such as the Place des Arts (home of the Montreal Symphony Orchestra), the Complexe Desjardins (offices, retail stores, and hotels), and the Palais des Congrès (Convention Center) that were wholly or partially funded by public dollars;
- Joint municipal-provincial public works projects such as the Montreal Métro, Expo '67 (the 1967 World's Fair held in Montreal), and the 1976 Summer Olympics.

These public works projects offered lucrative contracts to Francophone firms. For example, the Montreal Métro provided opportunities for Francophone construction companies, offered engineering contracts to firms such as BTM, and hired Francophone architects to design the Métro's distinctive stations. In 1974, the Société de transport de la Communauté urbaine de Montréal placed a $98 million order for subway cars with Bombardier at a time when the company was still mainly a snowmobile manufacturer. "Thanks to this first contract," one analyst has written, the company "could develop a new sector of activity that employs today 1,500 persons at its Montreal offices and La Pocatière factories."[65] Finally, based on the experience gained in designing the Métro, the Communauté urbaine de Montréal created BTM International, a firm with global clients specializing in the planning, construction, equipping, and implementation of mass transit systems.[66] In short, Montreal public projects provided a major impetus for the development of Francophone strength in the private sector.

Closing the Linguistic Education Gap

Economic development policy was one way the provincial government sought to advance the place of Francophones in the Montreal economy; a second key initiative involved investments in education. As numerous reports in the 1960s indicated, the Francophone lag in economic development, in part, flowed from the backward state of Quebec's French-language educational system.[67] Simply stated, Montreal's linguistic division of labor partially stemmed from an inadequate supply of skilled Francophone labor to occupy technical and managerial positions in the private sector. A study by three Université de Montréal economists for the RCBB put the matter with quantitative precision: 33 percent of the income differential separating Montrealers of British and French origin in 1961 was attributable to the inferior educational background of French Canadians.[68]

Educational reform was a central component of the Quiet Revolution. In large measure, the educational reform program of the Lesage administration was sold as a Francophone economic development initiative: *Qui s'instruit, s'enrichit* was the slogan as the provincial government promoted its massive school expansion and modernization program.[69] Expenditures for education increased dramatically in the 1960s, new institutions were created, and important changes occurred in curriculum, pedagogy, and educational standards.[70]

The results of these reforms were striking. Enrollments of sixteen-year-olds in secondary schools jumped from 51 percent in 1961 to 84 percent in 1971 and to nearly 100 percent by 1983. Between 1976 and 1983, the percentage of high school graduates grew from 53.9 percent to 70.5 percent. By 1983, over half of Quebec's high school graduates attended some form of postsecondary education, with dramatically increased numbers enrolled in universities.[71] Moreover, the school attendance gap between An-

Table 7.1
Number of Degrees Conferred by Montreal Universities,
Anglophone and Francophone by Level, 1983

	Francophone		Anglophone	
Bachelor's	6,674	(51.3%)	6,314	(48.7%)
Master's	1,268	(51.4%)	1,201	(48.6%)
Doctoral	143	(45.8%)	169	(54.2%)

Source: Le Québec Statistique, 1985–86 (Québec: Éditeur officiel, 1986),
pp. 444–445.

glophones and Francophones virtually vanished by the 1980s (although a higher proportion of Francophone high school graduates received their diploma in "general studies," disproportionately more Francophones still attend CEGEPs, and a higher percentage of Francophones attend university part-time).[72] Although university diplomas in Montreal and elsewhere in Quebec were still disproportionately awarded from Anglophone universities in the early 1980s (see Table 7.1), the differences were much less than they were in the 1960s, and at the doctoral level, Francophone universities had made striking gains.[73] Even at Anglophone universities, the Francophone presence had become substantial. By 1987, the student body at McGill, historically the heart of Montreal's Anglophone intelligentsia, was 25 percent Francophone.[74]

Francophones had always eschewed enrollment in business schools, a seemingly rational choice given their limited openings in private enterprise. Also, French-Canadian cultural traditions discouraged business careers. As Montreal Bishop Alphonse Paquet put it, in a 1902 sermon typical of French-Canadian ideology prior to the Quiet Revolution: "Our mission is less to control capital than to stir up ideas; it is less to light the fire of factories than to maintain and spread afar the luminous hearth of religion and thought."[75]

By the 1980s, however, business had become *la nouvelle vogue* for Francophone students. By 1985, Quebec's programs were producing nearly one-third of Canada's MBAs. Under the dynamic deanship of Pierre Laurin, Montreal's École des Hautes Études Commerciales (HEC) became the largest business school in Canada, with enrollments over eight thousand.[76] In addition, many Francophones enrolled in business programs at McGill and American universities such as Harvard and the Wharton School of the University of Pennsylvania. The graduates of these programs are now emerging as Montreal's new managerial elite, and U.S.-trained, Francophone economists dot the faculty of HEC.

In short, by the 1970s and 1980s, government educational policy had helped generate a significant reservoir of Francophone "human capital" in Montreal, thus providing skilled, French-speaking personnel for managerial positions in Montreal's private sector. Initially, as we have seen, the expanded public sector absorbed significant numbers of these Francophones. By 1985, however, 95 percent of HEC's graduates secured employment in the private sector, a sign of how Montreal's economy had changed for skilled Francophones.[77]

Language Policy and Regulation of the Private Sector

Direct public regulation of the language practices of private corporations was the third main public policy aimed at eradicating Montreal's linguistic division of labor. As we have seen, hints of a language policy on the economy began to surface in the mid-1960s. The 1965 PLQ White Paper advanced the nebulous policy concept of French as a "priority" language, and called for the empowerment of the Office de la langue française to assure "the implanting of French as a common language in all sectors of human activity" in Quebec. In "certain" private enterprises, noted the White Paper ambiguously, "French will be the primary language in the preparation of work documents and the language of communication between management and staff."[78] As we saw, however, Premier Lesage strongly opposed even the hint of regulating the language practices of private corporations, and the White Paper was never released.[79]

The first of Quebec's language laws, Bill 63, centered around language policy in education. Moreover, the bill's legitimation of free choice in the language of instruction reflected more the concerns of the Montreal Anglophone establishment than of Francophone nationalists. Not surprisingly, then, on matters of language and the economy Bill 63 was vague and essentially innocuous: it encouraged corporate Montreal to use more French in the workplace, and authorized the Office de la langue française to hear Francophone employee complaints when their "right to use French as a language of work is not respected." No sanctions were mentioned in the bill.[80]

In the early 1970s, amendments to legislation such as the Consumer Protection Act (1971) and the Companies Act (1973) required, at a minimum, bilingual consumer contracts and company names in Quebec. But, the first tentative steps toward a comprehensive language policy on the economy came in 1974 with Bill 22, Robert Bourassa's ill-fated effort to design a language policy acceptable to Montreal Anglophones and Francophone nationalists. Bill 22 mandated a French presence in the external face of Quebec businesses, and promoted the use of French and the place of Francophones in the internal workings of private industry. However, the *francisation* provisions of Bill 22—those articles specifying how Quebec firms might satisfy the requirement that they promote the use of French in their operations— were sufficiently ambiguous that Francophone nationalists found the economic provisions of the law inadequate. Moreover, the law's enforcement mechanisms were weak. Despite the shift in the political economy of language in Montreal implied by Bill 22, the bill's net impact would depend considerably on administrative discretion and the options chosen by Montreal firms. The close ties between the Bourassa government and Montreal's English-speaking business elite left little expectation that *francisation* would be pursued vigorously or that Francophones and the use of French would rapidly penetrate the pinnacles of economic power in Montreal.

The Parti québécois defeated the Liberals in the November 1976 provincial elections, and shortly thereafter party leaders began floating ideas on a language policy that promised to eliminate the ambiguities of Bill 22 and establish a more rigorous program regulating the language practices of businesses in Montreal and across Quebec. The PQ, of course, had been critical of the insufficient vigor in Bill 22's *francisation* program. In December 1976, Camille Laurin promised legislation that would be "much harder and more demanding."[81] In the PQ White Paper outlining the Charter of the French Language, Laurin put the matter succinctly: "The Charter . . . makes up for what is lacking in Bill 22: clear objectives, explicit deadlines, and penalties for offenders."[82]

Before coming to power, the PQ did not have detailed policies on language and the economy. The core of the pre-1976 PQ program, of course, was Quebec independence, and the assumption was that the genuine *francisation* of the Quebec economy would naturally flow from the establishment of an independent Quebec in which French would be the official language. Businesses operating in a sovereign, officially French Quebec, it was assumed, would use French as their working language, just as English was naturally the language of work in English Canada or the United States. The party position before 1976 was that Francophones would become *maîtres chez nous* only in a sovereign Quebec. Independence and social democracy were the chief elements in the PQ approach toward eradicating Montreal's linguistic division of labor.[83] The PQ program specified that all Quebec workers had "the right to work in French" and that all consumers had "the right to be served in French";[84] thus, "a Parti québécois government would pledge to legislate so that French becomes effectively the language of work and communications in all businesses."[85] But there was little indication of precisely what the PQ would do about language and economy, in the event it came to power *without* a mandate for Quebec independence—which is, of course, exactly what happened in 1976 when the PQ won by decoupling the provincial election from independence with the promise of a future referendum on the party's sovereignty formula.

The main elements of the PQ language policy on the economy emerged in the first nine months of 1977, as the White Paper, Bill 1, and then Bill 101 were presented. Although the debate over language and the economy lacked

the emotion and vituperativeness of the battles over the language of education, it nevertheless was intense and frequently bitter. The original intent of
the architects of the PQ language policy was to promote the *francophonisation* of Quebec firms explicitly. Language policy would require private firms
to give priority to Francophones in hiring and promotion in an affirmative
action program à la *québécoise.*[86] As Laurin wrote in the March 1977 White
Paper, "business firms could set themselves the following objective: to reflect, at every level and in every function of their personnel, the ethnic
make-up of the population of Quebec."[87]

The idea of using government regulation to increase Francophone representation in the private sector was not a completely new departure. Bill
22, for example, suggested that one way firms could meet its *francisation*
requirements was with a "Francophone presence in management" (although
this "presence" remained undefined). As early as 1972, the Gendron Commission concluded that the existence of segregated Anglophone work units
in the upper levels of Quebec firms constituted an insurmountable impediment to advancing the status of French as a language of work in Montreal
and across the province:

> the use of French as the language of work and the bilingualization of
> English-speaking senior personnel will become truly possible only
> when there are larger numbers of French-speaking individuals working
> at all administrative levels (*francophonisation*). The overrepresentation
> of the English-speaking element and the segregation of the two groups
> on the basis of language, constitute obstacles which, if not removed, will
> prevent any change in language usage within enterprises.[88]

The Gendron Commission itself recommended an explicit *francophonisation* policy, complete with quotas and timetables (although without
any enforcement mechanisms). The commission argued that "in our atmosphere of linguistic laisser-faire . . . those in control positions tend to impose their language on workers under their authority. In sectors dominated
by English-speaking people, it is useless to attempt to correct the situation
and increase the use of French without bringing in more French-speaking
people—either at the upper echelons as in the case of manufacturing, or at
all occupational levels in the finance and head office sectors."[89]

Through spring, 1977, it appeared that PQ language policy on the
economy would attempt this "social promotion" of Francophones.[90] In Bill 1,
the first version of the PQ's language bill, Article 112b mandated "increased
numbers of Québécois at all the levels of business," with the understanding
that "Québécois" referred to those of French-Canadian ethnic origin.[91] It
soon became apparent, however, there were difficult and socially explosive
implementation problems with such a policy. How would a "Québécois" be

defined? Was it simply someone who could speak French? Someone born in Quebec who spoke French? An ethnic French Canadian? [92] These logistical difficulties were fraught with explosive sociopolitical implications: defining "Québécois" in one particular way or another—for example, excluding someone fluent in French but not of French-Canadian ethnic origin—would, in effect, be defining the Quebec political community in provocatively particularistic terms.

The deep-seated opposition of Anglophones and Francophone business leaders led the PQ to retreat from this aggressive *francophonisation* program. In the final version of Bill 101, the stipulation was that Quebec firms should increase "at all levels of business, including the Board of Directors, the number of persons having a good knowledge of the French language so as to insure its generalized utilization." [93] There was no mention of ethnic origins, quotas, or timetables, and l'Office de la langue française (OLF), the body eventually created in Bill 101 to administer the *francisation* program, acknowledged that Article 141b of Bill 101 could apply to individuals whose primary language was *not* French but who had "good knowledge" of it. Thus, as one OLF representative candidly admitted in 1978, Queen Elizabeth could qualify as a Francophone under this interpretation of Bill 101! [94]

Having abandoned direct *francophonisation,* the PQ settled on "linguistic promotion": policies to ensure the use of French as the language of work in the private sector. [95] The expectation, of course, was that such *francisation* would ultimately result in *francophonisation,* as Francophone job candidates would possess a superior *capital* with their native fluency in French.

In Bill 1, the PQ's *francisation* requirements were a good deal more coercive than those found in Bill 22. Unlike Bill 22, the provisions of which applied only to firms wishing to do business with the provincial government, Bill 1 made it compulsory for *all* firms in Quebec employing fifty or more persons to obtain a certificate of *francisation* by December 31, 1983. The OLF would negotiate acceptable *francisation* programs and timetables with companies, and companies were required to set up "worker–management" committees that would analyze language use in the firm and then negotiate an appropriate *francisation* program with the OLF.

The *francisation* requirements of Bill 1 encompassed almost all areas of firm activity. The logic behind such a comprehensive program was clear: requiring French as a language of internal communication in a firm would fail, for example, unless concomitant regulations assured the availability of French-language documents, manuals, instructions on the use of equipment, and so forth. *Francisation* could not occur in a piecemeal fashion. To make French the "general language of work at all levels of enterprise," Bill 1 required the following: knowledge of French by a firm's executives; increased numbers of "Québécois" at all levels of the firm (later softened in Bill 101); use of French as language of work and internal communication; use of French in the firm's written documents; use of French in communication with clientele, suppliers, and the general public; use of French terminology; use of French in advertising; and "appropriate" hiring and promotion policies. An employee could not be fired because he or she spoke only French, and employers would be required to prove that a position required knowledge of a language other than French: barring such proof, "bilingual" requirements were illegal. Stiff penalties were created for failure to comply with *francisation,* including the loss of government subsidies and perhaps even permits to operate a business. Whereas Bill 22 had established a rather informal monitoring of the *francisation* process, Bill 1 established a Commission de surveillance to assure compliance. The Commission could receive complaints from citizens about possible violations of the law, conduct investigations, attempt to work out appropriate compliance programs and, failing a satisfactory resolution, turn the names of offending companies over to the Ministry of Justice.

Business opposition to these provisions of Bill 1 was intense. Briefs submitted to the Parliamentary Committee studying Bill 1 by such groups as the Montreal Board of Trade, La Chambre de Commerce du District de Montréal, and firms such as Alcan, the Bank of Montreal. and Royal Bank of Canada all strongly denounced the *francisation* program.[96] In early June 1977, a group of 326 Francophone businessmen, including Claude Castonguay—now the president of Le Groupe La Laurentienne—and Paul Desmarais of Power Corporation, wrote an open letter to Camille Laurin expressing their concern that Bill 1 would "damage economic development and give free reign to intolerance inside and outside Quebec."[97] Laurin blasted back by accusing the businessmen of selling out to the "English establishment."[98]

Up to a point, this "establishment" was a useful enemy for the PQ as it attempted to build support among Francophones for Quebec independence. However, fearful that business opposition to language legislation might damage the economic climate for the upcoming referendum on independence, the PQ modified several features of its *francisation* program. The surveillance mechanisms of Bill 1 were softened in Bill 101; the Commission de surveillance was now required to consult with alleged violaters before initiating legal action, and an appeal commission was established.[99] Nevertheless, "linguistic surveillance" remained a lightning rod for criticism. Popular Montreal novelist Mordecai Richler, in various polemics, ridiculed the Commission de surveillance as the PQ's own "tongue troopers" and "language cops." PQ leaders, courting investment by American companies, were concerned about the impact these images were having on the United States; articles by Richler in *The Atlantic* conjuring up images of a Third-Reichian language police in Montreal were not part of the PQ's prereferendum strategy.[100]

Business elites also trotted out again the early 1970s warning that *francisation* of Montreal's economy would chase head-office jobs from the city. The Montreal Board of Trade produced a study in 1977 indicating that the headquarters of thirteen major firms in Montreal directly provided 13,000 jobs and $430 million to the provincial economy; indirect effects, including the advanced corporate services dependent on head offices, such as law, accounting, engineering and so forth, were estimated at 40,000 jobs and $1 billion.[101] Two management consultants, former advisers to the Bourassa government, suggested that the PQ's *francisation* project would cost 23,000 jobs, especially in firms the chief clientele or operations of which were located outside Quebec.[102]

PQ economic policymakers recognized that it was in head offices where "the critical decisions about the future . . . whether they concern investment, exports, research or marketing, are often made."[103] Thus, the PQ followed the conclusions of the Gendron Commission that English-dominated head offices in Montreal were a strategic impediment to the *francisation* of the Quebec economy. In examining the recruiting practices of ten head offices in Montreal in the early 1970s, the Gendron Commission found that such firms hired two Anglophones for each Francophone in Quebec, with 21.3 percent of their personnel recruited from outside Quebec (and this group was exclusively Anglophone). Francophones represented 35 percent of the head-office employees earning salaries under $10,000, but only 15 percent of those above $22,000. Thus, concluded the commission: "If, as is frequently claimed, the presence of head offices in a given region offers the advantage of allowing the local population access to decision and control positions, it must be concluded that Quebec's French-speaking people derive a scant share from such benefits. . . . The only equivalent situation for French-speaking persons lies in the public administration of the province."[104]

Nevertheless, faced with predictions of a massive Montreal head-office exodus, the PQ backed down from a comprehensive *francisation* program that would affect head-office operations. Bill 101 and subsequent regulations permitted corporate head offices and research operations to negotiate special *ententes* with the OLF exempting them from the law's *francisation* requirements. In 1978 regulations, it was further specified that all Quebec head offices of companies deriving more than 50 percent of their gross revenues from outside Quebec were eligible to apply for exemption from Bill 101 for the following reasons: (1) frequent business contacts outside Quebec; (2) complexity of office technology; (3) requirements for specially trained staff; (4) and, the effects that implementation of a *francisation* program in the head office may have on the firm's competitive position.[105] In

1983 amendments to Bill 101, "research centers" were granted eligibility for "special agreements" exempting them from *francisation,* as the PQ cultivated high technology economic development in the Montreal region.[106] Claimed Camille Laurin: "We believe that the regulations on the usage of French in head offices are such that no firm will be justified in leaving Quebec for linguistic reasons."[107] By 1986, the OLF had concluded 224 "special agreements" permitting head offices and research centers to function solely in English.[108]

In addition to the head-office exemptions, the PQ also slightly liberalized access to English-language schooling as a concession to Anglophone business. During the language debates in 1977, the PQ was warned that multinational firms might not invest in Montreal because senior executives and managers would be prevented by Bill 1 from sending their children to English-language schools. Regulations issued along with Bill 101 permitted "persons who prove that they are assigned to Quebec by their employer for a duration not exceeding three years" to enroll their children in English-language schools; such authorization could, under special circumstances, be renewed by the Minister of Education for an additional three years.[109] Under 1985 regulations, the initial authorization period was extended to five years, with only a one-year renewal permitted.[110]

With these important concessions to the business community in place, the formal *francisation* of Montreal and Quebec firms progressed steadily after 1977. By December 1987, 50 percent of Quebec's large corporations (those with a hundred or more employees in Quebec) and 70 percent of the province's small and medium-sized enterprises (those with fifty to ninety-nine employees) had obtained certificates of *francisation,* attesting that "French had attained a general level of usage in the firm." (For large firms, the rate of certification was 33 percent in 1984 and 43 percent in 1986; for small and medium-sized firms, the figures were 40 percent in 1984 and 62 percent in 1986.)[111] Almost all the remaining firms in the province covered by Bill 101 (that is, those with more than fifty employees) were reported by the OLF to be in the process of implementing approved *francisation* programs.[112] In addition, the OLF had moved ahead with several activities supporting the *francisation* process, such as the "terminology program" that identified proper French terms for the new vocabulary of a rapidly changing, global economy.

Francisation certificates were required by the end of 1983; thus many firms have technically violated Bill 101, and the government has obviously applied the *francisation* regulations flexibly. This is hardly surprising given the Quebec government's consistent concern about discouraging corporate investment and the persistent power of Anglophone capital in Montreal. Nevertheless, the steadily increasing rate of certification in the 1980s suggests that "the usage of French in the workplace has clearly progressed."[113]

We shall examine in the following chapter how much the increase in formally certified *francisation* has represented genuine change in patterns of language use in Montreal workplaces.

The costs of *francisation,* while not insignificant, have not been as onerous as critics of Bill 101 contended. The main direct costs involve translating and printing new documents, developing new lexicons, language training, and some company reorganization.[114] Yvan Allaire and Roger Miller estimated that by 1980 Quebec corporations had expended around $96 million to comply with the provisions of Bill 101.[115] Other studies[116] suggest that the direct costs of *francisation,* on average, have been less than 1 percent of firm sales; moreover, the costs significantly diminish after a transition period of around five years, during which period the basic stock of French-language documents and procedures can be created. For new firms, the costs of *francisation* are minimal.

The direct costs of *francisation* vary by economic sector—firms more heavily dependent on complex communications bear the heaviest costs. But Allaire and Miller conclude that the costs of *francisation* are comparable to those incurred by firms from other forms of social regulation, such as consumer protection or occupational safety.[117] Moreover, there is some evidence that the *francisation* of firms improves the productivity of Francophone employees, particularly in management positions, thus "paying the bill" for *francisation* through increased firm productivity.[118] In any event, it appears that the direct costs of *francisation,* on balance, had a minimal effect on the ability of corporations to operate profitably in Montreal.

Critics of PQ language policy also contended that a major economic cost of Bill 101 was a surge in disinvestment it allegedly promoted in the Montreal area. There are no reliable aggregate figures on the extent to which firms left Montreal as a result of the government's regulation of corporate language practices. In addition, it is difficult to disentangle departures *caused* by Bill 101 from the longer-term trend of head-office displacement toward Toronto and western markets.

Clearly, though, there was some increase in capital flight in the immediate aftermath of Bill 101 (although some was in response to Quebec's political climate rather than a corporate inability to function under Bill 101). The most visible corporate departure came in January 1978 when the Sun Life Assurance Company—a pillar of Montreal's Anglophone financial establishment—announced its intention to move its head offices from Montreal to Toronto.[119] Sun Life officials argued that the company could not operate under the new language policy, even though the PQ had already indicated that head offices would be treated flexibly.

Unquestionably, concern about the requirements of Bill 101 was but a pretext for Sun Life's decision; a larger unwillingness to accommodate Montreal's changing linguistic dynamics was at stake here. The first appointment of a French Canadian to a position of managerial authority at Sun Life came in 1964. By 1978, only two of Sun Life's twenty-one directors were French Canadians, and only two hundred of its two thousand Montreal employees were French Canadians—"hired for the sake of appearance."[120] The company and its board chairman Alistair Campbell were the quintessential symbols of the era of the "English city." Campbell never "learned to say more than '*merci*' and a few other trifling, patronizing words in French," and was deeply disturbed that the "Montreal he had known, from the Square Mile . . . to the anachronistic Staff Common Room in his own building, no longer carried meaning."[121] Corporate president Thomas Galt was equally wedded to the old order.

The Sun Life pull-out was deliberately engineered—and universally interpreted—as a symbolic statement by Montreal's Anglophone old guard that it would not accommodate the city's new linguistic order; the company intended to "teach the Parti Québécois a lesson." PQ leaders denounced Sun Life as an example of Anglophone exploitation, pointing out that the company had historically invested little in Quebec despite the premiums it collected in the province. The day after the company's dramatic announcement, Francophone graffiti artists spray-painted the Sun Life Building on Dominion Square with the words "*bon débarras*" (good riddance).[122] Many Anglophones, hardly supportive of PQ policies, nevertheless expressed concern that Sun Life's actions would further undermine the ability of English-speaking Montrealers to defend their position in the new Quebec.

Other companies such as Royal Trust moved their head offices with less fanfare than Sun Life. Still others disinvested in stages by quietly moving components of their Montreal activities out of the province; the Bank of Montreal, for example, first moved its Mastercharge operations to Toronto before eventually transferring head-office operations from the city after which the bank was named.[123] Aggregate estimates of disinvestment from Montreal after Bill 101 vary widely. Miller estimates that some fourteen thousand jobs were lost in Montreal as head offices shifted operations out of Montreal between 1977 and 1983.[124] Clifford Lincoln, a former PLQ member of Quebec's l'Assemblée nationale, maintained that seventy-two head offices had left Montreal in the first five years following passage of Bill 101, with many others transferring their head offices "in all but legal terms."[125] Conversely, a provincial government study implausibly claimed that in 1977 and 1978—peak years of post-PQ panic in English-speaking Montreal—only six head offices left Quebec, at a cost of 774 jobs.[126] Of Canada's top hundred corporations (measured by assets), the number headquartered in Montreal declined from 25 in 1977 to 20 in 1988 (see Table 3.1). This figure, however, reflects not only the departure of some head offices from Montreal, but also the tremendous growth of corporations headquartered in Toronto and Calgary (thus displacing some Montreal companies from the "top 100").

Whatever the full extent of "policy-induced" head-office exodus from Montreal, it also was unclear how much these departures constituted an *aggregate net cost* to the Montreal economy. As we analyze it in the next chapter, the exodus of Anglophone firms and personnel from Montreal, while creating much economic uncertainty and involving individual hardships, also opened up substantial economic opportunities seized by aspiring Francophone entrepreneurs and managers. Montreal's new linguistic regime also spawned new industries, such as a booming "*francisation* industry" that provided employment for Francophone translators, consultants, and French-language instructors.[127] In short, as Jacques Parizeau has stated: "When all those English-Canadian companies were pulling out during the PQ's first few years in power, I maintained my equanimity. I realized it would simply open the way for French Canadians to step in and take control over those fields."[128] In addition, as nationalism waned and Montreal's business climate warmed in the 1980s, some companies—such as Ultramar in 1986 and NAS Canada in 1988—actually moved their headquarters *back* to Montreal from Toronto, to be closer to their Quebec clients and developing markets in the region (and to escape labor shortages and high land costs in Southern Ontario).[129]

Despite the initial intensity of business opposition to Bill 101, a certain acceptance and even positiveness toward the legislation had emerged in business circles by the 1980s. Although a majority of Quebec's corporate elites considered Bill 101 an obstacle to recruiting qualified managers, by 1987 many Francophone economic elites such Ghislain Dufour of the Conseil du patronat du Québec spoke glowingly of the salutary consequences of *francisation* and cautioned against any wholesale changes in the law.[130] A 1982 survey found that 71.8 percent of Francophone corporate executives and managers believed that Bill 101 should be strengthened or left intact; only 29.2 percent believed it should be weakened.[131] Anglo-Québécois capital maintained its negative stance toward Bill 101, with almost three-fourths of the executives favoring a relaxation of its requirements, but multinationals appear to have adapted relatively quietly.[132]

Business could adapt to Bill 101 relatively easily because, in the last analysis, the PQ responded to the chief concerns of capital and the final version of Bill 101 represented but an incremental deepening of Bill 22 on language and the economy. The more radical dimensions of Bill 1—explicit *francophonisation*, including head offices in *francisation*, and aggressive surveillance—were removed or significantly modified in Bill 101.

In one area, however, the PQ did significantly depart from Bill 22 on language and the economy. Francophone nationalists had long been concerned about the external face of business in Montreal: the omnipresence of English commercial signs and advertising in the city and the irritating inability to receive service in French in some commercial establishments. On the latter point, Bill 101 essentially followed Bill 22 and guaranteed all consumers the right to be served in French.[133]

The persistent visibility of English as a language of commerce was a particular affront to the aroused sense of cultural self-esteem of Francophone nationalists in the PQ. Thus, in Bill 101, the PQ mandated French unilingualism in company names, commercial signs, and documents such as bills, receipts, and order forms. The Bill 22 formula, requiring French on all signs but permitting English, was abandoned. Gaston Cholette, an adviser to Camille Laurin and later president of the Commission de surveillance wrote of the psychocultural importance of the signs issue for the French-speaking community:

> For the Francophone community, on a psychological level, French unilingualism in public signs is one of the most important aspects of the Charter of the French Language. . . . One of the clearest signs of the alienation of Francophones in the area of language is the profound and generalized belief that French can only live in, by, or with English. . . . It could truly be a matter of a serious personality crisis, combining an agonizing doubt toward their own language with attitudes toward English that have become a fetish.[134]

Cholette's language makes clear that basic concerns of Francophone affirmation and self-esteem underlay the signs issue. Moreover, unilingual commercial signs were not mandated simply as an answer to Francophone "alienation": there was a message to immigrants and Anglophones as well. As René Lévesque wrote in 1982:

> In its own way, each bilingual sign says to an immigrant: "There are two languages here, English and French; you can choose the one you want." It says to the Anglophone: "No need to learn French, everything is translated." This is not the message we want to convey. It seems vital to us that all take notice of the French character of our society.[135]

Although the Commission de surveillance—later renamed less ominously the Commission de protection de la langue française—was created to monitor compliance with *all* aspects of Bill 101, the lion's share of its work centered on alleged violations of Chapter VII: the provisions on the language of commerce. Over 80 percent of all commission investigations, between 1979 and 1986, were in the Montreal region, and over 75 percent of those cases involved alleged infractions of Chapter VII.[136] In 1983–1984 for example, all forty-one of the cases sent by the Commission to the Attorney General for legal action on Chapter VII were from the Montreal area.[137]

The Commission de surveillance was particularly vigilant, especially during its early years of operation, in pursuing Montreal violators of the French-only signage policy. Over half of the dossiers opened by the Commission, between 1979 and 1986, involved infractions of Articles 58 and 69 of Bill 101, and the overwhelming majority of these cases came from the Montreal area. As we saw in Chapter 6, however, the language of public and commercial signs remains Montreal's most sensitive linguistic issue, as the Anglophone community has resisted accepting this "cultural" dimension of Quebec's policy on language and the economy.

Conclusion

Bill 101 culminated almost two decades of provincial public policy that sought, in various ways, to attack the historical Anglophone domination of Montreal's economy. During and after the Quiet Revolution, the Quebec provincial government undertook major initiatives in economic development, educational reform, and language policy. The expansion of public employment, improvement of public education, creation of state corporations, such as the Caisse de dépôt et placement, Hydro-Québec, and the SGF, and the *francisation* program of Bill 101, were the chief tools deployed by the Quebec government to reconquer the Montreal economy.

These policies had several economic goals: improving the availability of good jobs for Francophones, launching successful Francophone-controlled businesses, and making French the "normal and customary" language of work. Although the policies were implemented at the provincial level, Montreal was the main target of government action: it was there that the power of Anglophone capital most clearly limited Francophone opportunities in the private sector, and where the pressures for Francophones to work in English were the greatest. In the next chapter, we explore to what extent French has emerged as Montreal's language of work and, in particular, to what degree language policy has been responsible for transforming Montreal's linguistic division of labor.

Chapter 8

The *Francisation* of the Montreal Economy

In his 1976 analysis of Canadian cities, George Nader could still describe such downtown Montreal locations as Victoria Square as "the nerve center of the English-Canadian financial community" and Dorchester Boulevard as "the new heart of the English business community."[1] The Sun Life Building stood majestically at Dominion Square, a brawny symbol of Anglophone corporate power.

By mid-1989, Dorchester Boulevard had been renamed *boulevard René-Lévesque* and was lined with skyscrapers and offices symbolizing the ascendancy of Francophone economic power in Montreal. On the western, historically Anglophone edge of downtown along the boulevard stood l'édifice La Laurentienne, the Montreal headquarters for the financial giant Le Groupe La Laurentienne. Symbolically, l'édifice La Laurentienne towered over the Hotel Queen Elizabeth located across the street—the same hotel whose naming in 1955 epitomized continuing Anglophone power in Montreal. Farther east along boulevard René-Lévesque, in the traditionally Francophone sector of downtown, was the distinctive Place Félix-Martin, headquarters of the world-class engineering firm of SNC. Anchoring the eastern end of boulevard René-Lévesque were the Hydro-Québec Building and the Complexe Desjardins, a mall, office, and hotel complex financed by the tremendously successful Francophone *caisses populaires*. At Dominion Square, the Sun Life Building included among its occupants the rising Francophone brokerage house of Lévesque Beaubien Geoffrion.

These physical developments bespeak an underlying transformation in the political economy of language in Montreal. There is little question that in the four key areas of Montreal's linguistic economy—the language of work, the control of capital, income distribution, and the external face of business—the position of Francophones and of the French language has advanced significantly since the early 1960s.

Scholars and policy analysts disagree, however, about the role played by language policy—or other government actions, for that matter—in promoting this transformation. Michel Plourde, the former president of the Conseil de la langue française maintains that "it is clear that Bill 101, in giving the French language an unquestionable status at the highest level of firms, increased and reaffirmed the presence and the role of Francophones in the Quebec economy, stimulated the ambition and confidence of young graduates, raised the social prestige of French, and undermined the traditional belief that English would be the only language of business."[2]

On the other hand, economists such as Yvan Allaire, Jorge Niosi, Robert Lacroix, and François Vaillancourt argue that the *francisation* of the Montreal economy was well underway *before* the adoption of Bill 101 (and Bill 22, for that matter). They argue that "market forces" such as the growth of French-speaking consumer markets, the increasing importance of service activities in the Montreal economy, the declining role of Montreal in Canada's national economy and the concomitantly regional focus of economic activities in the city, and improving skill levels in the Francophone labor force chiefly account for the improved status of French in the Montreal economy.[3]

It is impossible to determine with quantitative precision the extent to which the position of French advanced in the Montreal economy because of "market factors" or "public policy." This is the case, in part, because policy and market became so closely enmeshed in Montreal after 1960, as the role of the provincial government in the economy dramatically expanded. Moreover, although some of the linguistic shifts in the economy can be shown to have antedated Bill 101, it is difficult to determine how much seemingly "voluntary" change may have occurred because businesses anticipated a more restrictive set of language regulations. In addition, many of the secular changes promoting the position of French and Francophones may have been accelerated by the passage of language bills.

In any event, here we examine the changes that have occurred in Montreal's linguistic division of labor since the 1960s, seeking, as much as possible, to evaluate the role played by language policy as well as other factors in this transformation.

The Language of the Workplace

There are several angles from which to examine changes in the language of the workplace in Montreal between 1970 and the 1980s. Did the use of French increase as a language of communication in Montreal workplaces?

Were more Francophones able to work exclusively in French, avoiding the historical "burden of bilingualism" that limited Francophone economic opportunity? To what extent did Anglophones, particularly insulated in the past from the need to know French at the upper echelons of Montreal's private sector, find it necessary to use French in their work?

Specialized surveys conducted through the early 1980s, as well as two full-scale surveys of the language of work in Montreal—one conducted by the Gendron Commission in 1971 and the other by the Conseil de la langue française in 1979—permit us to examine these questions. As Figures 8.1 and 8.2, and Table 8.1 indicate, French advanced solidly as a language of work in Montreal in the 1970s. Overall, the percentage of Francophones working almost exclusively in French increased from 48 percent in 1971 to 55.4 percent in 1979. Data collected for 1983 suggest that this trend continued into the 1980s, with 56.6 percent of Francophones reporting French as their "almost exclusive" language of work.[4]

On the other hand, the historical ability of Montreal Anglophones to work exclusively in English eroded dramatically in the 1970s. Between 1971 and 1979, the percentage of Anglophones working almost exclusively in English in metropolitan Montreal declined from 66.8 percent to 46.7 percent. An increasing but still small percentage of Anglophones even reported working exclusively in French in 1979. By the end of the 1970s, the typical Montreal Anglophone reported working in both French and English and, on average, these bilingual Anglophones reported that they used French at work between 30 percent and 40 percent of the time.[5]

As Table 8.1 shows, by the end of the 1970s, *francisation* had occurred at all occupational levels and in all types of economic activity in metropolitan Montreal. Across the occupational spectrum, many more Anglophones worked in French in 1979 than in 1971, while Francophones increasingly were able to work in their own language.

Despite these significant changes, the broad outlines of Montreal's historical pattern of linguistic segmentation in the labor market lingered into the 1980s. Important disparities in language use persisted by occupation and sector of the economy. In certain sectors, such as finance, Anglophones were still able to work in English to a greater extent than in commerce where more contact with a French-speaking clientele is required. (In 1979, 45.3 percent of Montreal Anglophones employed in finance worked exclusively in English, compared with 28.9 percent of Anglophones working in commercial activities.)[6] Table 8.1 shows that while pressures for Anglophones to use French at work clearly increased across a broad range of occupations in the 1970s, Anglophone managers were still roughly twice as likely as Anglophone salespeople to work in English in 1979. Conversely, only one-third of Francophone administrators worked exclusively in French in 1979, compared with 50.4 percent of Francophone office employees and

Figure 8.1
Patterns of Language Use at Work in Metropolitan Montreal,
among Francophones, 1971–1979

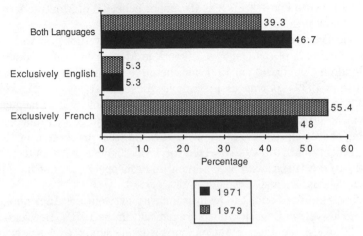

Source: Daniel Monnier, *L'usage du français au travail* (Québec: Éditeur officiel du Québec, 1983), p. 30.

Figure 8.2
Patterns of Language Use at Work in Metropolitan Montreal,
among Anglophones, 1971–1979

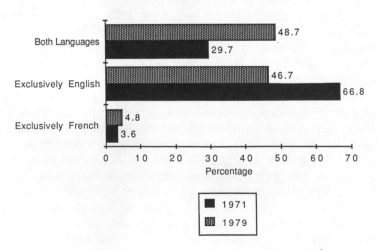

Source: Daniel Monnier, *L'usage du français au travail* (Québec: Éditeur officiel du Québec, 1983), p. 39.

Table 8.1
Patterns of Language Use at Work by Selected Occupations
in Metropolitan Montreal, 1971–1979

By Percentage of Time Working in French or English

Occupation	Francophones		Anglophones	
	1971	1979	1971	1979
Administrators				
EF	34.4	32.0	3.7	2.3
EE	3.9	7.5	62.3	50.3
2L	61.7	60.5	34.0	47.4
Office Employees				
EF	35.9	50.4	0.6	3.7
EE	8.2	7.4	74.1	48.6
2L	28.5	42.2	24.9	47.3
Salespeople				
EF	34.4	36.3	2.3	2.0
EE	3.0	5.8	66.1	24.5
2L	62.6	57.9	27.9	69.1
Transportation and Communications Workers				
EF	44.9	63.6	5.0	6.9
EE	5.0	3.1	67.3	44.8
2L	50.2	33.4	27.7	48.3

Source: Daniel Monnier, *L'usage du français au travail* (Québec: Éditeur officiel du Québec, 1983), pp. 97, 101.

EE = Almost exclusively in English.
EF = Almost exclusively in French.
2L = In both languages.

63.6 percent of Francophone transportation and communications workers. In short, while the gains in French were impressive—particularly the degree to which even Anglophone economic elites increasingly worked in French—English clearly remained a powerful force in the upper levels of the Montreal economy.

A 1982 study by Arnaud Sales and Noël Bélanger of the managers and executives in twenty-eight large Quebec firms and the state sector (public administration and state corporations) permits a more recent and detailed look at patterns of language use at the upper echelons of the Quebec economy. Roughly two-thirds of the Sales–Bélanger sample was drawn from Montreal firms; thus, we can infer much from their findings about language use in Montreal corporations.[7]

Taking the public, quasi-public, and private sectors as a whole, Sales and Bélanger found that by 1982 the majority of Anglophone *and* Francophone managers and executives were able to use their native tongue when

Table 8.2

Quebec Managers and Executives: Language Use at Work, 1982,
by percentage working in each linguistic pattern

	Oral		*Written*	
Language Used	*Francophone*	*Anglophone*	*Francophone*	*Anglophone*
French (exclusively)	55.2	2.3	54.0	3.0
English (exclusively)	3.0	59.9	6.0	77.7
Both	41.8	37.8	40.0	19.3

Source: Arnaud Sales et Noël Bélanger, *Décideurs et gestionnaires: Étude sur la direction et l'encadrement des secteurs privé et public* (Québec: Éditeur officiel du Québec, 1985), p. 215.

communicating with their immediate superiors, colleagues, and subordinates. Whereas 55.5 percent of all Francophone managers and executives reported working almost exclusively in French, 59.9 percent of Anglophone managers and executives reported working almost exclusively in English. As Table 8.2 shows, a substantial percentage of Anglophone and Francophone managers reported working in both languages, although the majority of "bilingual" managers indicated that they used their second language less than 25 percent of the time.[8]

There are, however, some important patterns masked in these aggregate figures. In state corporations and the Quebec public administration, almost 90 percent of managers and senior officials reported using French almost exclusively as their language of work. Thus, much of the status of French as a language of management in Quebec—reflected in Table 8.2— stems from the substantial public-sector managerial employment created by the expansion of the state after 1960.

However, when we look solely at the language use of managers and executives in the private sector through 1982, important linguistic disparities still remain. In firms controlled by English-Canadian or foreign capital,[9] Francophone managers and executives were much less likely to work exclusively in French than in either the public sector or in Francophone-controlled private corporations. In state corporations, for example, around 85 percent of Francophone executives and managers reported working almost exclusively in French, while in Francophone-controlled firms in the private sector, about 66 percent of Francophone managers and executives worked exclusively in French. By contrast, in English-Canadian firms, only 45 percent of Francophone managers and executives worked exclusively in French; in foreign-controlled companies, the figure was under 25 percent.[10]

Although the 1979 and 1982 surveys indicated substantial increases in the use of French as a language of work throughout the Montreal economy, the outlines of the city's historical linguistic division of labor remained. For

Francophones, the higher the managerial status, the less the ability to work exclusively in French and the greater the demands for bilingualism, especially in sectors controlled by non-Francophones. For Montreal Anglophones, the socioeconomic correlation with the use of French at work is reversed: the higher the occupational status, the *greater* the opportunity to use English exclusively at work and the less the demands for bilingualism. As Ian McKinnon and Roger Miller put it: "At the entry level, the pressure is on anglophones to demonstrate that they can function in French: at higher levels, there is pressure on francophones to demonstrate their facility in English."[11]

Changes in the language of work in Montreal also can be gauged from shifts in corporate recruiting practices and general labor market characteristics. The intent of Bill 101 was "to render exceptional" bilingualism as an employment requirement for Montreal Francophones. However, as the CLF noted in 1983, even a casual perusal of job advertisements in Montreal newspapers indicates that such a state of affairs has not yet been established.[12] The continuing status of English in the upper echelons of Montreal enterprises provides a clear incentive for upwardly mobile Francophones to learn English. In 1985, for example, in metropolitan Montreal's male labor force, unilingual French-speakers represented 42.4 percent of Francophones earning less than $15,000 annually, but only 12.8 percent of Francophones earning over $50,000 a year.[13]

Bilingualism as a precondition for Francophone economic advancement in Montreal *has* lessened: in local branches or corporate operations, serving essentially the Quebec market, "second-language" requirements for Francophones declined from 91 percent in 1964 to 23 percent in 1979 (it remained virtually unchanged, however, at 71 percent in head offices).[14] Quality employment possibilities have expanded for unilingual Francophones in metropolitan Montreal. Nevertheless, bilingualism requirements still face Francophones seeking work in corporate Montreal, and this situation is not likely to be eliminated in the near future. As McKinnon and Miller have noted:

> It remains quite possible for a unilingual francophone to pursue a career in Montreal; however, in a wide range of positions knowledge of English is essential for advancement. For a person who represents a company, whether to the public, or as a buyer or seller, there is usually a requirement to be able to work with English. For inter-corporate, or inter-divisional dealings there is, because of the nature of the North American economy, usually a necessity for English.[15]

On the other hand, the Montreal labor market has changed radically for Anglophones, especially when compared with the "English city" work ambiance that prevailed through the late 1950s. The days of the segregated, all-English work units described by the Gendron Commission are fading, and there is widespread recognition that knowledge of French is increasingly essential to socioeconomic advancement in the city. The "burden of bilingualism" is no longer exclusively shouldered by Francophones. In 1985, 67.6 percent of the Montreal Anglophone workforce declared itself bilingual, up from 43.4 percent in 1961.[16] More strikingly, unilingual Anglophones constituted, in 1961, 32 percent of Montreal's highest paid workers; by 1985, they represented only 7.8 percent of the city's best-paid employees.[17] In 1961, unilingual Anglophones represented 57.1 percent of the best-paid English-speaking workers in Montreal; by 1985, the unilingual component of highly paid Anglophones had declined to 31.7 percent.

By the 1980s, it had become increasingly difficult for Anglophones in the Montreal labor market to prosper without at least a working knowledge of the language of the city's majority. Anglophones working in local operations for Montreal corporations are expected to be bilingual. Even in head offices, generally exempt from the *francisation* provisions of Bill 101, 39 percent of Anglophone employees in 1979 had second-language job requirements, up from 10 percent in 1964.[18] Montreal corporations will recruit unilingual Anglophones, but the expectation is that these employees will undergo language training and gain a working knowledge of French. As *francisation* has progressed, job opportunities have diminished for unilingual Anglophones as office workers and sales personnel, occupations that involve either substantial public contact or linguistically heterogeneous workplaces. In short, as the 1981 SECOR study puts it, "It is still possible in Montreal to get a job without knowing French, provided one is willing to limit one's career. Bilingualism [has] . . . become virtually a necessary precondition in many firms for upward mobility."[19] This development represents a major transformation from only twenty-five years ago.

All the evidence suggests that Montreal workplaces increasingly functioned *en français* by the 1980s. Although French had not yet become by 1979 the "normal and customary" language of work envisioned by Bill 101, its status in the Montreal economy advanced considerably from the late 1960s. The fragmentary evidence presented by Monnier through 1983, and impressionistic evidence gathered by the CLF in its 1986 consultation, suggest that French has continued to make important, incremental gains as the language of work in Montreal through the 1980s.[20]

It is likely, however, that increased use of French in Montreal workplaces through the 1980s continued within the general pattern of sectoral and occupational variation of the 1970s. With the proximity of U.S. markets, the status of English as the international language of business in an increasingly global economy, and the historical roots of English in the Montreal economy, English will likely continue as a dominant language of management in Montreal.[21] In head offices and corporate activities oriented toward non-Quebec markets, English still prevails as a language of work; it is in local operations that French has made its most significant headway.

The Control of Capital

A central objective of Quebec government policy since the early 1960s has been to promote the growth of Francophone corporations and increase the number of Francophone managers and executives in the private sector, in Montreal and across the province. By the 1970s and 1980s, Quebec had witnessed the dynamic growth of Francophone corporations, most of them headquartered in Montreal, and many of them venturing beyond Quebec into Canadian and international markets. By the mid-1980s, there was a highly visible Francophone *garde montante* (rising guard) of economic elites—Pierre Laurin (Alcan), Pierre Lortie (Provigo), Bernard Lamarre (Lavalin), Laurent Beaudoin (Bombardier), and Claude Castonguay (Le Groupe La Laurentienne)—whose exploits filled the pages of Montreal's French-language press. Business has become practically a cultural obsession in much of French-speaking Montreal, and Francophones are involved in Montreal corporate life in ways that would have been unimaginable a mere twenty years ago.

The linchpin of the growing Francophone control of Montreal's economy was the "veritable breakthrough" in Francophone financial power that occurred in the 1970s.[22] As Fournier and Bélanger point out, "the regional financial hegemony of indigenous [Francophone] capital is no longer in question."[23] By the end of the eighties, it was rare for any major investments or deals to be made in Quebec without some participation by Francophone financial institutions. Moreover, the development of this financial power meant that Francophone businesses no longer lacked the access to capital that had historically limited their growth.

The new Francophone "financial network" includes the following sectors:

1. *Public capital.* The Caisse de dépôt et placement, with its active investment policy, its mandate to support Francophone economic development, and extensive holdings in Montreal firms, is the primary "quasi-public" pool of capital that has bolstered Francophone financial power in Montreal. In addition, tax-sheltered savings programs, such as the Régime enregistré d'épargne-retraite, have stimulated the growth of capital held by Francophone financial institutions.

2. *Private banks and credit unions.* The merger of the Banque Provinciale and the Banque Canadienne Nationale in 1979—creating the Banque nationale du Canada (BNC)—put a Montreal-headquartered, Francophone-

controlled bank within hailing distance of English-Canada's "Big Five"—at least in the Quebec market. The Banque nationale had assets of $31 billion in 1988 and, even though that is considerably less than the total assets of such English-Canadian banks as Royal Bank ($110 billion) and the Bank of Montreal ($78.9 billion), BNC is a major force in Quebec corporate finance.[24]

The explosive growth of the *caisses populaires*—credit unions of the Mouvement Desjardins—also injected new dynamism into Montreal and Quebec financial markets. The *caisses populaires* were founded in 1901 in the French-Catholic parishes of rural Quebec as a means of retaining local savings for local investment, and as a way of raising capital in Francophone communities neglected by Anglophone banks. After 1940, a substantial number of *caisses* were opened in Montreal and by 1974 the Fédération de Montréal des caisses Desjardins possessed over $325 million in assets.[25]

By the mid-1980s, the provincewide federation of *caisses* known as the Mouvement Desjardins contained more than fifteen hundred *caisses populaires* and, despite the localistic roots of the *caisses,* had become a Montreal-headquartered holding company. By 1988, helped by provincial government legislation permitting *caisses populaires* to finance subsidiaries with funds raised in the market, the Mouvement Desjardins held assets approaching $40 billion, including diversified holdings such as the Société d'investissement Desjardins, which buys shares in industrial firms, and the Crédit industriel Desjardins, which offers large business loans.[26] Other major enterprises connected with the expanding Desjardins empire include several insurance companies, substantial shares of the BNC, and a controlling interest in Culinar, Inc., a Quebec food-processor whose attempted takeover by the U.S. multinational Beatrice Foods was blocked by the Desjardins investment. The *caisses populaires* are particularly important in non-corporate finance, controlling, in 1987, 45 percent of Quebec's residential mortgage market, 32 percent of its consumer credit transactions, and 38 percent of its personal savings.[27] By 1988, the Mouvement Desjardins was Canada's sixth-largest deposit institution.

There still is a localistic, Francophone communal spirit underpinning the *caisses populaires:* "almost all Quebec Francophones, including their children"[28] have accounts in the *caisses.* But the Mouvement Desjardins has become one of the "mammoths" of Quebec's financial network, a financial and holding company of national and increasingly international scope that extends well beyond the rural "cooperative" ideology promulgated by its founder Alphonse Desjardins in 1901. The Complexe Desjardins, the architecturally-distinctive Montreal headquarters of the Mouvement Desjardins is as much a landmark of the Francophone ascendancy in the new Montreal economy as the Sun Life and Bank of Montreal buildings epitomized the era of the "English city."

3. *Insurance and trust companies.* Bolstered by PQ legislation de-

regulating the industry, Francophone insurance companies have become increasingly important participants in Quebec's financial markets. The most powerful of these insurance companies, Le Groupe La Laurentienne, has seen its assets grow from $100 million in 1975 to $4.5 billion in 1985 to almost $15 billion in 1988, chiefly through spectacular internal growth and numerous, remunerative acquisitions.[29] La Laurentienne has taken full advantage of deregulation, opening up Canada's first "full service, financial supermarket in its Montreal offices."[30] The company has diversified into banking (with the acquisition of La Banque d'épargne de la cité et du district de Montréal), trust companies, real estate, and financial services, and has penetrated markets in English Canada (with its control of the Toronto-based Eaton Financial Services), the United States, and Great Britain. As already indicated, the Mouvement Desjardins is also a major force in the Quebec insurance industry, with l'Assurance-Vie Desjardins, La Sauvegarde, and La Securité among its holdings.

Trust companies are Canadian financial institutions that act as fiduci-aries—managing private investment portfolios and estates—and financial intermediaries. Although Anglophone-controlled companies such as Royal Trust still dominate the Montreal market, major gains have been made by Francophone-controlled companies, such as the Trust générale du Canada and the Desjardins-controlled Fiducie du Québec. In addition, Francophones gained control of several formerly Anglophone companies in the 1970s and 1980s, such as the powerful Montreal Trust Co. that was controlled by Paul Desmarais' Power Corporation until it was sold to Bell Canada Enterprises in 1989.[31]

4. *The Montreal Stock Exchange.* A sign of the growing dynamism in Francophone-controlled financial markets was the revival in the 1980s of the Montreal Stock Exchange (ME). Historically, the ME was another bastion of Anglophone financial power, an important institution of the era when St. James Street was Canada's Wall Street, and Montreal was the financial capital of Canada. After the 1930s, however, as Toronto displaced Montreal as Canada's financial center, the importance of the ME waned. Fewer and fewer Anglophone companies listed their stock with the Exchange, and in the 1970s—with the dynamic growth of the Toronto exchange and the lin-guistic instability in Montreal and Quebec—the percentage of Canadian stock transactions taking place on the ME declined from 35.8 percent in 1971 to 11.9 percent in 1981.[32]

Despite the Exchange's alarming decline in the 1970s, the ground-work was being laid by the Exchange's first Francophone president, Michel Bélanger, to transform the ME from a declining, anachronistic Anglophone institution into a predominantly French-speaking operation increasingly serv-ing the investment needs of the Quebec regional market.[33] In the 1980s, under the innovative leadership of president Pierre Lortie, the Exchange began to rebound. Between 1979 and 1982, the ME reported only 58 new listings; by contrast, between 1983 and 1986, 335 new companies listed their stock on the Montreal Stock Exchange—177 in 1986 alone.[34] The new listings had a distinctly regional flavor, with over 60 percent of the companies headquartered in Quebec.

Lortie's efforts to rejuvenate the ME were decisively aided by a 1979 PQ program called the Régime d'épargne-actions (REA), the Quebec Stock Savings Plan that permitted Quebec investors to claim a tax deduction for buying new stock offered by Quebec companies.[35] By the mid-1980s, this program of "popular capitalism" had clearly promoted activity on the Montreal exchange. In 1986, so-called REA transactions accounted for 17.4 percent of the volume on the Montreal exchange, compared with only 6.3 percent in 1985. Eighty-nine of the 177 new companies listing stock on the ME in 1986 did so in conjunction with the REA.[36] Induced by the REA and a general Francophone surge of interest in the business world, Quebec rapidly became a province of stockholders. In 1978, only 2 percent of all Quebecers held stock; by 1985, over 15 percent were stockholders, the highest proportion found in any Canadian province. One survey reported that 11 percent of all adult Montrealers held REA stocks in 1987.[37]

The REA also boosted the growth of Francophone brokerage houses. With $3.7 billion in shares issued between 1979 and 1986 and $182 million in associated underwriters fees, the REA has been a major windfall for Francophone investment dealers. In 1985, Lévesque Beaubien and Geoffrion Leclerc managed or comanaged over half of all REA issues; boosted by REA business, both houses became major forces in Quebec finance.[38]

By the mid-1980s, as a result of all this activity, the ME had made somewhat of a comeback. The Montreal Stock Exchange's share of the total value of Canadian stock transactions rose from 11 percent in 1980 to 20 percent in 1986.[39] Although that is a far cry from 1960, when approximately one-third of the value of the Canadian stock transactions was exchanged in Montreal—let alone earlier in the century when Montreal was Canada's financial center—it does reveal the new strength of the city's Francophone financial sector. The REA market collapsed after the October 1987 stock market crash, but Montreal's Francophone financial network shows no signs of slowing down.

As a result of all of these developments in the financial sector, more and more capital has come under the control of Montreal Francophones, and a historical source of Francophone entrepreneurial weakness has been rectified. The amount of Quebec savings controlled by Francophone institutions tripled between 1977 and 1983.[40] Overall, according to Bélanger and Fournier, in 1984 Francophones controlled about one-third of the Quebec insurance, trust, and stock brokerage markets; over half the banking market; and 100 percent of the savings bank and credit union market.[41]

Moreover, as the "merger mania" of advanced capitalism came to French-speaking Montreal in the late 1970s, Francophone financial strength was enhanced by the concentration of power in giant, often interconnected financial empires: La Laurentienne, Banque nationale, the Mouvement Desjardins, and the Caisse de dépôt. Bélanger and Fournier count fifty major mergers or takeovers in the Francophone financial world between 1975 and 1983; Le Groupe La Laurentienne alone was involved in eight of these transactions.[42] This "paper entrepreneurialism" shows no sign of relenting. In 1988, for example, the Banque nationale took control of Lévesque Beaubien, Montreal's largest Francophone-controlled brokerage house, and in early 1989 acquired Geoffrion Leclerc, merging the two firms into a powerhouse of the Quebec securities industry.[43] The Bourassa government intends to deregulate Quebec's financial intermediaries with the explicit purpose of encouraging *further* concentration so that local "mammoths" such as the Mouvement Desjardins and Le Groupe La Laurentienne will reach the size to become more prominent participants in the international financial marketplace.[44] Thus, although English-Canadian financial institutions such as the Bank of Montreal, Royal Bank, Royal Trust, and the Canadian Imperial Bank of Commerce remain powerful forces in Montreal finance, linguistic control in the city's financial sector continues its radical transformation from the era when the Anglophone banks of St. James Street dominated Quebec's and Canada's financial markets.

The growth of Francophone financial power in the 1970s, along with provincial government loans and subsidies through the SGF, SDI, and other programs, created a sufficient pool of capital for the development of powerful Francophone firms in a number of other sectors. Some examples:

- In engineering, Montreal-headquartered Lavalin, SNC, and ABBDL–Tecsult have emerged as world-class firms, penetrating markets in the United States, English Canada, Europe, and Africa. Lavalin, the largest of the three, has more than seven thousand employees, $1 billion in revenues, and operations in more than ninety countries.[45]
- Montreal commerce, once dominated by Anglophone department stores and chains such as Eaton's, Steinberg's, and Simpson's, has become increasingly *francised*. In food retailing, Montreal's market was controlled as late as 1970 by two Anglophone-controlled firms: Steinberg's and Dominion. By 1989, Provigo and Métro-Richelieu controlled almost two-thirds of the Quebec market, Dominion had been sold (to Provigo), and Steinberg's, in deep financial difficulty, had been taken over by Francophone-controlled Socanav in tandem with the Caisse de dépôt.

In an era of corporate concentration, the increased availability of Francophone capital enabled small Francophone enterprises to form franchises and chains and gain the scale necessary to penetrate highly competitive markets.[46] Small Francophone hardware retailers joined together in the 1970s to form Ro-Na, a chain challenging the dominance of Anglophone-controlled Pascal, Inc. in Montreal. Similarly, the pharmaceuticals distributor Pharm-Escomptes Jean Coutu became one of Quebec's most important chains, controlling 45 percent of the province's pharmacy market by 1987; with its purchase of the Massachusetts-based Maxi-Drugs, Jean Coutu has begun penetrating the U.S. market.

- A 1983 study estimated that 60 percent of the transportation materials sector in Quebec was under Francophone control (up from 7.2 percent in 1961 and 44.5 percent in 1975).[47] Support from the Quebec government—from the Caisse de dépôt, SGF, and SDI—has been particularly important in the development of such companies in this sector as Bombardier, Prévost Car, and Canam-Manac.[48]
- Spawned by the *ébullition culturelle* of the Quiet Revolution and bolstered by PQ policies promoting Francophone control of Quebec's cultural industries, several Francophone communications "empires" have emerged: Unimédia, Québécor, Vidéotron, Télé-Métropole, Télé-Média, le groupe Civitas, and le groupe Beaudoin.[49]
- Francophone holding companies have become increasingly prominent participants in the paper entrepreneurialism of advanced capitalism. We have already mentioned the acquisitiveness of such companies as La Laurentienne and the Mouvement Desjardins. In addition, Bertin Nadeau of Unigesco has emerged as a kind of Québécois Boone Pickens, wheeling and dealing his way around the world of takeovers, greenmail, and golden parachutes; the jewel of Unigesco's empire is its controlling interest in Provigo.

The most powerful of the Francophone holding companies remains Paul Desmarais' Power Corporation. Using his close connections with the Trudeau government in the 1970s, Desmarais built a $50 billion media, energy, financial services, and forestry empire. Although Power Financial Corporation recently sold its interests in Montreal Trustco and Consolidated Bathurst, the corporation still controls Crédit Foncier, Great-West Life Assurance of Winnipeg, and *La Presse,* Montreal's major mass circulation French-language daily newspaper.[50]

In short, the evidence is clear that the linguistic segmentation of economic activity in Montreal has declined since the 1970s as Francophone firms have penetrated historically Anglophone sectors in finance, heavy industry, high technology, and advanced corporate services. Yet, despite these signs of Francophone economic power, the most recent systematic study of corporate control in Montreal revealed that, at least through 1978,

Francophones had not exactly become *"maîtres chez-nous."* Raynauld and Vaillancourt's survey found that only in the sectors of construction, printing and publishing, and recreational services, did a majority of Montreal employees work in firms controlled by Francophones, although in such significant sectors as business services, insurance and real estate, and wholesale trade, the rate of Francophone ownership approached that of Anglophones and foreigners.[51] In all of these sectors, and perhaps some others such as retail trade, transportation and communications, and metal products, the likelihood is that Francophone control increased sharply in the 1980s, though certainly not enough to assert that the Montreal economy was firmly under the control of Francophones. Across the province, the percentage of Quebecers working in establishments under Francophone control increased from 47.1 percent in 1961 to 54.8 percent in 1978, and 61.6 percent in 1987, with major leaps in the financial and construction sectors.[52]

Despite the emergence of world-class, Montreal-based Francophone enterprises, the main Francophone economic control in Montreal and across Quebec continues in small and medium-sized enterprises. This sector has created almost all of Quebec's jobs since the early 1980s, giving a sense of Francophone economic dynamism, and provincial government policies have focused on nurturing these "PME's" into market forces.[53] But, as Raynauld and Vaillancourt concluded, Francophone enterprises "are the smallest establishments, where productivity is the weakest, salaries are lower, the costs of production are higher, and which serve primarily a local market."[54]

In 1978, for example, for Quebec firms with shipments valued at under \$1 million, 53.8 percent of the total "value added" was from firms under Francophone control. By contrast, for firms with shipments exceeding \$10 million, only 15.8 percent of the total value added was produced in firms under Francophone control (35.0 percent was from Anglophone firms and 49.2 percent from firms under foreign control).[55] Moreover, as Figures 8.3 and 8.4 show, although the exports of Francophone manufacturers in 1978 were less tied to regional markets than in 1961, Francophone firms still produced substantially more for local markets than did Anglophone or foreign-owned firms in the province. Nevertheless, the impact of government export-promotion programs and the penetration of international markets by Provigo, Bombardier, La Laurentienne, Banque nationale, Lavalin, SNC, and Canam-Manac suggest a growing globalization of Francophone enterprise in the 1980s.

The situation observed by Raynauld and Vaillancourt in 1978 has clearly changed in the past decade. Francophone firms are no longer predominantly "family" enterprises or relegated to regional, low value-added sectors of the economy. Nevertheless, Anglophone capital still occupied commanding heights in the Montreal economy through the late 1980s. Several major Anglophone-controlled firms, Seagram, Pratt and Whitney, Bell

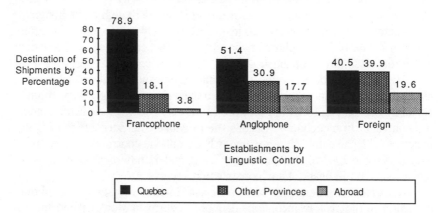

Figure 8.3
Destination of Manufacturing Shipments
by Linguistic-Group Ownership, Quebec, 1961

Source: André Raynauld, *Le propriété des entreprises au Québec: les années 60* (Montréal: Les Presses de l'Université de Montréal), p. 112.

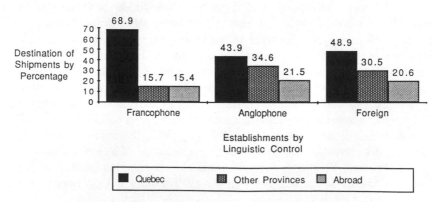

Figure 8.4
Destination of Manufacturing Shipments
by Linguistic Group Ownership, Quebec, 1979

Source: André Raynauld and François Vaillancourt, *L'appartenance des entreprises: le cas du Québec en 1978* (Québec: Éditeur officiel du Québec, 1984), p. 110.

Canada, and Canadian Pacific, remained headquartered in Montreal, while others whose headquarters were no longer in the city, the Bank of Montreal and Molson's, for example, retained substantial operations in Montreal and remained powerful economic forces in Quebec. Even Sun Life, whose loud movement of its head office from Montreal fueled linguistic tensions in the city, retains the largest share of Quebec's personal insurance market.[56] In 1988, six Montreal-headquartered companies, Seagram, Bell Canada Enterprises, Royal Bank, Canadian Pacific, Imasco, and Alcan Aluminum, ranked in the "Global 1000," a *Business Week* listing of the thousand leading corporations in the world according to market value.[57] Several other firms formerly headquartered in Montreal, such as the Bank of Montreal, also made the "Global 1000." All of these firms are Anglophone-controlled.

Another way to gauge changing patterns of economic power in Montreal is to examine the linguistic composition of management in the private sector. Although management and control are not synonymous, a growing presence of Francophone managers would suggest growing Francophone participation in private-sector decision-making.

Middle- and senior-level management in the Montreal and Quebec private sectors has been somewhat *francophonised* since the late 1960s. According to René Champagne, the proportion of Francophones among senior managers in Quebec grew from 19.3 percent in 1976 to 25.4 percent in 1982.[58] A Montreal Board of Trade study in 1979 revealed that the Francophone percentage of managers in Montreal area firms grew from 44.6 percent to 57.7 percent between 1967 and 1979.[59]

Yet, important variations by linguistic group remain. The 1982 Sales and Bélanger survey found, for example, that the linguistic composition of managers and executives varied strongly according to the linguistic background of the owners or chief stockholders of a company. Francophones constituted only 53.9 percent of the management of English-Canadian-controlled firms in 1982 and 58.3 percent of the management in foreign-owned firms. By contrast, 91.4 percent of the managers and executives in French-Canadian-controlled firms were Francophone.[60] This finding was confirmed in a 1986 study by Léo-Paul Lauzon that hinted at linguistically segmented corporate management in Montreal: nearly 100 percent Francophone "decision-makers" in firms such as Bombardier, Provigo, La Laurentienne, and Banque nationale, but less than 10 percent Francophone representation in "decisional positions" in firms such as Canadian Pacific, Royal Bank, Molson, Trizec, and the Bank of Montreal.[61] Thus, the increase in senior Francophone managers in 1980s Montreal seems to have stemmed mainly from the growth of Francophone corporations, rather than significant hiring of Francophones by Anglophone-controlled corporations.

In addition, *within* Quebec firms controlled by non-Francophones, a linguistic division of labor still apparently exists. As Figures 8.5 and 8.6 re-

Figure 8.5
Linguistic Composition of Management in Quebec,
by Type of Operation, 1982

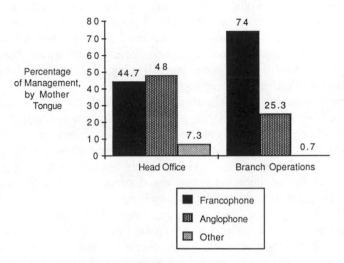

English-Canadian–Owned Firms

Source: Arnaud Sales et Noël Bélanger, *Décideurs et gestionnaires: étude sur la direction et l'encadrement des secteurs privé et public* (Québec: Éditeur officiel du Québec, 1985), p. 187.

veal, Francophone managers and executives are mainly concentrated in branch operations rather than head-office activity. Moreover, *within* head offices, Anglophones are much more likely to be involved with central administration tasks, while Francophones are disproportionately involved with the administration of branches and subsidiaries.[62] In summary, although Francophones are no longer limited to the proverbial "Vice-President for Public Relations" positions in Anglophone-controlled firms, linguistic segmentation of management remains an important part of Montreal's economy. Francophones are more involved in work activities linked to Quebec markets and regional administration, while Anglophones are involved in operations with wider scope, catering to English-speaking markets.

Nevertheless, the evidence seems clear that the *francisation* of Montreal workplaces *is* helping promote the *francophonisation* of private-sector economic decision-making. Francophone economic power in Montreal has been enhanced by the rise of a new generation of French-speaking corporate managers and executives in the city. There is now a genuine Francophone capitalist class headquartered in Montreal, strongly influencing not only the Quebec economy, but also emerging as powerful actors in the entire North American economic system. By 1987, another symbolic illustration of the

Figure 8.6
Linguistic Composition of Management in Quebec,
by Type of Operation, 1982

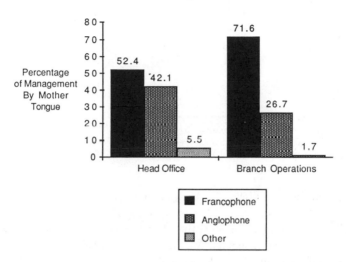

Foreign–Owned Firms

Source: Arnaud Sales and Noël Bélanger, *Décideurs et gestionnaires: étude sur la direction et l'encadrement des secteurs privé et public* (Québec: Éditeur officiel du Québec, 1985), p. 187.

changing Montreal economy could be seen: fully half of the 6,000 members of the Montreal Board of Trade were Francophone. A new sign hung outside the offices of this former preserve of Montreal's (and, indeed, Canada's) Anglophone *haute bourgeoisie:* Bureau de Commerce de Montréal.[63]

The Socioeconomic Status of Francophones

In the 1970s, the number of Quebec firms under the control of Francophones increased. Knowledge of French became a more important source of "human capital" on the Montreal labor market. Significant numbers of well-paid jobs became available to Francophones, first in the public sector and increasingly in the private sector during this decade.

Under these circumstances, the income gap separating Francophones and Anglophones in Montreal narrowed dramatically between 1960 and 1980. Male Anglophones in Montreal earned 51 percent more than their Francophone counterparts in 1961; by 1970, the gap had diminished to 32 percent and it shrank to 14 percent in 1980.[64] As Table 8.3 shows, by the 1980s there was only a small earnings gap separating bilingual Francophones

Table 8.3
Average Annual Earnings of Montreal Anglophones and Francophones,
by Linguistic Competence, 1970–1985

Average Male Earnings

	1961	*1970*	*1980*	*1985*
Francophones				
Unilingual	$2,975	$5,636	$14,351	$20,699
Bilingual	4,201	7,686	19,411	27,160
Anglophones				
Unilingual	5,749	9,123	19,840	27,601
Bilingual	5,931	9,367	19,920	29,071

Sources: Jac-André Boulet, *L'évolution des disparités linguistiques de revenus de travail au Canada de 1970 à 1980* (Ottawa: Conseil économique du Canada, 1983), p. 10; and Statistics Canada, Unpublished Special Tabulations, 1971, 1981, 1986.

and either unilingual or bilingual Anglophones (the gap was 39 percent in 1961 and 20 percent in 1970). Moreover, although unilingual Francophones were still clearly disadvantaged in the Montreal labor market, by 1985 the earnings gap between unilingual Anglophones and unilingual Francophones had fallen to 33 percent (from 96 percent in 1961 and 64 percent in 1970). Bilingual Anglophones remain Montreal's most prosperous linguistic group, and the narrowing of Montreal's linguistic earnings gap appears to have ceased after 1980. Nevertheless, Francophone socioeconomic gains since 1960 are impressive.

As we have seen, before the 1960s Anglophones held the bulk of Montreal's best-paying jobs.[65] By the 1980s, however, the linguistic composition of Montreal's earnings elite changed substantially. As Table 8.4 shows, although Francophones constituted over 67 percent of the region's labor force in 1961, they only represented 44 percent of Montreal's "best paid" workers (the top 15 percent of wage earners); by 1985, 75.3 percent of Montreal's high-paid workers were Francophone, roughly in proportion to the Francophone percentage of the overall labor force. Clearly, by this important indicator Francophone Montrealers experienced significant upward mobility between 1961 and 1985.

Changes in societal income distribution typically occur slowly and incrementally; thus, the steep reduction in the Anglophone–Francophone earnings gap in Montreal after 1960 was remarkable. In addition, during the 1970s a truly striking restructuring occurred in the distribution of earnings *within* Montreal's Francophone community. As Table 8.5 shows, an extraordinarily high percentage of Montreal's male Francophone labor force—particularly unilinguals—was clustered in 1970 in the lower end of the community's earnings distribution. Whereas 67.8 percent of Montreal Fran-

Table 8.4

Linguistic Composition of Well-Paid Montreal Labor Force, 1961–1985

% of total labor force

	1961	1970	1980	1985
Francophones	44.0	54.3	71.3	75.4
Unilingual	3.0	7.6	11.8	13.1
Bilingual	41.0	46.7	59.5	62.3
Anglophones	56.0	45.7	28.7	24.6
Unilingual	32.0	23.8	10.4	7.8
Bilingual	24.0	21.8	18.3	16.8

Sources: See Table 8.3.

Table 8.5

Distribution of Francophone Male Labor Force Among Earnings Classes,
Metropolitan Montreal, 1970–1985

% of total male labor force in each earnings class
(in 1985 constant $)

Annual Earnings	Unilingual Francophones			Bilingual Francophones		
	1970	1980	1985	1970	1980	1985
Under $15,000	39.9	33.3	33.9	26.1	24.2	26.7
$15,000–24,999	40.7	31.3	29.5	34.7	22.4	21.3
$25,000–39,999	17.1	29.4	29.6	29.7	35.1	32.7
$40,000–49,999	1.3	4.0	4.6	4.3	9.5	9.9
Above $50,000	1.1	1.9	2.4	5.2	8.9	9.4
	100.0	100.0	100.0	100.0	100.0	100.0

Source: Statistics Canada, Unpublished Special Tabulations, 1971, 1981, 1986.

cophones earned less than $25,000 annually in 1970 (in 1985 constant dollars), only 51.5 percent of Montreal Anglophones fell into this income category.[66] By 1980, however, the proportion of Francophones in the lower-end earnings class had fallen to 53.5 percent, with healthy increases in both middle- and upper-level earnings categories. This trend occurred for both unilingual and bilingual Francophones.

During the 1970s, cities in the United States experienced a distinct "bifurcation" in their earnings structure: an increase in low- and high-wage jobs, and a decline in middle-income employment.[67] The experience of Francophone Montreal was precisely the opposite during this decade. The 1970s saw a significant broadening of the middle class in French-speaking Montreal, as thousands of Francophones moved from lower-end to middle-

and upper-level earnings classes. For example, while the total male Franco-phone labor force in Montreal increased by 20.6 percent between 1970 and 1980, the number of male Francophones earning between $25,000 and $40,000 annually increased by *58.9 percent.* The number of unilingual Franco-phones in this earnings class jumped 123.1 percent between 1970 and 1980, while the number of bilinguals in this class increased 37.2 percent. These trends leveled off in the 1980s, but the Francophone gains from the earlier period remained largely intact.

It was not just a select few of Montreal's Francophone labor force who garnered upper-income jobs and hence narrowed the earnings gap between French- and English-speakers in the city. Aided by language policies and other programs promoting Francophone economic opportunity, and by de-parting Anglophones vacating middle-income positions in the city's econ-omy, Francophones were able to seize a broad range of "quality jobs" in Montreal in the 1970s. In this sense, those who argue that language policies and other policies of "ethnic promotion" are largely the tool of an aspiring economic elite [68] are wrong: the policies of the 1970s appear to have bene-fited broad elements in Montreal's French-speaking community.

Beyond language policy, several elements in Quebec political economy contributed to the broadening of the Francophone middle class in the 1970s. Educated Francophones began emerging from Montreal's revitalized school systems, prepared to assume quality jobs. Moreover, in contrast to trends in the United States and other advanced capitalist societies, the rate of unionization increased in Quebec, from 31.8 percent in 1970 to 37.6 percent in 1977. [69] By the early 1980s, almost two-thirds of Quebec's public-sector workers belonged to unions. [70] Throughout the 1970s, a surge in labor mili-tance yielded generous wage settlements, including increases in social bene-fits and the minimum wage, and legislation such as Bill 45, the "anti-scab" law of 1977, enhanced labor's bargaining position. It was not until the early 1980s, when the fiscal crisis of the Quebec state led the PQ to mandate a rollback of wage increases in the public sector, that Quebec labor began facing the anti-union environment endured by the U.S. workers a decade earlier. Prior to 1980, however, the rise of Francophone employment in the public sector, coupled with the generous wages paid in that heavily union-ized sector, helped thousands of Montreal Francophones earn middle-class incomes. For example, in 1961, the average salary of a Quebec provincial government employee was 98 percent that of an average private-sector worker; by 1978, the ratio had reached 129 percent, falling to 121 percent in 1985. The average Quebec elementary and secondary school teacher's sal-ary was 118.3 percent that of an average wage earner in 1970; by 1980, it had reached 138.3 percent, and it was 130.8 percent in 1985. [71]

All Francophones did not benefit materially from the shifting linguistic dynamics in the city's economy. In 1981, 20.1 percent of Montreal's Franco-

phone population remained below the poverty line,[72] and the rapid dein-
dustrialization of Montreal's east and southwest districts in the 1980s left
Francophone (and non-Francophone) workers in such neighborhoods as
Hochelaga, Maisonneuve, and Point-Saint-Charles in severe economic dis-
tress. (These neighborhoods reported unemployment rates exceeding 30
percent in the late 1980s.)[73] However, for thousands of Montreal Francophones—those individuals with the skills to take advantage of the changing
places of English and French in the city's economy—the new Montreal
economy offered an upward mobility that existed only for limited numbers
before 1960.

The External Face of Business

We only have impressionistic evidence regarding the "English face" of business in Montreal prior to the 1960s. But the evidence is compelling: photo-
graphs of downtown Montreal dotted with English-only commercial signs;
anecdotes of Francophone encounters with condescending, unilingual Anglophone clerks in the city's major department stores; stories of Francophone
tenants grappling with leases printed in English, or consumers frustrated
with English instructions on the use of a product.

By the 1960s, however, Montreal businesses began responding to the
city's growing French-speaking consumer market and nationalist complaints
over the use of English in commercial activities. The Gendron Commission reported in 1972 that Montreal business had made "a considerable effort . . . to serve its French-speaking clientele better. . . . A new practice
has come into being," noted the commission, "that of serving the client in
French or in English according to his choice, and that is becoming more
widespread."[74] Bilingual salespeople became commonplace in establishments
serving French-speaking clientele, and downtown department stores attempted to add a French face to their names (for example, Morgan's became
La Baie/The Bay; Eaton's became Eaton; Simpson's became Simpson, and
so forth). Nevertheless, despite seemingly greater attentiveness to Francophone consumers, in a 1971 survey 70 percent of Francophone Montrealers
reported having experienced "a great deal of difficulty" in obtaining service
in their own language in a restaurant or a store during the preceding six
months.[75]

Between 1970 and the early 1980s, facing increased expectations on
the part of French-speaking consumers as well as the regulations of Bills
22 and 101, the public face of Montreal businesses became increasingly
French. For example, in the 1971 Gendron survey, 42 percent of Montreal
Francophones reported purchasing a product with instructions for its use in
English only; in 1985, that figure had fallen to 30 percent.[76] Only 21 percent

of Montreal Francophones declared in a 1988 survey that they encountered "over the past twelve months, problems in receiving service in French in commercial transactions." (In that same survey, 23 percent of Montreal Anglophones reported difficulty in receiving service in English).[77]

A more exhaustive study by the CLF in 1988 found that only in some West Island establishments was there any difficulty in receiving service in French. Moreover, the survey reported that sales staff in department stores and shopping centers initiated transactions in French, on average, in 80 percent of the cases surveyed, with lower percentages in western Montreal neighborhoods such as Snowdon and West Island municipalities. Still, even in heavily Anglophone communities such as Dorval or Pointe-Claire, 50 percent of transactions began in French, and service was available in French in nearly 90 percent of the establishments surveyed in these communities.[78] These findings led Guy Rivard, at that time the minister responsible for the Charter of the French Language, to conclude: "No one can hereafter doubt that it is now possible, except in rare cases, to receive service in French in a commercial establishment in Montreal. Like many Montrealers, I am in a position to certify that French has progressed considerably in Montreal commerce during the past twenty years."[79]

As for the physical face of Montreal, Bill 101's regulations on French-only commercial signs seemed to promote a more "French" appearance in the city by the late 1970s. A 1970 survey by Guy Labelle estimated that 35 percent of the commercial signs in metropolitan Montreal were in French-only and 11.8 percent in English-only; by 1984, according to a CLF study, French unilingualism in commercial signs had grown to 78.5 percent and English unilingualism had fallen to 7.2 percent.[80] While the methodologies of the two surveys were sufficiently different to limit direct comparisons, the magnitude of the changes observed between 1970 and 1984 were large enough to confirm that a pronounced *francisation* had occurred in the external *visage* of Montreal businesses.[81] As the CLF concluded in 1983:

> Because of Articles 58 and 69 of Bill 101 [those regarding French-only commercial signs and company names], important changes have occurred . . . and it has not escaped notice that the external face of Quebec, notably that of Montreal, has become much more French. A survey of the Commission de surveillance de la langue française . . . shows that of 3,532 signs on the outside of establishments in downtown Montreal, 70% conform to the provisions of the Charter of the French Language, 25% utilise both French and English, and 5% are in English only.[82]

As we examined in Chapter 6, during the 1985 elections Robert Bourassa promised amendments to Bill 101 on the language of public signs, and after his victory progress toward the *francisation* of Montreal's external face appeared to stop. Bilingual and even unilingual English signs proliferated in downtown Montreal and the West Island. Stores such as Zellers openly displayed bilingual commercial signs in predominantly Anglophone West Island suburbs such as Pointe-Claire, claiming that since 1983 amendments to Bill 101 permitted municipal governments to serve Anglophones in English, then "what's good for municipalities is good for Zellers."[83] Between April 1986 and 1987, the Commission de protection de la langue française reported a 147 percent increase in complaints over violations of Bill 101, the overwhelming number regarding commercial signs and company names.[84] The 1988 CLF study found that the proportion of commercial establishments respecting Bill 101 and posting signs in French-only ranged from only 43 percent in some West Island and Central Montreal neighborhoods, to 93 percent in more French-speaking areas of the Island.

The continuing controversy over Bourassa's solution to the signs issue—unilingual French outside all establishments, bilingualism permitted inside some—makes this question the one great unresolved issue of *la question linguistique*. But, even with the problems over signs and occasional incidents in which Francophones have difficulties receiving service in French, the linguistic climate of commerce in Montreal has vastly *francised* from its early 1960s condition.

Public Policy, Market Forces, and Economic Change

Viewed from almost any angle, the position of French in the Montreal economy advanced considerably between 1960 and the 1980s. French was used more often in work and consumer activities, thousands of Francophones moved into positions of management and control in the private sector, the linguistic income gap all but vanished, and Montreal business took on a demonstrably more French face.

Public intervention in the economy was instrumental in this transformation. Government industrial policies promoted the development of Francophone enterprises, and the explosive growth of a French-speaking public sector in Quebec provided middle-income employment opportunities for Francophones. Educational reforms increased the number of Francophones qualified to assume well-paid positions in Montreal's private sector. Language policies also played an important role, in mandating changes in the external face of business, putting the force of law behind the right to work or be served in French, and generally accelerating the process of *francisation*.[85]

Several economists, however, downplay the impact of language policy particularly in transforming the places of English and French in Montreal's economy between 1960 and the mid-1980s, stressing instead the role of "natural market forces."[86] Yvan Allaire and Roger Miller, in several publications, maintain that "the process of *francisation* was well underway" before Bill 101, as Montreal businesses responded to a more prosperous Francophone consumer market and growing Francophone insistence on being served in French.[87] Firms more or less "voluntarily" began a process of *francisation*, they argue, as market shifts increased the profitability of operating in French.[88] Lacroix and Vaillancourt claim that "Quebec's language laws have not played an important role in the *francisation* of Quebec's labor market and thus are unlikely to have had an impact on the utilisation of French in the workplace."[89] Moreover, since income disparities based on language had closed significantly by 1977, "the policies could not have had a significant effect on the issue."[90] In their view, market forces, along with general political pressures beginning in the 1960s, generated increases in the supply of and demand for French-speaking labor that helped close the income gap between Anglophones and Francophones.

Three "market" or "structural" factors are most commonly cited as contributing to the post-1960 *francisation* of the Montreal economy. First, the focus of economic activity in Montreal continued to shift away from Canadian markets toward the Quebec region. The displacement of Montreal as Canada's preeminent urban economic center accelerated after 1960, as growing numbers of Canadian head offices and American branch plants opted for the Toronto region. By 1970, Toronto had supplanted Montreal in the number of head offices located there, and in the value and volume of stock transactions. Montreal's manufacturing investment slightly exceeded Toronto's in 1961; by 1981, as huge automobile investments came on-line in the Toronto region, Montreal's total manufacturing investment had fallen to 51 percent of Toronto's, and 1986 estimates were that the percentage had slipped to 28 percent.[91] In short, by the 1970s, Toronto had clearly become Canada's national economic center, while Montreal functioned increasingly as the urban node of the Quebec regional market.

The regional focus of economic activity in Montreal became even more pronounced during the 1970s. For example, managerial employment in Montreal head offices grew by 23 percent between 1967 and 1978 compared with a 49 percent increase in regional offices.[92] As Table 8.6 shows, there was a marked increase between 1970 and 1985 in the proportion of Montreal's labor force employed in economic activities oriented toward "internal markets" (Quebec) as opposed to "external markets" (primarily the U.S. and English Canada).

As economic activities in Montreal increasingly served a regional, predominantly French-speaking market rather than English-speaking continental markets, the "profitability" of knowing French concomitantly increased on the city's labor market—thus opening up greater economic opportunities for Francophones and increasing the usage of French as a lan-

Table 8.6

The Regionalization of the Montreal Economy, 1971–1985

% of Workforce Employed by Sector

Year	External Sector	Internal Sector
1971	45.2	54.8
1981	40.7	59.3
1985	37.5	62.5

Source: Pierre Lamonde, "La transformation de l'économie mon-treálaise, 1971–1986," unpublished study prepared for the Communauté urbaine de Montréal, 1988, pp. 23, 66.

Note: I have used Lacroix and Vaillancourt's classification scheme here in defining "internal" and "external" sectors. The internal sector includes construction, commerce and commercial services, and public services. The external sector includes manufacturing, transportation and communications, and finance.

guage of work in the city.[93] As Fernand Martin points out, "Montreal is more oriented toward Quebec and becomes by that fact more French. . . . A Montreal furnishing almost exclusively regional services becomes automatically a more Francophone Montreal."[94]

With more and more of Montreal's economic activity directed toward Quebec's overwhelmingly French-speaking market, it became increasingly rational for Anglophone workers to take their "capital" in English-language proficiency to labor markets where it would be more valued. Thus, between 1971 and 1981, over 15 percent of Montreal's male English-speaking labor force left the province, the vast majority for Ontario.[95] This departure of generally well-educated, middle-income Anglophones made available numerous managerial positions in Montreal's private sector that were garnered by Francophones, helping close the city's linguistic income gap in the 1970s. As Paul Bernard and his colleagues have described the process:

> Francophones almost totally monopolized the new positions that were . . . created. [This] was not the result of political intervention on the language question; instead, it resulted directly from the fact that Francophones constituted the only pool of new workers available on the Quebec market from 1971 to 1978.[96]

Second, as was the case throughout urban North America, between 1960 and 1986 the Montreal economy became increasingly based on services as opposed to manufacturing, and this sectoral shift had important implications for language use in the city's economy. Well over 95 percent of the

Table 8.7
Sectoral Composition of Workforce in Metropolitan Montreal,
1961–1986, in Percentages

Sector	1961	1971	1981	1986
Manufacturing	32.5	28.2	23.4	21.0
Construction	7.2	5.2	4.2	4.8
Services	59.6	66.0	72.1	73.6
Others	0.7	0.6	0.3	0.6

Source: See Table 8.6.

jobs created in metropolitan Montreal between 1961 and 1986 were in the service sector—government, finance, business and personal services, commerce, and so forth. As Table 8.7 shows, by 1986 almost three-fourths of Montreal's labor force was employed in service activities, compared with slightly less than 60 percent in 1961.

To a much greater extent than manufacturing, the service sector is characterized by intensive use of language. Whether employed as lawyers, advertising executives, office workers, or salespeople, service-sector employees are much more likely than manufacturing employees to be engaged in reading or writing or in public contact.[97] As Martin points out, "services, more than goods, are very sensitive to cultural and linguistic barriers, because of their basis in information exchanges and interpersonal communication."[98]

The shift to services has accentuated the growing linkage of Montreal's economy to French Quebec as opposed to English Canada. In the advanced corporate services sector, for example, the overwhelming percentage of business for Montreal firms in the 1980s was in Quebec. A 1980 survey found that 87.2 percent of the receipts for Montreal-based management consultants came from Quebec; information systems consultants and advertising agencies based in Montreal received 88.1 percent and 75.2 percent of their receipts respectively from Quebec.[99]

It is no accident that the most dramatic Francophone business successes have come in sectors involving the distribution of goods or the selling of services to Quebec's predominantly French-speaking clientele; it is in such activities that Montreal Francophone firms, provided they have adequate capital, *should* have a competitive advantage. According to Mario Polèse and Robert Stafford, the strength of Francophone firms is so evident in Montreal's corporate services sector that, far from a *satellisation* of Montreal to Toronto, "for most services it would be more accurate to talk about a sharing of markets because Montreal very clearly dominates Quebec territory, playing the same role vis-a-vis the rest of Quebec that Toronto does with the rest of Canada."[100] In short, the rapid growth of the service sector—and the linguistic segmentation of service activity—has created substantial economic opportunity for Montreal Francophones.

Finally, the establishment of a "critical mass" of French-speaking consumers, businesses, and managers in Montreal helped set in motion market processes that improved economic conditions in the Francophone community. As thousands of rural Francophones migrated to Montreal between 1900 and 1970, their urban concentration created an audience for the development of French-language cultural "industries" in the city—radio, television, print media, the performing arts, and literary activities. In addition, the growing number of Francophone consumers provided increased clientele for small Francophone firms in financial services, banking, investment, and real estate—industries that presented few barriers in the way of massive capital requirements or sophisticated production technology.[101] In turn, these initial private-sector ventures helped stimulate further Francophone economic development, especially as Francophone consumers demanded service in their own language. Aside from providing a geographically concentrated, French-speaking market for Francophone enterprise to target, Montreal's growth also meant that "jobs as car dealers, garage mechanics, insurance agents, telephone operators, or office clerks represented new possibilities for both long established Montrealers and for new arrivals in the metropolis."[102]

As Francophones entered the Montreal private sector, albeit initially in small numbers, a critical mass of French-speaking managers was formed, representing an important "information network" that would eventually promote further hiring of Francophones. As Jac-André Boulet has posited, an important reason that Anglophones were able to monopolize Montreal's well-paid jobs through the 1960s was that aspiring Francophones remained outside the private sector's "information network": Anglophones heard first about openings in various firms, Anglophones recruited other Anglophones, and so forth. By the early 1970s, however, Francophones were increasingly "plugged in" to Montreal's information network and advanced accordingly.[103]

There is little doubt that market trends such as regionalization and the growth of the service sector contributed heavily to the *francisation* of Montreal's economy after 1960, as did the development of "information networks" and "critical masses" of capital, consumers, and skilled labor. Nevertheless, market factors alone cannot possibly explain the shifting linguistic dynamics in the city's economy. Without the post-1960 investments in education, for example, Francophones would not have possessed the "human capital" necessary to take advantage of the openings created by the exodus of Anglophones in the 1970s. In that sense, educational reform was a "language policy that increased the supply of Francophones in the labor market."[104] Corporations may have partially *francised* in response to a growing Francophone consumer market, but that attractive consumer market was itself, in part, the product of the tremendous increase in public employment beginning in the 1960s that provided thousands of middle-income jobs to Francophones and injected millions of "Francophone dollars" into the Montreal economy. Finally, while Montreal firms may have begun *francisation* in response to changing consumer and labor markets, much of the business response also resulted from political pressures and anticipation of language policies—a politically induced market "climate" that hardly fits the "natural market forces" model of neo-classical economics.

Concomitantly, while market conditions in the 1970s may have been propitious for the development of Francophone corporate "success stories," almost all of the celebrated icons of Francophone free enterprise owe a large measure of their success to state policy. For example, we have already noted that Provigo was formed with government assistance (the Caisse de dépôt et placement), maintained under Francophone control as a result of the intervention of the Caisse, and was able to expand, in part, through government financial support and export assistance. Similarly, Bombardier received financing from the SGF and the Caisse, contracts from the Société de transport de la Communauté urbaine de Montréal, and export assistance from OQCE and SDI-Éxportation, while Lavalin, SNC, and numerous other firms developed through preferential purchasing by Hydro-Québec.

Government language policies did not single-handedly reshape Montreal's economy in the same, dramatic manner that they transformed schooling on the Island. Clearly, shifts in Montreal's linguistic division of labor were already occurring prior to the passage of Bills 22 and 101, with market forces and Quiet Revolution programs in education and economic development playing a major role. Nevertheless, language policy was instrumental in improving the economic prospects of Francophone Montrealers. For example, while educational reform has been credited with promoting Francophone mobility, through the early 1970s only 12.7 percent of the graduates of the Université de Montréal were working in the private sector, and over 90 percent of HEC's 1970 graduates took government positions.[105]

The failure of educational reform, by itself, to produce Francophone mobility in Montreal's private sector was not surprising. As long as English remained the working language of Montreal management, Francophones— even better-educated ones—would be at a disadvantage in competing for private-sector jobs. Thus, by helping change the language practices of Montreal firms, Bill 101 likely "increased both the demand for French-speakers and the recruitment of francophones . . . into high-wage occupations."[106] By 1985, the vast majority of HEC graduates found jobs in Montreal's private sector, the reverse of the pattern fifteen years earlier.[107] Closing the Anglophone/Francophone educational gap was a necessary condition for the *francisation* and *francophonisation* of Montreal corporations, but it was not a sufficient one. Language policy provided an important "encouragement" for Montreal firms to use French as a working language and an incentive to hire Francophones.

In addition, even though improvements in the condition of Francophones and the use of French in the Montreal economy antedated Bills 22 and 101, any rational businessperson operating in Montreal in the early 1970s could anticipate the passage of language policies of *francisation*. Thus, many of the pre-1974 developments, while not directly "caused" by language policy, may be understood as "anticipatory" *francisation*. Moreover, *francisation* was *not* all that far advanced at the time Bill 101 was passed. Even as late as 1984—one year *after* Bill 101's deadline for compliance—fewer than 40 percent of the Quebec firms covered by the legislation had *francised* sufficiently to receive certification from the OLF. By 1987, over 60 percent of the firms were in compliance.[108] Thus, it would appear that language policy played an important role in promoting a more conscientious and systematic program of *francisation* on the part of Montreal enterprises than had been operating before 1977.

Conclusion

A combination of market forces and public policy produced a stunning transformation of Montreal's linguistic division of labor between 1960 and the 1980s. Some of this transformation occurred as a result of long-term trends that favored the use of French in the city's economy, such as the growth of services and the decline of Montreal as a national economic center. But at the heart of Montreal's economic restructuring was deliberate government action. Public policies in employment, education, and economic development were instrumental in transforming the supply of and demand for Francophone labor, helping Francophone firms succeed in the private sector, and underwriting an attractive Francophone consumer market. By the early 1970s, these policies—along with the pressures of mobilized Québécois nationalism and the possibility of a more restrictive linguistic regime—had stimulated some business *francisation,* promoted the growth of successful Francophone firms, and helped close Montreal's linguistic earnings gap. The passage of Bill 22 in 1974, even with its lax implementation, nevertheless put Montreal firms further on notice that the days of English-only as the city's language of business were fading. Bill 101, while not initiating the *francisation* of the Montreal economy, clearly accelerated the process, forcing recalcitrant firms to adopt French systematically as the language of work and fostering an economic climate that increased the value of the French language in Montreal's labor and consumer markets.

Despite these changes, French was still not the dominant language of Montreal's economy in the 1980s, nor was the city's economic destiny firmly in the hands of Francophones. Although the hegemony of English Canadians over the city's economy had largely been broken, the status of English as an international language of business and high technology exerted strong Anglicization pressures. Through 1985, for example, 77 percent of the computer software employed by the *Quebec public administration*—the ultimate stronghold of French as a working language—operated in English.[109] As successful Montreal firms attempt to penetrate global markets, strong pressures will persist for Francophones to work in English. Moreover, Montreal's economic development strategy under Mayor Jean Doré is based on developing the city as an international business center, with the city's bilingual and bicultural tradition trumpeted as an *atout,* a unique "competitive advantage." Such a strategy assumes a continuing prominent place for English in the city.[110]

One economic development strategy explicitly calls for closer economic ties between Montreal and booming, high technology U.S. cities such as Boston.[111] Given the linguistic proclivities of most U.S.-based firms, the likelihood is that increased exchanges between firms in Montreal and Boston or any other U.S. city will bolster the importance of English in the Montreal economy. Thus, Francophone Montreal faces a supreme irony: the successes of Francophone firms in the Quebec market, and the increasing ability of many of these firms to penetrate markets in the United States, may yet impose English-language work requirements—with at least some Anglicization pressures—on upwardly mobile Francophones and Allophones. Moreover, as William Coleman has persuasively argued, greater integration of Francophone Quebec into the North American economy holds the real possibility of blurring Québécois cultural distinctiveness and turning the province—and its metropole—into the French-speaking branch of a homogenized North American consumer culture.[112]

Thus, even as the economic power of Anglophones has diminished in the city, English persists as a dominant language in the Montreal economy. Québécois culture will continue to face threats from the status of English in Montreal boardrooms, and from continental economic forces. These facts, however, should not obscure the tremendous changes that have occurred since the 1960s. Through political mobilization and public policy—and with some help from favorable market trends—the historically disadvantaged Francophone majority made remarkable progress in a twenty-five-year span. In the city's economic affairs, the days of the "English city" are clearly over.

Chapter 9

English and French in the New Montreal

When we want to know if French is in good shape in Quebec, it is not Chicoutimi or Quebec City where we should look but, above all, metropolitan Montreal. . . . It is this mixed setting where French is continually exposed to the pressures of English . . . and for which, above all, the Charter of the French Language was conceived.

Conseil de la langue française[1]

The quarter-century that has passed since the Quiet Revolution has been one of momentous change for Montreal's English- and French-speaking communities. Francophone political mobilization and the passage of two, far-reaching language laws fundamentally altered the city's linguistic balance of power. Virtually all major institutions in Montreal—schools, private corporations, public administration, and social service agencies—were transformed by this linguistic revolution, and French was firmly established as the only official language of public life. Two events, just twenty-two years apart, nicely capture the dimensions of Montreal's reshaped linguistic dynamics. In 1955, the Canadian National Railway could blithely ignore the protests of Francophone nationalists in giving its new downtown Montreal hotel the quintessentially British imperial name, The Queen Elizabeth. By 1977, Bill 101 would not only require that businesses and commercial establishments in Quebec possess French names, but also would proscribe the use of English on public signs throughout the province. In the 1950s, Montreal was a city in which an imperious Anglophone elite could safely disregard Francophone concerns over the cultural symbolism attached to the name of a major downtown building; by 1989, Montreal had become a city in which An-

209

glophones could no longer legally display their language—the language of Canada's majority—on public signs.

Montreal before 1960 was a city of "two majorities" and Anglophone elites, by virtue of their economic power, held an effective veto over all public decisions affecting language. These elites routinely acted, as in the case of the CNR hotel, as if Montreal were a British city that happened to be populated by many French-speaking citizens. By the 1980s, however, the city's linguistic hierarchies had been overturned: Francophone leaders regularly asserted the cultural and linguistic prerogatives of a majority, and Anglophones scrambled to defend community interests by invoking the principle of "minority rights."

Yet, notwithstanding indisputable signs of a Francophone reconquest of Montreal, the city's French character remained precarious through the 1980s. English persisted as a language of upward mobility in corporate Montreal, and even though linguistic income gaps were reduced, identifiably "English" areas on Montreal Island remained those with the highest property values and the greatest concentrations of wealthy individuals.[2] The omnipresence of North America's English-language mass culture exerted constant Anglicization pressures in the city. Moreover, the growing multicultural character of Montreal, along with the drive by an ascendant Francophone business class to integrate the city further into the global economy, raised a host of new problems for the future of French in Montreal that have only recently begun to receive serious attention in the Francophone community. As Daniel Latouche has perceptively noted, Montreal will always be more English than Paris: the problem for Francophones is to ensure that it does not "become less French than Geneva or Lyon."[3] Despite the changes since the 1960s, as the recrudescence of linguistic turbulence in 1988 over the issue of unilingual French signs made clear, Francophone anxieties over the linguistic character of Montreal remain far from resolved.

Linguistic Demography, 1971–1986

As we saw in Chapter 4, language policy became a mass political concern in Montreal in the late 1960s as Francophones worried that demographic trends might soon result in an English-speaking majority on the Island. Twenty years later, Bill 101 and an unprecedented out-migration of Anglophones have assured that metropolitan Montreal will remain predominantly French-speaking. As Table 9.1 shows, after steadily declining between 1961 and 1976, the French-speaking share of Montreal Island's population has increased slowly since 1976. The Francophone majority in *metropolitan* Montreal (69.7 percent in 1986) is even more pronounced than on the Island itself, because the rapidly growing off-Island suburbs on the North and South

Table 9.1
The Linguistic Composition of Montreal Island,
1961–1986, in Percentages by Mother Tongue

Year	French	English	Others
1961	62.7	24.0	13.3
1971	61.2	23.7	15.1
1976	59.4	25.6	15.0
1981	59.7	22.3	18.0
1986	60.1	21.6	18.3

Sources: Statistics Canada, *Census of Canada, 1971* (Catalogue 92–726); Statistics Canada, *Census of Canada, 1976* (Catalogue 92–822); Statistics Canada, *Census of Canada, 1981* (Catalogue 93–929); Statistics Canada, *Census of Canada, 1986* (Catalogue 95–130).

Shores are overwhelmingly (85 percent) French-speaking. The "demolinguistic" future of Montreal is now clear: with little prospect of significant Anglophone in-migration, and continued (albeit slowing) Francophone migration to the Montreal region from Quebec's hinterland, Francophones will represent a stable or increasing share of Montreal's population. The fear of Francophone *minorisation* in Montreal, if ever a credible one, no longer exists.[4]

A 1989 study by Michel Paillé of the CLF offers a dissenting view on the subject, suggesting that Francophones could make up as little as 56.5 percent of the population on Montreal Island by 1996. Paillé based his forecast on an influx of non-Francophone immigrants coupled with the plummeting Francophone birthrate, pointing out that since 1986 the number of non-Francophone immigrants arriving on the Island has exceeded the number of children born to Francophones. Paillé called the demographic situation of Francophones on the Island "fragile."[5]

Paillé's analysis, however, misses at least three important factors. First, thanks to Bill 101, the vast majority of immigrant children are now attending French-language schools; thus, their future status in Montreal's linguistic demography is at best problematical and cannot be assumed to be "non-Francophone." In fact, Paillé's analysis of the limited data on the subject suggests that slowly, but surely, Allophone children in Montreal's French-language schools are adopting French as their language to be spoken at home. Second, much of the "fragility" of the Francophone majority on the Island stems from the movement of Francophones off the Island to the North and South Shore suburbs (whereas Anglophones have remained largely concentrated in suburbs *on* the West Island). In 1986, metropolitan Montreal was 69.7 percent Francophone, and the City of Montreal was 66.9 percent Francophone; thus, it is somewhat misleading to focus simply on the Island of Montreal and conclude that the demographic position of French-speakers in Montreal is threatened in the near term. Finally, all predictions of a weakened Francophone demographic position assume a continuation of Quebec's depressed birthrate. But, birthrate projections are notoriously inaccurate, and with the growing political attention to Quebec's "fecundity crisis," it is not inconceivable that a Francophone mini "baby-boom" may be in the offing (indeed, through September 1989, Quebec's birthrate had increased 5.6 percent over 1988).[6]

However, even if analyses such as Paillé's seem unduly alarmist, it is undeniable that the English language remains a powerful assimilating force in the metropolis. In the parlance of demographers, net "linguistic transfers"—the balance of individuals changing their linguistic community—continued strongly in the direction of English in Montreal through the 1980s.[7] The Census of Canada has, since 1971, asked Canadians to identify not only their mother tongue ("the first language learned in childhood and still understood by an individual"), but also the specific language spoken at home. If the number of individuals using English as a home language exceeds the number of Anglophones in the population, then we can assume that non-"native Anglophones" have adopted English as their language of use, a clear indication of assimilation.[8]

As Table 9.2 shows, the number of Montrealers speaking English in their homes has consistently exceeded the number of Montreal residents reporting English as their mother tongue. In 1986, even as the number of Anglophones in metropolitan Montreal continued to decline, over 100,000 *more* Montrealers reporting using English in the home than were of English mother tongue.[9] Whereas 21.6 percent of Montreal Island's population was of English mother tongue in 1986, 25.2 percent of the population reported using English as the home language, a difference of 3.6 percent that represents net linguistic transfers to English. By contrast, in indisputably Francophone cities such as Quebec City, Trois-Rivières, and Chicoutimi, net linguistic transfers favor French and 50 percent of the Anglophones living in these cities report using French as their home language.[10]

Tables 9.3 and 9.4 reveal more precisely the sources of linguistic transfer in Montreal. While the vast majority of Allophones report using their native tongue at home, more than 70 percent of those reporting a "transfer" to one of Montreal's two main languages chose English. Table 9.3 displays the patterns of linguistic transfer among Montreal Allophones in various areas of the Island. Even though most of these communities contained substantially more Francophones than Anglophones in the population, only in overwhelmingly French-speaking Rosemont on the East End did Allophone transfers toward French exceed those to English. In predominantly Anglophone areas, such as Côte-St-Luc and Mont-Royal, Allophone transfers were overwhelmingly toward English, as they were in such areas as Côte-des-Neiges, Parc-Extension, Saint-Laurent, and Saint-Léonard, communities with high concentrations of Allophones.

Table 9.2

Net Linguistic Transfers on Montreal Island, 1971–1986

Percentage of the Population Declaring

Year	EMT	EHL	(EHL–EMT)	FMT	FHL	(FHL–FMT)
1971	23.7	27.4	+3.7	61.2	61.2	—
1981	22.3	27.0	+4.7	59.7	60.0	+0.3
1986	21.6	25.2	+3.6	60.1	61.8	+1.7

Sources: See Table 9.1.

EMT = English mother tongue   FMT = French mother tongue

EHL = English home language   FHL = French home language

Table 9.3

Allophone Linguistic Transfers in Montreal, 1986

Percentage distribution of Allophones by language spoken at home, in selected Montreal Island communities

Area	Toward English[a]	Toward French[b]	Tri-lingual[c]	Mother Tongue[d]
Metro Montreal	26.3	9.9	3.6	59.2
City of Montreal	21.1	9.4	3.3	65.7
Côte-des-Neiges	32.8	8.9	1.8	55.8
Rosemont	15.9	17.2	4.0	62.7
Parc Extension	14.1	3.2	2.1	80.2
Saint-Laurent	25.7	6.7	2.1	62.5
Saint-Léonard	22.0	7.5	4.1	66.4
Ville LaSalle	32.9	4.9	2.1	60.0
Montréal-Nord	13.8	13.1	7.2	65.9
Côte-Saint-Luc	58.6	1.7	4.0	34.9
Mont-Royal	42.5	10.2	4.2	41.2

Source: Statistics Canada, Unpublished Special Tabulations, 1986.

[a] Includes those reporting only English, or English plus the mother tongue, as language(s) spoken in the home.

[b] Includes those reporting only French, or French plus the mother tongue, as language(s) spoken in the home.

[c] Includes those reporting French, English, and the mother tongue as the languages spoken in the home.

[d] Includes those reporting only their mother tongue as the language spoken in the home.

In the aggregate, the number of *Francophones* transferring to English in metropolitan Montreal is not significant (2.1 percent of the metropolitan area's Francophones reporting using English as a home language in 1986, down from 3.2 percent in 1981).[11] Yet, as Table 9.4 shows, in the English ambiance of the West Island, the rate of Francophone "Anglicization" is

Table 9.4
Francophone Linguistic Transfers in Montreal, 1986

Language(s) Spoken at Home by Persons of French Mother Tongue,
in Selected Western Montreal Communities,
by Percentage Distribution

Area	French-only	English-only	English and French[a]
Côte-Saint-Luc	72.8	15.6	11.6
Westmount	75.9	16.1	8.0
Snowdon	83.3	9.8	7.0
Pointe-Claire	78.1	15.9	6.0
Beaconsfield	74.6	17.1	8.2
Dollard-des-Ormeaux	80.7	11.8	7.5
Hampstead	78.5	10.7	10.7
Montréal-Ouest	57.5	26.4	16.1

Source: See Table 9.3.
[a] All other responses omitted.

rather high for a metropolis bent on preserving its French character—especially when we realize that the percentage of Francophones using English regularly as a home language in *Ontario* is only slightly higher (27.5 percent in 1986) than in Montreal's West Island communities.[12]

In short, the assimilationist pull of English remained strong in Montreal through the 1980s, even as the city's linguistic politics and overall linguistic demography shifted sharply in favor of French. The linguistic transfers favoring English have been much too small to counterbalance the giant Anglophone deficit in interprovincial migration that occurred after 1976. Nevertheless, linguistic transfers offer an important sign that English remains a powerful force in the new Montreal.

The End of the Two Solitudes?

The changes in language-group relations that have occurred in Montreal since the 1960s have led some observers to herald a virtual end to the linguistic segmentation that historically characterized life in the city. "There's a new mentality in Montreal," stated Alfred Rouleau of the Mouvement Desjardins on the subject of Francophone–Anglophone relations. "When we speak together we understand each other better than when we stayed apart."[13] By the late 1980s, both of Montreal's major French-language newspapers had run series whose main theme was: linguistic barriers in Montreal were falling as Anglophones increasingly accepted a *Québec français.*[14] Combined with the postreferendum deflation of Francophone nationalism, many proclaimed a new era of linguistic *rapprochement.*

There are impressive behavioral indicators of this linguistic *rapproche-ment* in Montreal. Bilingualism among Montreal Anglophones is up dramatically, from an estimated 24 percent in 1960, to 36 percent in 1971 and 53 percent in 1981.[15] Surveys in the 1980s suggest that as many as two-thirds of Montreal Anglophones under the age of twenty-five may now be bilingual.[16] Table 9.5 shows rates of bilingualism in various areas of metropolitan Montreal. Although bilingualism varies markedly by the linguistic composition of an area (Anglophones living on the heavily English-speaking West Island are less likely to be bilingual than Anglophones living in predominantly Francophone suburbs), the data nevertheless show a much higher level of bilingualism, particularly among Anglophones, than existed in the 1960s.

In addition to the growing percentage of Montrealers capable of conversing in French or English, the "two solitudes" seem to be fading in other areas of Montreal life. English-language schooling in Montreal, which we examined in Chapter 6, has become contoured to Quebec's French fact, with huge increases in French immersion programs and with some Anglophones even sending their children to regular French-language schools. In municipal politics, the Rassemblement des citoyens de Montréal (RCM) emerged in the 1970s as a political party in which Anglophones and Francophones worked together in promoting a reformist, social-democratic urban agenda. Language has never been a seriously divisive issue in the RCM, and when the party took control of Montreal city government in 1986, members of both linguistic communities occupied key policymaking positions. The Doré–Fainstat government has solid roots in English- and French-speaking Montreal, a far cry from the era after 1900 when Anglophones essentially withdrew from municipal politics.[17]

These developments all bespeak a new linguistic climate in Montreal. Nevertheless, notions of Francophone–Anglophone *rapprochement* should not be overdrawn. The intense conflict in 1988–1989 over the issue of unilingual signs, and Anglophone support for the Equality Party in 1989, made clear that strong linguistic cleavages remain in Montreal. A comprehensive 1987 survey on the state of the language question "confirmed the presence

Table 9.5
Percentage of Bilinguals in Selected Areas of Metropolitan Montreal, by Mother Tongue, 1986

Area	Anglophones	Francophones
Metropolitan Montreal	54.7	43.8
City of Montreal	54.1	44.4
East Island Suburbs	70.4	41.1
West Island Suburbs	52.2	63.4
Off-Island Suburbs	59.1	38.8

Source: See Table 9.3.

in Quebec of two societies, two peoples, two nations."[18] This dualism was revealed, most clearly, in radically different senses of national identification: the overwhelming majority of Francophones called themselves "Québécois" or "French Canadians," while Anglophones tended to think of themselves as simply "Canadians." Moreover, Francophones and Anglophones articulated sharply divergent views on the places of English and French in Quebec life. Francophones strongly supported the concept of a Quebec as a "French society," while Anglophones favored, with near unanimity, the reestablishment of official bilingualism. In short, "the two communities hold radically contradictory visions of Quebec society."[19]

Beyond these fundamental ideological cleavages, there is some evidence that the celebrations of increased Francophone–Anglophone "understanding" and social interaction have been, at the least, overstated. An in-depth survey by sociologist Uli Locher found that, while Montreal Anglophones expressed greater attitudes of "social openness" toward Francophones between 1978 and 1983, these words were not matched by actual behavior. Only 15.5 percent of the Anglophones in Locher's survey reported "regular and intense contacts" with Francophones, leading Locher to conclude that sufficient social distance remains in Montreal to sustain "the old notion of the 'two solitudes.'"[20]

In short, as Peter Leslie accurately predicted in 1977, "the integration of Anglophones into a society they acknowledge must henceforth be predominantly French does not mean that they will be absorbed by it, or that the end of the 'two solitudes' is at hand."[21] Nevertheless, even if linguistic segmentation persists in the new Montreal, many of the elements historically associated with the city of "two solitudes" have been attenuated: linguistic hierarchy, English unilingualism, and an ability on the part of Anglophones to ignore the predominantly Francophone society around them. Social distance between Montreal's language groups will always exist—that is one way they remain distinct communities. But the context of language-group relations has changed enormously since the 1960s, and in that sense the era of the "two solitudes," connoting Anglophone hegemony and obliviousness to the interests of the Francophone majority, has emphatically ended. Anglophones may not interact extensively with Francophones, but they are acutely aware that the Francophone majority now controls the agenda for language relations in Montreal and that defense of "Anglophone rights" in the city requires patterns of accommodation far different from those that prevailed during the era of the "two solitudes."

The New Ethnicity and Francophone Montreal

New patterns of intergroup accommodation also will have to develop as Montreal adjusts to large-scale ethnic diversity. Through 1900, Montreal was almost exclusively composed of British- and French-origin residents, and even as late as 1951, 86 percent of the Island's residents were from these two "Charter" groups (with a thoroughly Anglicized Jewish community representing another 5 percent of the population).

By 1986, however, the British ethnic component of Montreal's population had fallen under 10 percent, and over 30 percent of Montreal Island's population was now composed of "cultural communities."[22] Italians (160,000) and Jews (73,000) represent Montreal's largest non-British, non-French ethnic minorities, while a sizable number of Greeks and Portuguese also emigrated to the city primarily between 1945 and 1970. Since the late 1970s, a new wave of immigration further transformed Montreal's ethnic make-up, as refugees fleeing war, political repression, and poverty in the Third World emigrated to the city. Fifty percent of Montreal's immigrants since 1978 have come from Africa, Asia, and the Caribbean, adding racial diversity to the Island's growing multicultural character. Montreal's black population, around 4,000 in 1961, totaled an estimated 120,000 in 1987 with Haitians (45,000) the largest single group; the Island's population is now estimated at 7 percent black.[23]

As we have seen, through the 1960s—in Montreal's era of linguistic freedom of choice—immigrants gravitated toward the English-speaking community, sending their children to English-language schools and utilizing English-language social and health services. Through the mid-1960s, Francophone interest in integrating immigrants into Montreal's French-language institutions had ranged from indifference to outright opposition. By the 1970s, however, Francophone nationalists focused on Montreal's ethnic minorities as the vital "third force" in the city's "demo-linguistic" balance. Some of Montreal's most bitter linguistic confrontations, such as the Saint-Léonard school crisis, pitted Francophone nationalists against ethnic minorities reluctant to send their children to French-language schools or otherwise be forcibly "integrated" into Francophone society.

Bill 101, by establishing French as Quebec's official public language, brought Montreal's ethnic minorities within the ambit of the city's French-language institutions and, for the first time, into large-scale interaction with Francophone society. As we saw in Chapter 6, the result has been "culture shock," as French-speaking Montreal experiences the processes of ethnic and racial conflict and accommodation typical of big cities in the United States. Through the late 1970s, the provincial government had no strategy and few institutions to help ethnic minorities find a place in Francophone society. Initially, the PQ's attitude was plainly assimilationist: in the Quebec it sought to build, it assumed that immigrants would naturally blend in with the French majority in the same fashion that immigrants assimilated into English in the United States and Canada. Ironically, for a party created by individuals deeply committed to preserving their language and culture, the PQ seemed oblivious to the possibility that ethnic minorities might want to maintain their "specificity" within a framework that acknowledged French as Quebec's official language and majority culture. The major PQ statement on cultural development policy, issued in 1978, focused largely on ways to strengthen Quebec's core French culture. The document included vague references to the "contributions" of Quebec's minorities, but clearly the PQ concept of Quebec culture in 1978 was rooted in the French-Québécois heritage and concepts of nationhood; it was decidedly *not* based on the notion of "multiculturalism."[24]

However, by the early 1980s, as Bill 101 inexorably promoted greater interaction between ethnic minorities and French-language institutions, the PQ began to incorporate "multiculturalism" in its approach to cultural development. In a 1981 White Paper on cultural minorities entitled *Autant de façons d'être québécois* (So many ways to be a Quebecer), the PQ sketched ways to preserve minority subcultures while integrating ethnic groups into Quebec public institutions.[25] Moreover, in 1981 the provincial Ministry of Immigration was renamed to include "Cultural Communities" in its mission, and the ministry became an active arm of the provincial government in promoting programs for Montreal's ethnic minorities.[26] The attention to cultural diversity continued under the Bourassa government; in 1987, the so-called Sirros Commission issued a report calling for "training in multiculturalism" for Montreal hospital and social services employees and increased ethnic community representation in the management of these institutions.[27] At the local level, municipal governments on Montreal Island began addressing the needs of the new minorities; in early 1989, for example, the STCUM announced a hiring goal of 25 percent ethnic and racial minorities for the Island's bus and metro systems, and the City of Montreal announced a program of municipal hiring quotas to reflect ethnic numbers in the workforce.[28] In short, by the end of the 1980s, the concept of "multi-ethnicity within a French framework" was "in" among Quebec policymakers.

Despite these efforts, Montreal faced new and troubling ethnic and racial tensions in the 1980s. Ethnic minorities remained woefully underrepresented in Montreal city government and in Quebec's provincial bureaucracy, constituting under 4 percent of the workforce in both.[29] In particular, Montreal's transit system and police forces were the targets of complaints by ethnic and racial minorities regarding employment discrimination.[30] Through 1987, only 6 of the 4,500 officers in Montreal's almost exclusively Francophone police force were black and, not surprisingly, police–community relations emerged as a flash point between Montreal's racial minorities and the Francophone community.[31] Reports of police brutality toward blacks surfaced with some regularity by the mid-1980s.[32] In 1987, Anthony Griffin, the teenage son of a Jamaican immigrant, was shot and killed while in police custody following an altercation over a taxi fare. Griffin allegedly was attempting to flee when he was shot, although the police later acknowledged that the youth had stopped and turned around before he was killed. Allan Gossett, the police officer who killed Griffin, was tried and acquitted of manslaughter.[33] Two thousand demonstrators, black and white, marched in protest, prompting the formation of a commission to investigate police treatment of racial minorities. The commission found widespread discrimination in police behavior—blacks were much more likely to be apprehended and held than were whites—and recommended that the Montreal Urban Community appoint a coordinator of Intercultural-Race Relations, with special focus on police activities. Members of the Montreal City Council pushed for civilian review of complaints over police behavior.[34]

Beyond problems in police–minority relations, there were signs by the mid-1980s that U.S.-style racial inequality and discrimination were becoming part of the social and economic fabric of Montreal life. Seventy percent of Montreal's Haitian community, largely confined by housing bias to ghettos in Montréal-Nord and Saint-Léonard, lived on unemployment compensation or social welfare payments, and 80 percent earned below $10,000 a year in 1981.[35] In language familiar to observers of racial inequality in urban America, a Haitian community leader complained that "Haitians are the last hired and the first fired."[36] Haitians lacked the educational background to gain employment in "high-end" service-sector jobs in Montreal, and even for the low-skill jobs available in the city's growing hotel and tourism industry, they faced discrimination. The socioeconomic profile of Montreal's Haitian community looked disturbingly similar to that labeled "underclass" in urban America.

Although Haitians were the largest nationality in Montreal's black community, an estimated 60 percent of Montreal's black community emigrated from English-speaking societies such as Jamaica and Grenada. In many cases, employment prospects for these immigrants, particularly in Montreal's public sector, were limited by inadequate knowledge of French (although group leaders asserted that linguistic deficiencies were used to cloak employment discrimination against blacks).[37] Thus, a vast array of problems—social, institutional, and linguistic—face Montreal's loosely knit and internally differentiated racial minorities.

Despite provincial government pronouncements in favor of cultural diversity, as we saw in examining the new challenges of the multi-ethnic French-language school in Chapter 6, many Francophones are uncomfortable with the ethnic and racial diversification underway in Montreal. This uneasiness has been exacerbated by the decline since the 1950s in the birthrate of native Francophone Québécois, a trend that raises the specter that "ethnic" Francophones will outnumber Francophones *de souche* in the not-too-distant future, with potentially profound consequences for the nature of Quebec culture and society. While nothing has emerged in Montreal or Quebec resembling the nativist movement headed by Jean-Marie LePen in

France, there are signs that many Francophones *de souche*—particularly in the eighteen- to twenty-four-year-old age bracket—fear the effects of cultural diversity on French-speaking society and are susceptible to xenophobic appeals. Sixty percent of Francophones surveyed in March 1987 labeled immigrants an "important threat to the French language," and by overwhelming numbers Francophones favored "making more babies" over "immigration" as the solution to Quebec's depopulation crisis.[38] Nativist sentiment was more pronounced in areas outside of metropolitan Montreal, suggesting a nascent cleavage between multicultural Francophone Montreal and Francophones *de souche* in the hinterland. But *neither* region appeared particularly open to concepts of cultural pluralism and diversity, leading one Montreal editorialist to bemoan that "ten years of Bill 101 have not dissipated the collective insecurity of the Francophone majority."[39] Quebec, wrote another, "remains a chilly society."[40]

The New Francophone Class Structure

While ethnic diversity promises major changes in the culture of Francophone Quebec, the class structure of Francophone society has already undergone a remarkable transformation since the early 1970s. As I have argued, the reconquest of Montreal was engineered by a new Francophone middle class that used the Quebec state to simultaneously displace traditional Francophone elites as well as dislodge Montreal's dominant Anglophone business class. From the early 1960s through the PQ referendum of 1980, this new middle class was unquestionably the ascendant group in Montreal and Quebec society, controlling the province's political agenda and promoting policies of economic nationalism and governmental intervention in linguistic matters that reshaped the province.

As we noted in Chapters 7 and 8, one of the objectives of post-1960 *étatisme* in Quebec was the creation of a viable Francophone capitalist class, and the policies promoted by the new middle class—in programs such as the Caisse de dépôt et placement, the SGF, Hydro-Québec, and Bill 101— were instrumental in establishing a visible Francophone presence in Montreal and Quebec's private sector. By the early 1980s, however, as the neo-nationalist project of the new middle class ran aground and as the conservatism sweeping all industrialized countries undermined the role of the state, this new Francophone business class clearly displaced the state-centered new middle class as the dominant group in Quebec society. The hegemony of this largely Montreal-headquartered Francophone business class—and the eroding position of the new middle class—became apparent during the second Lévesque administration. In 1982–1983, facing double-digit unemployment and skyrocketing deficits as Quebec wallowed in a deep recession, the PQ government adopted a classic pro-business strategy to the fiscal crisis of the state: it turned on its state middle-class constituency, particularly the teachers' unions, and imposed wage rollbacks in the public sector. The PQ offensive prompted a showdown with public-sector unions and when the teachers went on strike, the government passed Bill 111 containing back-to-work measures "that were unprecedented in their withdrawal of the rights of union members."[41]

In addition, the second Lévesque administration became Canada's most "business-oriented" government, aggressively using the Caisse de dépôt to support Francophone businessmen, and enacting programs such as the REA and Bill 75 that directly benefited the new Francophone *entrepreneuriat*. Ironically, the language policies promoted by the new middle class also played an important, if unintended, role in the process of building mass acceptance of pro-business policies and the political ascendancy of Francophone capitalists. As William Coleman points out, by taking the "foreign" (that is, English) face off of capitalism in Quebec, language policy helped reduce the anticapitalist sentiment in the French-speaking community (particularly in Montreal) that seemed linked to the language question in the early 1970s. In this context, pro-business policies appeared more legitimate from an "ethnic" perspective.[42]

The defeat of the PQ and the inauguration of the third Bourassa government in 1985 marked the full eclipse of the Francophone new middle class and an unabashed celebration of Francophone capitalism and capitalists.[43] In mid-1986, the Bourassa government released three task-force reports outlining its plans to "roll back" the Quebec state. These task forces, on deregulation, privatization, and streamlining government functions and structures, were composed of leading members of the ascendant Francophone business class: Pierre Lortie, Michel Bélanger, Claude Castonguay, and Raymond Cyr, to name a few. Not surprisingly, then, the reports of these groups reflected the radical *anti*state perspective of these businessmen: recommendations included the elimination of numerous government agencies, drastic reductions in the network of state enterprises built up since the Quiet Revolution, and deep cuts in public spending and public employment. While the Bourassa government did not enact all the proposals of these task forces, public policy after 1986 clearly followed the priorities of the Francophone business class. As Gérard-D. Lévesque, Bourassa's finance minister, put it in 1986:

> In Quebec, we have made great use of this instrument [state enterprises] during the last twenty-five years. It was, in particular, a means by which Francophones could rapidly establish themselves in a domain that history has led them to neglect, that of large enterprises.
> It is clear today that the role of state enterprises in Quebec's eco-

nomic development no longer needs to be as important. There now exists a class of extremely dynamic and competent Francophone entrepreneurs who are able to take over from the state and who aspire to assume more and more responsibility. Moreover, the pressing need of our enterprises to be more and more competitive should lead us to count more on the private sector.[44]

The dominance of the Montreal-based Francophone business elite over Quebec's policy agenda in the 1980s, coupled with the *francisation* of Montreal's private sector, has had important consequences. The trimming back of the state has undermined the structural basis for a powerful Francophone state middle class, reducing the ability of that group to pursue its agenda: neo-nationalism, social-democracy, and language policy. Concommitantly, as Francophone engineers and managers increasingly find employment in Montreal's private rather than public sector, the base of Francophones with a strong material interest in an interventionist state will continue to shrink, further eroding the political influence of the *étatiste* social scientists and policy intellectuals in the state middle class.

Finally, the political hegemony of Francophone capitalists may have important cultural-linguistic consequences. As we noted in Chapter 8, the leading "success stories" of Francophone capitalism—companies such as Lavalin, Provigo, and Bombardier—have expanded their economic activities beyond Quebec to continental and global markets. For example, Bernard Lamarre (Lavalin), Claude Castonguay (La Laurentienne), and Laurent Beaudoin (Bombardier) were among the biggest supporters of the Canada–U.S. free trade agreement, and, reflecting the views of Montreal's new business elite, Robert Bourassa was Brian Mulroney's main ally among provincial premiers in promoting the pact. This global orientation of the Francophone economic elite places them firmly in opposition to "particularist" projects such as *indépendantisme* or elements of language policy that might be construed as "protectionist" barriers to international economic exchanges. Moreover, the global economic integration promoted by these elites carries an additional possibility: by drawing Quebec more tightly into the economic orbit of the United States, the likelihood of increased "Americanization" of Quebec culture increases (an influence already troubling to many Francophones).

On the issue of language policy, although Francophone businessmen strongly opposed Bill 101, organizations such as the Chambre de Commerce du Québec and the Chambre de Commerce de Montréal have adopted a "pragmatic" position. These Francophone business organizations now trumpet Montreal as a "French city" with a bilingual/bicultural heritage. During the post-1986 anxieties over the Bourassa government's language policies, the Chambre de Commerce de Montréal warned the government not to tamper with the core of Bill 101: linguistic turmoil would be bad for business.[45] In short, while Francophone capitalists did not support Bill 101 and many of these businessmen still regard some of the law's restrictions on English as a "hindrance" to Montreal's business climate,[46] there is little sentiment among Francophone capitalists to dismantle this crowning public policy statement of the Francophone new middle class.

Whither the Language Question?

The outbreak of linguistic conflict in late 1988 over the question of unilingual French signs was a vivid reminder that language policy remains a divisive and potent issue in Montreal. The key items in the language dossier, schooling and the economy, are, for all intents and purposes, settled. There are periodic efforts to tamper around the margins of Bill 101 on these issues— for example, to extend the certification process for the *francisation* of businesses to firms with under fifty employees. However, the main provisions of the law—limiting access to English-language schools and promoting French as the language of work—are no longer matters of public debate.

One thorny issue bearing on language and education remained unresolved as the 1980s ended: the problem of reorganizing the confessional structure of Montreal's public schools. As we examined, Montreal's religious and linguistic rifts more or less overlapped when the confessional structure of schooling was established in the nineteenth century. But, by the 1960s, with the rise of a sizable Anglo-Catholic sector and the secularization of Protestant education, confessionally based schooling was both anachronistic and illogical. Nevertheless, efforts to reorganize the Island's schools, either by creating unified school boards or organizing school governance on the basis of language, were consistently thwarted in the 1960s and 1970s by a coalition of Anglophone business elites and groups of English-Protestant and French-Catholic teachers and school administrators.

Several developments in Montreal in the late 1970s made confessional schooling seem increasingly obsolete and gave new impetus to the idea of school reform. As we have seen, Francophone concern grew over the rise of a significant French-Protestant sector within the *Anglophone*-controlled PSBGM and numerous instances of linguistic cohabitation in commissions across the Island. In addition, within the CECM, parents in the multicultural neighborhood of Côte-des-Neiges attempted without success to establish a nondenominational school. The École Notre-Dâme-des-Neiges controversy brought renewed attention to the problem of school organization on the Island.

Thus, between 1982 and 1984, the PQ attempted to overcome the obstacles historically blocking school reform and enact a comprehensive restructuring of Montreal and Quebec public education.[47] The original PQ plan was drafted by Camille Laurin who had become minister of education in the second Lévesque administration. In Laurin's second celebrated White Paper—his first was the language policy paper of 1977—the government outlined a far-reaching reform plan that included replacing confessional school boards with unified boards outside Montreal Island and with linguistic commissions on the Island.[48] The true reformist content of the Laurin plan was not in its linguistic proposals, but in its vision of a radically decentralized structure in which genuine educational policymaking power would devolve from school commissions to autonomous individual schools, run by "councils" composed of parents and teachers.[49] In June 1983, Laurin presented Bill 40, which was largely based on the recommendations in the White Paper, although some of the radical proposals such as "corporate status" for individual schools were eliminated.[50]

Bill 40 was denounced by most Anglophone groups and opposed by the French-Catholic and English-Protestant education groups that had stymied school reform in the past. Part of the Anglophone opposition was visceral: "Because it comes from me," said Laurin, "some will oppose it."[51] More specifically, Anglophone groups feared the new structures would weaken the power of local boards and enhance the influence of the Francophone-controlled provincial Ministry of Education over local schooling. In the last analysis, notwithstanding the guarantees of linguistic community control in the bill, Anglophones were unwilling to relinquish the Constitutional guarantees of Section 93 of the BNA Act[52] for "mere" legislative assurances of linguistic autonomy that could always be withdrawn. As in the past, the old-guard French-Catholic educational establishment joined Anglophones in opposition to school reform. In the aftermath of the 1980 referendum defeat, Constitutional debacle of 1981,[53] and economic crisis of 1982–1983, the PQ was a weakened government, and in no position to challenge the determined efforts of this antireform coalition; thus, Bill 40 was withdrawn. Eventually, the PQ passed a watered-down version of its school reform plan, Bill 3, but in May 1985 the Superior Court of Quebec ruled the law an unconstitutional violation of Article 93.

In 1988, the Bourassa government offered yet another plan that would establish linguistic school boards on Montreal Island. Bill 107, the handiwork of PLQ Education Minister Claude Ryan, proposed solving the Article 93 conundrum by maintaining confessional boards alongside the new linguistic boards. Only Protestants and Catholics would be permitted access to PSBGM and CECM schools (in both English and French); all others would attend secular French- or English-language schools in their region. Protestants constitute only 45 percent of the PSBGM's English-language students and 37 percent of the commission's French-language students; therefore, depending on how it is implemented, Bill 107 could reduce the PSBGM's enrollments from 31,000 to 13,400 and presumably mitigate the importance of that board as the cornerstone of the Montreal Anglophone educational establishment.[54] The bill was adopted at the end of 1988, with school reform groups and the PQ assailing the government's "maintenance of obsolete confessional structures" and failure to "escape the iron collar of Article 93 . . . by regulating this problem in a true and lasting fashion."[55] Thus, no matter what the courts decide on the constitutionality of Bill 107, it seems safe to conclude that school reorganization will remain a contentious issue in Montreal in the near future.

Aside from lingering policy questions such as unilingual signs or school reorganization, English and French in the new Montreal also will be affected by several long-term developments. The most pressing, of course, is the looming constitutional impasse over the Meech Lake Accord. Quebec's political class is deeply committed to the accord, which adds to the Canadian Constitution recognition of Quebec as a "distinct society." At various points, Premier Bourassa has hinted that defeat of the accord—it must be ratified by all provinces by June 1990 or die—could rekindle separatism in Quebec. As 1990 began, with opposition to Meech Lake in English Canada apparently solidifying, many observers in both Quebec and English Canada were openly discussing the "inevitability" of an independent Quebec, with all of the uncertainty that would entail for language relations in Montreal and across Canada.

The *quality* of written and spoken French in Quebec, long a concern of Francophone intellectuals, also has received renewed attention in the 1980s. A 1987 report of the CLF detailed numerous deficiencies in the teaching of French in the public schools—problems such as illiteracy and poor grammar, spelling, and syntax—and called for a more active school commitment to "language planning" in Quebec.[56] Several surveys revealed growing mass support for improvements in French-language education and Education Minister Claude Ryan, long identified with concerns about the quality of French in Quebec, has promised action on the issue. Linguistic activists such as Jean-Marc Léger and Michel Plourde, while focusing on the importance of schools, also continue to push for a societywide "revalorisation" of French in Quebec.[57]

The international status of English as a language of science and technology also will influence the futures of French and English in Montreal. Many "high tech" and "research" centers in Montreal, exempt from Bill 101, function in English and are often closely connected to activities in the United States (and, as we saw in Chapter 8, an explicit economic development strategy in Montreal is to tighten links to high-tech centers such as Boston). For the most part, high-tech equipment in Montreal functions in English: estimates are that only 25 percent of Quebecers working on microcomputers use French-language software.[58] In short, French Quebec's entry into the global economy, combined with the current linguistic status of new and advanced technologies, introduces a new range of Anglicization influences in Montreal life.

Finally, Montreal exists in what Michel Plourde has aptly called a "state of permanent linguistic and cultural immersion in the Anglo-American universe."[59] Urban growth between 1920 and 1970 facilitated the availability of American cultural products in Montreal, and by the 1970s American newspapers, magazines, books, films and records were as generally accessible in Montreal as in U.S. cities.[60] Even in the *francised* Montreal of the 1980s, American and English-language cultural influences were ubiquitous. Forty percent of the films shown on Radio-Canada as well as in Montreal theaters were from the United States (including versions in French and English). French-language versions of such U.S. television products as "Dallas," "Little House on the Prairie," and "L.A. Law" ranked among Montreal's most widely watched programs.[61] In 1985, among Francophones between eighteen and thirty years of age, almost two-thirds regularly purchased English-language records and cassettes, and 45 percent of the television watched by Montreal Francophones was on English-language channels.[62] Advances in communications technology—for example, the mass diffusion of video cassette recorders and cable television—will only further the penetration of "made in the U.S.A." culture in Montreal.

In short, Francophones in Montreal and across Quebec face challenges in safeguarding and nurturing a distinctive Québécois language and culture that go well beyond the policy questions legislated in Bill 101. As former PLQ Communications Minister Richard French has perceptively noted:

A reorientation of ethnic consciousness is leading many Francophones to recognize that the health of the French language and culture will not be determined by the number of non-Francophones in Quebec, but by the behavior of Francophones themselves, as consumers of popular culture and information technologies.

Which is more important, the ever-diminishing number of students in English schools or the impact of cable television with American television channels . . . ?

Which is more important, the principle of unilingual signs or the impact of Boy George or Michael Jackson on the Quebec recording industry?

What does it mean for Québécois that English is the language of international technology, for example, of most computer software?[63]

The answer, of course, is that *all* of these questions matter for the future of French in Montreal. In one sense, the kinds of issues raised by Richard French reflect how much linguistic dynamics in Montreal have changed since the 1960s: the main threats to French in the city no longer flow from the presence of a privileged Anglophone minority but from the influences of "Americanism" that even concern culture planners in Paris. The big difference, of course, is that Montreal's proximity to English-language influences and the presence of a sizable non–French-speaking population in the city make English influences all the more immediate and pervasive. There is no denying the Francophone reconquest of Montreal in domains such as schooling, commerce, and the workplace. But the ultimate cultural and linguistic character of the new Montreal remains to be determined, subject to influences that originate from beyond the Island and constitute formidable challenges for Quebec's language policymakers.

Notes

Chapter 1

1. Jane Jacobs, *The Question of Separatism: Quebec and the Stuggle over Sovereignty* (New York: Vintage Books, 1980), pp. 11–12.

2. Robert Dahl, "Some Explanations," in Robert Dahl, ed., *Political Oppositions in Western Democracies* (New Haven: Yale University Press, 1966), p. 357.

3. Peter Leslie, "Ethnic Hierarchies and Minority Consciousness in Quebec," in Richard Simeon, ed., *Must Canada Fail?* (Montreal: McGill–Queen's University Press, 1977), p. 107.

4. Jac-André Boulet, "Les disparités linguistiques de revenu sur le marché montréalais: quelques éléments d'analyse," in François Vaillancourt, ed., *Économie et langue* (Québec: Éditeur officiel du Québec, 1985), p. 160.

5. Michael Hechter, *Internal Colonialism: The Celtic Fringe in British National Development, 1536–1966* (Berkeley: University of California Press, 1975), p. 37.

6. During the middle third of the nineteenth century, when the great British migration created Montreal's brief English-speaking majority, Quebec City also contained a large British-origin population (reaching nearly 40 percent by 1851). A substantial number were Irish Catholics. By 1931, however, as a result of intermarriage and out-migration, the non-Francophone proportion of Quebec City's population had fallen to only 7 percent. Similarly, in the Eastern Townships, where counties with names such as Brome, Richmond, Sherbrooke, and Stanstead bespeak a British-Protestant heritage, the English-speaking share of the population declined from 58 percent in 1861 to 18 percent in 1931 and only 9 percent in 1981. Clearly, by the 1960s the French language was demographically secure in these regions, and only the Montreal situation posed any threat to the future of French in Quebec. See Ronald Rudin, *The Forgotten Quebecers: A History of English-Speaking Quebec, 1759–1980* (Québec: Institut québécois de recherche sur la culture, 1985), pp. 63, 117. The 1981 language data is from Statistics Canada, *Census of Canada 1981* (Catalogue 93–929).

7. For the classic statements on the tendency in bilingual settings for speakers to shift to the more prestigious or powerful language, see Charles A. Ferguson,

"Diglossia," *Word* 15 (1959): 325–340; and Joshua A. Fishman, "Bilingualism with and without Diglossia; Diglossia with and without Bilingualism," *Journal of Social Issues* 23:2 (1967): 29–38. See also Fishman, "Language Maintenance and Language Shift," in Joshua A. Fishman, *Language in Sociocultural Change* (Stanford: Stanford University Press, 1972), pp. 76–134.

8. For an examination of the Brussels case, which contains many interesting parallels to Montreal, see Jeffrey Obler, "Assimilation and the Moderation of Linguistic Conflict in Brussels," *Administration* 22 (Winter 1974): 400–432; Kenneth D. McRae, *Conflict and Compromise in Multilingual Societies: Belgium* (Waterloo, Ontario: Wilfrid Laurier University Press, 1986), pp. 300–317; and Elizabeth Sherman Swing, *Bilingualism and Linguistic Segregation in the Schools of Brussels* (Laval: Centre international de recherche sur le bilinguisme, 1980). On the debates over language policy in the United States, the best historical overview is Heinz Kloss, *The American Bilingual Tradition* (Rowley, Mass.: Newbury House, 1977). A good, multidisciplinary overview of contemporary issues is provided in Kenji Hakuta, *Mirror of Language: The Debate on Bilingualism* (New York: Basic Books, 1986).

9. Sheila McLeod Arnopoulos and Dominique Clift, *The English Fact in Quebec* (Montreal: McGill–Queen's University Press, 1980), p. 202.

10. See Jean A. Laponce, *Langue et territoire* (Québec: Les Presses de l'Université Laval, 1984); and Kenneth D. McRae, "The Principle of Territoriality and the Principle of Personality in Multilingual States," *International Journal of the Sociology of Language* 4 (1975): 33–54.

Chapter 2

1. Fernand Ouellet, *Lower Canada, 1791–1840: Social Change and Nationalism* (Toronto: McClelland and Stewart, 1980), p. 360.

2. Paul-André Linteau, "La montée du cosmopolitisme montréalais," *Questions de culture* 2 (1982): 23–53.

3. On the number of British immigrants, their ethnic composition, and estimates on their ultimate destination, see Helen Cowan, *British Emigration to British North America* (Toronto: University of Toronto Press, 1961), pp. 183–185; and Ouellet, *Lower Canada*, p. 355. On the ethnic–linguistic composition of Montreal during this period, see Linteau, "La montée du cosmopolitisme montréalais," p. 25; and Ouellet, *Lower Canada*, p. 162.

4. The phrase is borrowed from Ronald Rudin, *The Forgotten Quebecers: A History of English-Speaking Quebec, 1759–1980* (Québec: Institut québécois de recherche sur la culture, 1985), p. 59.

5. Linteau, "La montée du cosmopolitisme montréalais," p. 26.

6. R. Cole Harris and John Warkenton, *Canada before Confederation: A Study in Historical Geography* (New York: Oxford University Press, 1974), p. 102. While there were some important episodes of religious conflict in nineteenth-century Montreal, tensions between Irish Catholics and English Protestants in the city do not appear to have been as intense as in U.S. cities between 1840 and 1860. Ouellet's conclusion, which seems amply supported by the evidence, is that linguistic cleavages superseded those of religion and class in pre-Confederation Montreal; the internal differences within the English-speaking community, at crucial junctures such as the Rebellions of 1837–1838, were overridden by linguistic concerns. See Ouellet, *Lower Canada*, p. 332.

7. The economic crisis of rural Quebec not only drew Francophones to Montreal, but also propelled more than 500,000 to New England between 1850 and 1900 in search of industrial employment. Assimilated into Anglo-American culture, these migrants became a "lost generation" of French-Canadians, and their departure prompted the Quebec Catholic church, for reasons of cultural survival, to promote a "colonisation" program to keep rural Francophones on "the land." See Yoland Lavoie, "Les mouvements migratoires des Canadiens entre leurs pays et les États-Unis au XIXe siècle: étude quantitative," in Hubert Charbonneau, ed., *La population du Québec: Études retrospectives* (Montréal: Éditions Boréal Express, 1973), pp. 78–288.

8. For the purposes of definitional clarity, there are three jurisdictions that will be mentioned at various points in this book: the city of Montreal; the Island of Montreal, which includes all other municipalities on the island; and the Montreal region (a post-1950s concept), which includes the city, other Island municipalities, and off-Island suburbs on the North and South shores.

9. The Eastern Townships contained 34 percent of Quebec's English-speaking population in 1861; by 1931, that figure had declined to only 13 percent, and by 1971 only 7 percent of Quebec Anglophones lived in the area originally settled by British Loyalists in the 1780s. In 1861, 58 percent of the population in the Eastern Townships was British; by 1931 the English-speaking component of the population had declined to 18 percent, and by 1971 it was only 11 percent (Rudin, *Forgotten Quebecers*, p. 179).

10. Census data, presented by Hubert Charbonneau and Robert Maheu, *Les aspects démographiques de la question linguistique* (Québec: Éditeur officiel de Québec, 1973).

11. The 1931 census was the first presenting data on the "mother tongue" of the population (English, French, other) rather than simply ethnic origin (British, French, other), thus permitting, for the first time, analysis of language-use patterns in the city. However, the absence of this data for years preceding 1931 is not terribly serious. In 1931 well over 90 percent of Montreal's English mother-tongue population was of British ethnic origin; thus, for prior census years, it seems legitimate to use British ethnic origin as a surrogate for Montreal's English-speaking population. After 1931, however, with a more polyglot English-speaking community, the more refined census data available after 1971 permits better analysis of Montreal's linguistic dynamics.

12. More than anyone, Ronald Rudin has argued persuasively for a more subtle understanding of the diverse histories of English-speaking Quebec. See Rudin, *Forgotten Quebecers*. On the lack of a historical sense of Anglophone communality, see Gary Caldwell, "Anglo-Quebec on the Verge of Its History," *Language and Society* 8 (August 1982): 3–11.

13. Robert Sweeney, "A Brief Sketch of the Economic History of English Quebec," in Gary Caldwell and Eric Waddell, eds., *The English of Quebec: From Majority to Minority Status* (Québec: Institut québécois de recherche sur la culture, 1982), p. 83; and Harris and Warkenton, *Canada before Confederation*, pp. 100–102.

14. See, for example, Norbert Lacoste, *Les caractéristiques sociales de la population du grand Montréal* (Montréal: Les Presses de l'Université de Montréal, 1958); and Jean Laponce, "The City Centre as Conflictual Space in the Bilingual City: The Case of Montreal," in Jean Gottman, ed., *Centre and Periphery: Spatial Variation in Politics* (Beverly Hills, Calif.: Sage Publications, 1980), pp. 149–162.

15. These lines should not be overdrawn: there have always been identifiable Francophone enclaves in Montreal's western neighborhoods, and the city's new eth-

nic minorities initially tended to settle in neighborhoods just east of boulevard St-Laurent—the street traditionally viewed in twentieth-century Montreal as the dividing line between the English- and French-speaking sectors of the city. See Linteau, "La montée du cosmopolitisme montréalais," who argues that these exceptions call "into question the image of ethnic encapsulation that we often accept without nuance" (p. 33).

16. See, for example, Paul-André Linteau, *Maisonneuve ou comment des promoteurs fabriquent une ville* (Montréal: Éditions Boréal Express, 1981); and Paul-André Linteau, "Suburbanization in Canada: Does the Border Make a Difference," *Journal of Urban History* 13:3 (May 1987): 252–274.

17. Andrew Sancton, *Governing the Island of Montreal: Language Differences and Metropolitan Politics* (Berkeley: University of California Press, 1985), pp. 26–28.

18. Ibid., p. 25.

19. Jean-Claude Marsan, *Montreal in Evolution* (Montreal: McGill–Queen's University Press, 1981), p. 183.

20. Stephen Leacock, *Leacock's Montreal*, rev. ed. (Toronto: McClelland and Stewart, 1963), p. 238; and Marsan, *Montreal in Evolution*, pp. 257–258.

21. Joshua Wolfe and Cécile Grenier, *Discover Montreal: An Architectural and Historical Guide* (Montréal: Éditions Libre expression, 1983), p. 294.

22. Andrew Sancton, "Montreal," in Warren Magnusson and Andrew Sancton, eds., *City Politics in Canada* (Toronto: University of Toronto Press, 1983), p. 66.

23. Linteau, "La montée du cosmopolitisme montréalais," p. 44.

24. See Paul-André Linteau et al., *Le Québec depuis 1930: Histoire du Québec contemporain* (Montréal: Les Éditions du Boréal Express, 1986), pp. 495–502.

25. Linteau, "La montée du cosmopolitisme montréalais," pp. 49–50. The consociational model, developed particularly by political scientist Arend Lijphart in the 1970s, posits that social peace can be maintained in culturally divided democracies through a combination of elite accommodation and group autonomy. In the model, institutional separation limits potentially conflict-producing intercultural contacts at the mass level, while stability-conscious elites keep ethnic passions from rising too high. See Lijphart, *Democracy in Plural Societies: A Comparative Exploration* (New Haven: Yale University Press, 1977).

26. Douglas Fullerton, *The Dangerous Delusion* (Toronto: McClelland and Stewart, 1978), pp. 9–10, 18.

27. Leacock, *Leacock's Montreal*, p. 235.

28. George Monro Grant, ed., *Picturesque Canada: The Country as It Was and Is: I,* cited in Marsan, *Montreal in Evolution,* p. 198.

29. Sancton, *Governing the Island of Montreal,* p. 73.

30. Ministère de l'Industrie et du Commerce du Québec, *Annuaire de la section finance publique, 1970* (Québec, 1970).

31. Terry Copp, *The Anatomy of Poverty: The Condition of the Working Class in Montreal, 1897–1929* (Toronto: McClelland and Stewart, 1974).

32. Raw data from Charbonneau and Maheu, *Les aspects démographiques* p. 75; calculations by author.

33. André Siegfried, *The Race Question in Canada* (1906; reprint, Toronto: McClelland and Stewart, 1966), p. 188.

34. Quoted in Jean-Pierre Proulx, "Tocqueville a lancé le débat sur l'affichage en . . . 1831," *Le Devoir* (Montréal), 12 décembre 1988.

35. Everett C. Hughes and Margaret MacDonald, "French and English in the Economic Structure of Montreal," *Canadian Journal of Economics and Political Science* 7 (1941): 496.

36. Leacock, *Leacock's Montreal*, p. 268.
37. Fullerton, *The Dangerous Delusion*, p. 14.
38. Charbonneau and Maheu, *Les aspects démographiques*, p. 75. Census data on bilingualism should always be viewed with some caution: it relies on self-declarations by the respondent rather than any test of genuine ability to converse in both English and French.
39. Richard Joy, *Languages in Conflict* (Toronto: McClelland and Stewart, 1972), p. 104.
40. Leacock, *Leacock's Montreal*, p. 274.
41. Data compiled from Charbonneau and Maheu, *Les aspects démographiques*, pp. 71–73.
42. Rudin, *Forgotten Quebecers*, p. 72.
43. Sancton, "Montreal," p. 60.
44. See, for example, Pierre Harvey, "La perception du capitalisme chez les canadiens français: une hypothèse pour la recherche," in J.-L. Migue, *Le Québec d'aujourd'hui* (Montréal: Éditions Hurtubise HMH, 1971), pp. 129–138; Pierre Harvey, "Pourquoi le Québec et les Canadiens-français occupent-ils une place inférieure sur le plan économique," in René Durocher and Paul-André Linteau, eds., *Le "Retard" du Québec et l'infériorité économique des Canadiens français* (Montréal: Éditions Boréal Express, 1971), pp. 113–127; N. W. Taylor, "The Effects of Industrialization, Its Opportunities and Consequences, Upon French-Canadian Society," *Journal of Economic History* 20 (December 1960): 638–647; and Donald Creighton, *The Empire of the St. Lawrence* (Toronto: University of Toronto Press, 1956), p. 154.
45. Kenneth McRoberts, "Internal Colonialism: The Case of Quebec," *Ethnic and Racial Studies* 2 (July 1979): 297.
46. Ronald Rudin, *Banking en français: The French Banks of Quebec, 1835–1925* (Toronto: University of Toronto Press, 1985), pp. 9–12.
47. See, for example, Harvey, "Pourquoi le Québec," pp. 113–127; and Michel Brunet, "La conquête anglaise et la déchéance de la bourgeoisie canadienne, 1760–1793," in Michel Brunet, *La présence anglaise et les Canadiens* (Montréal: Beauchemin, 1964). The most forceful argument in French-Canadian historiography *against* the collective trauma thesis is Fernand Ouellet, *Economic and Social History of Quebec*. For a critical analysis of Ouellet, as well as a useful overview of the entire debate, see Serge Gagnon, *Quebec and Its Historians* (Montreal: Harvest House, 1985), pp. 81–163.
48. Ouellet, *Lower Canada*, p. 164.
49. Rudin, *Banking en français*, pp. 78–140.
50. Yves Bélanger and Pierre Fournier, *L'Entreprise québécoise: développement historique et dynamique contemporaine* (Montréal: Éditions Hurtubise HMH, 1987), p. 27.
51. Ouellet, *Lower Canada*, p. 368. These occupations include: laborers, tradesmen (that is, blacksmiths, carpenters, tailors, etc.), and carters.
52. William Roy, "The French-English Division of Labor in Quebec," (M.A. thesis, McGill University, 1935), cited in Everett C. Hughes, *French Canada in Transition* (Chicago: University of Chicago Press, 1943), p. 205.
53. Rudin, *Forgotten Quebecers*, p. 140.
54. George Nader, *Cities of Canada: Profiles of Fifteen Metropolitan Centres* (Toronto: Macmillan of Canada, 1976), pp. 129–130.
55. Paul-André Linteau et al., *Quebec: A History, 1867–1929* (Toronto: James Lorimer and Company, 1983), p. 132.

56. Lorenzo Prince, Charles Gordonsmith, M. M. Marcy, and Ben Deacon, *Montreal: Old and New* (Montreal: International Press Syndicate, 1915), p. 80.

57. Siegfried, *The Race Question in Canada*, p. 187.

58. Murray Ballantyne, quoted in Marsan, *Montreal in Evolution*, p. 190.

59. Rudin, *Banking en français*, p. 16.

60. Hughes and MacDonald, "French and English in the Economic Structure of Montreal," pp. 493–505.

61. Bélanger and Fournier, *L'Entreprise québécoise*, p. 67.

62. Jorge Niosi, *La bourgeoisie canadienne: la formation et le développement d'une classe dominante* (Montréal: Éditions Boréal Express, 1980), p. 186.

63. André Raynauld, *La propriété des entreprises au Québec: les années 60* (Montréal: Les Presses de l'Université de Montréal, 1974), p. 116.

64. Ibid., p. 50.

65. Report of the Royal Commission on Bilingualism and Biculturalism, *Book III: The Work World* (Ottawa: Queen's Printer, 1969), p. 55 (Hereafter cited as RCBB).

66. Ibid., pp. 57–58.

67. Ibid., p. 44.

68. Ibid., p. 457.

69. Jac-André Boulet, *L'évolution des disparités linguistiques de revenus de travail au Canada de 1970 à 1980* (Ottawa: Conseil économique du Canada, 1983), pp. 16–17. Boulet defines the best-paid workers as the top 15 percent of wage-earners.

70. Jac-André Boulet, "Les disparités linguistiques de revenu sur le marché montréalais: quelques éléments d'analyse," in François Vaillancourt, ed., *Économie et langue* (Québec: Éditeur officiel du Québec, 1985), p. 166.

71. RCBB, *Work World*, p. 81.

72. Ibid., p. 458

73. Ibid., p. 45.

74. The average annual income for various linguistic groups in metropolitan Montreal in 1961 was as follows:

Bilingual Anglophones	$5,931
Unilingual Anglophones	$5,749
Bilingual Francophones	$4,201
Unilingual Francophones	$2,975

See Boulet, "Les disparités linguistiques," p. 160.

75. Stanley Lieberson, *Language and Ethnic Relations in Canada* (New York: John Wiley and Sons, 1970), p. 140.

76. Michel Brunet, "The Historical Background of Quebec's Challenge to Canadian Unity," in Dale C. Thomson, ed., *Quebec Society and Politics: Views from the Inside* (Toronto: McClelland and Stewart, 1973), pp. 40–41.

77. Quoted in Rudin, *Forgotten Quebecers*, p. 50.

78. Emile Gosselin, "L'administration publique dans un pays bilingue et biculturel," *Canadian Public Administration* 6 (1963): 411.

79. Sheila McLeod Arnopoulos and Dominique Clift, *The English Fact in Quebec*, 2d ed. (Montreal: McGill–Queen's University Press, 1984), p. 54; and Kenneth D. McRae, "The Structure of Canadian History," in Louis Hartz ed., *The Founding of New Societies* (New York: Harcourt, Brace, and World, 1964), pp. 234–242.

80. Ouellet, *Lower Canada*, p. 10.

81. Ibid., p. 207.

82. Mason Wade, *The French Canadians, 1760–1967* (Toronto: Macmillan and

Company, 1968), p. 103; and Roger Magnuson, *Education in the Province of Quebec* (Washington, D.C.: Government Printing Office, 1969), p. 13.

83. Quoted in Wade, *French Canadians,* p. 103.

84. Ibid., p. 104.

85. Magnuson, *Education in Quebec,* pp. 13–14; Benoit Gendreau and André Lemieux, *L'Organisation scolaire au Québec: Référential de connaissance* (Montréal: Éditions France-Québec, 1979), pp. 10–11; and Louis Phillip Audet, *Histoire de l'enseignement au Québec, 1840–1971* (Montréal: 1971), pp. 11–20.

86. See, in particular, Ouellet, *Lower Canada,* pp. 275–341.

87. Ibid., p. 332. For a description of revolutionary activity around Montreal from 1837 to 1838, see Robert Rumilly, *Histoire de Montréal,* tome 2 (Montréal: Éditions Fides, 1970), pp. 217–252.

88. Gerald M. Craig, ed. *Lord Durham's Report: An Abridgment of "Report on the Affairs of British North America"* (Toronto: McClelland and Stewart, 1967), p. 28.

89. My account of the Union period draws heavily on the first-rate study by J. M. S. Careless, *The Union of the Canadas: The Growth of Canadian Institutions, 1841–1867* (Toronto: McClelland and Stewart, 1967).

90. Careless, *Union of the Canadas,* p. 5; Arnopoulos and Clift, *The English Fact in Quebec,* p. 56.

91. Careless, *Union of the Canadas,* p. 7.

92. See William Ormsby, "The Province of Canada: The Emergence of Consociational Politics," in Kenneth D. McRae, ed., *Consociational Democracy: Political Accommodation in Segmented Societies* (Toronto: McClelland and Stewart, 1974), pp. 269–274.

93. Rumilly, *Histoire de Montréal 2,* p. 319.

94. All quotations are from Careless, *Union of the Canadas,* pp. 124–126.

95. Rumilly, *Histoire de Montréal 2,* p. 321.

96. Careless, *Union of the Canadas,* p. 126; Rumilly, *Histoire de Montréal 2,* pp. 322–325; and Michel Brunet, "La minorité anglophone du Québec: de la Conquête à l'adoption du Bill 22," in Michel Brunet, *Notre passé, le présent, et nous* (Montréal: Éditions Fides, 1976), p. 198.

97. Brunet argues that moving the capital from Montreal had lasting implications for French–English relations in Canada. In Brunet's view, had Montreal remained Canada's capital, French Canadians might have developed a stronger sense of national identification. See Brunet, "La minorité anglophone du Québec," pp. 198–199.

98. Linteau et al., *Quebec: A History,* p. 232.

99. Ralph Heintzman, "The Political Culture of Quebec, 1840–1960," *Canadian Journal of Political Science* 16:1 (March 1983): 35. As André Bernard has documented, through the late 1960s the average rate of nonvoting in provincial elections among Montreal Anglophones was almost twice the rate registered by the Island's Francophones. These differences, Bernard claims, reflected a "certain lack of integration by the minority community" into Quebec's political life. See André Bernard, "L'Abstentionisme des électeurs de langue anglaise du Québec," in Daniel Latouche et al., *Le procéssus électorale au Québec* (Montréal: Éditions Hurtubise HMH, 1976), pp. 159–160, 165.

100. Brian Young, *George-Étienne Cartier: Montreal Bourgeois* (Montreal: McGill–Queen's University Press, 1981), p. 64. See also Rumilly, *Histoire de Montréal 2,* pp. 343–363.

101. Bernard Vigod, *Quebec before Duplessis: The Political Career of Louis-Alexandre Taschereau* (Montreal: McGill–Queen's University Press, 1986).

102. Linteau et al., *Quebec: A History,* p. 538.

103. Conrad Black, *Duplessis* (Toronto: McClelland and Stewart, 1977), pp. 304, 603–624. See also Hubert Quinn, *The Union Nationale,* 2d ed. (Toronto: University of Toronto Press: 1979), pp. 73–102.

104. Dale C. Thomson, *Jean Lesage and the Quiet Revolution* (Toronto: Macmillan and Company, 1984), p. 14.

105. Kenneth McRoberts, *Quebec: Social Change and Political Crisis,* 3d ed., (Toronto: McClelland and Stewart, 1988), p. 108.

106. See, for example, the concerns of Eastern Townships Anglophone Christopher Dunkin, expressed during the debates on Confederation, in P. B. Waite, ed., *The Confederation Debates in the Province of Canada: 1865* (Toronto: McClelland and Stewart, 1963), pp. 118–120. See also A. I. Silver, *The French-Canadian Idea of Confederation* (Toronto: University of Toronto Press, 1982), pp. 51–66.

107. RCBB vol. 2, *Education* (Ottawa: Information Canada, 1967), p. 25; and Linteau et al., *Quebec: A History,* pp. 460–466.

108. Rudin, *Forgotten Quebecers,* p. 230.

109. Ibid., p. 232.

110. Copp, *The Anatomy of Poverty,* pp. 68–69; and the Report of the Royal Commission of Inquiry on Education in the Province of Quebec vol. 3, *Educational Administration* (Quebec: Government of the Province of Quebec, 1966), pp. 93–95. (Hereafter cited as the Parent Commission.)

111. Parent Commission 3, pp. 91–100.

112. Guy Bouthillier, "Aux origines de la planification linguistique québécoise," in Office de la langue française, *L'État et la planification linguistique,* tome 2, *Études de cas particuliers* (Québec: Éditeur officiel du Québec, 1981), p. 7.

113. Étienne Blanchard, *En garde! Termes anglaises et anglicismes* (Montréal: Imprimerie Bilendeau, 1912), p. 106.

114. On the ideology of "la survivance," see: Denis Monière, *Le développement des idéologies au Québec: des origines à nos jours* (Montréal: Éditions Québec-Amérique, 1977), pp. 159–188; Michel Brunet, "Trois dominantes de la pensée canadienne-française: l'agriculturisme, l'anti-étatisme, et le messianisme," in Michel Brunet, *La présence anglaise et les Canadiens: Études sur l'histoire et la pensée des deux Canadas* (Montréal: Beauchemin, 1964), pp. 113–166; and Ramsay Cook, "Quebec: The Ideology of Survival," in Ramsay Cook, *Canada and the French-Canadian Question* (Toronto: Macmillan of Canada, 1966), pp. 79–106.

115. Heintzman, "The Political Culture of Quebec," pp. 3–59.

116. Ibid., p. 35. On the limited development of the Quebec state before 1960, see James Ian Gow, *Histoire de l'administration publique québécois, 1867–1970* (Montréal: Les Presses de l'Université de Montréal, 1986).

117. See Jean-Louis Roy, *Les programmes électoraux du Québec. Un siècle de programmes politiques québécois,* tome 2, *1931–1966* (Montréal, Lémeac, 1970).

118. Vigod, *Taschereau,* pp. 241–246.

119. Guy Bouthillier and Jean Meynaud, "Une première loi timide et contestée," in Bouthillier and Meynaud, *Le Choc des langues au Québec, 1760–1970* (Montréal: Les Presses de l'Université du Québec, 1972), pp. 326–328.

120. Bouthillier and Meynaud, "Une capitulation linguistique," in Bouthillier and Meynaud, *Le Choc des langues,* p. 563.

121. Guy Bourassa, "The Political Elite of Montreal: From Aristocracy to Democracy," in Lionel D. Feldman and Michael D. Goldrick, eds., *Politics and Government of Urban Canada* (London: Methuen, 1969), p. 125.

122. Ironically, as Francophone leader Henri Bourassa remarked, the understandable "explosion" of French-Canadian ethnic politics in the aftermath of the events in Ontario "assured the victory of a fifth-rate man, incapable of acting for the honor or rights of his race, and the defeat of a rare Anglo Canadian who had manifested genuine sympathies for French Canadians." Quoted in Robert Rumilly, *Histoire de Montréal,* tome 3 (Montréal: Editions Fides, 1972), p. 461.

123. Quoted in Leslie Roberts, *Montreal: From Mission Colony to World City* (Toronto: Macmillan, 1969), p. 313; see also Robert Rumilly, *Histoire de Montréal,* tome 4 (Montréal: Éditions Fides, 1974), p. 87; and Rumilly, *Histoire de Montréal 3,* pp. 458–461.

124. Guy Bourassa, *Les relations ethniques dans la vie politique montréalaise,* Documents de la Commission royale d'enquête sur le bilinguisme et le biculturalisme, num. 10 (Ottawa: Information Canada, 1971), p. 40.

125. On the position of the Montreal Light, Heat, and Power Company in the city, see Linteau et al., *Quebec: A History,* p. 310; Linteau et al., *Le Québec depuis 1930,* p. 253; and Rumilly, *Histoire de Montréal 4,* pp. 108–109.

126. For an excellent analysis of the role of linguistic issues in governance on the Island of Montreal and the functioning of public institutions in the city and its suburbs, see Sancton, *Governing the Island of Montreal.*

127. Report of the Royal Commission of Inquiry on Constitutional Problems (Quebec: 1953).

128. William Coleman, "The Class Basis of Language Policy in Quebec, 1949–1975," *Studies in Political Economy* 3 (Spring 1980), p. 97.

129. Ibid., p. 104.

130. Quoted in Jean-Claude Corbeil, *L'aménagement linguistique du Québec* (Montréal: Éditions Guérin, 1980), p. 34.

131. Linteau et al., *Le Québec depuis 1930,* p. 366.

132. Pierre Laporte, "Queen Elizabeth? . . . Jamais!," *l'Action nationale* 44:8 (avril 1955): 668–678 (reprinted in Bouthillier and Meynaud, *Le Choc des langues,* quotation from page 630). See also Pierre Laporte, "Château Maisonneuve," *l'Action nationale* 44:9 (mai 1955): 754–762.

133. Coleman, "The Class Basis of Language," p. 97; Robert Rumilly, *Histoire de Montréal,* tome 5, *1939–1967* (Montréal: Éditions Fides, 1974), pp. 177–178. Drapeau recommended the name of "Place Ville-Marie" to project developer William Zeckendorf as a more acceptable name for the CNR hotel. During Drapeau's next term as mayor, in the early 1960s, a major Zeckendorf development complex in Montreal was named Place Ville-Marie.

134. Gordon would achieve even greater notoriety in 1962 when he remarked that no Francophone was a vice-president of the CNR because he had never met one who was qualified. This comment set off Francophone nationalist demonstrations in front of the Queen Elizabeth Hotel in December 1962, culminating in Gordon's hanging in effigy and burnings of the Union Jack. As the language issue in Montreal became politicized, and as French Québécois nationalism developed in the 1960s, Gordon's statement would become a classic symbol of Montreal Anglophone arrogance. See Louis Fournier, *F.L.Q.: Histoire d'un mouvement clandestin* (Montréal: Éditions Québec/Amérique, 1982), p. 23.

135. It was not until 1964 that Canada adopted its own flag with the maple leaf symbol—in part, a concession to growing nationalism in Quebec that found the existing flag a repugnant symbol of British dominance.

Chapter 3

1. Sheila McLeod Arnopoulos and Dominique Clift, *The English Fact in Quebec,* 2d ed. (Montreal: McGill–Queen's University Press, 1984), p. 153.

2. François-Pierre Gingras, "Le Rassemblement pour l'Indépendance Nationale ou l'indépendance: du mouvement sociale au parti politique," in Réjean Pelletier, ed., *Partis politiques au Québec* (Montréal: Éditions Hurtubise HMH, 1976), p. 238.

3. Louis Fournier, *F.L.Q.: Histoire d'un mouvement clandestin* (Montréal: Éditions Québec/Amérique, 1982), p. 46. Despite these efforts, the RIN organized demonstrations in Quebec City, provoking police violence and publicity on what became known as "le samedi de la matraque" ("The Saturday of the Billy-Club").

4. Ibid., pp. 108–109.

5. Ibid., pp. 13–29.

6. FLQ pamphlet, quoted in Gérard Pelletier, *The October Crisis* (Toronto: McClelland and Stewart, 1971), p. 224.

7. George Nader, *Cities of Canada.* vol. 2, *Profiles of Fifteen Metropolitan Centres* (Toronto: Macmillan of Canada, 1976), p. 131.

8. P. Dagenais, "La métropole du Canada: Montréal ou Toronto?," *Revue de Géographie de Montréal* 23: 1 (1969): 36.

9. Jacques Léveillée, *Développement urbain et politiques gouvernementales urbaines dans l'agglomeration montréalaise, 1945–1975* (Montréal: Société Canadienne de Science Politique, 1978), p. 202.

10. Jane Jacobs, *The Question of Separatism* (New York: Vintage Books, 1980), p. 15.

11. Arnopoulos and Clift, *English Fact in Quebec,* pp. 120–121.

12. Paul-André Linteau et al., *Le Québec Depuis 1930* (Montréal: Éditions Boréal Express, 1986), pp. 691–710.

13. As Michael Behiels points out, these cultural impulses had been building as Montreal grew throughout the twentieth century; pent up under the repression of Duplessis, they broke through in the 1960s. See Behiels, *Prelude to Quebec's Quiet Revolution* (Montreal: McGill–Queen's University Press, 1985).

14. Kenneth McRoberts, *Quebec: Social Change and Political Crisis,* 3d ed. (Toronto: McClelland and Stewart, 1988), pp. 147–159. There is a substantial scholarly debate over the role of the new middle class as opposed to other groups in promoting the Quiet Revolution. William Coleman and Dorval Brunelle, for example, argue that Francophone businessmen took the lead in promoting the *étatiste* policies of the Quiet Revolution, and that the development of a new middle class was a *consequence* rather than a *cause* of these policies. My argument on the relative weights of the Francophone new middle class versus the incipient Francophone capitalist class in shaping 1960s policies mainly follows McRoberts (see, in particular, Chapter 7). In fact, the Francophone business class opposed many of the most celebrated initiatives of the Quiet Revolution, such as the Hydro-Québec nationalization. The relative strength of the new middle class would become most obvious on the language question.

15. Kenneth McRoberts and Dale Posgate, *Quebec: Social Change and Political Crisis,* 2d ed. (Toronto: McClelland and Stewart, 1980), p. 99.

16. Ibid., p. 100.

17. Linteau, et al., *Le Québec Depuis 1930,* p. 277.

18. Lysiane Gagnon, "Les Conclusions du Rapport B.B.: De Durham à Laurendeau-Dunton: Variation sur le Thème de la Dualité Canadienne," *Économie Québécoise* (Montréal: Les Presses de l'Université du Québec, 1969), p. 251.

19. Charles Taylor, "Nationalism and the Political Intelligentsia: A Case Study," *Queens Quarterly* 72 (Spring 1965): 150–168.

20. Marcel Fournier, "La Question nationale: Enjeux et impasses," in *La Chance au coureur: Bilan de l'action du gouvernement du Parti Québécois,* ed. Jean-François Léonard (Montréal: Éditions Nouvelle Optique, 1978), pp. 177–179.

21. Albert Breton, "The Economics of Nationalism," *Journal of Political Economy* 72 (August 1964): 381.

22. Henry Milner, *Politics in the New Quebec* (Toronto: McClelland and Stewart, 1978), p. 134.

23. Quoted in Mordecai Richler, *Home Sweet Home: My Canadian Album* (New York: Penguin Books, 1985), p. 237.

24. Calculated from data in André Blais and Kenneth McRoberts, "Public Expenditure in Ontario and Quebec, 1950–1980: Explaining the Differences," *Journal of Canadian Studies* 18:1 (Spring 1983): 30.

25. James I. Gow, "Modernisation et administration publique," in Edmond Orban et al., *La modernisation politique du Québec* (Montréal: Éditions du Boréal Express, 1976), p. 165.

26. Ministère de l'Éducation du Québec, *Livre vert: L'enseignement primaire et secondaire au Québec* (Québec: MEQ, 1977), p. 4.

27. McRoberts and Posgate, *Quebec: Social Change and Political Crisis,* pp. 104–105.

28. René Lévesque, *Attendez que je me rappelle . . .* (Montréal: Éditions Québec/ Amérique, 1986), pp. 227–253; and Dale Thomson, *Jean Lesage and the Quiet Revolution* (Toronto: Macmillan of Canada, 1984), p. 242.

29. Yves Bélanger and Pierre Fournier, *L'Entreprise Québécoise: Développement historique et dynamique contemporaine* (Montréal: Éditions Hurtubise HMH, 1987), pp. 134–135; Douglas Fullerton, *The Dangerous Delusion: Quebec's Independence Obsession* (Toronto: McClelland and Stewart, 1978), pp. 53–61; and Thomson, *Jean Lesage,* pp. 243–245.

30. It was in the 1960s that the term *Québécois,* connoting a forward-looking, dynamic *nationality* replaced *French Canadian* as the term of self-identification for many French-origin residents of Quebec. The phrase "normal society," in which Francophones were not second-class citizens in their own territory, was frequently articulated by René Lévesque.

31. Linteau et al., *Le Québec Depuis 1930,* pp. 691–711.

32. Michael Stein, "Bill 22 and the Non-Francophone Population in Quebec: A Case Study of Minority Group Attitudes on Language Legislation," in John R. Mallea, ed., *Quebec's Language Policies: Background and Response* (Québec: Les Presses de l'Université Laval, 1977), p. 258. Anglophone business leaders objected to *étatisme* not only for cultural reasons, but also because, as businessmen, they abhorred public regulation of private property.

33. Arnopoulos and Clift, *English Fact in Quebec,* p. 103.

34. *Report of the Royal Commission on Bilingualism and Biculturalism,* vol. 2, *Education* (Ottawa: Information Canada, 1967), p. 25.

35. Ibid.

36. Arnopoulos and Clift, *English Fact in Quebec,* pp. 83–86; Pierre Fournier, *The Quebec Establishment* (Montreal: Black Rose Books, 1978), p. 126.

37. Léon Dion, *Le bill 60 et la société québécoise* (Montréal: Éditions Hurtubise HMH, 1967), pp. 67–80.

38. Formally titled the Royal Commission of Inquiry on Education in the Province of Quebec, the commission chaired by Msgr. Alphonse Parent ultimately issued five

volumes that constituted a blueprint for Quebec's massive school reform program.

39. Parent Commission, vol. 3, *Educational Administration* (Quebec: Government of the Province of Quebec, 1966), p. 94.

40. Ibid., p. 196. See also Lise Duval and Jean-Pierre Tremblay, *Le projet de restructuration scolaire de l'île de Montréal et la question linguistique au Québec* (Québec: Centre international de recherche sur le bilinguisme, 1974), pp. 8–10.

41. Parent Commission, *Educational Administration,* p. 196.

42. Royal Commission on Bilingualism and Biculturalism, *Education,* p. 25.

43. William Coleman, "The Class Basis of Language Policy in Quebec, 1949–1975," *Studies in Political Economy* 3 (Spring 1980): 104.

44. Nader, *Cities of Canada,* p. 152.

45. Ibid., p. 150.

46. See Abe Limonchik, "The Montreal Economy during the Drapeau Years," in Dimitrios Roussopolous, ed., *The City and Radical Social Change* (Montreal: Black Rose Books, 1982), pp. 183, 187; and Andrew Sancton, *Governing the Island of Montreal: Language Differences and Metropolitan Politics* (Berkeley: University of California Press, 1985), pp. 73–74.

47. Quoted in Jean-Pierre Proulx, "Tocqueville a lancé le debat sur l'affichage en . . . 1831," *Le Devoir,* 12 décembre 1988.

48. SSJBM brief reprinted in Guy Bouthillier, "Éléments d'une chronologie politique de l'action linguistique du Québec pour la décennie 1960–1969, précedée d'une aperçu sur la periode 1935–1969," in *L'État et la planification linguistique,* tome 2, *Études de cas particuliers* (Québec: Éditeur officiel du Québec, 1981), p. 32.

49. Quoted in Réjean Pelletier, "Les militants du R.I.N. et les autorités politiques québécois," in R. Pelletier, ed., *Partis politiques au Québec,* p. 261.

50. Guy Bouthillier and Jean Meynaud, *Le Choc des langues au Québec, 1760–1970* (Montréal: Les Presses de l'Université du Québec, 1972), p. 45.

51. Quoted in R. Pelletier, "Les militants du R.I.N.," p. 261.

52. *Programme politique du Rassemblement pour l'indépendance nationale,* article 111 (Montréal: 1965), p. 37.

53. *Le Devoir,* 8 septembre 1967; L. Fournier, *F.L.Q.,* pp. 150–151.

54. Réal Pelletier, "Centre l'unilinguisme, Lévesque retient l'indépendance comme solution," *Le Devoir,* 4 novembre 1963. As we shall see, sensitivity to Anglophone rights was a consistent theme in Lévesque's political career.

55. Thomson, *Jean Lesage,* p. 319.

56. William Coleman, *The Independence Movement in Quebec, 1945–1980* (Toronto: University of Toronto Press, 1984), pp. 139–140.

57. Thomson, *Jean Lesage,* p. 317.

58. Ministère des Affaires culturelles, *Livre blanc sur la politique culturelle* (unpublished, 1965), pp. 4, 24.

59. Ibid., pp. 28, 35–36.

60. Thomson, *Jean Lesage,* p. 319.

61. Ibid., p. 320.

62. Jean-Louis Roy, *Les programmes éléctoraux du Québec: Un siècle de programmes politiques québécois,* tome 2 (Montréal: Éditions Lémeac, 1970), p. 433.

63. R. Pelletier, "Les militants du R.I.N.," p. 263.

64. Statistics Canada, *Census of Canada, 1971* (Catalogue 92-726).

65. Hubert Charbonneau et Robert Maheu, *Les aspects démographiques de la question linguistique* (study prepared for the Commission of Inquiry of the Position of French Language and Language Rights in Quebec, 1972), p. 269.

66. See Fernand Harvey, "La question de l'immigration au Québec: Genèse historique," in *Le Québec français et l'école à clientèle pluriethnique* (Québec: Conseil de la langue français, 1987), pp. 16–19; and Jean-Marc Léger, "Immigration: problème sociale, drame nationale," *Le Devoir,* 12 décembre 1957.

67. Commission des écoles catholiques de Montréal, "Memoire à la Commission d'enquête sur la situation de la langue française et sur les droits linguistiques au Québec," septembre 1969, p. 45.

68. Calculated from Report of the Commission of Inquiry of the Position of the French Language and Language Rights in Quebec, *The Ethnic Groups* (Québec: Éditeur officiel du Québec, 1972), p. 218. (Hereafter cited as Gendron Commission.)

69. Gendron Commission, *Ethnic Groups,* pp. 218–221.

70. Jeremy Boissevain, *The Italians of Montreal* (Ottawa: Queen's Printer, 1971), p. 38.

71. Paul Cappon, *Conflit entre les néo-Canadiens et francophones de Montréal* (Québec: Les Presses de l'Université Laval, 1974), pp. 17, 28.

72. Gendron Commission, *Ethnic Groups,* p. 239.

73. Ministère de l'Éducation et Ministère des Affaires culturelles, *Rapport du Comité interministériel sur l'enseignement des langues aux Néo-Canadiens,* 27 janvier 1967, pp. 34–36. (Hereafter cited as Gauthier Report.)

74. See Parent Commission, *Educational Administration,* pp. 95–101; and Gendron Commission, *Ethnic Groups,* pp. 193–194.

75. See Donat J. Taddeo and Raymond C. Taras, *Le débat linguistique au Québec* (Montréal: Les Presses de l'Université de Montréal, 1987), pp. 51–52.

76. Coleman, *Independence Movement,* p. 147.

77. Gary Caldwell, "Assimilation and the Demographic Future of Quebec," in John R. Mallea, ed. *Quebec's Language Policies: Background and Response* (Québec: Les Presses de l'Université Laval, 1977), p. 67.

78. See Taddeo and Taras, *Le débat linguistique,* pp. 60–75; and Michael D. Behiels, "The Commission des écoles catholiques de Montréal and the Néo-Canadien Question: 1947–63," *Canadian Ethnic Studies* 18:2 (1986): 38–64.

79. Behiels, "The Commission des écoles . . . ," p. 46; Taddeo and Taras, *Le débat linguistique,* p. 60.

80. Behiels, "The Commission des écoles . . . ," p. 46.

81. Ibid., p. 54.

82. Taddeo and Taras, *Le débat linguistique,* pp. 69–76.

83. Behiels, "The Commission des écoles . . . ," p. 55.

84. Henry Milner, *La reforme scolaire au Québec* (Montréal: Éditions Québec/Amérique, 1985), p. 33.

85. Harvey, "La question de l'immigration au Québec," pp. 16–19.

86. On the Jewish/PSBGM accommodation, see David Rome, *On the Jewish School Question in Montreal, 1903–1931* (Montreal: Canadian Jewish Congress, 1975).

87. Conseil scolaire de l'île de Montréal, *Prévision des populations scolaires du territoires du Conseil scolaire de l'île de Montréal* (Montréal: Conseil scolaire de l'île de Montréal, 9 septembre 1983); Statistics Canada, *Census of Canada 1971* (catalogue 92-726).

88. Caldwell, "Assimilation and the Demographic Future of Quebec."

89. Calculated from Conseil scolaire de l'île de Montréal, *Prévisions des populations scolaires,* for various years.

90. Gauthier Report, p. 44.

91. Reprinted in Jacques Henripin, "Quebec and the Demographic Dilemma of French-Canadian Society," in Dale C. Thomson, ed., *Quebec Society and Politics: Views from the Inside* (Toronto: McClelland and Stewart, 1973), p. 162.

92. Ibid., pp. 155–160.

93. Réjean Lachappelle and Jacques Henripin, *La situation démolinguistique au Canada* (Montréal: L'Institut de recherches politiques, 1980), p. 235.

94. Charbonneau and Maheu, "Les aspects démographiques," pp. 180–183; Lachappelle and Henripin, *La situation démolinguistique*, p. 235.

95. Gendron Commission, *Ethnic Groups*, p. 177.

96. Ibid., pp. 220–221.

97. Coleman, "The Class Basis of Language Policy," p. 107. Enrollment data calculated from Gendron Commission, *Ethnic Groups*, pp. 220–221; and CECM, "Memoire à la Commission d'enquête," p. 45.

98. Roy, *Les programmes éléctoraux*, p. 407.

99. Gauthier Report, p. 44.

Chapter 4

1. Statistics Canada, *Census of Canada 1971* (Catalogue 92-726).

2. Henry Égretaud, *L'Affaire Saint-Léonard* (Montréal: 1967).

3. Ibid. Through the 1960s, Montreal schooling was administered by a crazy-quilt of local boards and regional school commissions. Students in Saint-Léonard attended primary schools run by the Saint-Léonard Catholic School Board, but then moved on to secondary schools administered by the Jérôme Le Royer Regional School Commission that encompassed the municipalities of Anjou, Montréal-Est, Pointe-Aux-Trembles, and Saint-Léonard.

4. Calculated from data provided in Égretaud, *L'Affaire Saint-Léonard*, p. 7.

5. *Le Devoir* (Montréal), 10 avril 1968.

6. *Le Devoir*, 2 avril 1968.

7. Robert Issenman, "L'affaire St. Leonard put in perspective," *The Star* (Montreal), March 14–17, 1970.

8. *Le Devoir*, 28 octobre 1968.

9. On the links between the MIS and the FLQ, see Louis Fournier, *F.L.Q.: Histoire d'un mouvement clandestin* (Montréal: Éditions Québec/Amérique, 1982), p. 186.

10. *Le Devoir*, 11–13 juin 1968.

11. *Le Devoir*, 28 juin 1968. Under the June 27 resolution, students previously enrolled in the bilingual classes would be permitted to complete the program.

12. *Le Devoir*, 12 juin 1968.

13. *Le Devoir*, 14 septembre 1968.

14. *Le Devoir*, 13 septembre 1968.

15. *Le Devoir*, 12 juin 1968.

16. *Le Devoir*, 4 juin 1968. Other Anglophone supporters of the Saint-Léonard Italians included the Montreal Council of PTAs and the Quebec Parents Association for Catholic Education.

17. Gerald Clark, *Montreal: The New Cité* (Toronto: McClelland and Stewart, 1982), p. 96.

18. *Le Devoir*, 2 juillet 1968.

19. *Le Devoir*, 4 septembre 1968.

20. *Le Devoir*, 19 septembre 1968.

21. *Le Devoir,* 26 septembre 1968.

22. See *Le Devoir,* 28 août–12 septembre 1968.

23. *Le Devoir,* 5 septembre 1968.

24. Ibid.

25. René Lévesque, *Attendez que je me rappelle . . .* (Montréal: Éditions Québec/Amérique, 1986), p. 306. MIS leader Raymond Lemieux was reported as "ripping up" his MSA membership card when Lévesque refused to "speak out" in support of the action at *l'école Aimé-Rénaud* (*Le Devoir,* 5 septembre 1968).

26. This "solution" led René Lévesque, a critic of MIS actions, to declare that "nothing was won at Saint-Léonard. I don't speak of victory when Francophone students are given a ramshackle block of cement on boulevard Métropolitaine [*l'école Aimé-Rénaud*] while Anglophone pupils are going to have a modern and luxurious school, located in the most tranquil section of this suburb" (*Le Devoir,* 9 septembre 1968).

27. *Le Devoir,* 25 juin 1968.

28. L. Fournier, *F.L.Q.,* p. 186.

29. Don Murray and Vera Murray, *De Bourassa à Lévesque* (Montréal: Éditions Quinze, 1978), p. 81.

30. Lévesque, *Attendez que je me rappelle . . . ,* p. 306.

31. Vera Murray, *Le Parti québécois: de la foundation à la prise du pouvoir* (Montréal: Éditions Hurtubise HMH, 1976), p. 114.

32. *The Star,* 22 November 1968. See also William Tetley, "The English and Language Legislation: A Personal History," in Gary Caldwell and Eric Waddell, eds. *The English of Quebec: From Majority to Minority Status* (Québec: Institut québécois de recherche sur la culture, 1982), pp. 384–385.

33. *Le Devoir,* 23 novembre 1968.

34. Robert J. MacDonald, "In Search of a Language Policy: Francophone Reactions to Bill 85 and 63," in John R. Mallea, ed. *Quebec's Language Policies: Background and Response* (Québec: Les Presses de l'Université Laval, 1977), p. 221.

35. Report of the Commission of Inquiry on the Position of the French Language and on Language Rights in Quebec, *The Ethnic Groups* (Quebec: Éditeur officiel du Québec, 1972), p. 238. Hereafter cited as the Gendron Report.

36. Ibid. Any immigrant wishing to learn English in COFI had to be fluent in French.

37. Bill 85, *Loi modifiant la Loi du ministère de l'education, la Loi du Conseil supérieur de l'éducation et la Loi de l'instruction publique,* 9 décembre 1968.

38. Cited in MacDonald, "In Search of a Language Policy," p. 222.

39. Richard Arès, "Autour du Bill 85: langues parlées par les Néo-Québécois à Montreal," *Relations* 337 (avril 1969): 105.

40. *Le Devoir,* 14 décembre 1968. The purpose of the PQ "ceiling" plan was to limit the growth of English-language schools while permitting immigrant children who had already begun their schooling in English to complete their studies in that language.

41. MacDonald, "In Search of a Language Policy," p. 227.

42. Ibid.

43. *Le Devoir,* 14 décembre 1968.

44. Douglas H. Fullerton, *The Dangerous Delusion: Quebec's Independence Obsession* (Toronto: McClelland and Stewart, 1978), p. 24.

45. Ibid., p. 186. See also Mordecai Richler, *Home Sweet Home: My Canadian Album* (New York: Penguin Books, 1985), p. 239.

46. Fullerton, *Dangerous Delusion,* p. 24.

47. L. Fournier, *F.L.Q.*, p. 208.

48. The other French-language university, of course, was the Université de Montréal.

49. *Le Devoir*, 24 mars 1969.

50. *Le Devoir*, 29 mars 1969; and Fournier, *F.L.Q.*, p. 210.

51. Benoit Gendreau and André Lemieux, *L'Organisation scolaire au Québec: Référentiel de connaissances* (Montréal: Les Éditions France-Québec Inc., 1979), p. 225.

52. *Le Devoir*, 22 septembre 1969.

53. *Le Devoir*, 5 septembre 1969.

54. *Le Devoir*, 20 septembre 1969.

55. *Le Devoir*, 4 septembre 1969.

56. Issenman, "L'affaire St. Leonard"; *Le Devoir*, 11–13 septembre 1969.

57. *Le Devoir*, 18 septembre 1969.

58. Bill 63, *Loi pour promouvoir la langue française au Québec* (Sanctionée le 28 novembre 1969).

59. See MacDonald, "In Search of a Language Policy," p. 229.

60. See Bill 63, Article 2, which amended section 203 of the Education Act.

61. *Le Devoir*, 7, 10 novembre 1969.

62. Lévesque, *Attendez que je me rappelle . . .* , p. 318. The group was dubbed the "Circumstantial Opposition" because it was merely the "circumstance" of their opposition to Bill 63—rather than any long-standing political commonalities—that joined them together. In the 1970s, however, Michaud, Lévesque, and Flamand would come together as *péquistes*—joined, ironically, by Jean-Guy Cardinal.

63. *Journal des débats*, 30 octobre 1969, p. 3459.

64. *Journal des débats*, 4 novembre 1969, p. 3539.

65. Ibid., pp. 3527, 3541.

66. *Le Devoir*, 10 novembre 1969.

67. *Le Devoir*, 31 octobre 1969.

68. *Le Devoir*, 29 octobre 1969.

69. *Le Devoir*, 30 octobre 1969.

70. *Le Devoir*, 29 octobre 1969.

71. MacDonald, "In Search of a Language Policy," pp. 237–238.

72. *Le Devoir*, 1 novembre 1969.

73. René Lévesque wrote of encountering a tearful Bertrand, fully aware of the damage Bill 63 was causing, yet determined, as a matter of "honor," to fulfill his promises to "Anglophone circles" (Lévesque, *Attendez que je me rappelle . . .* , p. 318). Bertrand's commitment to the bill is all the more curious given the UN's rural, Francophone base and the historical aversion to the party by Anglophone voters. Pierre Fournier speculates that the UN needed funding for the next provincial elections, and was hoping for big Anglophone contributions. Another theory, floated by PQ activist Gérald Godin, was that "the UN offered to stabilize the language situation for a more receptive attitude of the financial markets toward Quebec bond issues." Fournier concluded: "Given that business or the economic elites, English as well as French, were the only major groups to support the legislation, it would seem a legitimate hypothesis to claim that the government responded to their pressures." See Pierre Fournier, *The Quebec Establishment* (Montreal: Black Rose Books, 1978), pp. 138, 118.

74. Henry Milner, *The Long Road to Reform: Restructuring Public Education in Quebec* (Montreal: McGill–Queen's University Press, 1986), p. 27.

75. For analyses of Bill 62, see Lise Duval and Jean-Pierre Tremblay, *Le projet de*

restructuration scolaire de l'île de Montréal et la question linguistique au Québec (Québec: Centre internationale de recherche sur le bilinguisme, 1974); P. Fournier, *Quebec Establishment*, pp. 126–128; Milner, *Long Road to Reform*, pp. 27–28; and Andrew Sancton, *Governing the Island of Montreal: Language Differences and Metropolitan Politics* (Berkeley: University of California Press, 1985), pp. 155–157.

76. P. Fournier, *Quebec Establishment*, p. 127; Duval and Tremblay, *La restructuration scolaire*, pp. 40–43.

77. Anglo-Catholics supported Bill 62, believing that they would be less isolated on the unified boards—with Anglo-Protestants as allies—than they were in the Francophone-dominated Catholic boards in Montreal.

78. Duval and Tremblay, *La restructuration scolaire*, pp. 40–43.

79. *Le Devoir*, 2 décembre 1969.

80. Quoted in Sancton, *Governing the Island of Montreal*, p. 157.

81. Joseph Pagé, *Rapport du Conseil de la restructuration scolaire de l'île de Montréal* (Montréal: CECM, 1968); *Le Devoir*, 10 octobre 1968.

82. P. Fournier, *Quebec Establishment*, p. 139. Fournier points specifically to the interlocking directorates (my term, not his) of the PSBGM and the Montreal Board of Trade.

83. Protestant School Board of Greater Montreal, "Memorial to the Standing Parliamentary Committee on Education" (March 1970).

84. Montreal Board of Trade, "Memorial to the Standing Parliamentary Committee on Education" (March 1970).

85. Ibid.

86. On the role of capital flight in "disciplining" urban governments in the United States, see John Mollenkopf, *The Contested City* (Princeton: Princeton University Press, 1983).

Chapter 5

1. "The Parti Québécois and Its Grave Defects," *The Star* 21 April 1974.

2. Pierre Saint-Germain, "Beaulieu: Nous ferons enquête sur la firme Lafferty, Harwood, et Co.," *La Presse* (Montréal), 4 avril 1970; and Francine Charest, "Lafferty, Harwood, et Co. revient à la charge," *La Presse*, 11 avril 1970.

3. Henry Milner and Sheilagh Hodgins Milner, *The Decolonization of Quebec: An Analysis of Left-Wing Nationalism* (Toronto: McClelland and Stewart, 1973), p. 200.

4. The April 27 headlines were the following: *La Presse:* "Inquiétude face aux éléctions: des Québécois démenagent leurs valeurs en Ontario"; *Le Devoir:* "Des valeurs mobilières sont transférées a Toronto"; and *The Star:* "Securities Shipment Confirmed."

5. The Union nationale paid the price for its disastrous handling of Bill 63 by finishing third in the popular vote; this was the beginning of a series of electoral setbacks for the party created by Maurice Duplessis that resulted, after the 1981 provincial elections, in its virtual dissolution.

6. Calculated from Rapport du président général des éléctions, *Éléctions, 1970* (Québec: Éditeur officiel du Québec, 1971).

7. Serge Carlos and Daniel Latouche, "La composition de l'éléctorat péquiste," in Daniel Latouche, Guy Lord, and Jean-Guy Vaillancourt, *Le procéssus éléctoral au Québec: les éléctions provinciales de 1970 et 1973* (Montréal: Éditions Hurtubise HMH, 1976), p. 202.

8. Robert Stewart, "The City's Forgotten Assets: Head Offices," *The Star* (Montreal), 25 May 1971.

9. Cited in John Saywell, *Quebec 70: A Documentary Narrative* (Toronto: University of Toronto Press, 1971), p. 26.

10. Ibid., p. 27.

11. Jean V. Dufresne, "Lévesque solicits English support," *The Star*, 22 April 1970.

12. "Lévesque hits *Star* editorial," *The Star*, 23 April 1970. The PQ also fulminated over the gerrymandered Quebec and Montreal electoral maps that left the party with 23 percent of the popular vote but only 7 of 108 seats in l'Assemblée nationale. One PQ tract referred to *Le Coup d'État du 29 Avril*, and Lévesque asked: "Is Montreal going to be annexed sufficiently year after year to make it impossible for the majority group in Quebec to win an increasing number of ridings in Montreal?" Cited in Saywell, *Quebec 70*, pp. 24, 27.

13. Louis Fournier, *F.L.Q.: Histoire d'un mouvement clandestin* (Montréal: Éditions Québec/Amérique, 1982), pp. 259–262.

14. This was the same Pierre Laporte who had led the battle against the naming of the Queen Elizabeth Hotel in 1955 and who was the author of the 1965 White Paper proposing a Quebec language policy that was suppressed by Premier Lesage as excessively nationalistic.

15. The FLQ Manifesto, reprinted in Saywell, *Quebec 70*, pp. 46–51.

16. For a description of these events, see L. Fournier, *F.L.Q.*, pp. 287–372. Evidence has trickled out in the 1980s suggesting that the Trudeau government deliberately overstated the magnitude of the crisis to attempt to crush the fledgling PQ and *indépendantisme* of all stripes.

17. Vera Murray and Don Murray, *De Bourassa à Lévesque* (Montréal: Les Éditions Quinze, 1978), p. 141.

18. For Trudeau's philosophy on this subject, see his *Federalism and the French Canadians* (Toronto: Macmillan Company of Canada, 1968).

19. *The Globe and Mail* (Toronto), 25 November 1976.

20. Some examples: after a genuinely dualistic beginning, the province of Manitoba abolished any official status for French in 1890 and, in 1916, ended all bilingual education and declared English the sole language of instruction in the public schools. Similar policies eliminated French as a language of instruction in Alberta and Saskatchewan as they became provinces in 1905. In 1912, the Ontario legislature declared English the sole language of instruction in the province and even limited instruction in French as a subject. See Robert Craig Brown and Ramsay Cook, *Canada, 1896–1921: A Nation Transformed* (Toronto: McClelland and Stewart, 1974), pp. 1–26, 256–262.

21. K. D. McRae et al., *The Federal Capital: Report Prepared for the Royal Commission on Bilingualism and Biculturalism* (Ottawa: The Queen's Printer, 1967).

22. Report of the Royal Commission on Bilingualism and Biculturalism, *Book I: The Official Languages* (Ottawa: The Queen's Printer, 1967), p. 56. (Hereafter cited as RCBB.)

23. Cited in William Coleman, *The Independence Movement in Quebec, 1945–1980* (Toronto: University of Toronto Press, 1984), p. 194.

24. RCBB, *The Official Languages*, pp. 173–174.

25. The Official Languages Act, An Act respecting the status of the official languages of Canada, assented to 9th July 1969. In the Constitutional Accord of 1981, sections 16–22 incorporate guarantees on the official languages, and section 23 delineates minority-language educational rights.

26. Alfred Olivier Hero, Jr., and Louis Balthazar, *Contemporary Quebec and the United States, 1960–1985* (Boston: University Press of America, 1988), p. 157.

27. Ibid. See also Christopher Beattie, *Minority Men in a Majority Setting* (Toronto: McClelland and Stewart, 1975), and the comments of Max Yalden, commissioner of Official Languages, reported in *Le Devoir,* 22 octobre 1980.

28. This was the body appointed to implement the Official Language Act's provisions on bilingual districts.

29. See Kenneth D. McRae, "Bilingual Districts in Finland and Canada: Adventures in the Transplanting of an Institution," *Canadian Public Policy* 4 (Summer 1978): 331–351. For nationalist critiques of the concept of Montreal as a bilingual district, see Charles Castonguay, "Pour une politique des districts bilingues au Québec," *Journal of Canadian Studies* 11:3 (August 1976): 50–58; and Claude Jasmin, "Notre culture en peril coin de Peel et Sainte-Catherine," *Le Devoir,* 19 décembre 1968.

30. Report of the Bilingual Advisory Board, 1975 (Ottawa: Minister of Supply and Services, 1975).

31. Denis Turcotte, *La culture du Mouvement Québec français* (Québec: Les Presses de l'Université Laval, 1976).

32. Sheila McLeod Arnopoulos and Dominique Clift, *The English Fact in Quebec* 2d ed. (Montreal: McGill–Queen's University Press, 1984), p. 115; Gilles Gariepy, "Créer 100,000 emplois durant l'année 1971," *La Presse,* 7 avril 1970.

33. Règlement Numéro 6 du Ministre de l'Éducation, Approuvé par l'arrête en conseil numéro 155 en date du 13 janvier 1971; Bill 63, Loi pour promouvoir la langue française au Québec, Sanctionée le 28 novembre 1969, article 1.

34. Ibid.

35. Jean-Marie Mathieu and Edmund J. Malone, "Quelques aspects de la situation linguistique dans les huits commissions scolaires de l'île de Montréal" (Conseil scolaire de l'île de Montréal, 1976), pp. 39–47.

36. Donat J. Taddeo and Raymond C. Taras, *Le débat linguistique au Québec* (Montréal: Les Presses de l'Université de Montréal, 1987), p. 117.

37. Lise Duval and Jean-Pierre Tremblay, *Le projet de restructuration scolaire de l'île de Montréal et la question linguistique au Québec* (Québec: Les Presses de l'Université Laval, 1974), pp. 18–19.

38. Ibid.

39. Pierre Fournier, *The Quebec Establishment: The Ruling Class and the State* (Montreal: Black Rose Books, 1976), p. 128.

40. Duval and Tremblay, *Le projet de restructuration scolaire,* pp. 36–37.

41. Andrew Sancton, *Governing the Island of Montreal: Language Differences and Metropolitan Politics* (Berkeley: University of California Press, 1985), p. 162.

42. Projet de loi 71, Loi pour favoriser le développement scolaire dans l'île de Montréal, Sanctionée le 21 décembre 1972.

43. P. Fournier, *The Quebec Establishment,* p. 130; Duval and Tremblay, *Le projet de restructuration scolaire,* p. 52.

44. Robert J. McDonald, "Education, Language Rights, and Cultural Survival in Quebec: A Review Essay," *Journal of Educational Thought* 9 (April 1975): 53.

45. Duval and Tremblay, *Le projet de restructuration scolaire,* p. 30.

46. Ibid., p. 63.

47. Low voter participation in school board elections—typically under 15 percent of eligible voters—enabled dedicated Catholic-Confessionalist activists to consistently defeat "secularist" opponents and maintain control of Montreal's school policymaking. In 1973 and 1977, for example, Catholic-Confessionalist slates handily

defeated those connected with the Parti québécois and committed to school reorganization. See Duval and Tremblay, *Le projet de restructuration scolaire,* pp. 60–68; and *Le Devoir,* 9 juin 1977.

48. Rapport du Comité de Restructuration au Conseil scolaire de l'île de Montréal (1 novembre 1976); and Jules Leblanc, "Par un vote très serrée le conseil scolaire de l'île choisit les commissions confessionelles," *La Presse,* 1 février 1977.

49. Gendron Commission, *Ethnic Groups,* p. 271.

50. The Commission suggested that English as a "national language" might entail official status as: (1) a language of instruction in the public schools and (2) a language of communication with government.

51. Gendron Commission, *Ethnic Groups,* pp. 271, 274–275.

52. Ibid., pp. 271, 274.

53. P. Fournier, *The Quebec Establishment,* pp. 122–123. See, for example, the briefs of Bell Canada and Molson before the commission, warning of the dangers of imposing "unilingualism" (*Le Devoir,* 30 septembre 1969). The Gendron Commission hearings in Montreal, held in late 1969 and early 1970, were dominated by Anglophone corporate groups and were generally boycotted by Francophone nationalist groups. See Claude Ryan, "Le dilemme de M. Bertrand," *Le Devoir,* 3 octobre 1969.

54. Clement Trudel, "Un nouveau 'cheval de Troie,' dit Lévesque," *Le Devoir,* 14 février 1973; Pierre O'Neill, "La commission Gendron voit juste mais ses recommendations sont froussardes (le MQF)," *Le Devoir,* 20 février 1973; and "MQF: La philosophie inacceptable du rapport Gendron," *Le Devoir,* 20 février 1973.

55. See Claude Ryan, "Sur un sujet capital, un document raté," *Le Devoir,* 28 février 1973.

56. "La loi 63 doit être amendée: Gendron," *Le Devoir,* 26 février 1974; "M. Gendron s'en tient aux conclusions de son rapport," *Le Devoir,* 22 février 1974.

57. Eric Molson, quoted in Gerald Clark, *Montréal: The New Cité* (Toronto: McClelland and Stewart, 1982), pp. 89–90.

58. P. Fournier, *The Quebec Establishment,* p. 123. The "crazy things" mentioned in this quotation may refer to repeal of Bill 63. Arnopoulos and Clift argue that the increasingly Toronto-based Anglophone economic elite was willing to accept restrictions on access to Montreal's English-language schools in exchange for no interference in corporate operations, general linguistic peace, and a stable business climate. See Arnopoulos and Clift, *English Fact in Quebec,* pp. 117–118. This argument seems exaggerated, given the vehement public opposition of business groups such as the Board of Trade to the education restrictions in Bill 22 and especially in 1977 to Bill 101.

59. Ibid.

60. Guy Bouthillier, "Tenants et aboutissants de l'action linguistique," in Edmond Orban, ed. *La modernisation politique du Québec* (Montréal: Éditions du Boréal Express, 1976), p. 223.

61. *Rapport préliminaire—Éléctions générales 1973* (Québec: Président général des éléctions, 1974).

62. Murray and Murray, *De Bourassa à Lévesque,* p. 183.

63. Bouthillier, "Tenants et aboutissants," p. 216.

64. Murray and Murray, *De Bourassa à Lévesque,* pp. 181–183.

65. *Le Devoir,* 14 février 1974.

66. *The Star,* 14 February 1974.

67. "L'hésitation du Québec pourrait conduire à un affrontement brutal," *Le Devoir,* 28 février 1974. Claude Ryan, in his *Le Devoir* editorials, also questioned the

proposed legislation. See "Ce que pourrait être une solution realiste," *Le Devoir*, 26 février 1974; and "Où tracer la ligne de demarcation?" *Le Devoir*, 25 février 1974.

68. Bill 22, Loi sur la langue officielle, Sanctionée le 31 juillet 1974, préambule.

69. Ibid.

70. Bill 22, Chapitre II et Chapitre IV.

71. Bill 22, Articles 26–29.

72. Kenneth McRoberts, "Bill 22 and Canadian Language Policy," *Queen's Quarterly* 83 (Fall 1976): 464–477.

73. Bill 22, Article 29.

74. *Débats de l'Assemblée nationale du Québec,* Commission permanente de l'éducation, des affaires culturelles, et des communications. Étude du projet de loi no. 22: Loi sur la langue officielle, 20 juin 1974, p. B–3973 (hereafter cited as *Débats*).

75. Ibid. p. B–3974.

76. Ministère de l'Éducation du Québec, *Fichier élèves standard* (1973–1974).

77. In fact, between 1971 and 1974, the number of Francophone pupils in the Anglophone sector of the CECM declined from 5,724 to 5,103. See Taddeo and Taras, *Le débat linguistique*, p. 44.

78. Calculated from Conseil scolaire de l'île de Montréal, "Série de données d'inscription depuis 1970 et prévision des populations scolaires du territoire du Conseil scolaire de l'île de Montréal," 20 juin 1986; CECM data cited in Taddeo and Taras, *Le débat linguistique*, p. 44; and Gendron Commission, *Ethnic Groups*, pp. 484–485.

79. Conseil scolaire de l'île de Montréal, "Série de données . . . ," p. 6.

80. Ibid., pp. 12–14.

81. "La CEQ multiplier les feux contre la bilinguisme," *Le Devoir*, 5 avril 1974.

82. Cited in Taddeo and Taras, *Le débat linguistique*, p. 106.

83. "Bourassa craint des tensions s'il retarde l'adoption du projet 22," *Le Devoir*, 5 juillet 1974.

84. Bill 22, Article 40.

85. Bill 22, Article 43.

86. *The Gazette*, 22 May 1974.

87. See, for example, *Débats*, 17 juin 1974, pp. B–3577–3589 (Quebec Association of Protestant School Boards); 19 juin 1974, pp. B–3910–3919 (Federation of English-speaking Catholic Teachers, Inc.); 20 juin 1974, pp. B–3985–3995 (Provincial Association of Protestant Teachers of Quebec); 20 juin 1974, pp. B–4026–4037 (Quebec Association of School Administrators); 26 juin 1974, pp. B–4241–4252 (PSBGM); and 27 juin 1974, pp. B–4269–4277 (Provincial Association of Catholic Teachers).

88. *Débats*, 17 juin 1974, B–3562–3576. On the concern about splitting brothers and sisters, see Taddeo and Taras, *Le débat linguistique*, p. 150.

89. See, for example, *Débats*, 25 juin 1974, pp. B–4124–4141 (Alliance des professeurs de Montréal); 25 juin 1974, pp. B–4112–4124 (Société Saint-Jean Baptiste de Montréal); 26 juin 1974, pp. B–4228–4240 (CECM); and 27 juin 1974, pp. B–4303–4314 (Mouvement Nationale des Québécois).

90. *Débats*, 18 juin 1974, pp. B–3762–3786.

91. Gérald LeBlanc, "La fièvre linguistique s'empare du Parlement," *Le Devoir*, 23 mai 1974.

92. Arnopoulos and Clift, *The English Fact in Quebec*, p. 117.

93. *The Star*, 24 May 1974.

94. Michael Stein, "Bill 22 and the Non-Francophone Population in Quebec: A

Case Study of Minority Group Attitudes on Language Legislation," ed. John R. Mallea, *Quebec's Language Policies: Background and Response* (Québec: Les Presses de l'Université Laval, 1977), p. 253.

95. *Débats,* 25 juin 1974, pp. B–4069–4079; and Lysiane Gagnon, "Les Libéraux clouent le bec des adversaires du Bill 22," *La Presse,* 11 juillet 1974.

96. "La loi 22 ne rallie pas encore le caucus libéral," *Le Devoir,* 4 juillet 1974.

97. Taddeo and Taras, *Le débat linguistique,* pp. 155–192.

98. These exemptions included the students who: (1) had been in an English-language school the year earlier; (2) were of English mother tongue; or (3) had a brother or sister in an English-language school. See ibid., p. 152.

99. Bill 22, Article 40.

100. Angele Dagenais, "Bourassa engage le dialogue avec le Consiglio," *Le Devoir,* 21 septembre 1976; and Choquette's resignation letter, reprinted in *Le Devoir,* 27 septembre 1976. Curiously, Choquette had a complete change of heart and ran as a candidate committed to freedom of choice in the language of instruction in the 1976 provincial elections.

101. Loi sur la langue officielle (L.Q. 1974, ch. 6). Texte règlementaire, A.C. 1347–75 du 2 avril 1975; Règ. 75–129 du 2 avril 1975.

102. Taddeo and Taras, *Le débat linguistique,* pp. 175–183.

103. Ministère de l'Éducation, *Fichier élèves standard* (1976–1977).

104. Conseil scolaire de l'île de Montréal, "Série de données. . . ."

105. Conseil scolaire de l'île de Montréal, "Prévisions des populations scolaires de l'île de Montréal pour 1980 et 1985," 23 juin 1976, p. 8.

106. Pierre Dupont, *15 Novembre 76 . . .* (Montréal: Les Éditions Quinze, 1976), pp. 84–86. Bourassa's changes, meant to placate the restive Anglophone and Italian electorate in Montreal, included exempting all siblings of children currently in English-language schools from the Bill 22 tests and strengthening the early teaching of English in French-language schools.

107. For an excellent analysis of the Anglophone "majority" psychology in Montreal, see Stein, "Bill 22."

108. Montreal's Anglophones failed to understand that nothing in the BNA Act guaranteed language rights in education.

109. MNA Kenneth Fraser stated: "We're staring into the same thing as the Nazis did in Germany when they stopped the Jews from going to school there," *The Gazette,* 23 May 1974.

110. André Bernard, *Québec: éléctions 1976* (Montréal: Éditions Hurtubise HMH, 1976), pp. 110–111.

111. Ibid., p. 117.

Chapter 6

1. Election data are from *Rapport préliminaire des présidents d'élection—Éléctions générales 1976* (compilation du 30 novembre). For an analysis of the historic 1976 election, see André Bernard, *Québec: éléctions 1976* (Montréal: Éditions Hurtubise HMH, 1976). In addition to the controversies surrounding Bill 22, nationalist sentiment was boosted in the fall of 1976 by a conflict between Anglophone and Francophone pilots over bilingualism in Quebec air space.

2. Roger Lemelin, quoted in Henry Milner, *Politics in the New Quebec* (Toronto: McClelland and Stewart, 1978), p. 17.

3. Quoted in Mordecai Richler, *Home Sweet Home: My Canadian Album* (New York: Penguin Books, 1985), p. 232.

4. Ibid.

5. Lionel Albert and William Shaw, *Partition* (Pointe-Claire, Que.: Thunder Hill Publishing, 1981), pp. 27–28.

6. Activists in the radical Montréal-Centre branch of the PQ and affiliated Montreal-based groups such as the Société Saint-Jean Baptiste de Montréal and the Mouvement Québec français advocated no official status for English in an independent Quebec.

7. The PQ referendum question, requesting a popular mandate to begin negotiations on "sovereignty association" (the party's independence option that combined political sovereignty with economic association with the rest of Canada), was defeated by a provincewide vote of 59 to 41 percent. A slender majority of Francophones voted *non* to the PQ position.

8. Gouvernement du Québec, *La politique québécoise de la langue française* (mars 1977), p. 34. Emphasis added.

9. See Vera Murray, *Le Parti québécois: de la fondation à la prise du pouvoir* (Montréal: Éditions Hurtubise HMH, 1976), pp. 109–116.

10. René Lévesque, *Attendez que je me rappelle . . .* (Montréal: Éditions Québec/Amérique, 1986), p. 388.

11. Ibid.

12. Laurin's now secure position in history as the PQ's preeminent hard-liner on language policy is ironic in view of his early 1970s position, along with Lévesque, as a vocal opponent of unilingualist resolutions as PQ *congrès general*. See Murray, *Le Parti québécois*, p. 116.

13. See, for example, Laurin's press conference comments upon presenting Bill 1, in *La Presse*, 28 avril 1977.

14. Graham Fraser, *PQ: René Lévesque and the Parti Québécois in Power* (Toronto: Macmillan of Canada, 1985), p. 96.

15. Ibid.

16. For an excellent analysis of the sociolinguistic underpinnings of PQ language policy, particularly on the relationship of that policy to the controversial linguistic theories of Benjamin Whorf, see William Coleman, *The Independence Movement in Quebec, 1945–1980* (Toronto: University of Toronto Press, 1984), pp. 184–186.

17. *La politique québécoise de la langue française*, p. 21.

18. Ibid., p. 35.

19. Ibid., p. 34.

20. Ibid., pp. 6, 8. As several critics noted, the White Paper's use of demographic data was especially slippery, relying mainly on the dated 1972 study Charbonneau and Maheu produced for the Gendron Commission (which itself forecast a solid Francophone majority in Montreal and Quebec through the 1990s given prevailing migration patterns and birthrates).

21. On Lévesque's opposition, see Fraser, *PQ*, pp. 101–102.

22. *La politique québécoise de la langue française*, pp. 36–38. The White Paper and subsequent legislation left the matter of defining "appropriate knowledge" of French to future regulations.

23. Ibid., pp. 46–47.

24. *Édition 1973 du programme du Parti québécois*, p. 23.

25. *La politique québécoise de la langue française*, pp. 47–48.

26. Ibid., p. 47.

27. Ibid.

28. Ibid.

29. Kenneth McRoberts, *Quebec: Social Change and Political Crisis*, 3d ed. (Toronto: McClelland and Stewart, 1988), p. 276.

30. See "Le cabinet ne fait pas l'unanimité," *La Presse*, 31 mai 1977; Vera Murray and Don Murray, *De Bourassa à Lévesque* (Montréal: Éditions Quinze, 1978), p. 236; and Fraser, *PQ*, pp. 105–110.

31. Lévesque's offer was rejected first in August 1977 at the provincial premiers conference at St. Andrews, N.B., and again in February 1978 when the premiers met in Montreal. See "Pas de 'clause Canada' dans la loi 101," *Le Devoir*, 20 août 1977; and "Premiers Slam Door on Language Trade-off," *The Star*, 24 February 1978.

32. By 1984 this bureaucracy would employ more than six hundred persons (half of whom were based in Montreal) and have combined annual budgets over $20 million. *Le Québec Statistique, Édition 1985–1986* (Québec: Éditeur officiel du Québec, 1985), p. 261; Office de la langue française, *Rapport d'activité, 1983–84* (Québec: Éditeur officiel du Québec, 1984); Conseil de la langue française, *Rapport d'activité 1985–1986* (Québec: Éditeur officiel du Québec, 1986); and Commission de protection de la langue française, *Rapport d'activité 1985–1986* (Québec: Éditeur officiel du Québec, 1986).

33. For an interesting analysis of the treatment of Bills 1 and 101 in Montreal's English-language newspapers, see Nadia Bredimas-Assimopoulos and Michel Laferrière, *Législation et perceptions ethniques: Une étude du contenu de la presse anglaise de Montréal au vote de la Loi 101* (Québec: Office de la langue française, 1980).

34. Protestant School Board of Greater Montreal, "Brief Presented to the Parliamentary Committee Studying Bill 1," June 1977, p. 1.

35. See Bredimas-Assimopoulos and Laferrière, *Législation et perceptions ethniques,* p. 58.

36. Société Saint-Jean Baptiste de Montréal, "Mémoire à la Commission parlementaire étudiant le projet de Loi 1," juin 1977, p. 23; and Mouvement Québec français, "Mémoire à la Commission parlementaire étudiant le projet de Loi 1," juin 1977, p. 15.

37. See, for example, "La communauté italienne a tout juste pu presenter son mémoire," *La Presse*, 18 juin 1977.

38. The business class's reaction to Bill 1 is examined in detail in Chapter 7.

39. "PQ Attacks Anglophone Resistance," *The Star*, 20 July 1977.

40. Quoted in Murray and Murray, *De Bourassa à Lévesque*, p. 241.

41. Ryan's editorials on Bill 1 are conveniently collected in *Une Société Stable* (Montréal: Éditions Heritage, 1978), pp. 193–208.

42. Ibid., p. 197.

43. Lévesque, *Attendez que je me rappelle . . .* , p. 389.

44. "La Charte de la langue française," Sanctionée le 26 août 1977, Préambule (hereafter cited as Bill 101).

45. Bill 101, Article 113f.

46. Bill 101, Article 73, contained the "Quebec clause."

47. Quoted in Murray and Murray, *De Bourassa à Lévesque,* p. 244.

48. *La Presse*, 27 août 1977.

49. François-Albert Angers, "La montée vers un Québec maître de sa destinée," *L'Action nationale* 68 (1978): 28.

50. For a similar perspective on Bills 22 and 101, see William Coleman, "From Bill

22 to Bill 101: The Politics of Language Under the Parti Québécois," *Canadian Journal of Political Science* 14: 3 (September 1981): 459–485.

51. Ibid., p. 481.

52. Ibid., p. 463.

53. Surveys taken since 1977 have consistently shown solid support among Francophones for the bill. A 1988 *Le Devoir*/CRÉATEC survey reported that "93 percent of Francophones think that a law will always be necessary to protect French in Quebec (Gilles Lesage, "La loi 101: une police d'assurance pour les francophones," *Le Devoir*, 20 juin 1988).

54. See, for example, Daniel Monnier, *La Question linguistique: L'état de l'opinion publique* (Montréal: Conseil de la langue française, 1984), pp. 11–21.

55. Uli Locher, *Les anglophones de Montréal; émigration et évolution des attitudes, 1978–1983* (Québec: Éditeur officiel du Québec, 1988), p. 21.

56. Defined here as English mother tongue.

57. For 1966–1976 interprovincial migration data, see Réjean Lachapelle and Jacques Henripin, *La situation démolinguistique au Canada: evolution passée et prospective* (Montréal: Institut de recherches politiques, 1980), p. 235. The concept of linguistic transfer refers to members of one linguistic group adopting the language of another (for example, Francophones or Allophones adopting English as their language of use). Chapter 9 evaluates linguistic transfers in Montreal in the 1970s.

58. Statistics Canada, *Census of Canada 1981* (catalogue 93–929) and Statistics Canada, *Census of Canada 1986* (catalogue 94–109). The comparability of 1986 and 1981 census data on language is complicated by the fact that in 1986, for the first time, Statistics Canada recorded multiple mother tongues when these were reported. I have distributed these multiple responses according to the editing rules used by Statistics Canada, but a caution on the direct comparability of the data is necessary.

On interprovincial migration, for Quebec as a whole there were 198,000 Anglophone out-migrants between 1976 and 1986 and 52,000 English-Canadian immigrants for a net interprovincial balance of negative 146,000 during this decade (−106,000 during the fateful 1976–1981 period). The Montreal region accounted for around 75 percent of Quebec's interprovincial migration flows between 1966 and 1976; if that ratio held during the following decade, then we can estimate a net loss of 110,000 Anglophones in Montreal through interprovincial migration. See Mireille Baillargeon, *Évolution et caractéristiques des échanges migratoires interprovinciaux du Québec depuis 1971* (Québec: Conseil de la langue française, 1983), p. 51; and Michel Paillé, "Le Québec anglophone: Une comparaison sommaire avec les Franco-Ontariens," *Bulletin du Conseil de la langue française* 5: 2 (été 1988): 5.

59. For example, Beaconsfield fell from 82.5 percent Anglophone in 1976 to 67.5 percent in 1986; Pointe-Claire from 76.1 percent to 67.4 percent; Kirkland from 71.0 percent to 54.7 percent; and Mont-Royal from 55.2 percent to 40.6 percent; Statistics Canada, *Census of Canada 1976* (Catalogue 92–822) and Statistics Canada, *Census of Canada 1986* (Catalogue 95–130).

60. Locher, *Les anglophones de Montréal*, p. 44.

61. Ibid., pp. 42–43.

62. See ibid., p. 121; and Alliance-Quebec, "Brief on Demographic Tendencies Presented to the Standing Committee on Culture of the National Assembly," November 1984, pp. 41–42.

63. United States urban observers are painfully aware of this process in the racial turnover of urban neighborhoods in the 1960s and 1970s.

64. For example, Michel Paillé estimates that over one-third of the decline in Anglophone school enrollments since 1977 stems from the shrinking pool of potential pupils caused by out-migration. See Paillé, *Conséquences de politiques linguistiques québécois sur les effectifs scolaires selon la langue d'enseignement* (Québec: Conseil de la langue française, 1985), p. 12.

65. "PSBGM to Offer Freedom of Choice," *The Star,* 30 August 1977; and "Pupils Enroll Illegally as Teachers Defy Quebec," *The Star,* 7 September 1977.

66. "Police Won't Evict Children," *The Star,* 3 September 1977.

67. Michel Roy, "De la protestation à la désobéissance," *Le Devoir,* 20 mars 1978. Emphasis added.

68. "PSBGM Loses Court Fight over $9 Million," *The Gazette* (Montreal), 21 July 1978.

69. "Illegal Pupils to Stay with Us," *The Gazette,* 22 July 1978.

70. "PSBGM Ends Language Defiance," *The Gazette,* 1 August 1978. For Board President Joan Dougherty's defense of PSBGM behavior, see "Le BEPGM n'a jamais pratique le guerilla," *Le Devoir,* 17 mars 1978.

71. See Donat J. Taddeo and Raymond C. Taras, *Le débat linguistique au Québec* (Montréal: Les Presses de l'Université de Montréal, 1987), p. 197; and "Les écoles anglo-catholiques sont prêtes a defier encore la loi 101," *Le Devoir,* 17 mars 1978.

72. Ibid., pp. 202–204.

73. Ibid., p. 198. Fewer than fifty pupils were enrolled in these classes by 1978.

74. Michael Stein, "Changing Anglo-Quebecer Self-Consciousness," in Gary Caldwell and Eric Waddell, eds., *The English of Quebec: From Majority to Minority Status* (Montreal: Institut québécois de recherche sur la culture, 1982), p. 117. The "freedom of choice" candidate, a political novice named Dr. David DeJong, ran against Reed Scowen in the 1978 by-election in the heavily Anglophone riding of Notre-Dame-de-Grâce. De Jong captured about 33 percent of the Anglophone vote, running on a single issue: Bill 101 as "the greatest social crime ever legislated in this country," *The Gazette,* 4 July 1978.

75. Reed Scowen, "Il y a deux nations au Québec," *Le Devoir,* 14 septembre 1981.

76. Fred Reed, "Les anglophones: du status de majorité canadienne à celui de minorité québécoise," *Le Devoir,* 31 janvier 1985 (supplément), p. 50. See Alliance-Quebec Program, "A Policy for English-Speaking Quebec," April 1983 and June 1987.

77. *Le Devoir,* 2 mai 1978.

78. These enrollment data are calculated from Conseil scolaire de l'île de Montréal, "Série de données d'inscriptions depuis 1970 et prévision des populations scolaires du territoire du Conseil scolaire de l'île de Montréal," 20 juin 1986; and Conseil scolaire de l'île de Montréal, "Les inscriptions officielles au 30 septembre 1987" (hereafter cited as CSIM).

79. *Le Devoir,* 24 septembre 1978. These two commissions contained only 9 percent of Quebec's total school enrollments. Lakeshore is metropolitan Montreal's other major Protestant school commission.

80. Sheila McLeod Arnopoulos and Dominique Clift, *The English Fact in Quebec* (Montreal: McGill–Queen's University Press, 1980), p. 92.

81. Edith Bedard and Claude St. Germain, *La cohabitation linguistique en milieu scolaire au Québec* (Québec: Conseil de la langue française, 1980), p. 10; CSIM, "Serie de données d'inscription," p. 3.

82. Jean-Pierre Proulx, "Le communauté anglophone en declin," *Le Devoir,* 24 mars 1981; Lise Bissonnette, "Le bilinguisme béni par Québec," *Le Devoir,* 24 jan-

vier 1980; and Lise Bissonnette, "De Penetangue à Ville Mont-Royal," *Le Devoir,* 13 octobre 1979.

83. Bissonnette, "Le bilinguisme béni par Québec."

84. Bedard and St. Germain, *La cohabitation linguistique,* p. 7.

85. "Enfants de 4 ans et anglophones ne seront plus admis en classe d'accueil," *Le Devoir,* 21 février 1981.

86. Alliance-Quebec, "A Policy for the English-Speaking Community," April 1983, pp. 26–27.

87. W. E. Lambert and G. R. Tucker, *Bilingual Education of Children: The St. Lambert Experiment* (Rowley, Mass.: Newberry House, 1972).

88. There is some academic debate over the level of fluency attained in these immersion classes. Some studies suggest that the homogeneous setting of the classes—composed of non-Francophone pupils in English-language schools—precludes the sociocultural immersion necessary to achieve "instinctive bilingualism" and that immersion graduates have trouble with complex conversations in French. See Kathleen Connors et al., "Testing Linguistic and Functional Competence in Immersion Programs," in Michel Paradis, ed. *Aspects of Bilingualism* (Columbia, S.C.: Hornbeam Press, 1979), pp. 65–75.

89. *Le Devoir,* 3 juillet 1974.

90. Danielle Bonneau, "Les classes d'immersion français plus populaires que jamais," *La Presse,* 13 avril 1987.

91. Ibid. The difference between French immersion and the regular French-language school is that gradually English is introduced as a language of instruction for some subjects in immersion, whereas it is only taught as a subject in the regular French-language schools.

92. Ibid.

93. See "Avis du Conseil de la langue française au Ministre responsable de l'application de la Charte de la langue française sur la situation linguistique actuelle," 1985, pp. 1–5.

94. Repatriation meant creating a Canadian Constitution to replace the British North America Act as Canada's governing document so that, among other things, constitutional amendments would not require assent of the British parliament.

95. Article 23 also guaranteed this right in French across Canada.

96. CLF, "Avis," p. 5. For an analysis of the projected impact of Article 23, see Rapport du groupe de travail interministériel, "Effets démolinguistiques de l'article 23 du projet federal de charte des droits et libertés," CLF, 1981.

97. Monnier, *La question linguistique,* p. 9.

98. *The Gazette,* 1 October 1983.

99. Alliance-Québec, "Audition de personnes et d'organismes sur la Charte de la langue française," *Journal des débats, Assemblée nationale du Québec* (26 octobre 1983), #159, pp. B–8556–8557.

100. *The Gazette,* 22 November 1983.

101. *Journal des débats* (19 octobre 1983), #154.

102. *Journal des débats* (26 octobre 1983), #156.

103. Alliance-Québec, "Audition de personnes . . . ," pp. B–8539–8576.

104. *La Presse,* 27 octobre 1983.

105. See "Projet de loi 57: Loi modifiant la Charte de la langue française."

106. Ibid., Articles 20, 23.

107. Ibid., Article 26.

108. *The Gazette,* 17 December 1983.

109. *La Presse,* 17 décembre 1983.

110. Michel Plourde, *La politique linguistique du Québec: 1977–1987* (Québec: Institut québécois de recherche sur la culture, 1988), p. 65.
111. Clement Trudel, "Le PLQ entend conserver l'essentiel de la loi 101," *Le Devoir*, 20 octobre 1985.
112. Clement Trudel, "Les 'illégaux' ont jusqu'à septembre 1982," *Le Devoir*, 4 novembre 1981.
113. *Journal des débats* (3 juin 1986), #37, p. 2111.
114. Plourde, *La politique linguistique du Québec*, p. 70.
115. Paul-André Comeau, "Et un pas en arrière," *Le Devoir*, 15 novembre 1986; and Jean-Pierre Proulx, "Les enjeux du projet de loi 140," *Le Devoir*, 12 décembre 1986.
116. Jean-Pierre Proulx, "Anglais par referendum," *Le Devoir*, 8 décembre 1986.
117. See Jean-Bernard Robichaud, "Assurer l'équité linguistique sur un base territoriale," *Le Devoir*, 10 décembre 1986; and Andrew Sancton, *Governing the Island of Montreal: Language Differences and Metropolitan Politics* (Berkeley: University of California Press, 1985), pp. 184–189.
118. "La loi 142 mécontente le MQF," *Le Devoir*, 23 décembre 1986.
119. Robichaud, "Assurer l'equité linguistique . . ." and "Les hôpitaux ne veulent pas être obligés d'offrir des services en anglais," *Le Devoir*, 3 décembre 1986.
120. See Paul-André Comeau, "Faut-il une loi 142," *Le Devoir*, 11 décembre 1986; and Gilles Lesage, "Québec n'assurera pas les services en anglais partout," *Le Devoir*, 10 décembre 1986.
121. Monnier, *La question linguistique*, p. 17; and Monnier, *La perception de la situation linguistique* (Québec: CLF, 1980), p. 28.
122. See Rudy Le Cours, "Bourassa: créer des districts bilingues en étendant la loi 101," *Le Devoir*, 29 novembre 1986; and Plourde, *La politique linguistique du Québec*, pp. 66–69.
123. See letters from Gaston Cholette to Lise Bacon, Quebec's Minister of Cultural Affairs, published in Commission de protection de la langue français, *Rapport d'activité 1985–1986*, pp. 24, 29–30.
124. Sylvain Blanchard, "Le PQ deposéra 101 demandes d'enquête," *Le Devoir*, 3 octobre 1987.
125. Pierre Cayouette, "Sous l'égide du MQF, un week-end pour galvaniser la défense de la loi 101," *Le Devoir*, 11 décembre 1986; "La loi 101 attise 5,000 défenseurs," *Le Devoir*, 15 décembre 1986.
126. Rollande Parente, "La maniféstation géante n'a pas surpris Bourassa," *Le Devoir*, 19 avril 1988.
127. Bernard Descôteaux, "La paix sociale passera avant tout amendement à la loi 101," *Le Devoir*, 30 septembre 1987.
128. See Michel C. Auger, "L'affichage unilingue est inconstitutionel," *Le Devoir*, 16 décembre 1988; Bernard Descôteaux, "Bourassa penche vers le bilinguisme partiel," *Le Devoir*, 16 décembre 1988; and Descôteaux, "Bourassa repousse l'application de la loi 178 après les elections," *Le Devoir*, 24 décembre 1988.
129. Benoit Lauzière, "La solution de M. Bourassa," *Le Devoir*, 19 décembre 1988.
130. Bernard Descôteaux, "Une importante majorité rejette la solution linguistique de Bourassa," *Le Devoir*, 24 décembre 1988. A SORECOM survey taken December 19–21, 1988 found 69 percent of Anglophones and 60 percent Francophones opposed to Bourassa's solution.
131. Bernard Descôteaux, "In n'y aura pas de bilinguisme sur les routes, dit Bourassa," *Le Devoir*, 17 février 1989; Jean-Pierre Proulx, "Le bilinguisme peut s'afficher sans délai dans certains commerces," *Le Devoir*, 27 décembre 1988.

132. "Bourassa n'est nullement inquiét," *Le Devoir,* 24 janvier 1989.

133. Claude Ryan, "La loi 178 et la politique linguistique: Bilan et perspectives du gouvernement québécois," *Le Devoir,* 17 mars 1989.

134. Bernard Descôteaux, "'Deux pour un' pour l'affichage: une route où il devra être facile de circuler, dit Ryan," *Le Devoir,* 4 mai 1989.

135. Léon Dion, "La loi 178: acceptable mais d'application aléatoire," *Le Devoir,* 6 janvier 1989.

136. Michel Auger, "L'arrivée de Ryan n'a pas accru la confiance des Québécois," *Le Devoir,* 23 mars 1989.

137. Monnier, *La question linguistique,* p. 14.

138. Gilles Lesage, "L'affichage en français est considérée peu important," *Le Devoir,* 21 juin 1988; and Jean-Pierre Proulx, "Une nette majorité pour l'affichage bilingue," *Le Devoir,* 22 juin 1988.

139. Ibid.

140. These numbers again underscore the extent to which immigrant Anglicization bolstered Montreal's English-speaking community. In 1977–78, while 41.5 percent of the Island's schoolchildren were in English-language schools, only 25.6 percent of the population reported English as its mother tongue. Even in 1987–1988, while the Anglophone share of total school enrollments had dropped to 30.3 percent, that total still exceeded the Island's English mother-tongue population of 20.8 percent.

141. Bureau de la statistique, CECM, Service de l'équipement, "Origines ethniques des élèves," 1986.

142. Paillé, "Consequences de politiques linguistiques. . . ."

143. CSIM, "Serie des données."

144. Danielle Bonneau, "Les anglophones tiennent à leurs écoles," *La Presse,* 13 avril 1987. Even this total understates the shift toward French. By 1980, for ex ample, fourteen of the PSBGM's forty-five Anglophone primary schools were "French immersion" schools. All told, the number of English-language schools in the PSBGM dropped from ninety-three in 1976 to forty in 1986.

145. Système de Planification, CSIM, "Répartition des élèves pour chacun des réseaux de chaque commission scolaire selon la religion, le niveau, le degré, et la langue maternelle," Année scolaire 1986–1987. These data also show that the proportion of Anglo CECM pupils reporting French as their mother tongue fell from 12 percent in 1974 to 4.6 percent in 1987. Albert Côté of the CSIM advises that these data should be viewed cautiously because there is no verification of the mother tongue reported and, given the controversies surrounding access to English-language schooling, there is a tendency for non-Anglophones to declare English as their mother tongue.

146. Ironically, by its second term, the PQ would break its bonds with Francophone teachers as it embraced austerity policies that mandated wage rollbacks for teachers. The result was a bitter strike and authoritarian back-to-work legislation in 1983 (Bill 111) that drove a wedge into the PQ coalition. For an excellent discussion of this turn to PQ policy, see McRoberts, *Quebec: Social Change and Political Crisis,* pp. 371–375.

147. Jean-Pierre Proulx, "Moins bien desservi que le secteur anglais, le secteur français craque partout," *Le Devoir,* 10 novembre 1987.

148. Ibid.

149. Jean-Pierre Proulx, "A l'école Van Horne, les élèves sont entassés comme des sardines," *Le Devoir,* 11 novembre 1987.

150. A further irony, highlighting the confusion inherent in Montreal's structure of school governance, is that only 21 percent of the students in the French-Protestant schools are French-speaking Protestants. See Proulx, "Moins biens désservi. . . ."

151. Calculated from data in: Commission des Écoles Catholiques de Montréal, "Rapport sur la population scolaire d'origine ethnique en 1985–1986," décembre 1986; and CLF, *Vivre la diversité en français: Le défi de l'école française à clientèle pluriethnique de l'île de Montréal* (Québec: CLF, 1987), pp. 163–173. The category "non-Francophone" here refers to all students reporting mother tongues other than French.

152. André Lachance, "Tiraille entre deux cultures," *Le Devoir,* 9 août 1986.

153. CECM, "Rapport sur la population scolaire," p. 2.

154. Ibid., p. 28.

155. CLF, *Vivre la diversité en français,* p. 23. The clientele in the French-language schools in the Lakeshore Commission is 84 percent non-Francophone (64 percent Anglophone and 20 percent Allophone); clearly, these schools are simply a more intensive form of French immersion for non-Francophones.

156. CLF, *Vivre la diversité en français,* pp. 47–52, 105–110.

157. Ibid., pp. 66–70.

158. Françoise Coulombe, "Données factuelles concernant le personnel d'origine ethnique étrangère," CECM, mars 1986, p. 5.

159. Ibid. See also CLF, *Vivre la diversité en français,* pp. 127–128.

160. A 1988 MEQ study showed encouraging results from the *classes d'accueil.* Once integrated into regular French-language classes, Allophone "graduates" of the *classes d'accueil* did as well as "regular" students. See Jean-Pierre Proulx, "Intégrés en classes françaises, les allophones cheminement souvent plus vite que les autres," *Le Devoir,* 3 mars 1988.

161. CLF, *Vivre la diversité en français,* pp. 69–70. PELO stands for Le Programme d'enseignement des langues et des cultures d'origines.

162. Ibid., p. 25; and André Beauchesne and Helen Hensler, *L'école française à clientèle pluriethnique de l'île de Montréal: situation du français et intégration psychosociale des élèves* (Québec: Éditeur officiel du Québec, 1987), pp. 504–505.

163. CLF, *Vivre la diversité en français,* pp. 84–85.

164. Beauchesne and Hensler, *L'école française,* p. 49.

165. For a collection of "reflections" on the subject by Québécois scholars, see CLF, *Le Québec français et l'école à clientèle pluriethnique: contribution à une reflexion* (Québec: CLF, 1987).

166. Arnopoulos and Clift, *English Fact in Quebec,* p. 191.

167. Jean-Marc Léger, "Primauté du français et pluralisme culturel," *Le Devoir,* 25 octobre 1988.

168. Pierre Laplante, "Que sera donc le Québec de demain," *Le Devoir,* 3 septembre 1988.

169. Ibid.

170. Ibid.

171. Signs of Francophone xenophobia, particularly outside the Montreal region, appeared in a 1987 CRÉATEC survey on attitudes toward immigration, *Le Devoir,* 11 mars 1987.

172. Fraser, *PQ,* p. 111.

173. Lévesque, *Attendez que je me rappelle.* . . .

174. Mario Fontaine, "Les anglophones montréalaise acceptent le Québec français," *La Presse,* 11 avril 1987.

175. John O'Meara, editor of the NDG Monitor, quoted in George Tombs, "Les Anglo Québécois: Une minorité en quête d'une nouvelle identité," *Le Devoir,* 6 octobre 1988.

176. Mario Fontaine and Roch Côté, "Le grand exodus des anglophones est terminé," *La Presse,* 11 avril 1987.

Chapter 7

1. André Raynauld, *La propriété des entreprises au Québec: les années 60* (Montréal: Les presses de l'Université de Montréal, 1974), pp. 116, 147–148.

2. Report of the Commission of Inquiry on the Position of the French Language and Language Rights in Quebec, *Book I: The Language of Work* (Québec: Éditeur officiel du Québec, 1972), p. 77 (hereafter cited as the Gendron Commission).

3. See Jules-Paul Tardival, "Dénonciation du Franglais," in Guy Bouthillier and Jean Meynaud, eds., *Le Choc des langues au Québec, 1760–1970* (Montréal: Les Presses de l'Université du Québec, 1972), pp. 206–213 (reprint of excerpts from Tardival, "L'anglicisme, viola l'ennemi!," causerie faite au Cercle catholique de Québec, le 17 décembre 1879); and Gouvernement du Québec, *La politique québécoise de la langue française* (Québec: Éditeur officiel du Québec, 1977).

4. Peter Leslie, "Ethnic Hierarchies and Minority Consciousness in Quebec," in Richard Simeon, ed., *Must Canada Fail?* (Montreal: McGill–Queen's University Press, 1977), p. 113.

5. Quoted in Edward Corbett, *Quebec Confronts Canada* (Baltimore: Johns Hopkins University Press, 1967), p. 95.

6. Leslie, "Ethnic Hierarchies and Minority Consciousness," p. 113.

7. James I. Gow, "Modernisation et administration publique," in Edmond Orban et al., *La modernisation politique du Québec*, p. 167; *Le Québec Statistique, Édition 1985–1986* (Québec: Éditeur officiel du Québec, 1986), p. 250.

8. See André Blais and Kenneth McRoberts, "Public Expenditure in Ontario and Quebec, 1950–1980: Explaining the Differences," *Journal of Canadian Studies* 18: 1 (Spring 1983): 28–53.

9. Paul-André Linteau et al., *Le Québec Depuis 1930* (Montréal: Les éditions du Boréal Express, 1986), p. 427.

10. Arnaud Sales and Noël Bélanger, *Décideurs et Gestionnaires: Étude sur la direction et l'encadrement des secteurs privé et public* (Québec: Éditeur officiel du Québec, 1985), p. 217.

11. Public-sector employment is determined from data in Pierre Lamonde and Mario Polèse, "L'évolution de la structure économique de Montréal, 1971–1981: Désindustrialisation ou reconversion," *L'Actualité économique* 60: 4 (décembre 1984): 483; *Le Québec Statistique: Édition 1985–1986*, pp. 246, 249, 254.

The workforce in the Quebec public administration and the city of Montreal has been consistently 90 percent Francophone since 1960 (see Guy Bourassa, *Les relations ethniques dans la vie politique montréalaise*, Documents de la Commission royale d'enquête sur le bilinguisme et le biculturalisme, no. 10 (Ottawa: Information Canada, 1971), pp. 156–157; and Denise Turgeon, "Répartition des employées à l'intérieur des ministères québécois selon l'origine ethnique" (miméo, prepared for the Gendron Commission, 1972). Federal employment in Montreal also favored Francophones, though to a lesser extent than the municipal or provincial sectors. See François Vaillancourt, "Revenus et langues au Québec, 1961–1971," *Journal of Canadian Studies* 13: 1 (Spring 1978): 66.

My estimate of the percentage of Francophones employed by the public sector in Montreal in 1981 is based on the following assumptions: 90 percent of the provincial and municipal employment in Montreal was Francophone, 80 percent of the federal employment was Francophone, and 70 percent of the employment in the parapublic sector was Francophone.

12. Kenneth McRoberts, *Quebec: Social Change and Political Crisis*, 3d ed. (Toronto: McClelland and Stewart, 1988), p. 178.

13. See William Coleman, *The Independence Movement in Quebec, 1945–1980*

(Toronto: University of Toronto Press, 1984), pp. 94–100; and Dorval Brunelle, *La Désillusion tranquille* (Montréal: Les Éditions Hurtubise HMH, 1978), pp. 79–80.

14. Michael Behiels, *Prelude to Quebec's Quiet Revolution* (Montreal: McGill–Queen's University Press, 1985), p. 17.

15. Brunelle, *La Désillusion tranquille*, pp. 79–80.

16. Dale C. Thomson, *Jean Lesage and the Quiet Revolution* (Toronto: Macmillan of Canada, 1984), pp. 197–199.

17. *Guide des programmes d'aide offerts aux entreprises québécoises* (Québec: Direction générale des services aux entreprises, Ministère de l'Industrie et du Commerce du Québec, 1979).

18. Gouvernement du Québec, *The Technology Conversion* (Québec: Éditeur officiel du Québec, 1982), p. 44.

19. Ibid., p. 170.

20. Linteau et al., *Le Québec Depuis 1930*, p. 431.

21. Gouvernement du Québec, *Challenges for Quebec: A Statement on Economic Policy* (Québec: Éditeur officiel du Québec, 1979), p. 52.

22. Thomas Courchène, "Le Québec se demarque du reste du Canada par son ouverture du jeu du marché," *Le Devoir*, 16 juillet 1986.

23. A. Brian Tanguay, "Business, Labor, and the State in the 'New' Quebec," *The American Review of Canadian Studies* 17:4 (Winter 1987–88): 403.

24. Gouvernement du Québec, *The Technology Conversion*, p. 44.

25. Gouvernement du Québec, *Challenges for Quebec*, p. 53.

26. Report of the Consultative Committee to the Ministerial Committee on the Development of the Montreal Region (Ottawa: Minister of Supply and Services, 1986), p. 278.

27. See, for example, Gilles Bourque, "Class, Nation, and the Parti Québécois," in Alain Gagnon, ed., *Quebec: State and Society* (Toronto: Methuen, 1984), pp. 124–147; Bourque and Anne Legaré, *Le Québec: la question nationale* (Paris: Maspéro, 1979); Pierre Fournier, "Les nouveaux parametres de la bourgeoisie québécoise," in Pierre Fournier, ed., *Le Capitalisme au Québec* (Montréal: Éditions Cooperatives Albert Saint-Martin, 1978), pp. 135–181.

28. *Le Devoir*, 14 janvier 1978.

29. Laurent Beaudoin, "Un sursis d'une moi s'impose pour reviser le dossier," *Le Devoir*, 23 decémbre 1977.

30. Parizeau, "Au Québec, l'État doit intervenir," *Québec-Presse*, 15 février 1970, quoted in Pierre Fournier, *The Quebec Establishment* (Montreal: Black Rose Books, 1981), p. 210.

31. Thomson, *Jean Lesage*, p. 37.

32. See also McRoberts, *Quebec: Social Change and Political Crisis*, pp. 174–175.

33. Fournier, *Quebec Establishment*, p. 183.

34. Alain G. Gagnon and Khayyam Z. Paltiel, "Toward Maîtres chez-nous: The Ascendancy of a Balzacian Bourgeoisie in Quebec," *Queen's Quarterly* 93:4 (Winter 1986): 739; Bombardier Inc., *Rapport annuel, 1988;* and Sheila McGovern, "Bombardier Lands Short Brothers," *The Gazette*, 8 June 1989.

35. Yves Bélanger and Pierre Fournier, *L'Entreprise québécoise: Développement historique et dynamique contemporaine* (Montréal: Éditions Hurtubise HMH, 1987), p. 123.

36. Diane Francis, *Controlling Interest: Who Owns Canada* (Toronto: McClelland and Bantam, 1987), p. 246.

37. McRoberts, *Quebec: Social Change and Political Crisis*, p. 163.

38. Fournier, *Quebec Establishment*, p. 183.

39. Martin Shefter, *Political Crisis/Fiscal Crisis* (New York: Basic Books, 1985).

40. Thomson, *Jean Lesage*, p. 115.

41. Quoted in Francis, *Controlling Interest*, p. 246.

42. Thomson, *Jean Lesage*, p. 115.

43. Bélanger and Fournier, *L'entreprise québécoise*, p. 135; Thomson, *Jean Lesage*, pp. 246–247; and Douglas Fullerton, *The Dangerous Delusion* (Toronto: McClelland and Stewart, 1978), pp. 59–60.

44. Alain Pinard, "Your Money at Work for Quebec," *The Star*, 11 January 1972.

45. Caisse de dépôt et placement, *Rapport annuel, 1988*, p. 20.

46. See Jacques Parizeau, "Le Québec remet-il en cause le role même du secteur public?" *Le Devoir*, 30 décembre 1970.

47. Caisse de dépôt et placement, *Rapport annuel, 1988*, pp. 1, 26.

48. Caisse de dépôt et placement, *Rapport annuel, 1987*, p. 31.

49. Fournier, *Quebec Establishment*, p. 215.

50. "Provigo restera québécoise," *Le Devoir*, 24 septembre 1977.

51. *The Economist* (London), 27 May 1989.

52. Lise Bissonnette, "Le Relais," *Le Devoir*, 10 septembre 1986.

53. Bélanger and Fournier, *L'entreprise québécoise*, p. 175.

54. Peter Hadekel, "Caisse de dépôt has outlived its usefulness," *Gazette*, 6 December 1989.

55. Francis, *Controlling Interest*, p. 246.

56. Ibid.

57. Royal Commission on Bilingualism and Biculturalism, *The Work World* (Ottawa: Queen's Printer, 1969), p. 496.

58. Jean Chartier, "Hydro-Québec et la Caisse de dépôt: Les succès ont depassé les espoirs," *Le Devoir*, 31 janvier 1985, p. 66.

59. Fournier, *Quebec Establishment*, p. 213.

60. RCBB, *Work World*, p. 497.

61. Ibid., p. 498.

62. Ibid.

63. Sales and Bélanger, *Décideurs et gestionnairess*, p. 217.

64. André Bouthillier, "La naissance d'entreprises modernes mieux gerées et capable d'exporter leurs produits," *Le Devoir*, 31 janvier 1985, p. 64.

65. Angele Dagenais, "Le Métro de Montréal a 20 Ans," *Le Devoir*, 22 août 1987.

66. Communauté Urbaine de Montréal, *Rapport annuel, 1987*, p. 12.

67. RCBB, *Work World*, pp. 68ff. See also the Parent Commission report noted in Chapter 3.

68. Ibid., pp. 69–70.

69. Kenneth McRoberts and Dale Posgate, *Quebec: Social Change and Political Crisis*, 2d ed. (Toronto: McClelland and Stewart, 1980), p. 57; and Coleman, *Independence Movement in Quebec*, pp. 157–182.

70. Ministère de l'éducation du Québec, *Livre vert: L'enseignement primaire et secondaire au Québec* (Québec: Ministère de l'éducation du Québec, 1977), p. 4.

71. Ibid., p. 12; *Le Québec Statistique, Édition 1985–1986*, p. 425; and Jean-Pierre Proulx, "En éducation, un rattrapage quantitatif," *Le Devoir*, 31 janvier 1985, pp. 29–32.

72. Proulx, "En éducation, un rattrapage quantitatif," p. 32.

73. Raymond Duchesne, *La science et le pouvoir au Québec (1920–1965)* (Québec: Éditeur officiel du Québec, 1978), p. 23.

74. See Roch Côté, "McGill a bienfait quelques pas vers le Québec français, mais . . . ," *La Presse*, 14 avril 1987.

75. Quoted in Claude Turcotte, "Une nouvelle vocation québécoise: les affaires," *Le Devoir*, 31 janvier 1985.

76. Gagnon and Paltiel, "Toward Maîtres chez nous," p. 740; Graham Fraser, *PQ: René Lévesque and the Parti Québécois in Power* (Toronto: Macmillan of Canada, 1985), p. 212; and Ramsay Cook, *Canada, Quebec, and the Uses of Nationalism* (Toronto: McClelland and Stewart, 1986), pp. 87–104.

77. Gagnon and Paltiel, "Toward Maîtres chez nous," p. 740.

78. Ministère des Affaires Culturelles, *Livre blanc sur la politique culturelle* (n.p., 1965).

79. Thomson, *Jean Lesage*, p. 320.

80. Bill 63, Loi pour promouvoir la langue française au Québec, Sanctionée le 28 novembre 1969, article 4, section 14 et 14a.

81. Laurin, quoted in *Le Devoir*, 18 décembre 1976.

82. Gouvernement du Québec, *La politique québécoise de la langue française*, p. 39.

83. See, for example, Parti québécois, *Quand nous serons vraiment chez nous* (Montréal: Éditions du Parti québécois, 1972). See also Vera Murray, *Le Parti québécois: de la fondation à la prise du pouvoir* (Montréal: Éditions Hurtubise HMH, 1976), pp. 41–65.

84. Parti québécois, *Édition 1975 du programme du Parti québécois* (Montréal: Éditions du PQ, 1975), p. 25.

85. Ibid.

86. *Le Devoir*, 18 décembre 1976; Fraser, *PQ*, p. 99.

87. Gouvernement du Québec, *La politique québécoise de la langue française*, p. 61.

88. Gendron Commission, *Book I: Language of Work*, p. 63.

89. Ibid., p. 121.

90. Yvan Allaire, "La nouvelle classe politique et les pouvoirs économiques," in Jean-François Léonard, ed., *La chance au coureur: Bilan de l'action du gouvernement du Parti Québécois* (Montréal: Les éditions Nouvelle Optique, 1978), p. 63.

91. For an analysis of the more stringent *francisation* and *francophonisation* requirements of Bill 1, see William D. Coleman, "From Bill 22 to Bill 101: The Politics of Language Under the Parti Québécois," *The Canadian Journal of Political Science* 14:3 (1981): 467–472.

92. Fraser, *PQ*, p. 99.

93. Bill 101, *La Charte de la langue française*, Sanctionée le 26 août 1977, Titre II, Chapitre V, Article 141b.

94. *Le Devoir*, 1 février 1978.

95. Allaire, "La nouvelle classe politique et les pouvoirs économiques," p. 63.

96. Coleman, "From Bill 22 to Bill 101," p. 471.

97. *Le Devoir*, 4 juin 1977.

98. "Liberal Asks Laurin to Apologize," *The Star*, 8 June 1977.

99. "Règlement régissant la Commission d'appel de francisation des entreprises," A.C. 465–79, 21 février 1979; and Règlement fixant les modalités d'un appel interjeté auprès de la Commission d'appel de francisation des entreprises," A.C. 466–77, 21 février 1979.

100. Mordecai Richler, "Oh Canada! Lament for a Divided Country," *The Atlantic* 240:6 (December 1977): 41–55.

101. Cited in Leslie, "Ethnic Hierarchies and Minority Consciousness," p. 77.
102. William Johnson, "Language Bill Would Cost Quebec 22,900 Jobs, Study Finds," *The Globe and Mail* (Toronto), 13 June 1977.
103. Gouvernement du Québec, *Challenges for Quebec,* p. 149.
104. Gendron Commission, *Book I: Work World,* pp. 119–120.
105. See the following: Bill 101, *La Charte de la langue française,* Sanctionée le 26 août 1977, Titre II, Chapitre V, Article 144; and "Règlement de l'Office de la langue française relatif à la définition de 'siège social' et a la reconnaissance des sièges sociaux pouvant faire l'objet d'entente particuliers avec l'Office," *La Charte de la langue française,* A.C. 3646–78, 30 novembre 1978, in "Règlements adoptés en vertu de la Charte de la langue française," mars 1980, pp. 7125–7126.
106. Bill 101, *La Charte de la langue française,* Article 144, L.R.Q., Chapitre c–11, a jour au 30 juin 1987. On the PQ's interest in high technology, see Gouvernement du Québec, *Technology Conversion.* A 1986 federal government committee chaired by Laurent Picard of McGill also targeted high tech as a cornerstone of Montreal's economic development strategy and, even as late as 1986, still explicitly mentioned Bill 101 as a potential impediment to economic development in Montreal. Although, for obvious political reasons, the report avoided extended discussion of the role of Bill 101 on local economic development, the implication was that Bill 101 makes it difficult to attract non-Francophone, high-tech researchers to Montreal. The apparent reticence of English-Canadian scientists to move from Ottawa to Montreal's South Shore suburbs with the new Canadian Space Agency in June 1989 may be seen as an instance of this phenomenon. See *Report of the Consultative Committee to the Ministerial Committee on the Development of the Montreal Region* (Ottawa: Minister of Supply and Services Canada, 1986), p. 32.
107. Françoy Roberge, "Les sièges sociaux n'ont plus de raison de bouder Québec (Laurin)," *Le Devoir,* 21 juillet 1978.
108. Conseil de la langue française, *Les enjeux actuels de la francisation des entreprises,* Notes et documents 57 (Québec: Conseil de la langue française, 1986), p. 32.
109. Bill 101, *La Charte de la langue française,* Sanctionée le 26 août 1977, Titre I, Chapitre VIII, Article 85; and "Règlement relatif à la langue d'enseignement des personnes séjournant temporaire au Quebec," A.C. 2851–77, 24 août 1977; Règlement 77–487, 26 août 1977.
110. "Language of Instruction (Temporary Residents) Regulation," O.C.2820–84 (1985).
111. Office de la langue française, *Rapport annuel, 1985–1986* (Québec: Les publications du Québec, 1986), pp. 13–14; Conseil de la langue français, *Les enjeux actuels de la francisation des entreprises,* pp. 31–32; and Office de la langue française, Direction des programmes de francisation, décembre 1987, cited in Michel Plourde, *La politique linguistique du Québec, 1977–1987* (Québec: Institut québécois de recherche sur la culture, 1988), p. 87.
112. Office de la langue française, *Rapport annuel, 1985–1986,* pp. 13–14.
113. Conseil de la langue française, *Les enjeux actuels de la francisation des entreprises,* p. 67.
114. Éconosult Inc., *Étude sur les avantages et les coûts de la francisation* (Montréal: Office de la langue française, 1981), p. 429.
115. Yvan Allaire and Roger Miller, *L'entreprise canadienne et la Loi sur la francisation du milieu de travail* (Montréal: Institut de recherches C. D. Howe, 1980).

116. See Éconosult, *Étude sur les avantages et les coûts de la francisation;* and Conrad Sabourin, "Procéssus de francisation et de certification des entreprises" (Montréal: Office de la langue française, 1977 [miméo]).

117. Roger Miller, "The Response of Business Firms to the Francization Process," in Richard Y. Bourhis, ed., *Conflict and Language Planning in Quebec* (Clevedon, England: Multilingual Matters, 1984), p. 124.

118. Éconosult, *Étude sur les avantages et les coûts de la francisation,* p. 300; and Laurent Cloutier, "La francisation de l'entreprise payante," *La Presse,* 28 août 1980.

119. Gerald Clark, *Montreal: The New Cité* (Toronto: McClelland and Stewart, 1982), p. 58.

120. Ibid., p. 56.

121. Ibid., p. 57.

122. Marie-Agnès Thellier, "Le départ de Sun Life, un dur coup pour la métropole,"*Le Devoir,* 10 janvier 1978; and René Lévesque, *Attendez que je me rappelle . . .* (Montreal: Éditions Québec/Amérique, 1986), pp. 392–393.

123. For a list of firms leaving Quebec in 1977 and 1978, see Raymond Breton and Gail Grant, *La langue de travail au Québec* (Montréal: l'Institut de recherches politiques, 1981), pp. 80–81.

124. Miller, "The Response of Business Firms," p. 127.

125. "Head Offices Leaving and Bill 101 Is the Major Cause," *The Gazette,* 18 October 1982.

126. Bernard Descôteaux, "Sièges sociaux: des départs certes mais pas d'éxode," *Le Devoir,* 16 décembre 1978.

127. Ian Anderson, "Cashing in on Languages," *The Gazette,* 9 December 1978.

128. Quoted in Gagnon and Paltiel, "Toward Maîtres chez nous," p. 742.

129. George Haim, "Montreal Cashes in on Ontario's Woes," *Globe and Mail,* 24 October 1988.

130. *La Presse,* 12 janvier 1987. Of the Francophone managers and executives surveyed by Sales and Bélanger in 1982, 47.5 percent called Bill 101 a hindrance to recruitment; nearly all Anglophone managers and executives—96.4 percent—still regarded Bill 101 as a major recruitment obstacle. See Sales and Bélanger, *Décideurs et Gestionnaires,* p. 248.

131. Sales and Bélanger, *Décideurs et Gestionnaires,* p. 233.

132. See Pierre Fournier, "Projet national et affrontement des bourgeoisies québécoise et canadienne," in Jean-François Léonard, ed., *La chance au coureur: Bilan de l'action du gouvernement du Parti Québécois* (Montréal: Les éditions Nouvelle Optique, 1978), pp. 39–59.

133. Bill 101, *La Charte de la langue française,* Sanctionée le 26 août 1977, Titre I, Chapitre II, Article 5.

134. Commission de surveillance de la langue française, *Rapport d'activité, 1982–1983* (Québec: Les publications du Québec, 1983), p. 18.

135. Letter of 5 November 1982 from René Lévesque to Eric Maldoff, President of Alliance-Quebec, quoted in Plourde, *La politique linguistique au Québec,* p. 61.

136. See Commission de surveillance de la langue française and Commission de protection de la langue française, *Rapport d'activité* for each year, 1979 through 1986. In 1986, for example, the Montreal region represented 84.1 percent of all commission dossiers, and 83.6 percent of the investigations by the commission involved alleged violations of the language of commerce clauses of Bill 101. See Commission de protection de la langue française, *Rapport d'activité, 1985–1986,* p. 11.

137. ꙅee Commission de protection de la langue française, *Rapport d'activité, 1983–1984,* pp. 25–27.

Chapter 8

1. George Nader, *Cities of Canada: Vol. 2* (Toronto: Macmillan of Canada, 1976), p. 154.

2. Michel Plourde, *La politique linguistique du Québec: 1977–1987* (Québec: Institut québécois de recherche sur la culture, 1988), p. 41.

3. See Yvan Allaire, "La nouvelle classe politique et les pouvoirs économiques," in Jean-François Léonard, ed., *La chance au coureur: Bilan de l'action du gouvernement du Parti Québécois* (Montréal: Les éditions Nouvelle Optique, 1978), p. 62; Ian McKinnon and Roger Miller, "Some Aspects of Recruitment Policies of Firms in Quebec" (Montreal: SECOR mimeo, 1981), pp. 24–26; François Vaillancourt, *Le français, les francophones, et les législations linguistiques au Québec: Une analyse économique* (Québec: Conseil de la langue française, 1983); Robert Lacroix and François Vaillancourt, *Le revenus et la langue au Québec (1970–1978)* (Québec: Éditeur officiel du Québec, 1981), pp. 82–83; and Jorge Niosi, *La bourgeoisie canadienne: La formation et le developpement d'une classe dominante* (Montréal: Les Éditions du Boréal Express, 1980), pp. 186–187.

4. Daniel Monnier, *La situation de la langue française au Québec: Statistiques récentes,* Notes et documents 40 (Québec: Conseil de la langue française, 1984), pp. 11, 19–20. The sample in the 1983 survey was too small, thus containing too large an error margin, for definitive comparison with the statistically significant 1971 and 1979 surveys. The 1983 data are presented here merely for suggestive purposes and because, on the basis of other evidence, they appear plausible.

5. Daniel Monnier, *L'usage du français au travail* (Québec: Éditeur officiel du Québec, 1983), p. 40.

6. Ibid., p. 101.

7. Arnaud Sales and Noël Bélanger, *Décideurs et gestionnaires: Étude sur la direction et l'encadrement des secteurs privé et public* (Québec: Éditeur officiel du Québec, 1985). Sales and Bélanger define large firms as those with over five hundred employees. Some care should be used in applying the Sales–Bélanger data to Montreal. Because the use of French is likely to be less frequent in Montreal firms than those elsewhere in Quebec, Sales and Bélanger's provincewide numbers on the use of French in mangement are likely higher than they would be for Montreal alone. Nevertheless, with two-thirds of the Sales–Bélanger sample drawn from Montreal, we can view their data as a reasonable approximation of the position of French as a language of management in the city in 1982.

8. Sales and Bélanger, *Décideurs et gestionnaires,* pp. 215–221.

9. Sales and Bélanger define linguistic control in terms of the linguistic background of a firm's owner, or a majority of the board of directors.

10. Sales and Bélanger, *Décideurs et gestionnaires,* pp. 221–226.

11. McKinnon and Miller, "Some Aspects of the Recruitment Policies of Quebec Firms," p. 40.

12. Conseil de la langue française, "Avis du Conseil de la langue française au ministre responsable de la Charte de la langue française sur la loi 101 et l'avenir de la langue française au Québec (novembre 1983)," in *L'état de la langue française au Québec,* Notes et documents 59 (Québec: Conseil de la langue française, 1986), p. 733. Hereafter cited as "Avis sur la loi 101 (novembre 1983)."

13. Data compiled by author from Unpublished Special Tabulations by Statistics Canada on language and income in metropolitan Montreal, 1971, 1981, 1986.

14. Pierre E. Laporte, "Status Language Planning in Quebec: An Evaluation," in

Richard Y. Bourhis, ed., *Conflict and Language Planning in Quebec* (Clevedon, England: Multilingual Matters, 1984), p. 65.

15. McKinnon and Miller, "Some Aspects of the Recruitment Policies of Quebec Firms," p. 40.

16. Jac-André Boulet et al., *L'évolution des disparités linguistiques de revenus de travail au Canada de 1970 à 1980* (Ottawa: Conseil économique du Canada, 1983), p. 51; Unpublished Special Tabulation, Statistics Canada, 1986 Census Data; calculations by author.

17. Boulet defines the "best-paid" workers as the top 15 percent of wage earners.

18. Laporte, "Status Language Planning in Quebec," p. 65.

19. McKinnon and Miller, "Some Aspects of the Recruitment Policies of Quebec Firms," p. 36.

20. Conseil de la langue française, *Les enjeux actuels de la francisation des entreprises*, Notes et documents 57 (Québec: Conseil de la langue française, 1986). The CLF concluded (p. 67) that "there has been effective progress in the usage of French in recent years." At this writing, the CLF is completing a full-scale survey on language use in Montreal and Quebec workplaces, replicating the surveys of the Gendron Commission in 1971 and the CLF in 1979. The new survey is expected to be published in 1990.

21. Pierre Gratton, "Business Talks English?" in Michel Amyot, ed., *Les activités socio-économiques et le français au Québec* (Québec: Éditeur officiel du Québec, 1982), pp. 304–309.

22. Paul-André Linteau et al., *Le Québec Depuis 1930* (Montréal: Les éditions du Boréal Express, 1986), p. 473.

23. Yves Bélanger and Pierre Fournier, *L'entreprise québécoise: développement historique et dynamique contemporaine* (Montréal: Les éditions Hurtubise HMH, 1987), p. 170.

24. "The Canadian Business 500," *Canadian Business* (June 1989): 151.

25. Bélanger and Fournier, *L'entreprise québécoise*, p. 140.

26. Ibid., pp. 169–170; Linteau et al., *Le Québec Depuis 1930*, pp. 468–470; and *The Report of the Consultative Committee to the Ministerial Committee on the Development of the Montreal Region* (Ottawa: Ministry of Supply and Services, 1986), p. 267.

27. Claude Turcotte, "L'actif de Desjardins atteint les $34 milliards," *Le Devoir*, 22 mai 1988.

28. Linteau et al., *Le Québec Depuis 1930*, p. 468. In 1987, 4.33 million Quebecers had *caisse* accounts. See Turcotte, "L'actif de Desjardins atteint les $34 milliards."

29. *Report of the Consultative Committee on the Development of the Montreal Region* (Ottawa: Minister of Supply and Services, 1986), p. 268; *Canadian Business*, "The Canadian Business 500" (June 1989): 151.

30. *Report of the Consultative Committee on the Development of the Montreal Region*, p. 268.

31. Linteau et al., *Le Québec Depuis 1930*, p. 471; *Report of the Consultative Committee on the Development of the Montreal Region*, pp. 267–268; and Bélanger and Fournier, *L'entreprise québécoise*, pp. 167–168.

32. *Report of the Consultative Committee on the Development of the Montreal Region*, p. 275.

33. Graham Fraser, *PQ: René Lévesque and the Parti Québécois in Power* (Toronto: Macmillan of Canada, 1984), p. 213.

34. Paul Durivage, "Une année record," *Le Devoir*, 31 décembre 1986; *Report of*

the Consultative Committee on the Development of the Montreal Region, p. 275. On Pierre Lortie, see Gerald Clark, *Montreal: The New Cité* (Toronto: McClelland and Stewart, 1982), pp. 127–131.

35. Thomas Courchène, "Montréal reprend son statut économique," *Le Devoir*, 17 juillet 1986.

36. Durivage, "Une année record."

37. Courchène, "Montréal reprend son statut"; and Robert Dutrisac, "Le marché du régime épargne-actions a fait son plein," *Le Devoir*, 22 octobre 1987.

38. *Report of the Consultative Committee on the Development of the Montreal Region*, p. 272.

39. Durivage, "Une année record."

40. François Roberge, "Dossier l'épargne québécoise: Une croissance phénoménale de contrôle économique depuis 1977," *Finance* 15 (août 1983).

41. Bélanger and Fournier, *L'entreprise québécoise*, p. 172.

42. Ibid., pp. 168–169.

43. Jean-Pierre Légault, "La Banque nationale prend le contrôle de Lévesque Beaubien pour \$100 million," *Le Devoir*, 2 juillet 1988; Robert Dutrisac, "Geoffrion Leclerc: Une décision lundi," *Le Devoir*, 4 février 1989; and Craig Toomey, "Geoffrion's head office is victim of merger," *The Gazette*, 12 May 1989.

44. Gilles Lesage, "Fortier se rejouit du consensus en faveur du décloisonment des intermédiaires," *Le Devoir*, 4 juin 1988.

45. Jean Chartier, "Hydro-Québec et la Caisse de dépôt: Les succès ont dépassé les espoirs," *Le Devoir*, 31 janvier 1985, p. 66; and Bélanger and Fournier, *L'entreprise québécoise*, p. 161.

46. Bélanger and Fournier, *L'entreprise québécoise*, p. 159.

47. Claude Painchaud, "Transport et matériel de transport: Étude monographique" (Montréal: miméo, 1983), cited in Bélanger and Fournier, *L'entreprise québécoise*, p. 158.

48. Bombardier is headquartered in Montreal; Canam Manac and Prévost Car are not.

49. Bélanger and Fournier, *L'entreprise québécoise*, p. 161; Linteau et al., *Le Québec Depuis 1930*, pp. 479–480.

50. Diane Francis, *Controlling Interest: Who Owns Canada?* (Toronto: McClelland and Bantam, 1987), p. 58.

51. André Raynauld and François Vaillancourt, *L'appartenance des entreprises: le cas du Québec en 1978* (Québec: Éditeur officiel du Québec, 1984), pp. 85–87.

52. Ibid., p. 81; and Carolyn Adolph, "Francophone control of Quebec's economy grows: study," *The Gazette*, November 1989. We do not have sectoral data on linguistic control for Montreal that would permit a comparison of employment patterns in 1961, 1978, and 1987, for the city or the metropolitan region, along the lines of the Raynauld and Vaillancourt provincewide findings. Again, from impressionistic data, we can infer that the trends in Montreal have been similar to those observed at the provincial level. Nevertheless, in view of the concentration of Quebec Anglophone strength in Montreal, as well as the fact that Montreal is still more closely connected to the rest of the North American economy than are other parts of Quebec, the likelihood is that Francophone control is less pronounced in Montreal than in the province as a whole. Put another way, the percentage of workers employed in Francophone-controlled establishments in the Saguenay/Lac Saint-Jean and Beauce regions—areas that emerged as models of Francophone entrepreneurialism in the 1970s—is undoubtedly higher than in Montreal. Nevertheless, the provincewide data give us at least some sense of the probable trends in Montreal.

53. André Bouthillier, "La naissance d'entreprises modernes mieux gerées et capables d'exporter leurs produits," *Le Devoir*, 31 janvier 1985, p. 64; and Jean-Pierre Nicaise, "L'entrepreneurship, un pouvoir createur actuel and indispensable," *Le Devoir*, 26 octobre 1987.

54. Raynauld and Vaillancourt, *L'appartenance des entreprises*, p. 118.

55. Ibid., p. 94.

56. Serge Truffaut, "Sun Life plus forte au Quebec qu'avant 1976," *Le Devoir*, 20 juin 1987.

57. Charles Gaffny, "The Global 1000," *Business Week*, 18 July 1988, p. 47.

58. René Champagne, *Évolution de la présence francophone parmi les hauts dirigeants des grandes entreprises québécoises entre 1976 et 1982* (Québec: Éditeur officiel du Québec, 1983), p. 1900.

59. Montreal Board of Trade, "Survey of Persons With French Mother Tongue in the Management Ranks of Montreal Area Firms" (mimeo, 1979), cited in Vaillancourt, *Le français, les francophones, et les législations linguistiques au Québec*, p. 22.

60. Sales and Bélanger, *Décideurs et gestionnaires*, p. 182.

61. Jean-Pierre Légault, "Les millieux d'affaires anglophones boudent toujours les francophones," *Le Devoir*, 22 octobre 1988.

62. Sales and Bélanger, *Décideurs et gestionnaires*, p. 189.

63. *La Presse*, 14 avril 1987.

64. Boulet et al., *L'évolution des disparités linguistiques*, pp. 8–11.

65. Jac-André Boulet, *Language and Earnings in Montreal* (Ottawa: Economic Council of Canada, 1980), pp. 28–31.

66. Data calculated by author from Unpublished Special Tabulations by Statistics Canada.

67. See, for example, Sassia Sassen-Koob, "The New Labor Demand in Global Cities," in M. P. Smith, ed., *Cities in Transformation* (Beverly Hills, Calif.: Sage Publications, 1984), pp. 139–170.

68. See, for example, Albert Breton and Peter Mieszowski, "L'investissement linguistique et la francisation du Québec," in François Vaillancourt, ed., *Économie et langue* (Québec: Éditeur officiel du Québec, 1985), pp. 83–102.

69. *Annuaire du Québec, 1979–1980* (Québec: Éditeur officiel du Québec, 1981), p. 491.

70. *Le Québec Statistique, 1985–1986*, p. 526.

71. Lacroix and Vaillancourt, *Revenus et langue*, pp. 72–73; and Statistics Canada, *Census of Canada 1986: Employment Income By Occupation* (Catalogue 93-116).

72. Russell Wilkins, "Income Adequacy in Relation to the Poverty Cutoff Lines by Family Size, Montreal Census Metropolitan Area, 1981: Location and Characteristics of the Poor" (Montreal, unpublished mimeo, 1984).

73. Statistics Canada, *Census of Canada, 1986: Montreal, Part 2* (Catalogue 95-130).

74. Report of the Commission of Inquiry on the Position of the French Language and Language Rights in Quebec, *Book I: The Language of Work* (Québec: Éditeur officiel du Québec, 1972), p. 236 (hereafter cited as the Gendron Commission).

75. Ibid., p. 225.

76. Ibid., p. 228; Daniel Monnier, *La perception de la situation linguistique par les Québécois* (Québec: Éditeur officiel du Québec, 1986), p. 25.

77. Jean-Pierre Proulx, "Les francophones jugent que la situation du français est bonne mais ils demeurent inquiets pour son avenir," *Le Devoir*, 21 juin 1988.

78. Daniel Monnier, "La langue d'accueil et la langue de service dans les com-

merces de Montréal," *Bulletin du Conseil de la langue française* 6:2 (Printemps 1989): 4–5.

79. Pierre O'Neill, "Le français impose de plus en plus dans les commerces," *Le Devoir*, 8 février 1989.

80. Jacques Maurais and Phillippe Plamandon, *Le visage français du Québec: Enquête sur l'affichage*, Notes et documents 54 (Québec: Conseil de la langue française, 1986).

81. For analysis of the discrepancies in research design that limit the comparability of the surveys, see Jean-Pierre Proulx, "L'étude du CLF sur l'affichage est biasée," *Le Devoir*, 15 décembre 1986.

82. Conseil de la langue française, "Avis sur la loi 101 (novembre 1983)," p. 739.

83. Gilles Lesage, "Lise Bacon invite au respect de la loi 101," *Le Devoir*, 25 septembre 1986.

84. Daniel Brosseau, "Les plaintes ont augmenté de 147%," *Journal de Québec*, 30 octobre 1987.

85. Raymond Breton and Gail Grant, *La langue de travail au Québec* (Montréal: L'Institut de recherches politiques, 1981), pp. 82–83.

86. Lacroix and Vaillancourt, *Les revenus et la langue*, p. 83.

87. Allaire, "La nouvelle class politique," p. 62.

88. McKinnon and Miller, "Some Aspects of Recruitment Policies," pp. 24–26.

89. Lacroix and Vaillancourt, *Les revenus et la langue*, pp. 82–83.

90. Ibid., p. 81.

91. *Report of the Consultative Committee on the Development of the Montreal Region*, p. 19.

92. Bureau de Commerce de Montréal, *Enquête sur les personnes dans les niveaux de direction des entreprises de la region de Montréal dont la langue maternelle est le français, 1977* (Montréal: 1979), cited in Lacroix and Vaillancourt, *Les revenus et la langue*, p. 66.

93. Lacroix and Vaillancourt, *Les revenus et la langue*, p. 66.

94. Fernand Martin, *Montréal: les forces économiques en jeu* (Montréal: Institut de recherche C. D. Howe, 1979), p. 42.

95. The data are calculated from an Unpublished Special Tabulation by Statistics Canada. On the destination of Montreal's Anglophone out-migrants between 1971 and 1976, see Réjean Lachapelle and Jacques Henripin, *La situation démolinguistique au Québec* (Montréal: L'Institut de recherches politiques, 1980), p. 235.

96. Paul Bernard et al., *L'évolution de la situation socio-économique des francophones et des non-francophones du Québec (1971–1978)* (Montréal: Office de la langue française, 1979), p. 132. For a similar argument, see Éconosult, *Étude sur les avantages et les coûts de la francisation* (Montréal: Office de la langue française, 1981), p. 300.

97. Lacroix and Vaillancourt, *Les revenus et la langue*, p. 64.

98. Martin, *Montréal: Les forces économiques en jeu*, p. 107.

99. Mario Polèse and Robert Stafford, "Le rôle de Montréal comme centre de services: Une analyse pour certains services aux entreprises," *L'Actualité Économique* 60:1 (mars 1984): 46.

100. Ibid., p. 51.

101. Niosi, *La bourgeoisie canadienne*, p. 186.

102. Paul-André Linteau et al., *Québec: A History 1867–1929*, pp. 361–362.

103. Boulet, *Language and Earnings in Montreal*, pp. 13–14.

104. Vaillancourt, *Le français, les francophones, et les législations linguistiques au Québec*, p. 33.

105. Kenneth McRoberts and Dale Posgate, *Quebec: Social Change and Political Crisis*, 2d rev. ed. (Toronto: McClelland and Stewart, 1980), p. 128; and Alain G. Gagnon and Khayyam Z. Paltiel, "Toward Maîtres chez-nous: The Ascendancy of a Balzacian Bourgeoisie in Quebec," *Queen's Quarterly* 93: 4 (Winter 1986): 740.

106. Daniel M. Shapiro and Morton Stelcner, "Economic Disparities Among Linguistic Groups in Quebec, 1970–1980," *Canadian Public Policy* 8: 1 (1987): 103.

107. Gagnon and Paltiel, "Toward Maîtres chez-nous," 740.

108. Office de la langue française, *Rapport annuel, 1984–1985;* and Office de la langue française, "Directions des programmes de francisation" (décembre 1987), cited in Plourde, *La politique linguistique au Québec,* p. 87.

109. Jean-Pierre Proulx, "La révolution informatique constitue le défi de l'heure," *Le Devoir,* 12 novembre 1985.

110. See Herbert H. Denton, "The New Mood in Montreal, Where Hospitality is Spoken," *Washington Post,* 8 December 1986; and *The Report of the Consultative Committee on the Development of the Montreal Region,* p. 32. The Committee stated: "The fact that Montreal is a bilingual and bicultural city is a unique asset for attracting international activities and widening the international horizons of the local business community in a multilingual, multicultural world. However, this is a strength which has not been well exploited in the past. Given the importance of English as an international language, some parts of Bill 101 are still a hindrance to certain international activities."

111. *The Report of the Consultative Committee on the Development of the Montreal Region,* p. 61 calls for the creation of "special ties with the Boston region," particularly in the area of high technology.

112. William Coleman, *The Independence Movement in Quebec: 1945–1980* (Toronto: University of Toronto Press, 1984), p. 228. Coleman concludes: "As Quebec's francophone community has come to participate more fully in the continental economy, its culture has become more similar to others active in that economy. In the view of many, this has led to a situation where that inner quality burning in the hearts of Québécois will soon be extinguished. If this does happen, then the nationalist movement in Quebec will have failed and may itself die."

Chapter 9

1. Conseil de la langue française, "Avis du Conseil de la langue française au ministre responsable de la Charte de la langue française sur la loi 101 et l'avenir de la langue française au Québec," 7 novembre 1983, reprinted in Conseil de la langue française, *L'État de la langue française au Québec* (Québec: Conseil de la langue française, 1986), p. 745 (the Conseil is hereafter cited as CLF).

2. Norman Délisle, "Salaires: Les Anglais demeurent au Sommet," *Le Devoir,* 1 décembre 1987.

3. Daniel Latouche, "La paradoxe de Montréal," *Le Devoir,* 13 mai 1988.

4. Other factors affecting Montreal's linguistic demography—birthrates, international migration, and linguistic transfers—all fail to seriously modify the "pro-Francophone" dynamics established by the inter- and intraprovincial migrations. See Marc Termotte and Danielle Gauvreau, *La situation démolinguistique du Québec* (Québec: Éditeur officiel du Québec, 1988); and Michel Paillé, *Aspects démolinguistiques de l'avenir de la population du Québec* (Québec: CLF, 1986).

5. "Island's Francophone Population Falling, Study Warns," *The Gazette,* 2 June 1989; and Michel Paillé, *Nouvelles Tendances Démolinguistiques dans l'île de Montréal: 1981–1986* (Québec: Conseil de la langue française, 1989).

6. Isabelle Paré, "La courbe de la natalité québécoise s'inverse: 5.6% plus de bébés en '89," *Le Devoir,* 7 septembre 1989.

7. In bilingual settings such as Montreal, individuals constantly "shift" and live in languages other than their mother tongue. In "mixed" Anglophone–Francophone marriages, for example, French may be used as the chief language of the household: in that case, there will have been a "linguistic transfer" by the Anglophone spouse to French. Conversely, as we shall see, some Francophones and many Allophones in Montreal adopt English as their language of usage in Montreal, representing linguistic transfers to English. *Net* linguistic transfers refers to the balance of these individual shifts.

8. In English Canada, for example, where Francophones are clearly under intense assimilationist pressures, 5 percent of the population was of French mother tongue whereas only 3.6 percent of the population reported using French in the home in 1986. This 1.4 percent difference represents Francophones who have "transferred" to English. See Statistics Canada, *Census of Canada, 1986: Language Retention and Transfer* (Catalogue 93–153).

The addition of the "home language" question in the census permits a much more refined analysis of the issue of linguistic transfers. Prior to 1971, the only way to estimate linguistic transfers was to examine the extent to which the number of individuals reporting English or French as their mother tongue exceeded the British- or French-origin numbers in the population (see Table 2.5 for these estimates in Montreal between 1941 and 1961). The assumption, of course, was that British and French represented the "true" Anglophones and Francophones, and that virtually all others were immigrants who had adopted either French or English. By the 1960s, however, with the British component of Montreal's Anglophone community much smaller than in 1941, such a procedure would be highly flawed.

9. Statistics Canada, "1986 Census of Canada: Adjusted Language Data," April 1988.

10. Statistics Canada, *1981 Census of Canada: Census Metropolitan Areas With Components* (Catalogue 95–943).

11. By way of comparison, 8.4 percent of metropolitan Montreal's Anglophones reported using French regularly as a home language in 1981 (4.5 percent in 1986). Because there are many more Francophones than Anglophones in Montreal, the *absolute* number of linguistic transfers from French to English (62,000) was higher than from English to French (43,000) in 1981; thus, there were 19,000 net linguistic transfers from French to English.

12. Statistics Canada, *Census of Canada, 1986: Language Retention and Transfer.*

13. Quoted in Gerald Clark, *Montreal: The New Cité* (Toronto: McClelland and Stewart, 1982), p. 237.

14. See *La Presse* series "Les Anglophones: Une Révolution discrète," 11–14 avril 1987; and George Tombs, "Les Anglo-Québécois: Une minorité en quête d'une nouvelle identité," *Le Devoir,* 6 octobre 1988.

15. Estimates from 1961 are derived from Hubert Charbonneau and Robert Maheu, *Les aspects démographiques de la question linguistique* (Québec: Éditeur officiel, 1973), p. 352. Other data are from *Census of Canada 1971* and *Census of Canada 1981* and unpublished 1986 census data; Statistics Canada defines bilingual, for the purposes of the census, as someone who can sustain a conversation in either French or English. The census-taker does not actually test the self-declaration by the respondent; thus, the bilingualism data must be viewed cautiously.

16. Daniel Monnier, *La perception de la situation linguistique par les Québécois* (Québec: Editeur officiel du Québec, 1986), pp. 13–19; CROP survey reported in "Les Anglophones: Une révolution discrète," *La Presse,* 11 avril 1987. Uli Locher's

survey of Montreal Anglophones in 1983 found slightly lower rates of bilingualism between 1978 and 1983. See Locher, *Les anglophones de Montréal; émigration et évolution des attitudes, 1978–1983* (Québec: Éditeur officiel du Québec, 1988), pp. 65–73.

17. For an analysis of the RCM, see Henry Milner, *Politics in the New Quebec* (Toronto: McClelland and Stewart, 1978), pp. 212–233; and Sheila McLeod Arnopoulos and Dominique Clift, *The English Fact in Quebec,* 2d ed. (Montreal: McGill–Queen's University Press, 1984), pp. 153–170.

18. Jean-Pierre Proulx, "Entre francophones et anglophones, les contradictions restent radicales," *Le Devoir,* 25 juin 1988.

19. Ibid.

20. Locher, *Les anglophones de Montréal,* p. 182.

21. Peter Leslie, "Ethnic Hierarchies and Minority Consciousness in Quebec," in Richard Simeon, ed., *Must Canada Fail?* (Montreal: McGill–Queens University Press, 1977), p. 131.

22. Statistics Canada, *Census of Canada, 1986: Montreal, Part 2.*

23. André Lachance, "Quand retournez vous?" *Le Devoir,* 7 août 1986.

24. See Gouvernement du Québec, *La politique québécoise du développement culturel,* 2 vols. (Quebec: Éditeur officiel du Québec, 1978). Fernand Dumont and Guy Rocher, whose Whorfian beliefs on the connections between language and culture underpinned the PQ language policy, also helped draft this cultural development White Paper. Thus, the PQ concept of culture was very much grounded in a monolingual, monocultural framework; multiculturalism was antithetical to the Dumont–Rocher analysis.

25. Gouvernement du Québec, *Autant de façons d'être québécois* (Québec: Éditeur officiel du Québec, 1981).

26. The Ministry of Immigration itself was established only in 1968. For a statement of the ministry's activities in the 1980s, see Ministère des Communautés culturelles et de l'Immigration, *Rapport annuel 1984–1985* (1986).

27. Comité Sirros, *Les services de santé et les services sociaux: pour une accessibilité multiculturelle* (Québec: Gouvernement du Québec, 1987).

28. Paul Wells, "City Unveils Plan to Increase Minority Hiring," *The Gazette,* 13 May 1989.

29. Isabelle Paré, "Les groupes ethniques occupent un maigre 4% des postes dans la fonction publique," *Le Devoir,* 22 mai 1988.

30. See Jean-Claude Leclerc, "Vers une CUM multiculturelle," *Le Devoir,* 17 février 1987.

31. Lachance, "Quand retournez vous?"

32. Michel C. Auger, "Les Montréalais croient que la police abuse son pouvoir," *Le Devoir,* 6 avril 1988.

33. Gossett was later removed from the force (and then reinstated by Court edict).

34. Martin Pelchat, "Les policiers se méfient davantage des Noirs," *Le Devoir,* 8 décembre 1988; Jean-V. Dufresne, "La police de Montréal et les minoritaires," *Le Devoir,* 8 décembre 1988.

35. André Lachance, "Être Haitien à Montréal: Davantage une affaire de bile que de ville," *Le Devoir,* 6 avril 1986. By contrast, only 26 percent of the labor force in metropolitan Montreal earned less than $10,000 a year in 1981. See Marc V. Levine, "Deindustrialization and Urban Inequality: A Preliminary Examination of Montreal, 1971–1986," paper presented at annual meeting of American Council for Quebec Studies, Quebec City, 23 October 1988.

36. Ibid.

37. Rollande Parent, "Le français sert d'alibi pour ne pas embaucher des Noirs," *Le Devoir,* 24 avril 1988.

38. See Jean-Claude Leclerc, "Les Québécois pronent la revanche des berceaux plutôt que l'immigration pour remédier la baisse de la natalité," *Le Devoir,* 11 mars 1987; Leclerc, "Les 18 à 24 ans: Une génération étonnante," *Le Devoir,* 11 mars 1987.

39. Jean-Claude Leclerc, "Une Choc nécéssaire," *Le Devoir,* 12 mars 1987.

40. Paul-André Comeau, "Une Société frileuse," *Le Devoir,* 10 mars 1987.

41. Kenneth McRoberts, *Quebec: Social Change and Political Crisis,* 3d ed. (Toronto: McClelland and Stewart, 1988), p. 372. See also A. Brian Tanguay, "Business, Labor, and the State in the 'New' Quebec," *The American Review of Canadian Studies* 17: 4 (Winter 1987–88): 402–403.

42. See William A. Coleman, *The Independence Movement in Quebec, 1945–1980* (Toronto: University of Toronto Press, 1984), p. 208.

43. For an excellent synopsis of the first years of the second Bourassa administration, see McRoberts, *Quebec: Social Change and Political Crisis,* pp. 404–416.

44. Quoted in ibid., p. 412.

45. *La Presse,* 1 décembre 1986.

46. See the *Report of the Consultative Committee to the Ministerial Committee on the Development of the Montreal Region* (Ottawa: Minister of Supply and Services Canada, 1986), p. 32.

47. For an in-depth study of the PQ's school reform efforts, see Henry Milner, *The Long Road to Reform: Restructuring Public Education in Quebec* (Montreal: McGill–Queen's University Press, 1986).

48. Gouvernement du Québec, Ministère de l'Éducation, *The Quebec School: A Responsible Force in the Community* (Québec: Gouvernement du Québec, 1982).

49. Ibid., pp. 51–58; Milner, *Long Road to Reform,* pp. 73–86.

50. Bill 40, "An Act respecting public elementary and secondary education," National Assembly, 32d legislature, 4th session, 1983.

51. Claude Arpin, "School Changes Help Anglos, Says Laurin," *The Gazette,* 25 June 1982.

52. These were the 1867 stipulations on the right to publicly supported Protestant schooling in Montreal that effectively safeguarded the existence of the Anglophone-controlled PSBGM. Section 93 said nothing about language rights in schooling, but Anglophones nevertheless viewed it as the best protection of their educational autonomy.

53. The Lévesque government was humiliated during the 1981 constitutional negotiations when, after forging a common front with English-Canadian provinces in opposition to Prime Minister Trudeau's repatriation plan, Quebec sat by helplessly on "the night of the long knives" when the Anglophone premiers cut a deal with Trudeau. Thus, despite Quebec's opposition, Trudeau's plan prevailed.

54. Jean-Pierre Proulx, "La loi 107 reduira de 55% les éffectifs de la CEPGM," *Le Devoir,* 5 décembre 1988.

55. Gilles Lesage, "Écoles: Ryan maintient la clause dérogatoire," *Le Devoir,* 22 décembre 1988.

56. CLF, *Le français à l'école, aujourd'hui et demain. Rapport du Conseil de la langue française sur l'enseignement du français langue maternelle* (Québec: CLF, 1987).

57. Michel Plourde, *La politique linguistique du Québec, 1977–1987* (Quebec: Institut québécois de recherche sur la culture, 1988), pp. 131–135.

58. Jean-Louis Roy, "La politique linguistique" *Le Devoir,* 11 janvier 1986.

59. Plourde, *La politique linguistique du Québec,* p. 124.

60. Alfred O. Hero, Jr., and Louis Balthazar, *Contemporary Quebec and the United States, 1960–1985* (Washington, D.C.: University Press of America, 1988), p. 209; and Yvon Lamonde, "American Cultural Influence in Quebec: A One Way Mirror," in Alfred O. Hero, Jr., and Marcel Daneau, *Problems and Opportunities in U.S.-Quebec Relations* (Boulder, Colo.: Westview Press, 1984), pp. 114, 119.

61. Ibid., pp. 116–119.

62. Edith Bedard and Daniel Monnier, *Conscience linguistique des jeunes québécois,* vol. 1. (Québec: Éditeur officiel du Québec, 1981), pp. 51–52; and Monnier, *La perception de la situation linguistique,* pp. 29–33.

63. Richard French, "The End of the Quiet Revolution," *The Gazette,* 5 December 1984.

Index

ABBDL-Tecsult, 189
Act of Union (1840), 28–29
A. E. Ames Group, 158
Aitken, Max, 21
Alcan, 159, 169, 193
Allaire, Yvan, 172, 178, 202
Allan, Hugh, 20, 30
Allemagne, André, 56
Alliance laurentienne, 38
Alliance-Quebec, 124–125, 127, 146;
  on amending Bill 101, 128–131; and
  language of commercial signs, 133,
  137; offices of, bombed, 135
Allophones, 117; access of children to
  English-language schools under Bill
  101, 115–116; and Bill 22, 103–106;
  classes d'accueil and, 125, 258n160;
  enrollment of children in English-
  language schools, 55–65, 106, 140;
  enrollment of children in French-
  language schools, 126, 139–144,
  211, 217; ethnic composition of,
  216–217; and Francophone community, 61–62, 68–72, 78–79,
  101–103, 216–220; "illegals" in English-language schools, 123–124,
  131–132; immigration to Montreal
  of, 4, 9–10, 55, 211, 216–
  220; integration into Anglophone institutions by, 60, 120; linguistic
  transfers by, 212–214

Angers, François-Albert, 81, 119
Anglophone business community, 47,
  70, 117, 202, 207–208; and Act of
  Union, 28–29; and Bill 1, 168–169;
  and Bill 22, 98, 100–101; and Bill 28,
  94–95; and Bill 62, 83–84; and Bill
  63, 79; and Bill 101, 170, 174; as
  Canada's economic elite, 20–21;
  efforts by, to annex Montreal to U.S.
  or English Canada, 27, 30; and Francophone politicians, 30–32; and
  Quebec state corporations, 156–157;
  threats of disinvestment by, 84, 88,
  89, 97, 98, 107–108, 117, 170,
  172–173
Anglophones, 26–27, 30, 215; bilingualism and unilingualism among,
  16–17, 25, 215–216; and Bill 1, 117;
  and Bill 22, 102–103, 107–108; and
  Bill 28, 94–95; and Bill 40, 224;
  and Bill 62, 83–84; and Bill 63, 80;
  and Bill 101, 118, 119–120,
  122–125, 131, 147; and Bill 178,
  137; British element among, 17,
  60–62, 217; changing class structure
  of, 122; concentration on West Island
  of, 12–13, 211; contacts with Francophones by, 14, 216; economic
  power of, 2, 3, 17–25, 47, 151–152,
  155, 158, 182, 187, 193–194, 208;
  and Equality Party, 137, 215; ethnic

275